D1556493

HFMA'S INTRODUCTION TO HOSPITAL ACCOUNTING

FIFTH EDITION

HFMA'S INTRODUCTION TO HOSPITAL ACCOUNTING

FIFTH EDITION

Michael Nowicki

Health Administration Press
Chicago, IL

Your board, staff, or clients may also benefit from this book's insight. For more information on quantity discounts, contact the Health Administration Press Marketing Manager at (312) 424-9470.

10   09   08   07   06   5   4   3   2   1

Library of Congress Cataloging-in-Publication Data

Nowicki, Michael, 1952-
    HFMA's introduction to hospital accounting / Michael Nowicki. — 5th ed.
        p. cm.
    A rendition of the 4th ed. by Steven H. Berger, published by Kendall/Hunt Pub. in 2002.
    Includes index.
    ISBN-13: 978-1-56793-254-6
    ISBN-10: 1-56793-254-1 (alk. paper)
    1. Hospitals—Accounting. I. Berger, Steven H. HFMA's introduction to hospital accounting, 4th ed. 2002. II. Title.

    HF5686.H7B47 2006
    657'.8322—dc22

                                                              2006041103

The paper used in this publication meets the minimum requirements of American National Standard for Information Sciences—Permanence of Paper for Printed Library Materials, ANSI Z39.48-1984. ∞™

Acquisitions editor: Audrey Kaufman; Project manager: Amanda Bove; Cover designer and layout editor: Robert Rush

Health Administration Press
A division of the Foundation
    of the American College of
    Healthcare Executives
One North Franklin Street
Suite 1700
Chicago, IL 60606
(312) 424-2800

Healthcare Financial Management
    Association
Two Westbrook Corporate Center
Suite 700
Westchester, IL 60154
(800) 252-4362

CONTENTS

DETAILED CONTENTS

FOREWORD

This fifth edition of *HFMA's Introduction to Hospital Accounting* marks a continuing commitment by the Healthcare Financial Management Association (HFMA) to introduce and maintain educational materials that together represent the body of knowledge of healthcare financial management—a profession still dedicated to providing the nation's healthcare in a cost-effective manner. It also marks a change of publishers to Health Administration Press, a division of the American College of Healthcare Executives; we are delighted to be working with such an excellent publisher and association on this important work.

The origins of this book date back 50 years, to a time when professor Stanley A. Pressler of the Indiana University Graduate School of Business encouraged one of his students, L. Vann Seawell, to study the accounting and financial management practices in hospitals. This study developed into a mimeographed booklet used in a correspondence course in hospital accounting offered by Indiana University and the American Association of Hospital Accountants (later to become HFMA). The success of the course and the encouragement of Sister Mary Gerald and Bob Shelton led Vann to write *Principles of Hospital Accounting*, which was published in 1960 by Physicians' Record Company and later revised and re-titled *Introduction to Hospital Accounting* and published by HFMA in three editions in 1971, 1977, and 1986, and was reprinted in 1992. After the book had been out of print for ten years, Michael Nowicki, who teaches healthcare accounting at Texas State University and began his teaching career under the tutelage of Allen Herkimer, a prolific author of HFMA-published textbooks himself, approached HFMA for permission to bring out a fourth edition, which was published by Kendall/Hunt in 2002. Nowicki has served HFMA in a number of local and national leadership capacities, including as a member of HFMA's board of directors, and is the author of *The Financial Management of Hospitals and Healthcare Organizations*, which was published in its third edition in 2004 by Health Administration Press, HFMA, and the Association of University Programs in Health Administration. Joining Nowicki in the fourth edition was Steven Berger, who has over 20 years of healthcare accounting experience and also has served HFMA in a number of local and national leadership capacities, as well as teaching HFMA seminars. (Due to increasing professional commitments, Steve was unable to participate in the preparation of the fifth edition.)

This fifth edition includes an all-new chart of accounts, glossary of healthcare accounting terms, as well as reference to HFMA's Principle and Practices (P & P) Board issue analyses, which provide the healthcare industry with short-term, practical assistance on emerging issues in healthcare accounting and financial management. Examples include the relationship of community benefit to hospital tax-exempt status and the accounting recognition of other-than-temporary declines in investments for tax-exempt organizations.

HFMA is grateful to Nowicki for continuing the Association's tradition of leadership in providing educational resources to the healthcare industry. We know that this fifth edition will be as successful as the previous four editions.

—Richard L. Clarke, DHA, FHFMA
President and CEO,
Healthcare Financial Management Association

PREFACE

Accounting is an essential service activity found in all economic entities and organizations, regardless of type or size. Accounting is generally divided into two major fields: financial accounting and managerial accounting. The primary purpose of financial accounting is to provide useful financial information, generally historical in nature, about an organization's financial activities and affairs. This information is intended to be used for purposes of intelligent decision making by interested external groups, such as investors, creditors, other resource providers, governmental agencies, and the general public. The primary purpose of managerial accounting is to provide useful financial information, generally current or prospective in nature, to internal users to improve management decision making. Because such decisions directly affect the manner in which limited resources are allocated and employed in our economy, the information generated by the accounting process plays a significant role in determining the types and quantities of products and services that are produced and consumed. With this in mind, the recording and reporting of adequate and reliable financial information relevant to users' needs clearly must be viewed as a function of extreme importance in our economic system.

The economic entity with which this book is specifically concerned is the hospital, organized and operated on a not-for-profit basis. This emphasis on accounting as related to the hospital organization in particular seems warranted because, although the basic principles of accounting are substantially the same for all types of organizations, not-for-profit hospitals have many unique characteristics that require specialized applications of accounting principles and procedures. In addition, the healthcare business has grown to have massive economic and social significance, demanding an increasingly higher order of accounting and financial reporting practices. It seems reasonable to assume that this requirement will be realized most effectively and quickly through educational materials and programs dealing specifically with the particular accounting and financial reporting problems of hospitals and other healthcare entities. Healthcare organizations of all types can benefit greatly from the use of time-proven accounting techniques, reporting practices, and business methods that have been developed by commercial organizations. It also should be noted that, although this book is focused largely on hospitals, the principles and practices described generally are applicable to most other entities comprising the healthcare industry.

In seeking solutions to the serious problems being encountered currently in the provision of high-quality healthcare at reasonable costs, hospital managers and other interested groups are more heavily dependent than ever before on the information provided by highly sophisticated accounting systems. The effectiveness of hospital managers at all levels is directly related to the quality of the information developed by accountants, including business office personnel engaged in the least glamorous bookkeeping tasks. A similar dependency on, and need for, more and better financial information about hospitals also exists with respect to third-party payers, lending institutions, federal and state agencies, and other external groups.

Your interest in hospital accounting may arise from a desire to become a hospital accountant or auditor, or from a need to increase your capabilities in these areas. On the other hand, you may be preparing yourself for a career in hospital administration as a non-accounting executive, recognizing that your preparation would not be adequate or complete without a study of accounting principles. In each case, this book is intended to serve as an introductory course emphasizing the methodology of hospital accounting but also providing an understanding of the meaning and managerial uses of accounting information. The broad coverage of subjects enables this book to be used as a complete course for those having no interest in an accounting career. The depth of coverage, however, is sufficient to permit others to continue their accounting education at an intermediate level.

ACKNOWLEDGMENTS

I would like to gratefully acknowledge those who assisted me in this project. First, I would like to thank Dick Clarke for entrusting me with this project; second, I would like to thank Rob Fromberg, editor-in-chief of *Healthcare Financial Management*, for masterminding an orderly transition from our previous publisher to Health Administration Press. Next, I would like to thank Audrey Kaufman and Amanda Karvelaitis of Health Administration Press, who were as helpful and patient with me during this project as they have been with me in other projects. I would like to thank my students at Texas State University, who generally encourage me to find more effective ways to teach accounting material and who, more specifically, found better ways of saying things in the fourth edition. Two students, my graduate assistants Teresa Prigmore and Laura Speer, provided special assistance with the slide presentation and instructor's manual that accompany this edition.

I would also like to thank my family, who have always supported my scholarly endeavors. I am most grateful for the time they allow me to spend teaching classes, traveling to workshops, and writing articles and books.

But most of all, I would like to acknowledge the original work of L. Vann Seawell. Earlier editions of this book were his labor of love for the healthcare accounting profession. I feel humbled to have been given the opportunity to follow his very good work, and I trust that I have done a creditable job in updating the book.

NATURE AND FUNCTION OF HOSPITAL ACCOUNTING

This chapter examines some of the characteristics of the hospital as an accounting entity, the economic environment in which it pursues its objectives, and the role of accounting in hospital management. You will see that there is a critical and continuous need for financial information about hospital activities and affairs, that this information is required for internal management purposes and also by external users, and that the accounting process provides that information. Then, in introductory fashion, the chapter explores the nature and content of financial statements developed by the accounting process. Your concern will be to obtain a general knowledge of the hospital business and a basic understanding of the end product of accounting—the financial statements—before you get involved in the details of accounting methodology introduced in the next chapter.

The Economic Environment

The importance of the healthcare business in this country is indicated in part by its size and rate of growth. Healthcare is said to be the second largest industry (after construction) in the United States, with annual expenditures projected to be $2,077.5 trillion in 2006 (see Figure 1.1). No other nation spends so much (more than 16 percent) of its gross domestic product for healthcare as does the United States. In addition, while expenditures were somewhat under control in the 1990s due to competition introduced by managed care and to federal reductions in reimbursement mandated by the Balanced Budget Act of 1997, healthcare has remained one of the nation's fastest growing industries. It is generally agreed that this trend is not likely to change significantly in the near future (see Figure 1.1). An even greater emphasis, however, will be placed on efforts to ensure maximum returns from this huge investment in terms of the quality and accessibility of healthcare services.

Looking at the $2,077.5 trillion in health expenditures projected for 2006, the single largest funding source of healthcare changes for the first time from private insurance, projected to fund 34.8 percent of the $2,077.5 trillion, to the federal government, projected to fund 35.1 percent

FIGURE 1.1

Economic
Environment

Year	Health Expenditures	Per Capita	Percent GDP
1950	12.7 billion	82	4.4
1960	26.9 billion	146	5.3
1970	73.2 billion	341	7.1
1980	247.3 billion	1,052	8.9
1990	699.5 billion	2,691	12.2
2000	1,311.1 trillion	4,681	13.1
2006*	2,077.5 trillion	6,830	16.0
2014*	3,585.7 trillion	11,046	18.7

*projected

SOURCE: Hefler, S., S. Smith, S. Keehan, C. Borger, M. K. Clemens, C. Truffer. 2005. "Trends: U.S. Health Spending Projections for 2004–2014." *Health Affairs* web exclusive [Online information; retrieved 2/23/05.] http://content.healthaffairs.org/cgi/content/abstract/hlthaff.w5.74.

FIGURE 1.2

Sources of
Healthcare
Expenditures,
2006*

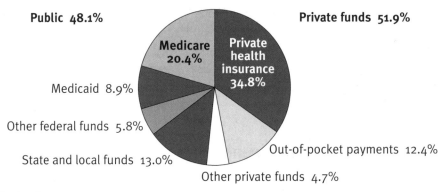

*projected

SOURCE: Hefler, S., S. Smith, S. Keehan, C. Borger, M. K. Clemens, C. Truffer. 2005. "Trends: U.S. Health Spending Projections for 2004–2014." *Health Affairs* web exclusive [Online information; retrieved 2/23/05.] http://content.healthaffairs.org/cgi/content/abstract/hlthaff.w5.74.

(see Figure 1.2). Where is the money going? The single largest consumer of healthcare funds continues to be professional services—including physicians, dentists, and other personal providers—spending 32.1 percent of the $2,077.5 trillion (see Figure 1.3).

Hospital Statistics

A significant component of the U.S. healthcare industry is the network of over 6,000 hospitals, whose annual expenses represent about 30 percent of the total annual healthcare expenditures. Approximately 97 percent of these hospitals are registered with the American Hospital Association (AHA). The Hospital Data Center of the AHA conducts an annual survey of hospitals to obtain

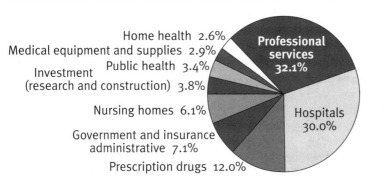

FIGURE 1.3
Consumers of Healthcare Expenditures, 2006*

*projected

SOURCE: Hefler, S., S. Smith, S. Keehan, C. Borger, M. K. Clemens, C. Truffer. 2005. "Trends: U.S. Health Spending Projections for 2004–2014." *Health Affairs* web exclusive [Online information; retrieved 2/23/05.] http://content.healthaffairs.org/cgi/content/abstract/hlthaff.w5.74.

information pertaining to (among other things) the utilization, personnel, and finances of hospitals; the results are published in the *American Hospital Association Guide to the Healthcare Field*, with a separate statistical supplement entitled *Hospital Statistics*. Much of the following information is drawn from the 1992, 2002, and 2005 editions of *Hospital Statistics*. (You are urged to refer to these AHA publications for more detailed and complete information.)

Figure 1.4 presents selected information relating to the utilization, personnel, and finances of all AHA-registered hospitals in the United States. This information is provided for 1990, 2000, and 2003 to highlight some of the important changes that have taken place. Note, for example, the decreases in number of hospitals, beds, average daily census, and occupancy percentage. Also, observe the increases in expenses and outpatient visits.

Breakdown of Hospitals by Ownership

Of the 5,764 hospitals included in Figure 1.4 for 2003, 4,918 (85 percent) are referred to as community hospitals. The AHA defines such hospitals as all nonfederal short-term general and other special hospitals whose facilities and services are available to the public. Of these 4,918 hospitals, 3,007 (61 percent) are nongovernmental not-for-profit hospitals, 1,121 (23 percent) are state and local governmental hospitals, and 790 (16 percent) are investor-owned hospitals.

Contributing Factors to Increased Healthcare Costs

Aside from inflation, the rather dramatic rise in hospital expenses since World War II can be attributed in part to a vastly greater demand for an increasingly wide range of hospital services. Expanded hospital services require an increase in hospital personnel. The average earnings of hospital employees

FIGURE 1.4

Selected
Information,
All AHA-
Registered
Hospitals in the
United States

	1990	2000	2003
Number of hospitals:			
Federal	337	275	239
Nonfederal psychiatric	757	590	477
Nonfederal respiratory diseases	4	3	4
Nonfederal long-term	131	125	126
Nongovernmental not-for-profit short-term	3,202	3,191	3,007
For-profit short-term	749	771	790
State and local governmental short-term	1,469	1,218	1,121
Total number of hospitals	6,649	6,173	5,764
Number of beds (in thousands)	1,226	1,013	965,256
Admissions (in thousands)	33,742	33,766	36,610
Average daily census (in thousands)	853	662	657
Outpatient visits (in thousands)	352,248	545,481	648,560
Full-time equivalent personnel (in thousands)	3,937	4,407	4,651
Expenses (in millions of dollars):			
Labor	99,256	157,573	213,209
Total expenses	214,886	355,450	498,103

SOURCE: American Hospital Association. 1992, 2002, 2005. *AHA Hospital Statistics*. Chicago: Health Forum.

also have risen substantially because of unionization, the application of minimum wage laws to hospitals, an increasing competition for the available labor force, and an increasing degree of training and education necessary for hospital employees. The last several decades have produced technological changes requiring the use of extremely sophisticated and expensive equipment operated by skilled and highly paid technicians.

One of the most important environmental influences on hospital operations is, of course, the third-party reimbursement system. Whereas most commercial businesses are paid directly by their customers for services and products sold to them, hospitals receive payment for a large majority of their services through reimbursement from third-party payers, including governmental agencies for Medicare and Medicaid, BlueCross plans, and commercial insurers, usually in the form of managed care payments. For many years, most reimbursements for inpatient services were made on a retrospective actual cost basis, or on the basis of the rates hospitals charged for their services. In the 1980s, however, many inpatient cost-based and charge-based payment mechanisms were discarded in favor of

- Prospective payment systems (PPS) based on a predetermined fixed price per case, or
- Prospective per diem (i.e., per day) systems based on established all-inclusive daily payments for services.

Medicare reimbursement, for example, consists of predetermined amounts based on diagnosis-related groups (DRGs). These innovations in payment systems were designed to reduce the utilization of inpatient services and encourage greater utilization of less expensive alternative services (such as outpatient care) to promote cost efficiency in the healthcare system.

On an outpatient basis, reimbursements have also changed substantially, primarily since the late 1990s. In the 1997 Balanced Budget Act, Medicare was mandated to change its cost-based outpatient reimbursement system to one of predetermined rates for services under the Ambulatory Payment Classification (APC) system. This became effective across the country on August 1, 2000. In the same time period, the managed care companies were moving from 100 percent fee-for-service reimbursement to a discount from gross charges and ultimately into fee schedules and, in some cases, capitation.

The full financial needs of many hospitals generally have not been met under either previous or existing reimbursement systems. Hospitals, facing increasing competition for patients, have found themselves in a price war. Greater attention has been given to marketing and public relations programs. The number of hospital acquisitions and mergers has increased, and many hospitals that were not cost efficient have been forced to close.

As a result, hospital managers are engaged in a desperate struggle to maintain the financial integrity of their institutions. Individual philanthropy and community fundraising drives have increased in recent importance as sources of supplementary funds, as some hospitals have difficulty financing their long-term capital needs through bond issues and other forms of debt.

Hospital Organization

The largest category of American hospitals comprises short-term, general hospitals usually referred to as community hospitals. Most of them are voluntary, not-for-profit organizations operated under corporate charters granted by the states. Other community hospitals are governmental institutions or investor-owned businesses conducted on a for-profit basis. Although major emphasis in this book is given to nongovernmental, not-for-profit community hospitals, much of the discussion is relevant to all types of hospitals and to other healthcare entities as well.

Objective and Purpose of the Hospital

Regardless of the type of ownership, the essential function and primary mission of all hospitals is patient care. This is the basic objective and purpose of the hospital: the provision of quality service at reasonable costs to persons needing medical attention and hospital care. In addition, hospitals also perform vital roles in the areas of healthcare research and education.

In carrying out these tasks, hospitals employ many different types of physical, financial, and human resources. These resources, if they are to be used economically and effectively, must be segregated into manageable organizational units in which authority is centralized and responsibility is clearly assigned for each function. The duties of each employee should be carefully defined, and interrelationships among individuals and organizational units should be soundly structured so that all personnel may work together in a coordinated, cooperative effort. Only through a well-conceived plan of organization can the hospital achieve its service and financial objectives.

Organization of Hospital Management

A hospital's organizational pattern is generally expressed in a formal organization chart such as the one shown in Figure 1.5. You should understand that this chart is illustrative only; there is no single plan of organization applicable to all hospitals. Different organizational structures arise because of differences in hospital size, range of services, personnel capabilities, management style, and other characteristics.

At the top of the organizational structure is the hospital's governing body, which often is called the **board of trustees** in a not-for-profit hospital and

FIGURE 1.5
Hypothetical Hospital Organization Chart

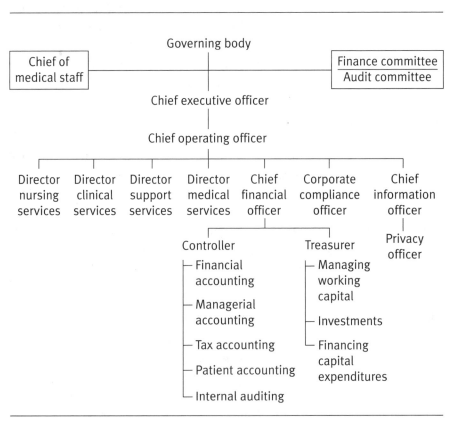

the **board of directors** in a for-profit hospital. The ultimate authority and responsibility for the proper and prudent management of the hospital's affairs rests with this group. Typically, the board carries out its function through a number of standing committees, such as finance, medical affairs, and public relations. The board members, however, do not directly manage the day-to-day operations of the hospital; this authority is delegated to the hospital's chief executive officer (CEO), who often has the title of president, administrator, or executive director. Similarly, authority and responsibility for the medical aspects of hospital activity are assigned to a physician known as the medical director (usually appointed by the governing board) and/or chief of staff (usually elected by the medical staff). The administrator and medical director, because their responsibilities are interdependent, must work always in close cooperation.

It is not possible, even in small hospitals, for the administrator to exercise continuous and direct personal supervision of all hospital activities. As indicated in Figure 1.5, hospital activities necessarily must be organized into major divisional units such as nursing services, other clinical services, support services, medical services, financial services, compliance services, and information services including privacy activities. Each of the divisional units is headed by a manager or director who has authority and clearly assigned responsibility for its operations. Each division head is responsible to the administrator who, in turn, is responsible to the governing board.

The nursing services division, headed by the director of nursing, is responsible for daily patient care activities. Employees of the division include nurses, nurses' aides, surgical technicians, ward clerks, and orderlies. The division comprises many departments, including nursing units generally organized by medical service classifications, operating rooms, delivery rooms, emergency rooms, and central supply.

The other clinical services division provides ancillary services to patients. This division is subdivided into several professional departments, such as laboratory; diagnostic imaging (radiology); pharmacy; electroencephalograms (EEGs); cardiology, including electrocardiograms (EKGs) and cardiac catheterization laboratories; and physical, occupational, and speech therapies. These departments, some of which are headed by physicians, provide essential diagnostic and therapeutic services.

The support services division is responsible for various support services necessary to patient care and to the operation of various other departments of the hospital. Departments organized within this division generally include food service (dietary), laundry and linen, environmental services (housekeeping), and plant operation and maintenance. Some hospitals have contracted with outside firms to perform certain of these support functions.

Medical services provides administrative support to the medical staff. This division is subdivided into several medical staff departments, such as internal medicine, surgery, and others.

A fifth division of the hospital is that of financial services. This division includes such departments as admitting, accounting, purchasing, personnel, and public relations. The accounting department itself is divided into subordinate organizational units, including the general accounting area (generally comprised of general ledger, accounts payable, and payroll), a financial analysis area (generally comprised of budgeting, reimbursement, cost, and, in some cases, the charge description master), and the revenue cycle area (generally comprised of patient registration, medical records, patient billing, follow-up, and collections). The entire division is generally managed by the hospital's chief financial officer (CFO).

While compliance is seldom considered a division, most hospitals now have a compliance officer who is responsible for ensuring that the hospital complies with the ever increasing number of federal and state laws and regulations.

Additionally, a seventh division that has grown dramatically in the 1990s is information services. Usually managed by a chief information officer (CIO), this division is responsible for all the sophisticated hardware and software used by the clinical, operating, and finance divisions. They are further responsible for the technological infrastructure, which are all the wires running behind the walls of the organization, allowing for data, voice, and video capabilities. This division has taken on greater importance since the early to mid-1990s, characterized by the elevation of the former information system manager (or director) to CIO status.

The Need for Statistical and Financial Information

Within any organization, there is an imperative need for statistical and financial information. This is particularly true of hospitals because of the large number of individual, yet interdependent, organizational units whose operations must be planned, coordinated, and supervised. Effective management of the hospital requires that definite objectives be established by each organized area of responsibility. These objectives initially are expressed in statistical terms, such as days of patient service, hours of nursing care, number of laboratory examinations, and pounds of laundry. These measurements of expected service volume then are translated into monetary terms, such as required dollars of expenditures and anticipated revenues. The service and financial objectives of each organizational unit are coordinated into an overall operating plan and budget for the hospital as a whole. Such plans typically are developed for a period of one year, broken down into monthly segments. Personnel at all levels in the hospital should participate in the development of the plan.

As the year progresses, each month's actual results are compared with the budgeted objectives so that the performance of each organizational unit of the hospital can be evaluated by department heads, divisional directors, the hospital

CEO, and the governing board. Variances from the budgeted objectives are watched closely, and tough questions must be answered when significant deviations are noted. Where, within the hospital, do material variations exist? Why have these variances occurred? Who is responsible? What can be done about them? Answers to these questions permit intelligent decisions to be made so that off-target operating units are redirected onto the planned and proper course.

Internal Uses of Financial Information

Hospital managers perform their function effectively through the use of statistical and financial information, both historical and projected. This information is essential to the manager in planning the hospital's operations, in evaluating the actual performance of hospital personnel, and in taking corrective action to overcome unfavorable conditions and trends. Of course, the information must be timely, adequate, relevant, and reliable, or the manager's decisions are likely to be unsound and ill advised.

External Uses of Financial Information

In addition to the internal use of statistical and financial data by management, groups external to the hospital also use much of the same information. These external groups include third-party payers, lending institutions, suppliers, planning agencies, and donors. Hard economic decisions are made by all these groups, and they have a direct impact on the ability of the hospital to pay its expenses, borrow money, obtain credit, acquire new plants and equipment, add new services, and pursue research and educational programs. You can be sure that these decisions will not favor a hospital that is unable or unwilling to supply the kinds of statistical and financial information required by these various external groups.

The Accounting Function

The hospital accounting function, simply stated, is to provide useful information about the hospital's activities and affairs. This information is of a statistical and financial character; it is both historical and projected in nature. As you have seen, this information has vitally important uses in the internal management of the hospital and equally important uses in the decisions made by parties external to the hospital. In short, accounting is an *information* system; it is the source of information absolutely essential to the management of the individual hospital and to the functioning of the hospital industry.

Hospital Accounting Defined

Hospital accounting can be defined as the accumulation, communication, and interpretation of historical and projected economic data relating to the financial position and operating results of a hospital enterprise, for purposes of decision making by its management and other interested parties. Take a moment to examine the parts of this definition.

Accumulation refers to the process of recording and classifying the business transactions and financial events that occur in the economic life of the hospital. This, if you wish, is the "bookkeeping" aspect of the accounting function. It consists of several procedural operations that you will discover in subsequent chapters.

Communication is the process of reporting recorded information to those who use it. There are many types of accounting reports, and they contain different kinds of information. The content of these reports generally depends on the particular needs of users, but there is a substantial body of information that is believed to serve certain common interests of all users. So this general purpose information is routinely reported in financial statements, such as balance sheets and statements of operations. There are other basic, required reports, but you will not need to concern yourself with them at this time.

Interpretation refers to the effort made by accountants to analyze and evaluate reported information so that it may be better understood and more easily used by decision makers. It is not enough for the accountant merely to record and report; the accountant's responsibility extends to the function of assisting users in the interpretation of reported data. This is necessary if users are to fully comprehend the significance of the information and use it in an intelligent manner. More will be said about this matter at various points later in this book.

Much of the information recorded and reported through the accounting process, of course, is historical in nature. Historical economic data can serve many purposes, including substantiation of revenues and expenses for reimbursement and payroll tax reports. At least an equal share of the accountant's time, however, is spent developing annual budgets, long-range plans, and other projections of data. Financial forecasting is a significant part of the accounting task.

Types of Information Produced by Accounting
The information generated by the accounting process is of four basic types. **Balance sheets** report financial position information, **statements of operation** report information relating to operating results, **statements of changes in net assets** report the summary reason for the changes in the three most common net assets, and **statements of cash flows** report the basic reasons for the changes in the organization's short-term balance sheet cash. The financial position of a hospital at a particular point in time is measured in terms of the hospital's resources (assets), obligations (liabilities), and difference between assets and liabilities (net assets). The operating results of a hospital for a given period of time are measured in terms of revenues earned and

expenses incurred during that period. These terms—*assets, liabilities, net assets, revenues,* and *expenses*—are defined and described later in this chapter.

Finally, the definition of accounting indicates that the financial statements developed in the accounting process are intended to be useful for decision-making purposes. If accounting information were not useful, there would be no need for accounting and no demand for accountants.

The Value of Good Internal Control Systems

To be useful, accounting information must be not only relevant but also accurate and reliable. The accuracy and reliability of the monetary and statistical data provided in accounting reports is dependent on an effective system of internal control. This system was defined well many years ago, and the definition remains valid and useful: **Internal control** comprises the plan of organization and all of the coordinated methods and measures adopted within a business to safeguard its assets, check the accuracy and reliability of its accounting data, promote operational efficiency, and encourage adherence to prescribed managerial policies.

Such a system greatly reduces the possibility of serious errors in the accumulation and communication processes of accounting, thereby giving the hospital manager more confidence in accounting information and in decisions based on such information. The hospital accountant is responsible for the development and operation of the internal control system as an integral part of the accounting process. Specific internal control methods and procedures are discussed at various points throughout this book.

Ethics and Public Confidence

The accounting profession is based on the public's perception that accountants will act in an ethical manner. Recent events, including the Enron collapse, have prompted the American Institute of Certified Public Accountants (AICPA) to take an active role in restoring public confidence in the accounting profession. In a letter to members, the AICPA expressed zero tolerance for violations of ethics and standards of the accounting profession and focused scrutiny on what it believes to be the basic problem—the current and outdated financial reporting model and the accounting principles that support it. The AICPA has already begun to focus on the benefits of a reporting model for "information age" companies whose earning assets cannot be accurately valued using the traditional, manufacturing-based measures.

Because scope of services has become such an issue with the Securities and Exchange Commission (SEC), the congressional committees investigating Enron, and therefore the public, the AICPA has approved a resolution to support prohibitions on auditors of public companies from also providing consulting services (it is reported that Arthur Andersen provided Enron with $25 million in audit services and $27 million in consulting services during 2001). However, AICPA does not believe that such prohibitions will improve the quality of audits but will help restore public confidence in the financial reporting process.

Also designed to restore public confidence, the Sarbanes-Oxley Act of 2002 was passed by Congress and signed by the president. Described as federal corporate accountability legislation to improve governance and corporate practices, the legislation includes ten standards that apply only to publicly held companies, though many states (like New York) have adopted similar legislation that also applies to not-for-profit organizations. In addition, some not-for-profits are voluntarily holding themselves to Sarbanes-Oxley-type standards.[1]

Financial Statements

As you have learned, hospital accounting is a service activity whose primary function is the provision of useful quantitative information about the financial position and operating results of the hospital enterprise. Financial statements are the product of the accounting process. They are the means by which the information developed by the accounting process is communicated to hospital managements, creditors, third-party payers, and others who use the information as a basis for economic decision making. Your understanding of the accounting process will be considerably enhanced by briefly examining the basic financial statements before you deal with the procedures through which financial information is accumulated by accountants.

Generally Accepted Accounting Principles (GAAP)

The particular elements to be included in financial statements, and the dollar amounts at which they are stated, are determined by the application of a body of rules, conventions, concepts, and standards known as **generally accepted accounting principles** (GAAP). For the present purpose, it is enough that you understand that there is an authoritative body of GAAP that accountants must observe in reporting financial information.

The primary source of GAAP is an independent organization called the Financial Accounting Standards Board (FASB). Since its formation in 1973, the Board has issued statements of financial accounting standards (SFAS), several statements of financial accounting concepts, numerous interpretations, and many other documents. Various other groups also have made significant contributions to the development of GAAP. The Accounting Standards Executive Committee (ACSEC) of the AICPA, for example, has issued a large number of statements of position. The AICPA Committee on Healthcare regularly revises and publishes the *Hospital Audit Guide*, which includes GAAP as well as auditing standards. The work of the Healthcare Financial Management Association (HFMA) through its Principles and Practices (P & P) Board also should be noted. To date, the P & P Board has issued more than 20 statements relating to financial accounting and reporting practices of hospitals and other healthcare entities (see Appendix A for P &P Board statements as of the printing of this book and see the HFMA website at www.hfma.org for the current statements). Appendix B includes P & P Board issue analyses provided to the healthcare industry to provide short-term, practical assistance on emerging healthcare financial management issues.

Illustrative Balance Sheet and Statement of Operations

The several types of financial statements usually prepared by accountants are illustrated and described at appropriate points in this book. For the present, however, you should be concerned only with two: the balance sheet and the statement of operations. In the following sections, Figures 1.6 and 1.7 present these statements for a hypothetical facility, Happy Valley Hospital. Certain simplifications and condensations of the data have been made to facilitate an introductory discussion of the essential elements and features involved. More detailed and real-world illustrations appear in subsequent chapters. Regarding the statement of operations, Figure 1.7a shows the statement in worksheet, or non-GAAP, format. Such a statement presents gross service revenues and would be used for internal purposes only. Figure 1.7b shows the statement of operations in GAAP format. Such a statement presents service revenues net of contractual adjustments (discounts to third-party payers) and charity care (the policy for and amount of charity care must be disclosed in the notes to the financial statements) in accordance with FASB Concepts Statement No. 6, published in 1992. (Statement No. 6 also requires that bad debt be presented as an operating expense.)

The Balance Sheet

A balance sheet is a presentation of the financial position of a hospital at a particular point in time. It also may be referred to as a statement of financial condition (or position). Financial position is measured in terms of resources (assets) owned and obligations (liabilities) owed by the hospital at a given date. The difference between these resources and obligations is the hospital's net assets. Thus, in the simplest terms, a balance sheet indicates how "well off" a hospital is on a particular date by listing the things of value the hospital owns in relation to its debts to suppliers, employees, and other creditors. The excess of things owned over things owed is the hospital's net assets on that date. A sample of a balance sheet is shown in Figure 1.6.

The Accounting Equation

The balance sheet gets its name from the fact that it depicts a balance (an equality) between total assets on one side, and the total of liabilities and net assets on the other side. This equality is known as the accounting equation:

Assets			Liabilities and Net Assets	
Cash	$ 540		Accounts payable	$ 300
Accounts receivable	2,500		Notes payable	275
Inventory	200		Accrued expenses payable	795
Prepaid expenses	60		Deferred income	30
Total current assets	3,300		Total current liabilities	1,400
Long-term investments	400		Long-term liabilities	3,200
Land, buildings,				
and equipment $7,200			Total liabilities	4,600
Less accumulated				
depreciation 2,100	5,100		Hospital net assets	4,200
			Total liabilities and	
Total assets	$8,800		net assets	$8,800

Assets = Liabilities + Net Assets

or

Assets – Liabilities = Net Assets

To put it in personal terms, say that today you have $25,000 of assets (cash and other property) and $10,000 of liabilities (unpaid bills and other debts). By subtracting your liabilities from your assets, you determine that your net assets (net worth) are $15,000. You could, of course, prepare a personal balance sheet for yourself, listing $25,000 of assets on the left side and reporting $25,000 of liabilities and net assets on the right side. This relationship of total assets to total liabilities and net assets is fundamental to the debit-and-credit methodology employed in accounting operations, as you shall see in the next chapter.

The dollar amounts included in Figure 1.6 are not intended to be realistic. Obviously, no hospital is as small as the balance sheet in Figure 1.6 suggests. The magnitude of the dollar amounts is purposely minimized for clarity and ease of exposition. It is easier to read, discuss, and otherwise work with small numbers than with large numbers, and this practice will be followed throughout this book. If you wish, assume that the numbers in Figure 1.6 are stated in thousands (or millions) of dollars.

Elements of Balance Sheets

Figure 1.6 presents the balance sheet of Happy Valley Hospital on December 31, 20X1. Notice that the statement heading consists of (1) the name of the accounting entity, (2) the name of the statement, and (3) the date of the statement. These three elements should always be included in the heading of the balance sheet.

The accounting entity in this case is Happy Valley Hospital. This is one of the most important and basic accounting concepts. Under this concept, the hospital is personified as an entity (being) separate and distinct from its governing board, management, and employees. The hospital is regarded as a "person" capable of owning property, incurring debts, buying and selling, rendering services, and taking other economic actions. Thus, you can say that "the hospital purchased equipment," "the hospital borrowed $100,000 from the local bank," or "the hospital paid $160,000 of salaries and wages to its employees last month." The accountant thinks of the hospital as an entity for whose economic activity a financial record must be kept. The object of the accountant's attention and effort is the hospital itself, not the personal affairs of board members, managers, and employees. Activity recorded in the hospital accounting records is limited to the financial affairs and business transactions of the hospital as an economic unit or entity in its own right.

As noted earlier, the name of this financial statement is balance sheet, but you should be aware of alternate titles, such as statement of financial position. The name most widely used, however, is balance sheet, and this term will be used throughout this book.

The date of the Happy Valley Hospital balance sheet is December 31, 20X1, a specific point in time. A balance sheet is analogous to a snapshot that portrays a situation existing at a given moment. It is a "picture" of the financial position of Happy Valley Hospital on December 31, 20X1, only. The picture likely was somewhat different on December 30 and probably will be different again on January 1, 20X2. This is true because business transactions occur every day, and consequently the dollar amounts of assets and liabilities also change daily.

Assets may be defined as the economic resources of the hospital that are recognized and measured in conformity with GAAP. As indicated in Figure 1.6, the assets of Happy Valley Hospital total $8,800 at December 31, 20X1. The following is a brief explanation of each of the assets included in that balance sheet. **Assets**

There are seven types of assets appearing on a hospital's balance sheet. They include the following: *Types of Assets*

1. **Cash** is the amount of money on hand and in bank checking accounts maintained by the hospital.
2. **Accounts receivable** represent the amount of money due the hospital from patients and their third-party sponsors for services provided to them but for which the hospital has not yet been paid.
3. **Inventory** is the cost of food, fuel, drugs, and other supplies purchased by the hospital but not yet used or consumed.
4. **Prepaid expenses** include expense items such as insurance, interest, and rent that have been paid in advance. These items are assets in the sense that their prepayment will provide future benefits (e.g., insurance

protection, use of borrowed money, use of space or leased equipment) to the hospital.

5. **Long-term investments** represent the cost of governmental and corporate securities that the hospital owns and intends to hold for a period of time in excess of one year.

6. **Land, buildings, and equipment** consist of the original acquisition costs of tangible plant assets used in hospital operations.

7. **Accumulated depreciation** reflects the amount of plant asset costs consumed by the use of the assets and treated as an operating expense of the hospital during the time that has elapsed since the assets were acquired. Notice that accumulated depreciation is deducted from the cost of the plant assets and that only the remaining "undepreciated" balance of cost is included in the total assets reported in the balance sheet.

Items 1 through 4 are totaled and presented in the balance sheet as total current assets. For the present, think of **current assets** as consisting of cash plus other assets that will be converted into cash or consumed by operations within one year from the balance sheet date. All other assets (items 5 through 7) are referred to as **noncurrent assets**, or **long-term assets**.

You have noticed that most assets are reported in the balance sheet at historical acquisition costs rather than current market values. Valuation of assets at cost is a basic accounting principle. This basis of valuation generally is employed in accounting because it is a permanent and objective measurement and because accountants assume that the monetary unit is reasonably stable; that is, that the purchasing power of money does not change materially over time. This assumption, because of earlier inflationary trends, naturally has been challenged by various groups who argue that assets should be presented in balance sheets at either current fair values or estimated replacement costs. In fact, the FASB moved off the concept of historical costs for balance sheets in a major way in the mid-1990s when it issued SFAS No. 124, which says that not-for-profit organizations are required to report their investment balances at "market." This was a significant change in authoritative accounting pronouncements with which all organizations had to comply. There will be an expanded discussion of SFAS No. 124 later in the book.

Sequencing of Assets

Another point worth noting at this time concerns the sequence in which the assets are listed on the balance sheet. Observe that the sequence is generally in the order of liquidity. The most liquid asset (cash) is listed first; the least-liquid assets (land, buildings, and equipment) are last in sequence. This is standard practice in financial reporting.

Finally, you should understand that certain economic resources of the hospital are not included as assets in the balance sheet. A hospital may enjoy good public relations and high employee morale, but although these things may be regarded as valuable resources, they are not formally recognized as assets in hospital accounting. These items are excluded from reported assets because of the great difficulty involved in making an objective measurement of them in monetary terms. This problem is being studied, and perhaps someday a satisfactory solution will be forthcoming.

Liabilities may be defined as the economic obligations of the hospital that are recognized and measured in conformity with GAAP. Following is a brief description of the liabilities presented in the Happy Valley Hospital balance sheet.   **Liabilities**

There are five types of liabilities appearing on a hospital's balance sheet. They include the following: ***Types of Liabilities***

- **Accounts payable** are amounts owed by the hospital to suppliers and other trade creditors for merchandise and services purchased from them but for which the hospital has not yet paid.
- **Notes payable** generally consist of short-term borrowings by the hospital from banks and other financial institutions. These debts usually are in the form of promissory notes issued by the hospital to the lender.
- **Accrued expenses payable**, sometimes known as accrued liabilities, are liabilities for expenses (employee salaries and wages, for example) that have been incurred by the hospital but for which the hospital has not yet paid.
- **Deferred income** represents income (e.g., nursing school tuition) that has been received in cash by the hospital but that the hospital has not yet earned and for which it is obligated to provide some specific service in the future.
- **Long-term liabilities** typically are mortgage loans or hospital bond issues that will not be retired by the hospital in the near future (usually well beyond one year from the date of the balance sheet).

As you can see in Figure 1.6, items 1 through 4 are totaled and reported as total **current liabilities**—that is, obligations that mature and will be paid by the use of current assets within one year from the balance sheet date. The other liabilities of the hospital therefore are referred to as **noncurrent liabilities**, or **long-term liabilities**. Liabilities, generally speaking, are measured in terms of the dollar amounts that will be required to discharge them. Long-term liabilities, however, generally are reported in the balance sheet at the present value of the future payments required for their liquidation; but again, a discussion of this matter is postponed until later in the book.

As was true of assets, recognition problems also exist for liabilities. When is an obligation a liability in the accounting sense? As you pursue your study of this book, you will discover items you may consider liabilities that are not so treated in accounting. Similarly, you may encounter accounting liabilities you have not previously regarded as such. This is but another example of the patience you must have in beginning your study of hospital accounting. Full explanations cannot be given of all matters in the first chapter; your complete comprehension of the various concepts and procedures mentioned in this chapter will eventually be achieved, but only through a gradual building-block process.

Sequencing of Liabilities   Liabilities are presented in the balance sheet more or less in the order in which they will be paid. The proper sequence, however, is not always easy to determine, and compromises often must be made. It is essential, however, that balance sheets report total current liabilities and total liabilities (current and noncurrent) as indicated in Figure 1.6. Users of the balance sheets of hospitals are entitled to this information.

Net Assets   Hospital **net assets** may be defined simply as the excess of hospital assets over hospital liabilities. They are the hospital's residual ownership interest in its own assets after the claims of creditors against these assets are satisfied. Hospital net assets are increased by net income (excess of revenues over expenses); they are decreased by net loss (excess of expenses over revenues). Net assets are sometimes referred to as equity, capital, or net worth.

Later on in this book, the subject of **fund accounting** is introduced. Fund accounting is employed by many hospitals and consists basically of a segregation of assets, liabilities, and net assets into self-balancing groups of funds. When this accounting procedure is used, a separate balance sheet can be prepared for each fund; or, a single balance sheet may be prepared in which assets, liabilities, and net assets are classified and reported according to the particular fund with which they are associated. In a fund-accounting system, the net assets account of each fund generally is referred to as the fund balance.

Statement of Operations

A **statement of operations** is a presentation of the operating results of a hospital for a specified period of time. It also may be referred to as the income statement, the statement of revenues and expenses, the profit-and-loss statement, or simply the operating statement. In any event, this statement reports the revenues earned and the expenses incurred by the hospital during a given period of time, such as a month, a quarter, or one year. The difference between the revenues and expenses of the period is reported as **excess of revenues over expenses**. It also may be referred to as net income or net margin (depending on its placement on the statement of operations). The statement of operations for Happy Valley Hospital is shown in non-GAAP format in Figure 1.7a and in GAAP format in Figure 1.7b.

Elements of Statements of Operations

Figure 1.7 presents the statement of operations for Happy Valley Hospital for the year ended December 31, 20X2 (the year following the hospital's balance sheet illustrated in Figure 1.6). The statement heading includes (1) the name

Gross patient services revenues:		
Daily patient services	$6,000	
Other professional services	4,000	
Gross patient services revenues		$10,000
Less deductions from patient services revenues	1,000	
Net patient services revenues		9,000
Other operating revenues		500
Total operating revenues		9,500
Less operating expenses:		
Nursing services	3,400	
Other professional services	2,700	
General services	1,800	
Fiscal and administrative services	1,400	
Total operating expenses		9,300
Operating income		200
Add nonoperating income		130
Excess of revenues over expenses		$ 330

FIGURE 1.7A
Happy Valley Hospital Statement of Operations, Non-GAAP Format, Year Ended December 31, 20X2

Net patient services revenues*	$9,000	
Other operating revenues	500	
Total operating revenues	9,500	
Less operating expenses:		
Nursing services	3,400	
Other professional services	2,700	
General services	1,800	
Fiscal and administrative services	1,400	
Total operating expenses	9,300	
Operating income	200	
Add nonoperating income	130	
Excess of revenues over expenses	$ 330	

FIGURE 1.7B
Happy Valley Hospital Statement of Operations, GAAP Format, Year Ended December 31, 20X2

*Net patient services revenue is net of $500 of charity care. Happy Valley Hospital provides charity care to patients with incomes less than 200 percent of the federal poverty level.

of the accounting entity, (2) the name of the statement, and (3) the period of time encompassed by the statement. These elements should always appear in the heading of statements of operations.

The accounting entity is identified here, as in the balance sheet previously discussed, as Happy Valley Hospital. It is the economic unit or organization whose activities are reported in the financial statement. A careful identification of the entity is required to clearly distinguish it from other entities, such as the Happy Valley college, church, nursing home, or manufacturing company. As previously stated, the hospital is personified as an economic being separate and distinct from its governing board, management, and employees.

The heading also includes the name of the statement—statement of operations. This indicates the nature and function of the statement.

Observe that the illustrative statement of operations is dated "year ended December 31, 20X2." This specifies the accounting period to which the statement of operations elements are related (that is, the 12 calendar months of 20X2). It is improper and misleading to date the statement "December 31, 20X2," as this would imply that the information relates to a single day or, at least, to an indeterminate period of time ending on that date. The statement of operations often is prepared for a period of one month or one quarter, as well as annually, and it is essential that the particular time period covered be clearly disclosed in the statement heading. Balance sheets also are prepared on a monthly or quarterly basis, as well as annually. When financial statements are issued during the course of a year, they are referred to as **interim** and/or **internal statements**. For the present, however, you will be concerned only with annual financial statements.

Some hospitals and other healthcare entities employ a fiscal year ending June 30 or September 30 rather than a calendar-year accounting or reporting period ending December 31. For ease of exposition, however, a fiscal year ending December 31 is assumed throughout this text.

The previously discussed balance sheet presented the assets, liabilities, and net assets of Happy Valley Hospital at December 31, 20X1 (see Figure 1.6). These resources and obligations, of course, became the opening balances for the 20X2 year. For example, the closing cash balance on December 31, 20X1, becomes the opening cash balance on January 1, 20X2. As the 20X2 year unfolds day by day, Happy Valley Hospital will complete thousands of individual business transactions. Services will be provided to patients, supplies will be purchased and used, employees will be paid salaries and wages, cash receipts will arise from billings to patients and third parties, and various other operating activities will take place.

At the end of 20X2, another balance sheet can be prepared, as shown in Figure 1.8. This statement presents the financial position of the hospital at December 31, 20X2. (A vertical, or report, format is used here simply to illustrate an alternative form of presentation; Figure 1.6 presented a balance sheet in

FIGURE 1.8

Happy Valley Hospital Balance Sheet, December 31, 20X2

Assets

Cash		$ 575
Accounts receivable		2,600
Inventory		420
Prepaid expenses		80
Total current assets		3,675
Long-term investments		380
Land, buildings, and equipment	$7,500	
Less accumulated depreciation	2,210	5,290
Total assets		$9,345

Liabilities and Net Assets

Accounts payable	$ 360
Notes payable	200
Accrued expenses payable	831
Deferred income	24
Total current liabilities	1,415
Long-term liabilities	3,400
Total liabilities	4,815
Hospital net assets	4,530
Total liabilities and net assets	$9,345

a horizontal format.) The December 31, 20X2, balance sheet does not reveal the details of the operating results for 20X2. A 20X2 statement of operations therefore is needed to disclose exactly what happened during the 12-month interval between December 31, 20X1, and December 31, 20X2. In this way, statements of operations serve as connecting links between successive balance sheets.

Revenues

Hospital **revenues** consist primarily of economic values earned by the hospital through the provision of services and sales of products to patients. Revenues also include receipts of unrestricted gifts and certain other donor contributions. Revenues typically are evidenced by an increase in hospital assets, either cash or receivables in most instances.

The revenues of a hospital are determined by the application of GAAP. In conformity with these principles, some increases in assets are recognized as revenues; other assets increases are not revenues. Cash received from an outpatient for a laboratory examination, for example, is revenue. A billing made to an inpatient for a day's room and board is recorded as an increase in accounts receivable and is recognized as revenue. In each case, the revenue is recorded when it is earned (that is, at the time the related service is rendered and the hospital has either received cash or has a claim against the patient for the value of the service provided). On the other hand, the receipt of cash arising from the borrowing of money from a bank is not revenue. Happy Valley Hospital provides care to patients who meet certain criteria under the hospital charity care policy without charge or at amounts less than the hospital's established rates; because the hospital does not pursue collection of amounts determined to qualify for charity care, the amounts are not reported as revenue. Happy Valley Hospital provided $450 in charity care during the reporting period.

Please note that the illustrative statement of operations shown in Figure 1.7a is in non-GAAP format. GAAP format—in this case, represented by the authoritative pronouncements of AICPA 1996 *Audit and Accounting Guide for Healthcare Organizations*—requires that the format of the statement of operations begin with the line "Net patient services revenues," as shown in Figure 1.7b. Note that "Gross patient services revenues" and "Less deductions from patient services revenues" are no longer presented on statements of operations distributed outside the facility; however, for teaching purposes, both are important and included. On statements distributed outside the facility, deductions from patient services revenues are reported as follows: Bad debt is reported as an operating expense based on rates; charity care is reported as a note based on rates, costs, or volumes and must include the hospital's policy for the provision of charity care; and contractual adjustments are not reported, though agreements with principle third parties must be reported in the notes to the financial statements.

Reporting Revenues on the Statement of Operations

Hospital revenues arising from patient care services generally are recorded at the value of those services as evidenced by the hospital's full, established rates (prices or charges) for those services. This is true whether the hospital actually collects its full charges, contracts to accept less than full charges from third-party payers, or collects nothing for the services provided. Most third-party payers, for example, pay less than established rates because their economic power permits them to negotiate lower rates. Hospitals also provide a considerable amount of service to indigent patients at nominal rates or on a free (charity) basis. Also, certain patients who are financially able to meet their obligations simply fail to pay the hospital for services they have received, and bad debts are recorded by the hospital.

Nevertheless, all patient care services rendered by the hospital are usually recorded as revenues measured in terms of full, established rates. Figure 1.7, for example, reports $10,000 of gross patient services revenues, of which $1,000 is estimated to be uncollectible for the reasons just indicated. This produces $9,000 of net patient services revenues or, if you prefer, "collectible" patient services revenues. You should understand, however, that much of this $9,000 has not yet been collected: The balance sheet at December 31, 20X2, reports $2,600 of accounts receivable!

There are two other categories of revenues in the illustrative statement of operations. "Other operating revenues" include cafeteria sales, television and parking lot fees, rentals received, tuition from educational programs, research grants, and similar items related to the hospital's mission in some way. "Nonoperating income" consists mainly of unrestricted contributions from donors and income from investments, net of nonoperating expenses and losses.

The statement of operations in Figure 1.7 presents the revenues of the hospital in condensed form. In actual practice, of course, much more detail would be required. Necessary details often are provided in supplementary schedules to accompany the summary statement of operations. The schedules supply detailed information about the revenues earned by each organizational unit (e.g., revenues of each nursing unit, laboratory revenues, pharmacy revenues). In addition, patient services revenues may be classified in various inpatient and outpatient categories. Detailed classifications of revenue deductions, other operating revenues, and nonoperating income also are provided in these supplementary schedules.

Supplementary Schedules for Summary Statements of Operations

Hospital expenses may be defined roughly as the costs of services, supplies, and other items purchased and consumed by the hospital in the provision of patient care services during a given period of time. In accordance with GAAP, expenses are measured and recognized in the period in which they are incurred or consumed in the production of hospital revenues. This may or may not be the same time period in which they are paid. When supply items are purchased for cash, for example, their costs are considered to be assets (inventory). Only when supply items are used or consumed in hospital activities are their costs recognized and reported as expenses by the hospital. Like most assets, expenses generally are measured in terms of historical costs.

Expenses

The operating expenses in Figure 1.7 are reported in a functional classification; that is, they appear according to the divisional organizational units of the hospital. In actual practice, these divisional expense totals usually are supported by supplementary schedules, in which details, classified by individual department and type of expense, are provided. General services expenses of $1,800, for example, could be reported by department (e.g., dietary, housekeeping, plant operation) and by type of expense (e.g., salaries and wages, supplies, purchased services). Illustrations of such schedules appear at a later point in this book.

Reporting Expenses on the Statement of Operations

    Rather than reporting expenses in a functional classification as shown in Figure 1.7, Happy Valley Hospital might report its expenses in an object-of-expenditure, or natural, classification in the manner indicated as follows:

Operating expenses:	
Salaries and wages	$5,080
Supplies	1,753
Purchased services	1,520
Depreciation	310

Interest	206
Other	431
Total operating expenses	$9,300

This natural classification of expense typically appears in the published financial statements of hospitals. In internal management reports, hospital expenses are classified primarily on a functional basis so as to associate the expenses with organizational units and individuals who are responsible for them. This procedure, known as **responsibility reporting**, is especially useful for managerial control purposes.

Effect of Excess of Revenues over Expenses on Net Assets Balance

The 20X2 excess of revenues over expenses of Happy Valley Hospital is $330, as indicated in Figure 1.7. As noted earlier, an excess (profit) increases the net assets of the hospital. So, by adding the 20X2 excess to the net assets balance at December 31, 20X1, we obtain the hospital net assets figure appearing in the balance sheet at December 31, 20X2:

Hospital net assets, December 31, 20X1 (Figure 1.6)	$4,200
Add excess for 20X2 (Figure 1.7)	330
Hospital net assets, December 31, 20X2 (Figure 1.8)	$4,530

Had there not been an excess (loss) in 20X2, the loss would be deducted in this computation. Recognize, however, that this is a simplification in that factors other than excess (or excess of expenses over revenues) may at times affect the hospital net assets balance. This point is discussed further at a later point in this book.

You should now have a general understanding of two of the principal financial statements comprising the end product of accounting. With this behind you, you can move on to a study of the accounting operations that produce the financial information contained in these statements.

Questions

Q1.1. What is the basic objective and purpose of the hospital enterprise?

Q1.2. Draw up a simple organization chart for a hypothetical hospital to indicate your understanding of the basic organizational structure generally found in hospitals.

Q1.3. State briefly the function of a hospital's governing board, medical director, and administrator.

Q1.4. Why is there a need for information about a hospital's financial position and operating results?

Q1.5. Describe briefly some of the major characteristics of the economic environment in which today's hospitals operate.

Q1.6. What is the primary function of hospital accounting?

Q1.7. State briefly the purpose of a balance sheet.

Q1.8. Define *assets*. List five examples of assets that appear in hospital balance sheets.

Q1.9. Distinguish between current and noncurrent assets. Give an example of each.

Q1.10. Define *liabilities*. List five examples of liabilities that appear in hospital balance sheets.

Q1.11. Distinguish between current and noncurrent liabilities. Give an example of each.

Q1.12. State the accounting equation in two alternative forms.

Q1.13. What is meant by GAAP? What is the primary source of GAAP?

Q1.14. What information should be provided in the heading of a balance sheet?

Q1.15. State briefly the purpose of the statement of operations.

Q1.16. Define *revenues*. List four examples of revenues that appear in hospital statements of operations.

Q1.17. Define *expenses*. List four examples of expenses that appear in hospital statements of operations.

Q1.18. Distinguish between a functional classification of expenses and a natural classification of expenses.

Q1.19. What information should be provided in the heading of the statement of operations?

Q1.20. "In a hospital balance sheet, assets are reported at their fair market values." Do you agree or disagree? Explain your answer.

Q1.21. "In a hospital statement of operations, revenues represent cash receipts, and expenses represent cash disbursements of the period." Do you agree or disagree? Explain your answer.

Q1.22. What are interim financial statements?

Q1.23. In hospital accounting, when should revenues and expenses be recognized and recorded?

Q1.24. What is the accounting entity concept?

Q1.25. What are two of the major objectives of an effective system of internal control in hospitals?

Exercises

E1.1.   Given the following, what are the missing dollar amounts?

Assets	Liabilities	Net Assets
1) $90,000	$60,000	$?
2) 80,000	?	30,000
3) ?	35,000	50,000

E1.2. Given the following, what is the total amount of current assets?

Prepaid expenses	$ 150
Long-term investments	600
Cash	260
Deferred income	110
Inventory	320
Plant assets, at cost	8,400
Accounts receivable	2,900
Accumulated depreciation	3,300

E1.3. Given the following, what is the amount of long-term (noncurrent) liabilities?

Current liabilities	$ 1,500
Current assets	3,400
Plant assets, net of accumulated depreciation	5,200
Hospital net assets	4,300
Long-term investments	400

E1.4. Given the following, what is the excess of revenues over expenses for the year?

Total operating expenses	$ 9,500
Gross patient services revenues	10,300
Nonoperating income	140
Deductions from patient services revenues	1,100
Other operating revenues	600

E1.5. Dippel Hospital's December 31, 20X2, balance sheet reported hospital net assets of $8,645. Dippel's 20X2 excess of revenues over expenses was $714.

Required: What was reported as hospital net assets in Dippel's balance sheet at December 31, 20X1?

Problems

P1.1. Keener Hospital provides you with the following information that relates to its financial position at September 30, 20X1:

Accrued expenses payable	$ 760
Inventory	480
Accumulated depreciation	2,800
Accounts payable	420
Prepaid expenses	90
Cash	600

Deferred income	15
Land, buildings, and equipment	8,800
Accounts receivable	2,450
Notes payable	150
Long-term investments	400
Bonds payable (due 20X9)	3,500

Required: Prepare, in good form, a September 30, 20X1, balance sheet for Keener Hospital.

P1.2. Alice Hospital provides you with the following information that relates to its operating results for the year ended December 31, 20X1:

Nursing services expenses	$3,900
Deductions from patient services revenues	1,200
Other professional services revenues	4,800
General services expenses	1,700
Nonoperating income	140
Fiscal and administrative services expenses	1,200
Daily patient services revenues	6,320
Other professional services expenses	2,610
Other operating revenues	450

Required: Prepare, in good form, a statement of operations for Alice Hospital for the year ended December 31, 20X1.

P1.3. McCart Hospital provides you with the following information that relates to its financial position at August 31, 20X2, and its operating results for the year then ended:

Accounts payable	$ 430
Nonoperating income	190
Accounts receivable	2,950
Deferred income	60
Long-term investments	590
Nursing services expenses	4,300
Bonds payable (due 20X9)	4,100
Daily patient services revenues	6,830
Fiscal and administrative services expenses	1,600
Cash	340
Notes payable	180
Land, buildings, and equipment	8,600
Deductions from patient services revenues	970
Prepaid expenses	70
Other professional services expenses	2,900

Other professional services revenues	4,560
Accrued expenses payable	820
Accumulated depreciation	3,200
Inventory	240
Hospital net assets, August 31, 20X1	3,660
Other operating revenues	630
General services expenses	2,100

Required: Prepare, in good form, (1) a statement of operations for McCart Hospital for the year ended August 31, 20X2, and (2) a balance sheet for McCart Hospital at August 31, 20X2.

P1.4. Clarke Hospital provides you with the following information that relates to its financial position at October 31, 20X1, and its operating results for the month then ended:

Bonds payable (due 20X6)	$2,500
Salaries and wages expenses	5,260
Prepaid expenses	40
Hospital net assets, September 30, 20X1	2,330
Daily patient services revenues	4,630
Interest expenses	120
Nonoperating income	110
Cash	170
Deferred income	20
Deductions from patient services revenues	420
Accounts payable	170
Land	250
Utilities expenses	980
Other operating revenues	380
Notes payable	200
Accounts receivable	1,930
Accumulated depreciation	1,580
Accrued expenses payable	490
Other professional services revenues	3,470
Supplies expenses	1,210
Buildings and equipment	5,000
Inventory	190
Depreciation expenses	240
Other operating expenses	70

Required: Prepare, in good form, for Clarke Hospital (1) a statement of operations for the month ended October 31, 20X1, and (2) a balance sheet at October 31, 20X1.

Note

1. See Bigalke, J. T., and D. Roach. 2005. "Corporate Responsibility: Not-for-Profits Prepare to be Held Accountable." *Healthcare Financial Management*, June, 70–76.

ANALYSIS OF BUSINESS TRANSACTIONS

The economic life of a hospital consists of a continuous stream of business transactions. At frequent intervals, for example, a hospital purchases medical and surgical supplies for its inventory. An invoice is received in due course from the supplier, and a check is written in payment of the billing. As required, the supplies are issued from inventory for use in the provision of patient care services. Certain supplies may not be itemized on the patient's bill separately; other supplies are directly chargeable. Eventually, patients' accounts will be collected, and the cash receipts are deposited in the hospital's bank accounts. The cycle then begins again.

Transactions of many different types occur daily in large numbers. Over a period of a few months, a hospital may complete thousands of individual transactions. Certainly, there must be a system by which this mass of activity can be efficiently processed and recorded so that the desired information about the hospital's business transactions can be produced on a timely and accurate basis. That system, of course, is the transaction segment of the hospital's accounting system. This chapter, and several of the chapters immediately following, describe the basic elements and operations found in all accounting systems.

Learning Accounting Techniques with Manual Systems

In addition to making certain simplifying assumptions, we also will assume that the accounting records involved are manually maintained in handwritten or typewritten form. It is true, of course, that virtually all hospitals today necessarily employ various types of accounting equipment ranging from computer systems designed for small- or medium-sized hospitals to large-scale information system devices that are designed to process enormous amounts of transaction-based data. Nevertheless, an exposition of the accounting process is greatly facilitated, and the procedural operations are more easily learned and clearly understood when a manual system is assumed. You also should be aware that accounting principles are not altered by the employment of accounting equipment or computers; the principles are the same for manual systems as for mechanized and electronic systems. You can better comprehend what various types of accounting equipment and computers do if you learn first how manual records are maintained. How to program and operate such electronic equipment, however, is beyond the scope of this book.

Documentary Evidence of Transactions

In creating records of business transactions, accountants must first be made aware that transactions have occurred. A system must be devised to document all business transactions as they occur, or at the earliest practicable point after their occurrence. It is of critical importance that no transaction is overlooked or goes unrecorded. A failure to recognize and record all transactions results in lost revenues and incomplete financial information.

Documentary evidences of transactions include purchase requisitions, purchase orders, receiving reports, invoices, checks written and checks received, patient services requisitions, charge tickets, cash register tapes, cash receipt slips, deeds and contracts, bank deposit slips, correspondence with patients and creditors, intrahospital memoranda, and many other forms and business papers. This documentary evidence is the "red tape" for which accountants often are blamed. Although these documents are vital to the accounting process, they often have primary purposes and supplemental uses that are not directly related to accounting.

The documentation should provide all essential facts involved in the transaction. Accountants are particularly interested in authorizations; dates; accurate identification of the services, supplies, and other items involved; quantities; and dollar amounts. Without this information, the integrity of the accounting records is subject to question.

Thus, accountants require verifiable and objective evidence of the occurrence of bona fide transactions and of all essential facts involved. Not everything recorded in the accounting records, however, can be documented or documented to the same degree. A certain amount of the information recorded and reported by accountants consists of approximations and estimates based on professional judgment and experienced opinion. This is one aspect of accounting that makes it interesting and challenging.

The Accounting Equation

The accounting equation, or model, was introduced briefly in Chapter 1. This equation, you may remember, was expressed as follows:

$$\text{Assets} = \text{Liabilities} + \text{Net Assets}$$

The left side of the equation represents assets—that is, the things of value owned by the hospital (e.g., cash, receivables, inventory, plant assets). The right side of the equation consists of liabilities—that is, claims against the assets of the hospital, and net assets. These claims consist of the amount of assets owed to creditors (e.g., accounts payable, wages payable to employees, loans payable to banks, other economic obligations) and the residual ownership interest in assets accruing to the hospital itself (net assets). The equation must always balance; it expresses an equality that exists throughout the accounting process.

When a business transaction occurs, the accountant must analyze the transaction in terms of its effect on the accounting equation. A determination is made of the increase and/or decrease effects of each transaction on each element of the equation. Each transaction is analyzed to determine the amounts by which it increased and/or decreased assets, liabilities, or net assets. The amounts are measured in terms of dollars. Documentary evidence provides the information needed to make this analysis.

The Initial Accounting Equation

Let us assume, as a starting point, that a hospital has $5,000 of assets, $2,000 of liabilities, and $3,000 of net assets. The equation is as follows:

Assets	=	Liabilities	+	Net Assets
$5,000	=	$2,000	+	$3,000

Effect of Borrowing on the Accounting Equation

Now assume that the hospital borrows $600 from a bank. What effects does this transaction have on the accounting equation? Which of the elements of the equation were increased or decreased?

The answer is as follows:

Assets	=	Liabilities	+	Net Assets	
$5,000	=	$2,000	+	$3,000	(Previous balances)
+ 600		+ 600		_____	(Effect of transaction)
$5,600	=	$2,600	+	$3,000	(Resulting balances)

As a result of the bank loan, the hospital has $600 more assets (cash received from the bank) and $600 more liabilities (the debt owed to the bank that must be paid in the future). The receipt of a cash loan has no effect on the hospital's net assets, nor is the cash receipt regarded as revenue.

Effect of Repaying a Loan on the Accounting Equation

Assume that the hospital repays $100 (disregarding interest) of the principal amount of the bank loan. The analysis is as follows:

Assets	=	Liabilities	+	Net Assets	
$5,600	=	$2,600	+	$3,000	(Previous balances)
- 100		- 100		_____	(Effect of transaction)
$5,500	=	$2,500	+	$3,000	(Resulting balances)

The hospital disbursed $100 cash, thereby reducing its assets and its liability to the bank (from $600 to $500). Repayment of the bank loan (disregarding interest) has no effect on the hospital's net assets, nor does this expenditure constitute expense.

Effect of Purchases on the Accounting Equation

Assume that the hospital purchases $300 of supplies on account (on credit). In this transaction, the hospital obtains a new asset (inventory) and incurs a liability (accounts payable) to pay the supplier at an agreed future date. The analysis then becomes the following:

Assets	=	Liabilities	+	Net Assets	
$5,500	=	$2,500	+	$3,000	(Previous balances)
+ 300		+ 300		_____	(Effect of transaction)
$5,800	=	$2,800	+	$3,000	(Resulting balances)

This transaction has no effect on the hospital's net assets; neither is it a transaction that requires the recognition of revenue or expense.

Assume that the hospital purchases a new item of equipment for $400 cash. The analysis is as follows:

Assets	=	Liabilities	+	Net Assets	
$5,800	=	$2,800	+	$3,000	(Previous balances)
+ 400					(Effect of transaction)
					(Capital purchase)
− 400		_____		_____	(Effect of transaction)
					(Cash payment)
$5,800	=	$2,800	+	$3,000	(Resulting balances)

The effect of this transaction is to increase one asset (equipment) and decrease another asset (cash). There is no effect on liabilities or net assets, nor is there any revenue or expense to recognize.

Effect of Revenue Transaction on the Accounting Equation

Now let us consider a transaction that affects the hospital's revenue and therefore its net assets. Assume that the supplies previously purchased in one of the transactions above are sold to patients for $350 and charged to their accounts (no cash is yet received from them). The analysis now becomes as follows:

Assets	=	Liabilities	+	Net Assets	
$5,800	=	$2,800	+	$3,000	(Previous balances)
+ 350		_____		+ 350	(Effect of transaction)
$6,150	=	$2,800	+	$3,350	(Resulting balances)

This transaction produces an increase in the hospital's assets (patients' accounts receivable). Every business transaction, however, has at least two effects. What is the other effect? Because liabilities are unaffected by the transaction, the other effect must be an increase in the hospital's net assets. The principle is this: Revenues, evidenced by increases in net assets, are recognized as increases in the hospital's net assets.

But you are probably wondering about the cost of the supplies that were sold and are no longer in the hospital's inventory. The accountant must recognize the related expense in addition to revenue, as follows:

Assets	=	Liabilities	+	Net Assets	
$6,150	=	$2,800	+	$3,350	(Previous balances)
− 300				− 300	(Effect of transaction)
$5,850	=	$2,800		$3,050	(Resulting balances)

Here, assets (inventory) are decreased by the cost of the supplies removed from inventory and sold to patients. The cost of supplies sold (or used) is treated as a reduction of the hospital's net assets. The principle is this: Decreases in net assets are expenses, and expenses are recognized as decreases in hospital net assets.

We could have recorded the revenue transaction and the expense transaction simultaneously. The analysis would have been the following:

Assets	=	Liabilities	+	Net Assets	
$5,800	=	$2,800	+	$3,000	(Previous balances)
+ 350				+ 350	(Effect of transactions)
− 300				− 300	
$5,850	=	$2,800	+	$3,050	(Resulting balances)

A point made in Chapter 1 was that excess of revenues over expenses (profit) increases hospital net assets. This is because revenues increase net assets, and expenses decrease net assets. As you can see in the simultaneous transactions just shown, hospital net assets increased by $50, the profit made on the sale of supplies ($350 − $300 = $50).

Expanding the Accounting Equation for Revenues and Expenses

Hospitals, however, have so many revenue and expense transactions that it is not feasible to attempt to record them individually as direct additions to and deductions from hospital net assets. Instead, we expand the accounting equation to include two additional elements: revenues and expenses. The expanded equation is as follows:

Assets = Liabilities + Net Assets + Revenues − Expenses

Here, net assets represent the net assets balance at the beginning of the period. This extension of the equation simply expresses the principle that the net assets balance at the beginning of the period is increased by revenues earned and is decreased by expenses incurred during the period. It also allows revenues and expenses to be treated as separate elements of the equation rather than as direct changes in the net assets balance.

The expanded equation will be easier to work with if we add expenses to each side to produce the following equation:

Assets + Expenses = Liabilities + Net Assets + Revenues

This avoids having positive and negative elements on the right side of the equation. Here again, net assets represents the net assets balance at the beginning of the period. Subsequent expressions will not mention that net assets means the net assets balance at the beginning of the period (year, for example), but keep this fact in mind.

Now, using the expanded equation, let us analyze a new set of transactions for a different hospital with assumed opening balances, including $300,000 of assets, $100,000 of liabilities, and $200,000 of net assets. The assumed transactions are as follows:

1. The hospital borrowed $25,000 from a bank.
2. The hospital purchased supplies on account for $12,000.
3. Half of the supplies were issued from inventory and used in patient care ($6,000). Patients were billed for $7,500.
4. The hospital paid $14,000 of salaries and wages to its employees.
5. Patients were billed (charged) for $15,300 of other services.
6. The bank loan was paid by a disbursement of $26,000, including interest of $1,000.
7. The hospital paid $9,000 on its accounts payable.
8. The hospital collected $18,400 on patients' accounts receivable.

Figure 2.1 analyzes the effects of these transactions on the expanded equation. Observe that each transaction has at least two effects and that the equation balances (left equals right) after each of the transactions are recorded.

Obtaining the Closing Net Assets Balance

At the bottom of Figure 2.1, you see that a closing entry has been made to eliminate the accumulated totals of revenues and expenses from the equation and to add the excess of revenues over expenses (the net income, or profit) to the opening net assets balance. This produces the closing net assets balance, as shown in Figure 2.2.

In actual practice, closing entries are made at the end of each annual period as a part of the procedure known as "closing the books." Extensive attention is given to this matter in Chapter 4.

After the closing entry has been made, the accounting equation consists only of the closing balances for assets, liabilities, and net assets. These balances are carried forward into the next accounting period and become the opening balances of that period. A new accounting cycle then begins.

Debit and Credit Methodology

In analyzing and recording the effects of business transactions, accountants employ a special method involving debits and credits. This method was first

	Assets	+	Expenses	=	Liabilities	+	Net Assets	+	Revenues
Opening balances	$300,000	+ $	-0-	=	$100,000	+	$200,000	+ $	-0-
Transaction 1	+25,000				+25,000				
Resulting balances	325,000	+	-0-	=	125,000	+	200,000	+	-0-
Transaction 2	+12,000				+12,000				
Resulting balances	337,000		-0-	=	137,000	+	200,000	+	-0-
Transaction 3 {	−6,000		+6,000						
	+7,500								+7,500
Resulting balances	338,500	+	6,000	=	137,000	+	200,000	+	7,500
Transaction 4	−14,000		+14,000						
Resulting balances	324,500	+	20,000	=	137,000	+	200,000	+	7,500
Transaction 5	+15,300								+15,300
Resulting balances	339,800	+	20,000	=	137,000	+	200,000	+	22,800
Transaction 6	−26,000		+1,000		−25,000				
Resulting balances	313,800	+	21,000	=	112,000	+	200,000	+	22,800
Transaction 7	−9,000				−9,000				
Resulting balances	304,800		21,000	=	103,000	+	200,000	+	22,800
Transaction 8 {	+18,400								
	−18,400								
Resulting balances	304,800	+	21,000	=	103,000	+	200,000	+	22,800
Closing entry (profit)			−21,000				+1,800		−22,800
Closing balances	$304,800	+ $	-0-	=	$103,000	+	$201,800	+ $	-0-

FIGURE 2.1
Transaction Analysis

Net assets, beginning of period		$200,000
Revenues of the period	$22,800	
Less expenses of the period	21,000	
Excess of revenues over expenses		
(the net income, or profit) for the period		+1,800
Net assets, end of period		$201,800

FIGURE 2.2
Closing Net Asset Balance

described in writing in a book published in 1494 by an Italian monk named Paciolo. Today, more than 500 years later, accountants throughout the world are still using the system described by Paciolo.

Let us assume, for the moment, that only five types of accounts are employed in accounting: (1) assets, (2) expenses, (3) liabilities, (4) net assets, and (5) revenues. The relationship among these accounts can be expressed by the basic accounting equation previously discussed:

Assets + Expenses = Liabilities + Net Assets + Revenues

Paciolo suggested that we refer to the left side of the equation as the *debit side*. The elements of the left side—assets and expenses—are therefore debit items (or debit balances). If the accountant makes an addition to the left side of the equation, the entry is a debit. In other words, increases in assets and expenses are recorded by making debits to those accounts.

Similarly, Paciolo indicated that the right side of the equation is called the *credit side*. The elements of this side—liabilities, net assets, and revenues—are therefore credit items (or credit balances). If the accountant makes an addition to the right side of the equation, the entry is a credit. In other words, increases in liabilities, net assets, and revenues are recorded by making credits to those accounts.

Thus, increases in assets and expenses are debits; increases in liabilities, net assets, and revenues are credits. It logically follows that decreases in assets and expenses are credits and that decreases in liabilities, net assets, and revenues are debits. In summary, the rules of debit and credit are as follows:

1. With respect to assets and expenses accounts:
    a. Debit to increase.
    b. Credit to decrease.
2. With respect to liability, net assets, and revenue accounts:
    a. Credit to increase.
    b. Debit to decrease.

Most introductory accounting students first memorize these rules. As they gain experience by applying the rules to business transactions, however, debit-and-credit analysis becomes almost second nature.

Real Meaning of Debits and Credits

Many people begin a study of accounting with certain preconceived (and incorrect) notions about debits and credits. It is widely believed, for example, that a debit is something "bad" and that a credit is something "good." There also exists an erroneous idea that the term debit always means "decrease," and that credits always "increase" a balance. These notions are incorrect and, if not discarded, impair the study of accounting. The word **debit**, standing alone, simply means an entry or balance on the left side of an accounting record. A debit means increase only with respect to assets and expenses; a debit to any other type of account is a decrease. Similarly, the word **credit** means nothing more than an entry or balance on the right side of an accounting record. Whether a debit or a credit is an increase or a decrease, then, depends on the type of account to which it is related.

Use of Accounts

Accountants have devised a standard way to record debits and credits in accounts. An account form is basically a "T" shape:

(Account Name or Title)	
(left)	(right)
Debit	Credit
side	side

The name or title of the account appears at the top of the form above the horizontal rule. For the purpose here, the terms *assets, expenses, liabilities, net assets,* and *revenues* serve as the account names. (More specific account titles are introduced in Chapter 3.) A vertical rule divides the account equally into a left side and a right side.

The Basic T-Account

No matter what the account name, however, the left side of a T-account is the debit side; the right side is the credit side. With respect to assets and expenses, entries made on the left (debit) side are increases (+), and entries made on the right (credit) side are decreases (–). The opposite is true in accounts for liabilities, net assets, and revenues. These debit and credit rules are presented here in account form:

Assets	+	Expenses	=	Liabilities	+	Net Assets	+	Revenues
Dr. | Cr.		Dr. | Cr.		Dr. | Cr.		Dr. | Cr.		Dr. | Cr.
(+) | (–)		(+) | (–)		(–) | (+)		(–) | (+)		(–) | (+)

Note that the word "debit" is abbreviated Dr., and the word "credit" is abbreviated Cr. These abbreviations are derived from equivalent words of the Latin language in which Paciolo wrote. They are not English abbreviations.

Figure 2.1 analyzed eight transactions in terms of the basic accounting equation. These same eight transactions now will be analyzed in T-account form, using debits and credits. You should recall the assumed balances, labeled (B), at the beginning of the period:

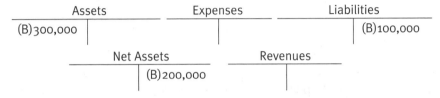

The five T-accounts, as a group, are referred to as the ledger. As you can see, the ledger is "in balance"—that is, total debits equal total credits.

The first transaction to be analyzed and entered in this ledger is one in which the hospital borrows $25,000 from a bank. This transaction creates

$25,000 of additional assets (cash) and $25,000 of additional liabilities (the amount now owed to the bank). The entry, numbered (1), is as follows:

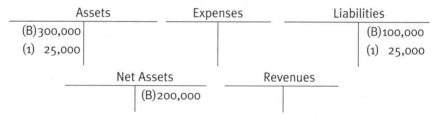

Assets	Expenses	Liabilities
(B)300,000		(B)100,000
(1) 25,000		(1) 25,000

Net Assets	Revenues
(B)200,000	

Thus, the required entry is a $25,000 debit to assets and a $25,000 credit to liabilities. The entry increases assets to a balance of $325,000 and increases the liabilities to a balance of $125,000, and the ledger remains in balance.

The second transaction is the purchase of supplies (inventory) on account for $12,000. The entry, numbered (2), is as follows:

Assets	Expenses	Liabilities
(B)300,000		(B)100,000
(1) 25,000		(1) 25,000
(2) 12,000		(2) 12,000

Net Assets	Revenues
(B)200,000	

This transaction, which produces a new asset (inventory) and a new liability (accounts payable) is recorded as a $12,000 debit to assets and a $12,000 credit to liabilities. Every transaction entry will have at least two effects; every entry will include at least one debit and one credit.

Maintaining a Balance in the Ledger

Do not fall into the trap of assuming that a transaction entry is always an increase in one account and a decrease in another. Each of the two entries made in the preceding accounts was an increase in one account and an increase in another. No decreases at all were recorded. Other types of transactions are recorded by a decrease in one account and a decrease in another (or the same) account, with no increase in any account. Still other transactions require an increase in one account and a decrease in another. It is possible to have any combination of increases and decreases.

Notice that the ledger is still in balance. The debit total of assets, $337,000 ($300,000 + $25,000 + $12,000) equals the credit totals of liabilities, $137,000 ($100,000 + $25,000 + $12,000), and net assets, $200,000. This equality of debit and credit balances must be maintained at all times.

The next transaction consists of the sale of half the supplies of inventory to patients for $7,500. Because all the supplies purchased in the second transaction cost $12,000 but only half of them were sold, the cost of the supplies sold is $6,000. This $6,000 must be removed from assets (inventory) and charged to expenses (supplies expense). The $7,500 billing to patients must be charged to patients' accounts receivable (debited to assets) and recorded as revenues earned by the hospital. The entry, numbered (3), is as follows:

Assets			Expenses	Liabilities	
(B)300,000	(3)	6,000	(3) 6,000		(B)100,000
(1) 25,000					(1) 25,000
(2) 12,000					(2) 12,000
(3) 7,500					

Net Assets	Revenues	
(B)200,000	(3)	7,500

This entry includes two debits and two credits. Entries having more than one debit or credit are referred to as **compound entries**. You also will encounter compound entries having two or more debits but only one credit, and entries having two or more credits but only one debit.

In the fourth transaction, the hospital pays $14,000 of salaries and wages to its employees. The entry, numbered (4), is as follows:

Assets			Expenses	Liabilities	
(B)300,000	(3)	6,000	(3) 6,000		(B)100,000
(1) 25,000	(4)	14,000	(4)14,000		(1) 25,000
(2) 12,000					(2) 12,000
(3) 7,500					

Net Assets	Revenues	
(B)200,000	(3)	7,500

This entry records a decrease in assets (cash) and an increase in expenses (employees' salaries and wages expense).

The fifth transaction is the billing of hospital patients for $15,300 of services (e.g., room and board, laboratory, pharmacy). This entry, numbered (5), is as follows:

Assets			Expenses	Liabilities	
(B)300,000	(3)	6,000	(3) 6,000		(B)100,000
(1) 25,000	(4)	14,000	(4)14,000		(1) 25,000
(2) 12,000					(2) 12,000
(3) 7,500					
(5) 15,300					

Net Assets	Revenues	
(B)200,000	(3)	7,500
	(5)	15,300

This entry records an increase in hospital assets (accounts receivable) and an increase in hospital revenues (revenues from services to patients). A portion of the accounts receivable established in this entry will be collected in cash in the eighth transaction.

The sixth transaction consists of the repayment of the bank loan of $25,000 plus $1,000 of interest assumed to be due to the bank. The required entry, numbered (6), includes two debits and one credit, as follows:

Assets		Expenses	Liabilities	
(B)300,000	(3) 6,000	(3) 6,000	(6) 25,000	(B)100,000
(1) 25,000	(4) 14,000	(4)14,000		(1) 25,000
(2) 12,000	(6) 26,000	(6) 1,000		(2) 12,000
(3) 7,500				
(5) 15,300				

Net Assets	Revenues	
(B)200,000	(3) 7,500	
	(5) 15,300	

Of this $26,000 cash disbursement, $1,000 is interest expense, and the remaining $25,000 is a reduction of liabilities (elimination of the bank loan payable).

The seventh transaction is the payment by the hospital of $9,000 of accounts payable to its suppliers. The required entry, numbered (7), is as follows:

Assets		Expenses	Liabilities	
(B)300,000	(3) 6,000	(3) 6,000	(6) 25,000	(B)100,000
(1) 25,000	(4) 14,000	(4)14,000	(7) 9,000	(1) 25,000
(2) 12,000	(6) 26,000	(6) 1,000		(2) 12,000
(3) 7,500	(7) 9,000			
(5) 15,300				

Net Assets	Revenues	
(B)200,000	(3) 7,500	
	(5) 15,300	

These accounts payable arose in the second transaction, when the liabilities account was credited for $12,000. Now, because $9,000 of the accounts payable is being paid, the liabilities account is debited. The difference of $3,000 remains unpaid as part of the credit balance in the liabilities account.

The last transaction is the receipt of $18,400 in payment of a portion of accounts receivable due from patients for supplies and services provided to them in previous transactions (the third and fifth transactions). The entry, numbered (8), is as follows:

Assets		Expenses		Liabilities	
(B)300,000	(3) 6,000	(3) 6,000		(6) 25,000	(B)100,000
(1) 25,000	(4) 14,000	(4)14,000		(7) 9,000	(1) 25,000
(2) 12,000	(6) 26,000	(6) 1,000			(2) 12,000
(3) 7,500	(7) 9,000				
(5) 15,300	(8) 18,400				
(8) 18,400					

Net Assets		Revenues	
	(B)200,000		(3) 7,500
			(5) 15,300

This transaction requires entering a debit and a credit to the asset account. The entry, in this case, debits (increases) one type of asset (cash) and credits (decreases) another type of asset (accounts receivable).

Now we should determine the balance of each account. Consider, for example, the assets account that consists of an opening balance at the beginning of the period, five debits for the increases in assets during the period, and five credits for the decreases in assets during the period. The balance of assets at the end of the period may be determined as follows:

	Assets	
	(B)300,000	(3) 6,000
	(1) 25,000	(4) 14,000
	(2) 12,000	(6) 26,000
	(3) 7,500	(7) 9,000
	(5) 15,300	(8) 18,400
	(8) 18,400	
(Totals)	378,200	73,400
(Less credit total)	73,400	
(Closing balance)	(B)304,800	

Notice that the opening balance of assets plus the debits (increases) during the period totals $378,200; the credits (decreases) during the period total $73,400. The difference between the debit and credit totals is the end-of-period balance of assets—that is, a debit balance of $304,800. It is a debit balance because the debit total in the account exceeds the credit total.

Generating a Trial Balance

A balance for each of the other accounts may be determined in a similar manner. To determine whether the ledger is in balance, the individual account balances may be arranged in a trial balance, as shown in Figure 2.3.

Notice that the accounts for assets and expenses have debit balances and that the accounts for liabilities, net assets, and revenues have credit balances.

FIGURE 2.3

Trial Balance

	Balances	
	Dr.	Cr.
Assets	$304,800	
Expenses	21,000	
Liabilities		$103,000
Net assets		200,000
Revenues		22,800
Totals	$325,800	$325,800

This is the normal state of affairs. Elements on the left side of the accounting equation are debit items; elements on the right side are credit items.

Obtaining the Net Assets Balance with a Closing Entry

To obtain the end-of-period net assets balance (taking into account the excess of revenues over expenses for the period), a *closing entry* is required, as indicated in the following, labeled (C):

Assets		Expenses		Liabilities	
(B)300,000	(3) 6,000	(3) 6,000	(C)21,000	(6) 25,000	(B)100,000
(1) 25,000	(4) 14,000	(4)14,000		(7) 9,000	(1) 25,000
(2) 12,000	(6) 26,000	(6) 1,000			(2) 12,000
(3) 7,500	(7) 9,000				
(5) 15,300	(8) 18,400				
(8) 18,400					

Net Assets		Revenues	
	(B)200,000	(C) 22,800	(3) 7,500
	(C) 1,800		(5) 15,300

Again, the closing entry eliminates the balances of revenues and expenses and records the $1,800 difference (excess of revenues over expenses) as an increase in the net assets account. The double rules in the accounts for revenues and expenses indicate that these accounts have been closed and have no balance. In the account for expenses, for example, debits equal credits; the account balance is zero.

The Need for More Detailed Information

If financial statements were prepared from the accounts developed in the previous discussion, the information in those statements would be highly

FIGURE 2.4
Condensed
Statement of
Operations and
Balance Sheet

Income Statement

Revenues	$ 22,800
Less expenses	21,000
Net income of the period	$ 1,800

Balance Sheet

Assets	$304,800
Liabilities	$103,000
Net assets	201,800
Total liabilities and net assets	$304,800

condensed data. The statement of operations for the period and the balance sheet at the end of the period would contain the information shown in Figure 2.4.

Whereas these are the general types of information required by financial statement users, the categories are much too broad to be useful. Much more detailed information must be provided.

From what services and other sources did the hospital earn its revenues, and how much revenue was derived from each source? What are the functional and natural breakdowns of the hospital's expenses, and how much expense was incurred in each classification? What specific assets are owned by the hospital, and how much money is invested in each of them? What specific liabilities does the hospital have, and what is the monetary amount of each of them? Which of these assets and liabilities are current, and which are noncurrent?

The next chapter begins to develop the detailed information necessary to answer such questions.

Questions

Q2.1. Indicate briefly the need for documentary evidence in accounting. Give five examples of documentary evidence used in hospital accounting.

Q2.2. Define the term *debit*.

Q2.3. Define the term *credit*.

Q2.4. "In accounting, debits represent something 'bad' (undesirable), whereas credits represent something 'good' (desirable)." Do you agree or disagree? Explain your answer.

Q2.5. State the rules of debit and credit with respect to asset and expense accounts.

Q2.6. State the rules of debit and credit with respect to liability, net assets, and revenue accounts.

Q2.7. What are compound entries?

Q2.8.   What is a trial balance? What is its purpose?

Q2.9.   Which of the following types of accounts normally have debit balances?
  a. Assets
  b. Liabilities
  c. Net assets
  d. Revenues
  e. Expenses

Q2.10. What is the purpose of a closing entry?

Exercises

E2.1.   On March 31, Hopi Hospital had assets of $500,000, liabilities of $300,000, and net assets of $200,000. During April, the following transactions were completed:

  1. Services rendered to patients, $100,000
  2. Collections on patients' accounts, $85,000
  3. Supplies purchased on account, $20,000
  4. Payments on accounts payable to suppliers, $16,000
  6. Supplies consumed in patient care services, $18,000
  7. Other expenses paid in cash, $54,000
  8. Purchased equipment for cash, $12,000

  Required: What were the amounts of Hopi Hospital's (1) assets, (2) liabilities, and (3) net assets at April 30?

E2.2.   On August 31, Zebra Hospital had $800,000 of assets, $500,000 of liabilities, and $300,000 of net assets. The following transactions were completed during September:

  1. Borrowed $75,000 from a local bank
  2. Repaid $25,000 of the bank loan, plus $750 interest for the month of September
  3. Provided $186,000 of services to patients
  4. Collected $193,000 on patients' accounts
  5. Other September expenses paid in cash, $184,000
  6. Purchased equipment for $15,000 cash

  Required: What were the amounts of Zebra Hospital's (1) assets, (2) liabilities, and (3) net assets at September 30?

E2.3.   At May 31, Tiger Hospital had $650,000 of assets, $350,000 of liabilities, and $300,000 of net assets. The following transactions were completed during June:

1. Charged patients for $204,000 of services
2. Collected $190,000 on patients' accounts
3. Purchased $31,000 of supplies on account
4. Used $28,000 of supplies in patient care activities
5. Paid $35,000 on accounts payable
6. Paid employee salaries and wages of $99,000
7. Paid other expenses of $60,000

Required: What were the amounts of Tiger Hospital's (1) assets, (2) liabilities, and (3) net assets at June 30?

E2.4.   Tarzan Hospital began operations on January 1, 20X1, with $10,000 of assets, $6,000 of liabilities, and $4,000 of net assets. Following are the ledger accounts at December 31, 20X1:

Assets		Expenses		Liabilities	
10,000	500	1,100		500	6,000
1,500	1,100	3,200			1,500
5,000	3,200				
4,200	4,200				

Net Assets		Revenues	
	4,000		5,000

Required: Reconstruct the 20X1 transactions of Tarzan Hospital to the extent possible.

Problems

P2.1.   Assume that Joy Hospital on May 1 had $29,000 of assets, $12,000 of liabilities, and $17,000 of net assets. Subsequently, the following transactions were completed:

1. The hospital borrowed $2,500 from a local bank.
2. The hospital repaid $1,000 of the bank loan (disregard interest).
3. Supplies costing $1,800 were purchased on account and placed in inventory.
4. A new item of equipment was purchased for $4,600 cash.
5. The hospital paid $800 on its accounts payable.
6. Supplies previously purchased for $700 were sold to patients for $960 cash.
7. Patients' accounts were charged for $1,770 of hospital services rendered to them.
8. Cash collections on patients' accounts amounted to $1,150.

Required: Taking into account the cumulative effects of the eight transactions and the May 1 balances, what are Joy Hospital's (1) total assets, (2) total liabilities, and (3) total net assets?

P2.2.   On October 1, Taylor Hospital had $450,000 of assets, $150,000 of liabilities, and $300,000 of net assets. Transactions completed during the month of October were as follows:

1. The hospital borrowed $50,000 from a bank.
2. The hospital purchased supplies on account for $20,000.
3. Seventy-five percent of the supplies were issued from inventory and used in patient care. Patients were billed for $21,000.
4. The hospital paid $45,000 of salaries and wages to employees.
5. Patients were billed for $48,500 of other services.
6. The hospital paid $30,400 (including $400 interest) on the bank loan.
7. The hospital paid $17,000 on its accounts payable.
8. The hospital collected $59,000 on patients' accounts.

Required: Prepare an analysis of these transactions using the format illustrated in Figure 2.1.

P2.3.   On December 1, Todd Hospital had $380,000 of assets, $120,000 of liabilities, and $260,000 of net assets. Transactions completed during the month of December were as follows:

1. The hospital borrowed $20,000 from a bank.
2. Supplies purchased on account amounted to $14,000.
3. Supplies issued from inventory and used in patient care amounted to $10,000. Patients were billed for $16,000.
4. Employees were paid $28,000 of salaries and wages.
5. New equipment was purchased for $4,000 cash.
6. Patients were billed for $26,000 of other services.
7. The bank loan was paid off with a disbursement of $20,300, including interest of $300.
8. Payments on accounts payable amounted to $11,000.
9. Collections on accounts receivable were $39,000.

Required: (1) Prepare a debit and credit analysis of the nine transactions in T-account form, including a closing entry at December 31. (2) Indicate the balance of each account at December 31.

P2.4.   On October 31, Iowa Hospital had $710,000 of assets, $230,000 of liabilities, and $480,000 of net assets. Transactions completed during the month of November were as follows:

1. Supplies purchased on account totaled $29,000.
2. Supplies that had cost $26,000 were issued from inventory and used in patient care. Patients were billed $31,000.
3. Employees were paid $84,000 of salaries and wages.
4. Patients were billed for November services as follows:

Daily patient services	$51,500
Other professional services	37,500
Total	$89,000

5. Other operating revenues received in cash amounted to $2,800.
6. Purchase of new equipment on account was for $12,000.
7. Payments on accounts payable amounted to $24,700.
8. Collections on accounts receivable totaled $102,600.
9. Miscellaneous other expenses paid in cash came to $14,300.

Required: (1) Prepare a debit and credit analysis of the above information in T-account form, including a closing entry at November 30. (2) Prepare an income statement for November that is as detailed as possible.

JOURNAL, LEDGER, AND TRIAL BALANCE

The preceding chapter was concerned with analyzing business transactions in terms of how they increase and decrease the basic elements of the accounting equation. Only five accounts were used in the analysis: assets, expenses, liabilities, net assets, and revenues. A much greater number of accounts is needed, however, to provide the detailed information required by hospital management and other financial statement users. Such information is developed by the use of a chart of accounts, sometimes called a classification of accounts. A relatively simple chart of accounts is introduced in this chapter; a more sophisticated set of accounts is presented in Chapter 10.

Also in the previous chapter, transaction entries were recorded directly in the accounts. This procedure is not feasible in actual accounting practice because of the large volume of transactions that must be recorded each day. Instead, the effects of business transactions are recorded initially in an accounting record known as a journal. The process of making records of transactions in a journal is called **journalizing**. Subsequently, the journalized information is transferred (by a process called posting) into the accounts in the hospital's ledger. The major part of this chapter is devoted to a discussion of these procedures.

Illustration Data

Let us assume that Smalltown is a rapidly growing community, but one without a hospital of its own. Because the nearest hospital is in a city some distance away, the citizens of Smalltown decide to build their own community hospital. A Civic Improvement Committee is established to raise the necessary money for construction, equipment, and initial operating needs (working capital). An extended fundraising campaign is completed on December 31, 20X0, when a goal of $100,000 is achieved. The hospital is incorporated under the laws of the state, and a corporate charter is duly obtained.

On receipt of the not-for-profit charter, Smalltown Hospital begins its corporate existence on January 1, 20X1. During the ensuing year, the following transactions are completed by the hospital:

1. On January 1, 20X1, the hospital receives its initial net assets of $100,000 from the citizens of Smalltown through the Civic Improvement Committee.

2. On January 2, 20X1, the hospital issues $50,000 of 8 percent, ten-year bonds at face value. Interest on these bonds is payable annually on December 31.

3. On January 3, 20X1, the hospital purchases plant assets for cash as follows:

Land	$ 25,000
Buildings	67,000
Equipment	45,000
Total cost	$137,000

The cost of the building includes the alteration and remodeling of an existing structure previously operated as a hotel.

4. During the year, total purchases of supplies on account by the hospital amount to $28,200. These include dietary supplies, pharmaceuticals, and other medical and surgical supplies.

5. As the year passes, $21,500 of these supplies are issued from inventory for use in hospital patient care activities.

6. Services rendered to patients over the course of the year total $120,300 and are billed to patients as follows:

Daily patient services	$ 72,180
Ancillary services	48,120
Total revenues	$120,300

Daily patient services include room, board, routine nursing care, and minor medications. Ancillary services are those provided by departments such as operating rooms, laboratory, radiology, and pharmacy.

7. During the year, collections on patients' accounts amount to $94,500. (We will assume no charity care, bad debts, or other deductions from revenues occur.)

8. Payments on accounts payable to suppliers are $22,600.

9. During 20X1, the hospital receives in cash $13,800 of revenues from other sources, including unrestricted contributions and gifts.

10. Over the course of 20X1, the hospital pays operating expenses as follows:

Salaries and wages	$ 76,400
Utilities	12,700
Insurance	3,600
Repairs	2,900
Other expenses	1,300
Total	$ 96,900

11. On October 1, 20X1, the hospital obtains a short-term, 10 percent loan of $12,000 from a local bank.

12. On December 31, 20X1, the hospital pays interest expense on the bonds and bank loan as follows:

Interest on bonds	$4,000
Interest on bank loan	300
Total	$4,300

You should understand that this list is largely a summary of the thousands of transactions the hospital had during 20X1. Except in a few instances, individual transactions are not indicated. This also means that, other than where particular dates are specified, the itemization is not in the chronological order in which the events occurred. Items 4 through 10, for example, each describe a series of transactions that took place over the entire year at periodic intervals. The hospital rendered patient services daily, cash was received and disbursed every day, supplies were purchased periodically, salaries and wages were paid biweekly, and so forth.

You now are aware of all of the financial activities of Smalltown Hospital during 20X1. Knowing this, what is the hospital's excess of revenues over expenses for the year? How much cash does Smalltown Hospital have in the bank at the end of the year? At December 31, 20X1, what is the amount of accounts receivable due from patients? Inventory? Accounts payable to suppliers? What are the amounts of other hospital assets and liabilities?

Users of Accounting Information

Who cares about these balances? As you learned in Chapter 1, management, creditors, third-party payers, bankers, bondholders, and governmental agencies all care. The citizens of Smalltown have a rather personal interest in the hospital's finances as well. All of these and other groups care very much indeed about these questions and the answers to them. Without such information, none of these groups would be able to make intelligent economic decisions.

So, once we agree that financial information about Smalltown Hospital is important and useful, how do we deal with the problems of accumulating, communicating, and using it? How do we develop and maintain the necessary accounting records, and how do we report the recorded information to those who use it?

Chart of Accounts

As noted in Chapter 2, competent documentary evidence of completed transactions is the first and fundamental requirement of the accounting system. Documentary evidence is essential, because the reliability and accuracy of the information produced by the accounting process rests largely on the extent to which that information is based on verifiable, objectively determined facts. You realize, of course, that accounting never can become fully objective or completely scientific. Accounting is an art that requires the exercise of judgment and the use of estimates. Wherever possible, however, business transactions are evidenced by independent and objective documentation, such as invoices, bank deposit slips, charge tickets, cash receipt slips, and other business papers.

Transaction Types Listed in the Chart of Accounts

Properly executed documentary evidences make the accountant aware that transactions have occurred. To record these transactions in an organized manner, an information classification system must be used. This system is set forth in a chart of accounts, such as the one illustrated in Figure 3.1. This chart depicts the manner in which transaction data will be classified and recorded in the accounting records of Smalltown Hospital. It is designed primarily to meet the informational needs of the hospital management, but accounting standards as well as legal, tax, and regulatory agency requirements also influence the design of the chart of accounts. The chart of accounts for Smalltown Hospital in Figure 3.1 has more detail than you need for Chapters 3 and 4, but it provides sufficient detail for Chapters 5 through 8. An expanded chart of accounts is discussed in Chapter 10. It is important to note that few hospitals use the same chart of accounts because of differences in information needs. The chart of accounts in Figure 3.1 is designed for teaching purposes only.

Coding Groups of Accounts

The illustrative chart is divided into six major groups of accounts: assets, liabilities, net assets, revenues, deductions from revenues, and expenses. Each account in the chart is assigned an identifying number; any account in the 100 series is an asset account, any account in the 200 series is a liability account, and so on. This numerical coding of the accounts saves clerical time and effort in that it is easier to pronounce, write, or type "601," for example, than it is to pronounce, write, or type "salaries and wages expense." The numerical coding also promotes accuracy and permits the accountant to readily identify the nature of any account. Data processing equipment requires the use of account numbers.

There are 43 accounts in Smalltown Hospital's chart. If the management of Smalltown Hospital required more detailed information about expenditures for, say, utilities, then separate accounts could be provided for water, heat, and electricity instead of combining all such expenditures into a single utilities account. Or, rather than a single revenue account for ancillary services, a number of separate accounts could be maintained for individual services, such as operating room revenue, laboratory revenue, and pharmacy revenue.

This, of course, is done in actual practice, where charts of accounts generally consist of several hundred individual accounts. The Smalltown Hospital's chart of accounts, however, is limited to 43 accounts for the purposes of this introductory discussion. Notice also that we introduced accounts for contractual adjustments, depreciation, prepaid and accrued

FIGURE 3.1

Smalltown
Hospital Chart
of Accounts

100   *Assets*
    101   Cash
    102   Temporary investments
    103   Accrued interest receivable
    104   Accounts receivable
    105   Allowance for uncollectible accounts
    106   Inventory
    107   Prepaid insurance
    108   Prepaid rent
    109   Prepaid interest
    120   Land
    130   Buildings
    131   Accumulated depreciation—buildings
    140   Equipment
    141   Accumulated depreciation—equipment

200   *Liabilities*
    201   Accounts payable
    202   Notes payable
    203   Accrued interest payable
    204   Accrued salaries and wages payable
    205   Deferred rental income
    206   Deferred tuition income
    250   Bonds payable

300   *Net Assets*
    301   Hospital net assets
    302   Revenue and expense summary

400   *Revenues*
    401   Routine services revenue
    402   Ancillary services revenue
    403   Interest income
    404   Rental income
    405   Tuition income
    406   Other operating revenues
    407   Premium revenue
    408   Nonoperating revenue

500   *Deductions from Revenues*
    501   Contractual adjustments
    502   Charity care adjustments

600   *Expenses*
    601   Salaries and wages expense
    602   Supplies expense
    603   Utilities expense
    604   Insurance expense
    605   Repairs expense
    606   Rent expense
    607   Depreciation expense
    608   Interest expense
    609   Bad debt expense
    610   Other expenses

FIGURE 3.2

General
Journal Form

Date			Accounts and Explanations	Acct. No.	Dr.	Cr.
Mo.	Day	Year	Account(s) debited	No.	Amounts	
			Account(s) credited	No.		Amounts
			Explanation of the transaction			
		X1	Cash	101	100,000	
			Hospital net assets	301		100,000
			Receipt of initial asset from Civic Improvement Committee			
1	2	X1	Cash	101	50,000	
			Bonds payable	250		50,000
			Issue of 8%, 10-year bonds at face value			

expenses, bad debts, and various other financial statement items that you may recall from Chapter 1. These complications will be further discussed at appropriate points in subsequent chapters.

Journal

Assuming that we have documentary evidence supporting the Smalltown Hospital's 20X1 transactions, and given the hospital's chart of accounts, we can proceed with the task of analyzing and recording the transactions for 20X1. Each of the 12 transactions previously listed will be analyzed in terms of its effects on the account classifications provided in the chart of accounts. Which account or accounts should be debited and which should be credited for each of these transactions? This debit and credit analysis will be recorded initially in an accounting record called a **journal**.

The General Journal
As you will see later, there are many types of journals: revenue journals, cash receipts journals, voucher registers, and so on. These special journals are illustrated in Chapters 11 through 14. We are concerned at this point, however, only with the general journal. This particular form of journal is illustrated in Figure 3.2.

The Journalizing Process
The process of recording transactions in the journal is called **journalizing**. It consists of a formal recorded analysis of the increase and decrease effects of

transactions on the specific account classifications provided in the chart of accounts. You might think of journalizing as maintaining a business diary for the hospital. The journal is a chronological record of financial events in the economic life of the hospital. As each event, or transaction, occurs, it is recorded in the journal. This record, as you can see in Figure 3.2, consists of several elements, which are entered in the following order:

1. The date of the transaction;
2. The titles of the accounts affected (increased and/or decreased) by the transaction—that is, the particular accounts to be debited and credited;
3. A brief explanation of the nature and salient facts of each transaction;
4. The account numbers of the accounts being debited and credited; and
5. The dollar amounts of the debits and credits.

These are the essential elements of a journal entry. All five of these elements must be provided for each entry.

Several different kinds of journal entries are made in accounting. Later in this book, you will learn how to make adjusting entries, correcting entries, reversing entries, and closing entries. At this point, however, we are concerned only with entries to record transactions—that is, transaction entries.

All of the transaction entries for Smalltown Hospital for 20X1 are presented in Figure 3.3. Note the following points:

1. The date on which each transaction occurred ordinarily appears in the column on the far left. For purposes of this illustration, however, we give each transaction entry a number rather than a specific date. Transactions of the same type—purchases of supplies, for example—are summarized for the entire year in this illustration. They are recorded by a single journal entry to simplify and shorten the presentation; this is why the journal entries are not dated with a specific month and day.
2. The titles of the accounts debited and credited, along with a brief explanation of the transaction being recorded, are indicated in the next section of the journal.
   a. The titles of the accounts debited in each entry are written first and are entered against the left margin.
   b. The titles of the accounts credited are written underneath the accounts debited and are indented about an inch or so. This indentation distinguishes the credits from the debits at a glance.
   c. The explanations or descriptions of the transaction follow the account titles and are indented about half an inch so that they will not be confused with account titles.
3. The account numbers of the accounts debited and credited in each journal entry are entered in the column provided for them. Do not "invent" new account numbers; use only the numerical coding provided by the chart of accounts.

Entry No.	Accounts and Explanations	Acct. No.	Debit	Credit
1	Cash	101	100,000	
	Hospital net assets	301		100,000
	Receipt of net asset funds from			
	Smalltown Civic Improvement Committee			
2	Cash	101	50,000	
	Bonds payable	250		50,000
	Issue of 8%, 10-year bonds at face value			
3	Land	120	25,000	
	Buildings	130	67,000	
	Equipment	140	45,000	
	Cash	101		137,000
	Purchase of plant assets			
4	Inventory	106	28,200	
	Accounts payable	201		28,200
	Purchase of supplies on account			
5	Supplies expense	602	21,500	
	Inventory	106		21,500
	Supplies used			
6	Accounts receivable	104	120,300	
	Routine services revenue	401		72,180
	Ancillary services revenue	402		48,120
	Charges to patients for services rendered			
7	Cash	101	94,500	
	Accounts receivable	104		94,500
	Collections on patients' accounts			
8	Accounts payable	201	22,600	
	Cash	101		22,600
	Payments on accounts payable			
	to suppliers			
9	Cash	101	13,800	
	Other operating revenues	406		13,800
	Receipt of miscellaneous revenues			
10	Salaries and wages expense	601	76,400	
	Utilities expense	603	12,700	
	Insurance expense	604	3,600	
	Repairs expense	605	2,900	
	Other expenses	610	1,300	
	Cash	101		96,900
	Payments of operating expenses			

Continued

FIGURE 3.3
(**CONTINUED**)
Smalltown
Hospital 20X1
Journal

Entry No.	Accounts and Explanations	Acct. No.	Debit	Credit
11	Cash	101	12,000	
	Notes payable	202		12,000
	Receipt of short-term, 10% loan			
	from local bank			
12	Interest expense	608	4,300	
	Cash	101		4,300
	Payment of interest as follows:			
	Interest on bonds $4,000			
	Interest on bank loan 300			
	Total $4,300			

4. The dollar amounts involved in the transaction are written in the debit and credit columns on the right side of the journal. Dollar signs ($) are not necessary in these columns.
5. One line is skipped between journal entries so that each entry is set apart from the others on the journal page.

Although some accounting may still be done manually in typewritten or handwritten form, most hospitals employ computerized accounting equipment. What you see in Figure 3.3 in manual form, however, is the same sort of record made by computerized accounting systems.

Let us quickly examine each of the 12 transaction entries appearing in Smalltown Hospital's 20X1 journal:

Entry
 No.
1. The transaction had the effect of increasing the hospital assets (cash) and increasing the hospital's net assets. Assets are increased by debits, and net assets are increased by credits; so, we record a debit to cash and a credit to hospital net assets.
2. The transaction increased the hospital's assets (cash) and its liabilities (bonds payable). Assets are increased by debits, and liabilities are increased by credits; so, we debit cash and credit bonds payable. (This entry is very similar to entry 11.)
3. The transaction increased three asset categories (land, buildings, and equipment) and decreased another asset (cash). Assets are increased by debits and decreased by credits; so, we debit the accounts for land, buildings, and equipment, and we credit the cash account.
4. The transaction was one in which the hospital acquired an asset (inventory) and incurred a liability (accounts payable); so, we record an addition to the hospital assets and an addition to hospital liabilities.

Later, you will see that purchased supplies sometimes may be debited directly to supplies expense rather than to inventory. For the present, however, we will debit inventory for purchases of supplies.

5. The transaction decreased an asset (inventory) and increased the hospital's expenses (supplies expense). Expenses are increased by debits; assets are decreased by credits; so, we record the cost of the supplies used as expense and reduce the inventory.

6. In this summary transaction, hospital services were rendered to patients who did not pay for the services at the time they were provided.

   Revenues earned by the hospital are recognized (recorded) when services are rendered. The transaction, then, increases the hospital's assets and its revenues. Because assets are increased by debits and revenues are increased by credits, we debit receivables and credit the appropriate revenue accounts.

7. Collections on patients' accounts increase cash and decrease accounts receivable. No revenue is recognized; the revenue to which these collections relate has already been recorded in entry 6.

8. When supplies were purchased on account (entry 4), accounts payable were established by a credit. Now, when a portion of these accounts is paid, accounts payable are debited (decreased) and cash is credited (decreased). This entry is a decrease in one account and a decrease in another; the transaction results in no increase in any account.

9. This transaction entry records the receipt of cash representing revenues collected from miscellaneous operating sources, such as sales by the hospital cafeteria. Some revenues may be recorded directly in this manner without using a receivables account.

10. This summary entry records the disbursements made during the year for various operating expenses. The appropriate expense accounts are debited, and cash is credited.

In actual practice, however, all hospital disbursements usually are run through liability accounts. Salaries and wages, for example, generally require two entries:

Salaries and wages expense	$XXX,XXX	
Salaries and wages payable		$XXX,XXX
Salaries and wages payable	$XXX,XXX	
Cash		$XXX,XXX

This procedure will be introduced later; for now, we will record expenses directly by debits to expense and credits to cash. We also are disregarding, at this point, matters such as payroll taxes, prepaid and accrued expenses, and depreciation.

11. This entry records the receipt of a short-term (less than one year) loan from a bank. Cash is debited, and the liability to the bank is established by the credit. A similar transaction was recorded in entry 2.

   Note that neither this entry nor entry 2 gave recognition to interest, either as a liability or as an expense. The point is that at the time the bank loan was received and at the time the bonds were issued, the hospital owed no interest and therefore had no interest expense. The interest on these obligations is recorded in entry 12.

12. Recall that the hospital issued $50,000 of ten-year, 8 percent bonds at the beginning of the year. These bonds have been outstanding all year, so the bond interest expense is $4,000 (8 percent of $50,000). The bank loan, on the other hand, was obtained on October 1, 20X1. Because the hospital has had the use of the bank's money for only three months (October, November, and December), the hospital's interest expense is $300 ($12,000 × 10 percent × 3 months ÷ 12 months).

   We are assuming that interest on the bonds and on the bank loan is paid on December 31, 20X1. So, the entry debits interest expense and credits cash for $4,300, or $4,000 + $300. If we assume, however, that the interest was payable on January 1, 20X2, the December 31 entry would be as follows:

Interest expense	$4,300	
Accrued interest payable		$4,300

   We are not yet ready to consider expense accruals, but this matter will be considered at a later point in this book.

What the Journal Reveals

Thus, Smalltown Hospital's 20X1 journal provides a chronological record of the effects of the year's transactions on the account classifications set forth in the hospital's chart of accounts. It presents an economic history of the hospital's financial activities for the year.

   To assist you in studying the transaction entries in the 20X1 journal of Smalltown Hospital, a classification of routine transaction entries is provided in Figure 3.4. Note the following points:

1. Transactions completed by a hospital may be basically classified as either cash transactions or noncash transactions. If the transaction produces a cash receipt or requires a cash outlay, it is a cash transaction. All other transactions, of course, are noncash transactions.
2. If the transaction does not involve a cash inflow or outflow, it may be (for example) the purchase of supplies on account, a charge to patients for services rendered, or the use of supplies from the hospital's inventory.

FIGURE 3.4
Classification
of Routine
Transaction
Entries

	Dr.	Cr.
Noncash Transaction Entries		
1. Purchases of supplies on account:		
Inventory	X	
Accounts payable		X
2. Charges to patients for services rendered:		
Accounts receivable	X	
Appropriate revenue accounts		X
3. Usage of supplies from inventory:		
Supplies expense	X	
Inventory		X
Cash Disbursement Transaction Entries		
1. Acquisition of an asset:		
Appropriate asset account	X	
Cash		X
2. Elimination of a liability:		
Appropriate liability account	X	
Cash		X
3. Payment of an expense:		
Appropriate expense account	X	
Cash		X
Cash Receipt Transaction Entries		
1. Collections on patients' accounts:		
Cash	X	
Receivables—patient services		X
2. Incurrence of a liability:		
Cash	X	
Appropriate liability account		X
3. Receipt of revenue:		
Cash	X	
Appropriate revenue account		X

Although there are many other types of noncash transactions, these three are the ones with which you should be most concerned at this point in your study of accounting.

3. If the transaction is a cash transaction, it is either a cash disbursement or a cash receipt transaction. This can be determined simply by reading the description of the transaction as given in the text or in end-of-chapter problems.

   a. If the transaction is a cash disbursement, you always make a credit to cash. Cash disbursements are decreases in cash, an asset. To decrease an asset, you credit the asset. To determine what is debited, simply ask yourself, "For what was the money spent?" Was it spent to acquire an asset? If so, debit the asset. Was it spent to eliminate or reduce a liability? If so, debit the appropriate liability account. Was it spent to pay an expense? If so, debit the appropriate expense account.

Cash disbursement transactions may require a debit to net assets or to a revenue account, but such transactions are rather unusual. You need not be concerned with such transactions at this time.

b. If the transaction is identified as a cash receipt, you will always make a debit to cash. To determine the proper credit, simply ask yourself, "What was the source of the cash receipt?" Did the cash arise from collections of patients' accounts? If so, credit accounts receivable. Was the cash obtained through the incurrence of a liability, such as bank loans or bond issues? If so, credit the appropriate liability account. Does the cash receipt represent revenues provided on a cash basis—that is, cash received at the time the service is rendered? If so, credit the appropriate revenue account.

Cash receipt transactions rarely require a credit to expense, but a credit to net assets sometimes is required, as you have seen in Smalltown Hospital's first journal entry. Also, hospitals occasionally sell plant assets that require a credit to land, buildings, or equipment. Later on, you will be introduced to some of these transactions.

Remember that Figure 3.4 is a classification of routine, regularly recurring transaction entries only. Such recurring transactions in practice are recorded in specialized journals that are illustrated in subsequent chapters. Until then, we will enter all transactions in a general journal. There also are other kinds of transactions not included in Figure 3.4. And, as mentioned earlier, entries other than transaction entries are made in journals—for example, adjusting entries and closing entries. You will be introduced to nontransaction entries shortly.

Ledger

At this point, we have a complete record of the transactions completed by Smalltown Hospital during 20X1. This record appears in chronological sequence in the hospital's journal. The journal, however, does not readily or directly provide the information needed for the development of financial statements. It does not provide individual account balances at the end of the year. Nowhere in the journal do we find, for example, the December 31, 20X1, cash balance. In actual practice, a general journal could consist of hundreds of pages and include perhaps thousands of transaction entries. Cash receipt and disbursement entries would appear in chronological order throughout the pages of the journal, and there would

FIGURE 3.5

Ledger Account

Account Title: Cash							Account No.: 101	
Date							Balance	
Mo.	Day	Year		Ref.	Dr.	Cr.	Dr.	Cr.
1	1	X1		GJ-1	100,000		100,000	
1	2	X1		GJ-1	50,000		150,000	
1	3	X1		GJ-1		137,000		13,000

be no indication of the year-end cash balance. How, then, do we determine the December 31, 20X1, balance of cash or any other account in Smalltown Hospital's chart of accounts?

Posting Journal Data to the Ledger

To determine year-end account balances, we must transfer the information recorded in the journal to another accounting record: the *ledger*. The process of making this transfer is called **posting**. By posting to the ledger, the journalized information is summarized according to account classification so that all recorded increases and decreases in each account are brought together to permit the determination of individual account balances at the end of the year.

A ledger account, as it might appear in actual practice, is illustrated in Figure 3.5. A single page ordinarily is used for each account. The title and number of the account appears at the top of the form. Within the form, columns are provided to indicate the various elements of each posting to the account as follows:

1. The date indicated generally is the date as of which the posting is being made. In other words, in posting the 20X1 journal entries, the postings to the ledger would be dated December 31, 20X1. Sometimes, however, the posting date may be the date the transaction occurred, as shown in Figure 3.5, but we will not do this in subsequent illustrations.
2. The next column may be used for memorandum entries or notations of supplemental information of value to the accountant. You may disregard this column for the time being.
3. The Ref. column, for reference (sometimes shown as LF, for leaf folio), is the posting reference. That means it contains the name of the journal and the page number of the journal from which the posting is made. This provides a cross-reference between the ledger and the journal.
4. The next two columns show the dollar amounts of debits and credits posted from the various journal entries affecting the account. In this way, all of the increases and decreases in each ledger account (as recorded in the journal) are brought together on a single page so that the balance of each account can be determined.

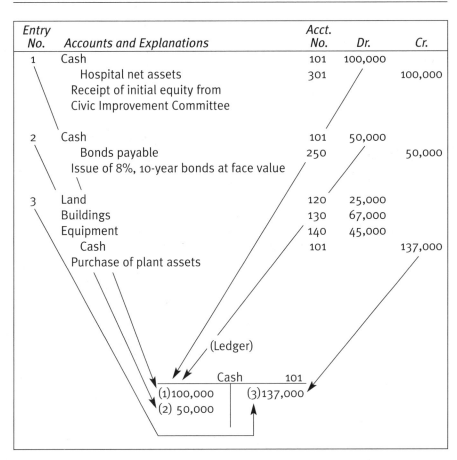

FIGURE 3.6

Illustration of Posting Procedure

5. The two columns on the far right are used to maintain a running balance (debit or credit, as the case may be) of the account. If debit postings exceed credit postings, the account will have a debit balance, and vice versa.

The example shown in the ledger account assumes that the account is the account for cash, account number 101. What you see in this example are the postings to the cash account of the cash debits and credits from the first three entries of Smalltown Hospital's general journal.

The ledger account form used in the remainder of this book, however, will be the T-account form introduced in the preceding chapter. Figure 3.6 illustrates how we will make postings to these accounts. Notice that no posting dates will be indicated; we will assume that all postings are made on December 31. Instead of using a journal page number as the posting reference, we will simply use the journal entry number. And instead of maintaining a running balance in each account, we will not compute an account balance until all debit and credit postings are made.

You should recognize that Figure 3.5 illustrates only the postings of the cash debits and credits from the first three journal entries. All of the debits and credits in the journal, of course, must be posted to the appropriate ledger accounts (as will be seen in Figure 3.7 later in this chapter).

Summary of Transaction Recording Process

To summarize, then, the transactions for the period are initially recorded as transaction entries in the hospital's journal. Although this provides a necessary chronological record of the transactions, it does not provide the account balances resulting from those transactions. These end-of-period account balances are needed to prepare the financial statements. So, the information recorded in the journal must be rearranged and summarized in such a manner so that these balances can be determined. This is accomplished by posting (transferring) the journal entries to the ledger accounts.

The ledger contains a separate account for each account listed in the chart of accounts. Because Smalltown Hospital's chart provides for 43 accounts, the hospital's ledger consists of 43 accounts. This ledger is referred to as the general ledger. Just as there are several different kinds of journals, so too are there several different kinds of ledgers. Ledgers other than the general ledger are called *subsidiary ledgers*. Such ledgers include the accounts receivable subsidiary ledger (or "patients' ledger"), the accounts payable ledger, the plant assets subsidiary ledger, and others. Subsidiary ledgers are discussed later, but for now we are concerned only with the general ledger.

Although you may have some difficulty at first with the journalizing of transactions in journals, you should have little trouble with postings to the ledger accounts. Posting is simply a matter of copying the journal debits and credits into the ledger accounts. If the journal indicates a cash debit, you debit the cash account in the ledger; if the journal indicates a credit to hospital net assets, you post a credit to the ledger account for hospital net assets. This procedure is easily learned. Be sure, however, that you post all debits and credits from the journal to the ledger; take care not to overlook any postings. And, unless you are attentive, you may find yourself posting debits as credits and credits as debits. If you do this, your ledger will not balance.

Figure 3.7 shows Smalltown Hospital's ledger after all postings of the 12 transaction entries have been made. It may be helpful for you to trace all of these postings from the hospital's journal (see Figure 3.3) to the ledger accounts. Notice in Figure 3.7 that where an account has more than a single posting and the account balance is not obvious, account balances at year-end have been determined. This was done by totaling the debits in the account, totaling the credits in the account, and computing the difference between the two totals. This difference, either a debit or a credit, is shown as the account balance, labeled (B). If it is a debit balance, it is shown on the left side of the account; credit balances are shown on the right side.

FIGURE 3.7

Smalltown Hospital 20X1 Ledger

Cash 101		Accounts Receivable 104		Inventory 106	
(1) 10,000	(3) 137,000	(6) 120,300	(7) 94,500	(4) 28,200	(5) 21,500
(2) 50,000	(8) 22,600	(B) 25,800		(B) 6,700	
(7) 94,500	(10) 96,900				
(9) 13,800	(12) 4,300				
(11) 12,000					
(B) 9,500					

Land 120		Buildings 130		Equipment 140	
(3) 25,000		(3) 67,000		(3) 45,000	

Accounts Payable 201		Notes Payable 202		Bonds Payable 250	
(8) 22,600	(4) 28,200		(11) 12,000		(2) 50,000
	(B) 5,600				

Hospital Nest Assets 301		Revenue and Expense Summary 302		Routine Services Revenue 401	
	(1) 100,000				(6) 72,180

Ancillary Services Revenue 402		Other Operating Revenues 406		Salaries and Wages Expense 601	
	(6) 48,120		(9) 13,800	(10) 76,400	

Supplies Expense 602		Utilities Expense 603		Insurance Expense 604	
(5) 21,500		(10) 12,700		(10) 3,600	

Repairs Expense 605		Interest Expense 608		Other Expenses 610	
(10) 2,900		(12) 4,300		(10) 1,300	

Only one posting appears in many of the ledger accounts because of the fact that the illustration is simplified. In actual practice, most ledger accounts have multiple postings. If, for example, the hospital pays salaries and wages to its employees on a monthly basis, the salaries and wages expense account contains 12 postings per year. We also have assumed annual postings to the ledger accounts, whereas general ledger postings are made monthly in actual practice. So do not be misled by the illustration; in an actual hospital, there typically is a considerable amount of activity in each ledger account.

One more point should be made with respect to Smalltown Hospital's ledger. You probably have noticed the revenue and expense income summary account (account number 302), wondering how and when it is used. The summary account is employed in the process of closing the books, a procedure that is discussed in Chapter 4. You need not be concerned about this account until then.

Trial Balance

At this point in Smalltown Hospital's accounting process, it would be interesting to determine whether the hospital's ledger is in balance. It should be in balance if we have made equal debits and credits in the journal, if we have posted these debits and credits correctly to the ledger accounts, and if we have made no mathematical errors in computing the balance of each account in the ledger. To ascertain whether the ledger is in balance, we can prepare a trial balance, as shown in Figure 3.8. The trial balance is a listing of all of the accounts in the ledger, with their debit or credit balances at the end of the year (or other period). The sequence in which the accounts are listed is the same as the sequence in which they appear in the ledger and in the chart of accounts.

Observe that the trial balance indicates that the Smalltown Hospital ledger is in balance. The debit balances total $301,700, as do the credit balances. A warning, however, is in order: The fact that the trial balance shows an equality of debit and credit balances is no guarantee that the dollar amounts are accurate. If the documentary evidence is incorrect or misinterpreted, the trial balance data will be incorrect. If debits and credits were made to the wrong accounts in the journal or ledger, the trial balance will include incorrect amounts. Thus, the trial balance is only a partial check on the accuracy of the accounting work of the period. Should the trial balance not balance, however, we know that an error has been made somewhere in the journal or ledger, or in the trial balance itself.

Smalltown Hospital's December 31, 20X1, trial balance is the starting point for the next chapter. In that chapter, we will use the trial balance figures to prepare a set of annual financial statements. Chapter 4 also illustrates and discusses the use of worksheets, and it describes and explains the process known as closing the books.

Questions

Q3.1.   Why is documentary evidence essential to the accounting process?

Q3.2.   What is the purpose of a chart of accounts? What factors influence the design of a hospital's chart of accounts?

Acct. No.	Account Titles	Dr.	Cr.
101	Cash	$ 9,500	
104	Accounts receivable	25,800	
106	Inventory	6,700	
120	Land	25,000	
130	Buildings	67,000	
140	Equipment	45,000	
201	Accounts payable		$ 5,600
202	Notes payable		12,000
250	Bonds payable		50,000
301	Hospital net assets		100,000
302	Revenue and expense income summary		
401	Routine services revenue		72,180
402	Ancillary services revenue		48,120
406	Other operating revenues		13,800
601	Salaries and wages expense	76,400	
602	Supplies expense	21,500	
603	Utilities expense	12,700	
604	Insurance expense	3,600	
605	Repairs expense	2,900	
608	Interest expense	4,300	
610	Other expenses	1,300	
	Totals	$301,700	$301,700

FIGURE 3.8

Smalltown Hospital Trial Balance, December 31, 20X1

Q3.3. Distinguish between a chart of accounts and a ledger.

Q3.4. How does a chart of accounts differ from a trial balance?

Q3.5. Why are numerical codes assigned to the accounts in a chart of accounts? Are these codes identical in all hospitals?

Q3.6. Define each of the following terms: (1) *journal*, (2) *journalizing*, and (3) *journal entry*.

Q3.7. What are the five essential elements of a journal entry?

Q3.8. In recording cash receipt transactions in the journal, debits are made to cash. What types of accounts generally would be credited?

Q3.9. In recording cash disbursement transactions in the journal, credits are made to cash. What types of accounts generally would be debited?

Q3.10. What is the purpose of posting journal entries to ledger accounts?

Q3.11. What are the five essential elements of a posting to a ledger account?

Q3.12. Distinguish between general and subsidiary ledgers. Give two examples of a subsidiary ledger.

Q3.13. What is the purpose of a trial balance?

Q3.14. "If a trial balance indicates an equality of debit and credit balances, this indicates that the journal and ledger are free of errors." Do you agree or disagree? Explain your answer.

Q3.15. "The ledger contains a separate account for each account in the hospital's chart of accounts. That is, if the chart of accounts contains 150 accounts, there will be 150 accounts in the ledger." Do you agree or disagree? Explain your answer.

Q3.16. In what sequence are accounts listed in the ledger? In a trial balance?

Exercises

E3.1.   Select the best answer for each of the following five multiple-choice questions.

1. The process of recording transactions in a journal is called
   a. Journalizing,
   b. Posting,
   c. Preparation of a trial balance, or
   d. Closing the books.
2. The process of transferring recorded information in the journal to the ledger is called
   a. Journalizing,
   b. Posting,
   c. Accumulating, or
   d. Reporting.
3. A chart of accounts is
   a. A listing of the accounts of a hospital with the account balances at the beginning of the fiscal year,
   b. A listing of the accounts of a hospital with the account balances at the end of the fiscal year,
   c. A listing of the accounts that will be used in recording and classifying the transactions of a hospital, or
   d. A diagram indicating the organizational structure of the hospital.
4. A trial balance is
   a. A listing of the accounts of a hospital with the account balances at a specified date;
   b. An accounting form that presents only the revenues and expenses of the hospital for a given period;
   c. An accounting form that presents only the assets, liabilities, and net assets of a hospital at a given point in time; or
   d. The balance of a particular ledger account the first time you attempt to compute it.
5. An accounting record that presents the transactions of the hospital in chronological order is
   a. A journal,

b. A ledger,

c. A trial balance, or

d. A statement of operations and a balance sheet.

E3.2.   Compass Hospital provides you with the following information:

Accounts receivable, December 31, 20X1	$150,000
Accounts receivable, December 31, 20X2	175,000
Collections on patients' accounts during 20X2	825,000

Required: What was the amount of charges to patients for services rendered to them in 20X2?

E3.3.   Catspaw Hospital provides you with the following information:

Accounts payable, December 31, 20X2 $	45,000
Purchases of supplies on account during 20X2	316,000
Payments on accounts payable during 20X2	301,000

Required: What was the balance of accounts payable at December 31, 20X1?

E3.4.   Contrail Hospital provides you with the following information:

Inventory, December 31, 20X1	$ 57,000
Inventory, December 31, 20X2	60,000
Cost of supplies purchased during 20X2	437,000

Required: What was the cost of supplies used during 20X2?

E3.5.   Convex Hospital provides you with the following information:

Cost of supplies used during 20X2	$855,000
Accounts payable, December 31, 20X1	200,000
Accounts payable, December 31, 20X2	246,000
Inventory, December 31, 20X1	191,000
Inventory, December 31, 20X2	100,000

Required: What was the total amount paid on accounts payable during 20X2?

Problems

P3.1.   Cupfull Hospital completed the following transactions during the month of October 20X1:

1. New equipment was purchased for $16,000 cash.

2. Supplies were purchased on account for $36,400.
3. Supplies that had cost $31,200 were issued from inventory for use in hospital activities.
4. Payments on accounts payable were $34,700.
5. Services rendered to patients during the month were billed as follows:

Routine services	$ 84,300
Ancillary services	47,900
Total	$ 132,200

6. Collections on patients' accounts totaled $105,750.
7. Other revenues collected in cash amounted to $13,600.
8. Operating expenses were paid as follows:

Salaries and wages	$ 82,400
Utilities	8,700
Insurance	2,900
Repairs	1,600
Other expenses	7,300
Total	$ 102,900

9. A short-term, 9 percent loan of $15,000 was obtained from a local bank (disregard interest).

Required: Using the chart of accounts provided in Figure 3.1, prepare, in good form, general journal entries for each of the preceding transactions.

P3.2.   Capstone Hospital began its corporate existence on January 1, 20X1. During the ensuing year, it completed the following transactions:

1. The hospital received initial capital of $250,000 from a fundraising committee established by the citizens of Capstone. This money was deposited in a bank checking account opened in the name of Capstone Hospital.
2. The hospital issued $150,000 of 6 percent, ten-year bonds at face value. Interest on these bonds is payable annually on December 31.
3. Plant assets were purchased for cash, as follows:

Land	$ 35,000
Buildings	200,000
Equipment	125,000
Total	$360,000

4. Purchases of supplies on account totaled $37,500.
5. Supplies that had cost $32,000 were issued from inventory for

use in hospital activities.

6. Services were billed to patients as follows:

Routine services	$ 91,000
Ancillary services	56,700
Total	$147,700

7. Cash collections on patients' accounts amounted to $121,600.

8. Payments on accounts payable totaled $24,900.

9. Other revenues received in cash amounted to $9,350.

10. Payments of operating expenses were as follows:

Salaries and wages	$ 79,250
Utilities	11,600
Insurance	4,200
Repairs	3,100
Other expenses	2,300
Total	$100,450

11. A short-term, 12 percent loan of $20,000 was obtained from a local bank.

12. On December 31, the following expense was paid:

Interest on bonds	$ 9,000
Interest on bank loan	600
Total	$ 9,600

Required: Using chart of accounts provided in Figure 3.1, (1) journalize the 20X1 transactions, (2) post the transaction entries to the general ledger, (3) prepare a trial balance at December 31, 20X1, (4) prepare a statement of operations for 20X1, and (5) prepare a balance sheet at December 31, 20X1.

P3.3.   Cocktail Hospital's trial balance at January 1, 20X1, includes the following accounts:

Cash	$ 10,500	
Accounts receivable	24,800	
Inventory	5,700	
Land	19,000	
Buildings	73,000	
Equipment	27,000	
Accounts payable		$ 6,600
Short-term notes and loans payable—banks	15,000	
Bonds payable		60,000
Hospital net assets		78,400
	$160,000	$160,000

The hospital completed the following transactions during the month ended January 31, 20X1:

1. Purchases of supplies on account were $4,900.
2. Supplies that had cost $5,200 were issued from inventory for use in hospital activities.
3. Services billed to patients were as follows:

Routine services	$ 40,800
Ancillary services	31,600
Total	$ 72,400

4. Cash collections on patients' accounts were $59,100.
5. Payments on accounts payable totaled $5,070.
6. Other revenues received in cash amounted to $7,300.
7. Operating expenses included these payments:

Salaries and wages	$ 53,200
Utilities	1,900
Insurance	1,200
Repairs	1,100
Other expenses	600
Total	$ 58,000

8. Payment of interest on bonds and bank loan totaled $870.

Required: Using the chart of accounts provided in Figure 3.1, (1) enter the January 1, 20X1, balances in ledger accounts, (2) journalize the January 20X1 transactions, (3) post the transaction entries to the ledger accounts, (4) prepare a trial balance at January 31, 20X1, (5) prepare a statement of operations for January 20X1, and (6) prepare a balance sheet at January 31, 20X1.

P3.4. Copper Hospital's trial balance at November 30, 20X2, which includes data accumulated since December 31, 20X1, is as follows:

Cash	$ 14,700	
Accounts receivable	34,900	
Inventory	7,400	
Land	30,000	
Buildings	200,000	
Equipment	105,000	
Accounts payable		$ 11,200
Notes payable		25,000
Bonds payable		75,000
Hospital net assets		274,300

Routine services revenue		85,800
Ancillary services revenue		31,300
Other operating revenues		9,400
Salaries and wages expense	95,000	
Supplies expense	13,000	
Utilities expense	3,600	
Insurance expense	1,200	
Repairs expense	1,700	
Interest expense	4,500	
Other expenses	1,000	
	$512,000	$512,000

The hospital completed the following transactions during the month of December 20X2:

1. Purchases of supplies on account amounted to $2,300.
2. Supplies that had cost $1,100 were issued from inventory for use in hospital activities.
3. Payments on accounts payable totaled $3,060.
4. Services billed to patients were as follows:

Routine services	$ 9,300
Ancillary services	6,070
Total	$ 15,370

5. Cash collections on patients' accounts totaled $16,140.
6. Other revenues received in cash totaled $980.
7. Payments of operating expenses included the following:

Salaries and wages	$ 9,100
Utilities	300
Insurance	150
Repairs	240
Other expenses	80
Total	$ 9,870

8. Payment of interest on bonds and bank loan amounted to $850.

Required: Using the chart of accounts provided in Figure 3.1, (1) enter the November 30, 20X1, balances in ledger accounts, (2) journalize the December 20X1 transactions, (3) post the transaction entries to the ledger accounts, (4) prepare a trial balance at December 31, 20X1, (5) prepare a statement of operations for the year ended December 31, 20X1, and (6) prepare a balance sheet at December 31, 20X1.

WORKSHEETS, FINANCIAL STATEMENTS, AND CLOSING ENTRIES

In the previous chapter, you had an opportunity to examine three of the initial steps in the accounting process: recording transaction entries in a general journal, posting these entries to a general ledger, and preparing a trial balance. The discussion centered around the business transactions completed by the hypothetical Smalltown Hospital during 20X1, the first year of that hospital's economic life. That illustration continues in this chapter as we explore worksheets, financial statements, and closing entries.

This chapter illustrates a simplified version of the **worksheets** (or, as they are sometimes called, working papers) widely used by accountants as a device to facilitate the preparation of financial statements. The worksheet you develop will lead to an illustration and discussion of Smalltown Hospital's 20X1 statement of operations and December 31, 20X1, balance sheet. The last section of this chapter describes and demonstrates the procedures performed to close the books for Smalltown Hospital.

The General Worksheet

After transaction entries have been journalized and posted, a trial balance is prepared of the ledger account balances. Financial statements may be prepared directly from the trial balance listing of accounts. In most cases, where a large number of accounts are involved, the development of the financial statements can be facilitated by the preparation of a general worksheet. A major purpose of the worksheet is to classify and segregate the trial balance figures according to the financial statements in which they will be presented. Other purposes of the worksheet will be shown in subsequent chapters. In addition, later chapters will introduce you to special-purpose worksheets.

A worksheet to develop financial statements for 20X1 for Smalltown Hospital is illustrated in Figure 4.1. Note the following points:

1. The trial balance at December 31, 20X1, is entered on the left side, with the dollar amounts being shown in the first two columns. This is the same trial balance that was developed in the preceding chapter and illustrated in Figure 3.8.

FIGURE 4.1 Smalltown Hospital Worksheet to Develop Financial Statements, Year Ended December 31, 20X1

Acct. No.	Account Title	12/31/X1 Trial Balance Dr.	Cr.	Statement of Operations Dr.	Cr.	Net Assets Dr.	Cr.	Balance Sheet Dr.	Cr.
101	Cash	9,500						9,500	
104	Accounts receivable	25,800						25,800	
106	Inventory	6,700						6,700	
120	Land	25,000						25,000	
130	Buildings	67,000						67,000	
140	Equipment	45,000						45,000	
201	Accounts payable		5,600						5,600
202	Notes payable		12,000						12,000
250	Bonds payable		50,000						50,000
301	Hospital net assets		100,000				100,000		
302	Revenue and expense summary	—							
401	Routine services revenue		72,180		72,180				
402	Ancillary services revenue		48,120		48,120				
406	Other operating revenues		13,800		13,800				
601	Salaries and wages expense	76,400		76,400					
602	Supplies expense	21,500		21,500					
603	Utilities expense	12,700		12,700					
604	Insurance expense	3,600		3,600					
605	Repairs expense	2,900		2,900					
608	Interest expense	4,300		4,300					
610	Other expenses	1,300		1,300					
	Totals	301,700	301,700	122,700	134,100				
	Net income for the year			11,400			11,400		
	Totals			134,100	134,100	-0-	111,400		
	Hospital net assets, 12/31/X1					111,400			111,400
	Totals					111,400	111,400	179,000	179,000

2. Next, the individual balances in the trial balance are extended to the appropriate financial statement columns. Debit balances are extended as debits, and credit balances are extended as credits, as follows:

   a. Assets and liabilities account balances are extended into the balance sheet section.

   b. The trial balance figure for hospital net assets is extended into the net assets statement section. This statement will be discussed in the next part of this chapter.

   c. Revenue and expense account balances are extended into the statement of operations section of the worksheet.

   d. The income summary account has no balance and can be disregarded in the preparation of the worksheet. The summary account is used only in the process of closing the books.

   In this way, the individual trial balance items are categorized or assembled into groups according to the financial statements in which the items will be presented.

3. Totals now are taken of the debits and credits in the statement of operations section; debits total $122,700, and credits total $134,100. Because the debits are expenses and the credits are revenues, the difference ($11,400) is the 20X1 excess of revenues over expenses. The excess of revenues over expenses figure ($11,400) is shown in the statement of operations section as a debit simply to balance the columns at $134,100. In addition, the $11,400 excess of revenues over expenses is extended as a credit to the net assets statement section of the worksheet.

4. Then, totals are taken of the debits (none) and credits in the net assets statement section. In certain situations, there could be debits to the net assets statement, but you need not be concerned with that possibility at this time. The credits to the net assets statement include the $100,000 of hospital net assets on January 1, 20X1, and the $11,400 excess of revenues over expenses for 20X1. This credit total of $111,400 is the amount of the hospital net assets on December 31, 20X1. The $111,400 figure is entered in the net assets statement section as a debit simply to balance the columns; the figure also is extended to the balance sheet section as a credit item.

5. A final step in completion of the worksheet is totaling the debits and credits in the balance sheet section. Notice that these columns balance with totals of $179,000.

Thus, a primary function of the worksheet is to assemble the account balances in financial statement groupings. This, of course, facilitates preparation of the formal financial statements.

Financial Statements

The assembled data provided by the worksheet can now be used in the preparation of 20X1 financial statements for Smalltown Hospital. These statements, in the order in which they usually are prepared, are as follows:

1. A statement of operations for the year ended December 31, 20X1, illustrated in Figure 4.2;
2. A balance sheet at December 31, 20X1, illustrated in Figure 4.3; and
3. A statement of hospital net assets for the year ended December 31, 20X1, illustrated in Figure 4.4.

As previously stated, financial statements are the final product of the accounting process. They are the means by which financial information is communicated to hospital management and interested external parties for use in making economic decisions.

Statement of Operations

The heading of the statement of operations (see Figure 4.2) identifies the accounting entity as Smalltown Hospital, indicates that the statement is a statement of operations, and specifies the time period covered by the statement as being the year ended December 31, 20X1. This statement presents the operating results of the hospital for 20X1 in terms of revenues earned and expenses incurred. The result of operations, measured as the difference between operating revenues earned and operating expenses incurred, is the **operating income**. Adding nonoperating income (typically interest on long-term investments minus an investment fee) produces the bottom line to the statement of operations called the excess of revenues over expenses (or net profit, or net loss, in some cases).

Accrual Versus Cash Basis Accounting Smalltown Hospital's statement of operations has been prepared in accordance with GAAP in that operating revenue is shown net of deductions and in accordance with the **accrual basis** of accounting. Under this basis of accounting, revenues are recognized and recorded in the time period in which they are earned by the hospital in rendering services and selling products to patients and others, regardless of when (if ever) the related inflow of cash occurs. Expenses are recognized and recorded in the time period in which they are incurred or consumed in revenue-producing activities of the hospital, regardless of when (if ever) the related outflow of cash occurs. The accrual basis is a GAAP that must be employed by all hospitals.

The alternative to the accrual system is the **cash basis** of accounting. In this system of accounting, revenues are recognized and recorded in the time period in which they are received in cash; expenses are recognized and recorded in the time period in which they are paid in cash. A statement of

Net patient services revenues:		
Routine services	$72,180	
Ancillary services	48,120	
Total net patient services revenues	120,300	
Other operating revenues	13,800	
Total operating revenues		$134,100
Less operating expenses:		
Salaries and wages	76,400	
Supplies	21,500	
Utilities	12,700	
Insurance	3,600	
Repairs	2,900	
Interest	4,300	
Other	1,300	
Total operating expenses		122,700
Operating income		11,400
Nonoperating income		-0-
Excess of revenues over expenses		$ 11,400

FIGURE 4.2

Smalltown Hospital Statement of Operations, Year Ended December 31, 20X1

operations prepared on a cash basis, then, is little more than a statement of cash receipts and cash disbursements (and an incomplete statement at that, because not all cash receipts are revenues and not all disbursements are expenses). Thus, the cash basis of accounting is not appropriate for hospitals or, for that matter, most other enterprises for external reporting purposes.

Smalltown Hospital's statement of operations, then, is a statement of revenues earned and expenses incurred during 20X1. It is *not* a statement of cash received and disbursed. The term "revenue" does not mean cash receipts, nor is the term "expense" synonymous with cash disbursements. Notice, for example, that the statement of operations of Smalltown Hospital, as shown in Figure 4.2, reports $120,300 of revenues earned from patient services. How much of this amount has been received in cash? Having seen the 20X1 transactions in Chapter 3, you know that only $94,500 was collected during the year on patients' accounts. And where is the other $25,800? It is presented in the balance sheet as "Receivables—patient services" (see Figure 4.3). Thus, $120,300 of patient services were rendered by Smalltown Hospital during 20X1, and this is the amount reported as revenues for the year, although $25,800 of that amount will not be collected until 20X2.

FIGURE 4.3

Smalltown Hospital Balance Sheet, December 31, 20X1

Assets		
Cash	$ 9,500	
Receivables—patient services	25,800	
Inventory	6,700	
Total current assets		$ 42,000
Land	25,000	
Buildings and building improvements	67,000	
Fixed equipment	45,000	
Total noncurrent assets		137,000
Total assets		$179,000
Liabilities and Net Assets		
Accounts payable	$ 5,600	
Short-term notes and loans payable—banks	12,000	
Total current liabilities		$ 17,600
Noncurrent liabilities		50,000
Total liabilities		67,600
Hospital net assets		111,400
Total liabilities and net assets		$179,000

Or consider the $21,500 supplies expense item in the statement of operations of Smalltown Hospital (see Figure 4.2). Is this the amount of supplies purchased and paid for during 20X1? No! Having worked with the 20X1 transactions in Chapter 3, you know that $28,200 of supplies were purchased on account during the year and that cash payments of only $22,600 were made to the suppliers of these items. The statement of operations of the year is charged only for the cost of supplies consumed in activities of the period. As a result of this accrual basis accounting, the balance sheet shown in Figure 4.3 reports a $6,700 inventory and $5,600 of accounts payable to suppliers. These items would not appear in the balance sheet if cash basis accounting were employed.

Relationship to Other Financial Statements

The excess of revenues over expenses is not directly linked to cash balance in the short run. This means that there is no necessary short-run relationship between reported excess of revenues over expenses and the change in the cash balance during the year. Smalltown Hospital begins the year with $100,000 of cash but ends the year with a cash balance of only $9,500. Thus, in a year when an $11,400 excess of revenues over expenses is reported, the

FIGURE 4.4
Smalltown
Hospital
Statement of
Hospital Net
Assets, Year
Ended
December 31,
20X1

Hospital net assets, January 1*	$100,000
Add excess of revenues over expenses for the year	11,400
Hospital net assets, December 31	$ 111,400

*This represents the contribution of initial net asset funds received on January 1, 20X1, from Smalltown's Civic Improvement Committee, when the hospital began its operations.

cash balance decreases by more than $90,000. Do not get the idea, therefore, that the statement of operations is a presentation of cash flows.

Cash flows, however, are vitally important in the management of a hospital. In addition to statements of operations and balance sheets, accountants also prepare statements of cash flows (cash receipts and disbursements) for internal management and external reporting purposes. A discussion of such statements will appear later in this book.

You should understand that the two-column format in which the statement of operations is presented in Figure 4.2 in no way implies a debit and credit relationship. The left column is not necessarily a debit column, nor is the right column is not necessarily a credit column. There are no debit or credit columns in financial statements. The number of columns employed is only a matter of presentation (display) style. The statement of operations, for example, could be formatted in a single column.

Statement of Net Assets

A statement of hospital net assets for the year ended December 31, 20X1, is illustrated for Smalltown Hospital in Figure 4.4. The statement begins with the net assets figure at January 1. To this figure, we add the 20X1 excess of revenues over expenses as indicated by the statement of operations. (If a net loss had been reported, the net loss would be subtracted from the January 1 net assets balance.) The resulting amount is the amount of hospital net assets at December 31. This dollar amount, of course, is the net assets balance to be reported in the December 31, 20X1, balance sheet.

For the present purpose, assume that the hospital's net assets are affected (changed) only by the excess of revenues over expenses of the period. Later in the book, you will see, however, that the hospital net assets balance is increased and decreased by other factors. When these factors are introduced, a more realistic net assets statement will be illustrated.

The net assets statement provides a connection between the statement of operations and the balance sheet. It also explains the change in the net assets balance from one balance sheet to the next. It is an essential financial statement, one that all hospitals should prepare and include in their annual financial reports.

**Relationship
to Other
Financial
Statements**

Balance Sheet

Smalltown Hospital's December 31, 20X1, balance sheet is illustrated in Figure 4.3. Notice that the heading provides the name of the accounting entity, the name of the statement, and the date of the statement. Unlike the dating of the statement of operations and net assets statement, the dating of the balance sheet specifies a particular point in time. The information in the balance sheet applies only to the financial position of the hospital at the "close of business" on December 31, 20X1. Most of the balance sheet figures were different on the preceding day and will also be different on the next day. The balance sheet is somewhat like a photographic snapshot, whereas the income and net assets statements are more like moving pictures covering a period of time.

Elements of Financial Position   The financial position of Smalltown Hospital is presented in terms of its assets, liabilities, and net assets on December 31, 20X1. Assets are the economic resources of the hospital that are recognized and measured in conformity with GAAP. Liabilities are the economic obligations of the hospital that are recognized and measured in conformity with GAAP. Net assets—sometimes called equity, fund balance, capital, or net worth—are the excess of assets over liabilities. Because most of the assets are reported in the balance sheet at cost rather than at what they are "worth," the use of the term *net worth* can be misleading. So, this book uses the term *net assets*, which is the common not-for-profit term.

Current and Noncurrent Assets   Smalltown Hospital's assets are listed in the sequence usually seen in actual practice. The assets are classified into two main groups: current assets and noncurrent assets (which, in this situation, consist only of plant assets). The current assets consist of cash plus those other assets that are likely to be converted into cash within a short period (one year or less). Normally, the plant assets are reduced by depreciation, but for simplicity we are disregarding the matter of depreciation for the time being.

Current and Noncurrent Liabilities   Smalltown Hospital's liabilities and net assets also are listed in the usual sequence. Like the assets, the liabilities are classified into two major categories: current liabilities and noncurrent (or long-term) liabilities. The current liabilities consist of debts that ordinarily are paid within a short time (one year or less). In this example, the noncurrent liabilities comprise a single item: the 8 percent bonds due in nine more years. A total of liabilities is obtained, and to it is added the hospital net assets balance as reported in the net assets statement. Then, of course, you see that total assets equal the total of liabilities and net assets (the accounting equation).

As this book proceeds, you will develop more sophisticated financial statements. Many additional accounts will be introduced into the statements, and the impact of net assets accounting and responsibility accounting on the statements will be described. We will also describe in more depth problems of terminology, classification, valuation, and disclosure. The subject of financial analysis and interpretation also is covered in subsequent chapters.

Closing the Books

Once the financial statements are prepared, the accountant can proceed to the last step in the accounting process. This procedure is known as **closing the books**. It consists of the closing of revenue and expense accounts in the hospital's ledger and the adjustment of the hospital net assets to the balance at which they are stated in the year-end balance sheet. The balances of revenue and expense accounts in Smalltown Hospital's ledger relate only to the 20X1 year. These balances therefore must be eliminated to prepare the ledger for the next accounting period and to avoid the commingling of revenue and expense balances of one year with those of the next year.

Real and Nominal Accounts

Balance sheet accounts, referred to as **real (permanent) accounts**, are not closed. The balances of these accounts—assets, liabilities, and net assets—are carried over into the next year as the opening balances for that year. The accounts to be closed are the statement of operations accounts, often called **nominal (temporary) accounts**. Thus, all revenue and expense account balances are closed; these accounts begin the next year with zero balances.

Closing Entries

A closing of the books is accomplished by making what are called **closing entries** in the hospital's journal and by posting these entries to the ledger accounts. Figure 4.5 presents the closing entries for Smalltown Hospital for 20X1.

The first closing entry is one to eliminate the revenue account balances. Recall that all revenue accounts have credit balances. The closing entry, therefore, debits each revenue account for its credit balance as shown in the hospital's ledger. A credit is made in this entry to the income summary account for the total revenues of the period. This credit balances the entry (entry number 13).

A second closing entry is made to remove the expense account balances from the ledger. Because the expense accounts have debit balances, this entry credits each of the expense accounts for its debit balance. The total of these credits (total expenses for the period) is debited to the income summary. This is entry 14.

The third and last closing entry (number 15) is one to close the revenue and expense summary account and to add the excess of revenues over expenses for 20X1 to the hospital net assets account (while the account

Entry No.	Accounts and Explanations	Acct. No.	Dr.	Cr.
13	Routine services revenue	401	72,180	
	Ancillary services revenue	402	48,120	
	Other operating revenues	406	13,800	
	Revenue and expense summary	302		134,100
	To close revenue accounts			
14	Revenue and expense summary	302	122,700	
	Salaries and wages expense	601		76,400
	Supplies expense	602		21,500
	Utilities expense	603		12,700
	Insurance expense	604		3,600
	Repairs expense	605		2,900
	Interest expense	608		4,300
	Other expenses	610		1,300
	To close expense accounts			
15	Revenue and expense summary	302	11,400	
	Hospital net assets	301		11,400
	To close revenue and expense			
	summary account, and to add excess			
	of revenues over expenses for 20X1			
	to the hospital net assets			

always carries the title "excess," the amount could in fact be a deficiency of revenues over expenses, in which case the number would be a loss represented by a negative number). Because the revenue and expense summary account has been debited (entry 14) for total expenses and credited (entry 13) for total revenues, that account now has a credit balance in the amount of the excess of revenues over expenses for the period. The debit to the summary account in entry 15 for the excess of revenues over expenses therefore will close that account. If the hospital had a loss for the period, of course, the debit and credit in this entry would be reversed.

The posting of these three closing entries from Smalltown Hospital's journal to its ledger accounts is shown in Figure 4.6. It is suggested that you trace the individual postings into the ledger. They are referenced as numbers 13, 14, and 15. Notice also that the closing of the revenue accounts, expense accounts, and the income summary account is indicated in the ledger by the "double-ruling" of the individual accounts.

Starting the Next Year's Books
Smalltown Hospital's ledger now contains balance sheet accounts only; all other accounts have been closed. These remaining ledger balances are left open

Cash 101		Accounts Receivable 104		Inventory 106	
(1)100,000	(3) 137,000	(6) 120,300	(7) 94,500	(4) 28,200	(5) 21,500
(2)50,000	(8) 22,600	(B) 25,800		(B) 6,700	
(7)94,500	(10) 96,900				
(9)13,800	(12) 4,300				
(11)12,000					
(B) 9,500					

Land 120		Buildings 130		Equipment 140	
(3)25,000		(3) 67,000		(3) 45,000	

Accounts Payable 201		Notes Payable 202		Bonds Payable 250	
(8)22,600	(4) 28,200		(11) 12,000		(2) 50,000
	(B) 5,600				

Hospital Net Assets 301		Revenue and Expense Summary 302		Routine Services Revenue 401	
	(1) 100,000	(14)122,700	(13)134,100	(13) 72,180	(6) 72,180
	(15) 11,400	(15) 11,400			
	(B) 111,400				

Ancillary Services Revenue 402		Other Operating Revenues 406		Salaries and Wages Expense 601	
(13)48,120	(6) 48,120	(13) 13,800	(9) 13,800	(10)76,400	(14)76,400

Supplies Expense 602		Utilities Expense 603		Insurance Expense 604	
(5)21,500	(14) 21,500	(10) 12,700	(14) 12,700	(10) 3,600	(14) 3,600

Repairs Expense 605		Interest Expense 608		Other Expenses 610	
(10)2,900	(14) 2,900	(12) 4,300	(14) 4,300	(10) 1,300	(14) 1,300

FIGURE 4.6

Smalltown Hospital 20X1 Ledger (with Closing Entries)

to become the beginning ledger balances of the ensuing year. None of the revenue or expense accounts have balances, so these accounts are ready to receive postings of the next year's revenues and expenses. In this way, the revenues and expenses of one year are not commingled with the revenues and expenses of the next year. This aids the measurement of operating income for each year.

FIGURE 4.7

Smalltown Hospital Postclosing Trial Balance, December 31, 20X1

Acct. No.	Account Titles	Dr.	Cr.
101	Cash	$ 9,500	
104	Accounts receivable	25,800	
106	Inventory	6,700	
120	Land	25,000	
130	Buildings	67,000	
140	Equipment	45,000	
201	Accounts payable		$ 5,600
202	Notes payable		12,000
250	Bonds payable		50,000
301	Hospital net assets		111,400
302	Revenue and expense summary		
401	Routine services revenue		
402	Ancillary services revenue		
406	Other operating revenues		
601	Salaries and wages expense		
602	Supplies expense		
603	Utilities expense		
604	Insurance expense		
605	Repairs expense		
608	Interest expense		
610	Other expenses		
	Totals	$179,000	$179,000

Checking Whether the Accounts Balance

At this point, another trial balance may be taken of the ledger to determine whether the accounts are in balance after the books are closed. This trial balance is called a **postclosing trial balance**; the trial balance illustrated in Chapter 3 as Figure 3.8 is referred to as a **preclosing trial balance**. A postclosing trial balance for Smalltown Hospital is presented in Figure 4.7. Notice that it contains balance sheet account balances only. These are the account balances with which Smalltown Hospital will begin 20X2.

Summary of the Accounting Procedure

It should be useful at this time to present a summary of the operations we have covered so far. All of the procedures or operations performed during the annual accounting period are together called the accounting cycle. The steps in this cycle discussed and illustrated up to this point are summarized in the diagram in Figure 4.8.

Assuming the existence of documentary evidences of transactions and a well-designed chart of accounts, the steps in the accounting cycle are as follows:

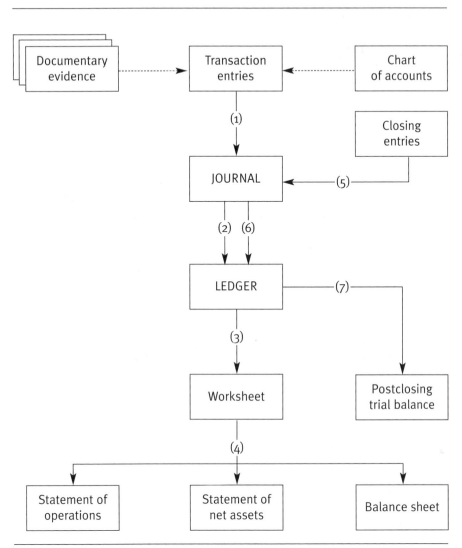

FIGURE 4.8

Summary of the Accounting Procedure

1. Journalize transaction entries in the journal.
2. Post transaction entries from the journal to the ledger and determine individual account balances.
3. Enter the preclosing trial balance on a worksheet and complete the worksheet.
4. Prepare financial statements from the information provided on the worksheet.
5. Journalize closing entries in the journal.
6. Post closing entries from the journal to the ledger.
7. Prepare a postclosing trial balance of the account balances now remaining in the ledger.

There are, however, additional steps involved in a complete accounting cycle. One of these additional steps is the journalizing and posting of another kind of journal entry called the **adjusting entry**. This procedure, often a matter of considerable difficulty for introductory accounting students, is treated in detail in the next three chapters.

Questions

Q4.1. What is the major purpose of a general worksheet?

Q4.2. Distinguish between the cash basis and the accrual basis of accounting.

Q4.3. Distinguish between revenues and cash receipts.

Q4.4. Distinguish between expenses and cash disbursements.

Q4.5. Why should cash basis accounting not be used by hospitals?

Q4.6. What is the purpose of the statement of hospital net assets?

Q4.7. Define briefly each of the following terms: (1) *assets*, (2) *liabilities*, and (3) *net assets*.

Q4.8. Describe briefly the procedure known as closing the books.

Q4.9. Distinguish between real and nominal accounts.

Q4.10. Distinguish between a preclosing trial balance and a postclosing trial balance.

Q4.11. List, in the sequence normally completed, the steps involved in an accounting cycle.

Q4.12. What is the significance of double rulings in ledger accounts?

Exercises

E4.1. Dowdy Hospital provides you with the following information:

Revenues for 20X2	$500,000
Expenses for 20X2	450,000
Hospital net assets, December 31, 20X1	860,000
Revenue and expense summary	-0-

Required: (1) Prepare closing entries for 20X2 in general journal form. (2) What is the hospital's net assets balance on December 31, 20X2?

E4.2. Doit Hospital provides you with the following information:

Assets	$350,000
Liabilities	150,000
Hospital net assets	180,000

Revenues	420,000
Expenses	400,000

Required: (1) Prepare a preclosing trial balance. (2) Prepare a postclosing trial balance.

E4.3. Devon Hospital provides you with the following information:

Revenue and Expense

Summary   302

787,000	800,000
13,000	

Required: Answer the following questions:

1. What were total revenues for the year?
2. What were total expenses for the year?
3. What was the excess of revenues over expenses for the year?
4. If hospital net assets were $400,000 at the beginning of the year, what were the hospital's net assets at the end of the year?

E4.4. Select the best answer for the following five multiple-choice questions.

1. Posting is an accounting procedure in which
   a. Information is transferred from the ledger to the journal,
   b. Information is transferred from the journal to the ledger,
   c. Information is transferred from the ledger to the hospital financial statements, or
   d. Information is transferred from the trial balance to the ledger.
2. A trial balance can be prepared
   a. Only before the books are closed,
   b. Only after the books are closed,
   c. Either before or after the books are closed, or
   d. Only at the end of the fiscal year.
3. In closing entries,
   a. Expense accounts are always debited,
   b. Expense accounts are always credited,
   c. Expense accounts may be debited in some cases and credited in other cases, or
   d. Expense accounts are not debited or credited.
4. Under the accrual basis of accounting, revenues are recorded
   a. In the period in which they are collected in cash,
   b. In the period in which they are earned through the provision of services or the sale of products,
   c. In the period in which management decides they should be recognized, or

d. In the period in which the income tax laws indicate that they are taxable.

5. Dawson Hospital provides you with the following information:
   - Services rendered to patients were valued at $600,000.
   - Cash collections on patients' accounts totaled $540,000.
   - Cash disbursements for expenses were $530,000.
   - Expenses incurred during the period totaled $550,000.

   Under the accrual basis of accounting, the excess of expenses over revenues (loss) of the period should be
   a. $(10,000),
   b. $10,000,
   c. $50,000, or
   d. $70,000.

Problems

P4.1.   The following balances, among others, appeared in the general ledger of Dent Hospital at the end of its fiscal year:

Acct. No.		
301	Hospital net assets	$143,674
302	Revenue and expense summary	-0-
401	Routine services revenue	85,375
402	Ancillary services revenue	52,939
406	Other operating revenues	21,655
601	Salaries and wages expense	101,488
602	Supplies expense	22,475
603	Utilities expense	13,880
604	Insurance expense	4,203
605	Repairs expense	1,922
608	Interest expense	3,077
610	Other expenses	1,249

Required: Prepare, in good form, general journal entries to close the books of Dent Hospital for the year.

P4.2.   The preclosing trial balance of Dunston Hospital on December 31, 20X2, is as follows:

Acct. No.		Dr.	Cr.
101	Cash	$ 11,200	
104	Accounts receivable	27,400	
106	Inventory	7,300	

120	Land	15,000	
130	Buildings	80,000	
140	Equipment	35,000	
201	Accounts payable		$ 6,900
202	Notes payable		14,000
250	Bonds payable		60,000
301	Hospital net assets		96,900
302	Revenue and expense summary		-0-
401	Routine services revenue		86,400
402	Ancillary services revenue		41,700
406	Other operating revenues		19,200
601	Salaries and wages expense	94,600	
602	Supplies expense	28,700	
603	Utilities expense	13,400	
604	Insurance expense	3,100	
605	Repairs expense	2,700	
608	Interest expense	4,400	
610	Other expenses	2,300	
	Totals	$325,100	$325,100

Required: (1) Prepare a general worksheet to develop financial statements for the year ended December 31, 20X2. (2) Prepare, in good form, financial statements for 20X2. (3) Prepare, in general journal form, closing entries for 20X2.

P4.3.   The following balances, among others, appeared in the general ledger of Dixon Hospital at the end of its fiscal year:

Acct. No.		
301	Hospital net assets	$294,600
302	Revenue and expense summary	-0-
401	Routine services revenue	121,800
402	Ancillary services revenue	87,500
406	Other operating revenues	26,300
601	Salaries and wages expense	155,400
602	Supplies expense	31,400
603	Utilities expense	18,700
604	Insurance expense	6,400
605	Repairs expense	3,900
608	Interest expense	7,500
610	Other expenses	3,300

Required: (1) Enter the balances in ledger accounts, (2) journalize the necessary closing entries for the year, and (3) post the closing entries to the ledger accounts.

P4.4. The following balances appeared in the general ledger of Deerly Hospital at December 31, 20X2:

Acct. No.		
101	Cash	$ 31,100
104	Accounts receivable	89,700
106	Inventory	11,200
120	Land	25,000
130	Buildings	240,000
140	Equipment	114,000
201	Accounts payable	22,800
202	Notes payable	28,000
250	Bonds payable	75,000
301	Hospital net assets	372,300
302	Revenue and expense summary	-0-
401	Routine services revenue	140,700
402	Ancillary services revenue	79,900
406	Other operating revenues	21,300
601	Salaries and wages expense	150,800
602	Supplies expense	38,500
603	Utilities expense	22,100
604	Insurance expense	4,700
605	Repairs expense	3,200
608	Interest expense	7,900
610	Other expenses	1,800

Required: (1) Prepare a general worksheet to develop financial statements for the year ended December 31, 20X2. (2) Prepare, in good form, financial statements for 20X2. (3) Prepare, in general journal form, closing entries for 20X2.

PREPAID AND ACCRUED EXPENSES

5

I n the two preceding chapters, Smalltown Hospital's 20X1 transactions were entered in the journal and posted to the ledger. A trial balance of the ledger accounts was then prepared. We assumed that the trial balance dollar amounts were the correct account balances at the end of the year, and these figures were used in the development of financial statements for 20X1. In actual practice, however, many of the account balances included in the trial balance are likely to be incorrect. This means that financial statements should not be prepared until the incorrect balances in the trial balance are adjusted to reflect the correct amounts. The necessary corrections are accomplished by journalizing and posting **adjusting entries**. All of the required adjustments must be made before financial statements are prepared.

Incorrect account balances will appear in the trial balance regardless of the amount of care exercised in recording the transactions of the period. Some of the reasons for this are as follows:

1. *Prepaid and accrued expenses.* The trial balance may include expense accounts whose balances are overstated or understated because of
   a. The prepayment of expenses during the period, or
   b. The failure to recognize expenses that were incurred during the current period but that will not be paid until the next period.
   Adjustments for prepaid and accrued expenses are illustrated and discussed in this chapter.
2. *Deferred and accrued revenues.* The trial balance may include revenue accounts whose balances are overstated or understated because of
   a. The receipt of revenues in advance, or
   b. The failure to recognize revenues that were earned during the current period but that will not be received until the next period.
   Adjustments for deferred and accrued revenues are illustrated and discussed in Chapter 6.
3. *Revenue deductions.* The trial balance may include incorrect balances in accounts representing revenue deductions, such as charity care. Chapter 7 deals with adjustments of this type.
4. *Depreciation.* The trial balance may not reflect the correct amount of depreciation expense relating to hospital buildings and equipment. Adjustments for depreciation are discussed in Chapter 7.

These are the types of adjusting entries that we will examine in this chapter and in Chapters 6 and 7. After we explore the types of adjusting entries, all of the various adjustments will be brought together in a comprehensive illustration in Chapter 8.

The Matching Principle

Chapter 4 made a very important distinction between cash basis accounting and accrual basis accounting: The accrual basis is a GAAP on which the financial statements of hospitals must be based. You have seen that the business life of the hospital entity is divided into time segments called accounting periods. So far, we have assumed that these accounting periods are calendar years—that is, the 12 months from January 1 through December 31. This is the fiscal year employed by Smalltown Hospital. Many hospitals have adopted a fiscal year or accounting period, however, that ends June 30 or September 30. Such a fiscal period generally is referred to as the **natural business year**. No matter what the annual period may be, it is broken down into monthly reporting periods. In actual practice, the hospital will prepare monthly as well as annual financial statements.

This brings us to the **matching principle**: The revenues of the hospital are "matched" with the accounting period during which they are earned. To put it another way, revenues must be recognized and recorded in the time period during which they are earned by the hospital through the provision of services and the sale of goods to patients and others. Revenues are earned when a hospital renders services to patients, when assets are sold, and when the hospital rents its assets to others. The hospital may receive cash prior to the earning of the revenue, at the time the revenue is earned, or after the earning of the revenue. Unfortunately, hospitals also may earn revenues for which they are never paid. Revenue deductions related to the matching principle are discussed in Chapter 6.

The matching principle also has important implications for recognition of hospital expenses. The expenses of the hospital are matched to the extent practicable with the revenues to which they are related. In other words, expenses are incurred in the production of revenues. Once the revenues of a given time period are measured and recorded, the expenses incurred in the production of those revenues should be recognized and recorded in the same period. There is, then, a matching of expenses with revenues in each accounting period to permit a meaningful and useful measurement of periodic operating income.

Not all hospital costs can be directly and easily associated with specific revenues. Yet, such costs must be charged as expenses to one or more accounting periods at one time or another. When no direct association of expenses with revenues can be made, the costs are matched with the accounting period or periods that they benefit. If more than one accounting period benefits from a cost expenditure, the cost is allocated to expense on some systematic and rational basis. If a cost expenditure is made during the current period and no future benefit is expected, that cost is charged in its entirety to expenses of the current period (the immediate recognition concept). Expense adjustments related to the matching principle are addressed later in this chapter and in Chapter 7.

Prepaid Expenses

Prepaid expenses, sometimes called *deferred expenses* or *deferred charges*, are expenditures made by the hospital for goods and services not yet consumed or used in hospital operations. They are therefore recognized as expenses in a future accounting period (or periods). Because these cost expenditures benefit one or more future accounting periods, they should be appropriately classified in the balance sheet as assets. Prepaid expenses, then, may be referred to as unexpired, or "unexpensed," costs. Some examples of prepaid expenses are prepaid insurance, prepaid interest, and prepaid rent.

Adjusting the Trial Balance for Prepayments
At the end of each accounting period, the trial balance must be scanned to determine the need for adjustments arising because of prepayments of expenses by the hospital. An analysis often must be made of the debits and credits in each of the accounts to develop the necessary adjusting entries. As a basis for illustration, we will assume a hypothetical Hoosier Hospital at the end of its first year of operations. This hospital's December 31, 20X1, trial balance is shown in Figure 5.1. From this point on, the trial balance taken after all transaction entries have been journalized and posted will be called a **preadjusted trial balance** (to distinguish it from an adjusted trial balance and from a postclosing trial balance). Certain of the accounts included in Figure 5.1 have not been specifically discussed before, but the nature and use of each of these accounts will soon become apparent to you.

Prepaid Insurance
Observe that Hoosier Hospital's preadjusted trial balance includes a prepaid insurance account (number 107) with a debit balance of $3,600. Normally, we would expect Hoosier Hospital also to have some amount of insurance expense for the 20X1 year, but the insurance expense account (number 604) has no balance whatever. It would seem obvious that an adjustment is needed here.

To determine the necessary adjustment, we need to examine copies of the hospital's insurance policies. Let us assume that we discover a single

Acct. No.	Account Titles	Dr.	Cr.
101	Cash	$ 38,300	
102	Temporary investments	12,000	
103	Accrued interest receivable	-0-	
104	Accounts receivable	96,600	
105	Allowance for uncollectible receivables		$ -0-
106	Inventory	10,500	
107	Prepaid insurance	3,600	
108	Prepaid rent	1,080	
109	Prepaid interest	720	
120	Land	25,000	
130	Buildings	180,000	
131	Accumulated depreciation—buildings		-0-
140	Equipment	60,000	
141	Accumulated depreciation—equipment		-0-
201	Accounts payable		29,840
202	Notes payable		18,000
203	Accrued interest payable		-0-
204	Accrued salaries and wages payable		-0-
205	Deferred rental income		4,200
206	Deferred tuition income		2,160
250	Bonds payable		80,000
301	Hospital net assets		225,000
302	Revenue and expense summary		-0-
401	Routine services revenue		151,300
402	Ancillary services revenue		137,400
403	Interest income		-0-
404	Rental income		-0-
405	Tuition income		-0-
406	Other operating revenues		27,100
501	Contractual adjustments	29,200	
502	Charity care adjustments	19,400	
601	Salaries and wages expense	139,600	
602	Supplies expense	28,600	
603	Utilities expense	14,400	
604	Insurance expense	-0-	
605	Repairs expense	8,300	
606	Rent expense	-0-	
607	Depreciation expense	-0-	
608	Interest expense	-0-	
609	Bad debt expense	-0-	
610	Other expenses	7,700	
	Totals	$675,000	$675,000

comprehensive insurance policy for which the hospital paid a three-year premium in advance on January 1, 20X1. The amount of the premium was $3,600, meaning that the hospital's insurance expense is $1,200 per year—that is, a third of the insurance premium expired in 20X1. The transaction entry made by Hoosier Hospital on January 1, 20X1, when the premium was paid, must have been as follows:

Prepaid insurance	107	$3,600	
Cash	101		$3,600
Payment of 3-year premium in advance			
on a comprehensive insurance policy			

At the end of the year, however, $1,200 of this prepayment has expired and should be included in the hospital's 20X1 expenses. Also at year's end, the amount of prepaid insurance to be reported as an asset is only $2,400 ($3,600 – $1,200).

An adjusting entry therefore must be made in the hospital's journal at December 31, 20X1. The required entry is the following:

Insurance expense	604	$1,200	
Prepaid insurance	107		$1,200
Adjustment for portion of prepaid			
premium that expired during 20X1			

When this entry is posted, it corrects the two account balances in the ledger of the hospital. The $1,200 of insurance expense will appear among the expenses in Hoosier Hospital's 20X1 statement of operations. The $2,400 adjusted balance of prepaid insurance will be presented as an asset in the hospital's December 31, 20X1, balance sheet. It is an asset because the insurance company "owes" Hoosier Hospital insurance protection for the next two years (20X2 and 20X3), and this asset is valued at the unexpired cost of the insurance. Prepaid insurance represents a future economic benefit (insurance protection).

The same adjusting entry will be required at the end of 20X2 and at the end of 20X3. Then, of course, it will be time to renew the insurance and make another premium payment. In this way, a $3,600 expenditure on January 1, 20X1, is charged or allocated to expense over the three-year period benefiting from the expenditure at the rate of $1,200 per year. (Had the entire $3,600 been charged to 20X1 expense, this would result in an overstatement of 20X1 expense and an understatement of expense in 20X2 and 20X3.) Because this hospital uses accrual basis accounting, expenses are recognized in the period in which they are incurred, regardless of when they are paid.

It is important that you clearly understand that this discussion of adjusting entries is presented in terms of an annual time frame. Well-managed hospitals, of course, prepare monthly statements of operations and balance sheets. For these monthly statements to be accurate and useful, all significant adjustments must be made at the end of each month. If we assume the preparation of monthly financial statements for Hoosier Hospital, an adjusting entry would be made at the end of each month to recognize $100 ($1,200 ÷ 12 months) of insurance expense and to reduce prepaid insurance by the same amount, as follows:

Insurance expense	604	$ 100	
Prepaid insurance	107		$ 100
Adjustment for monthly expiration of			
prepaid insurance premiums			

The illustration presented in Chapter 9 assumes monthly adjusting entries, but we will discuss adjustments in annual terms until then.

Adjusting for Insurance Expense Hospitals carry substantial amounts of many different types of insurance and have a large number of policies. Thus, the determination of the monthly and annual insurance expense figures can be somewhat difficult. It may be necessary to maintain an insurance register and perhaps an insurance expiration schedule or worksheet. Not only do these specialized records provide the necessary information for accounting adjustments, they also aid in the management of the hospital's insurance requirements to ensure that adequate coverage is maintained, that claims for insured losses are promptly reported and recovered, and so on.

Prepaid Rent

Let us assume now that Hoosier Hospital rented certain equipment for use in its business offices on May 1, 20X1. The transaction entry is as follows:

Prepaid rent	108	$1,080	
Cash	101		$1,080
Payment of a year's rent in advance for			
office equipment ($90 per month)			

The December 31, 20X1, preadjusted trial balance therefore includes $1,080 of prepaid rent (account 108) but no balance in rent expense (account 606).

Because the rent is $90 per month, Hoosier Hospital's 20X1 expenses therefore should include rent expense of $720 ($90 × 8 months). Prepaid rent at December 31, 20X1, should be $360 ($90 × 4 months), the rent that is prepaid for January through April of 20X2. The required December 31, 20X1, adjusting entry is as follows:

Rent expense	606	$ 720	
Prepaid rent	108		$ 720
Adjustment to record rent expense for			
May through December 20X1, at			
$90 per month			

In 20X2, the remaining $360 of prepaid rent will be charged to expense. In this way, the equipment rental cost is charged to expense during the periods in which the equipment is being used by the hospital. Had the entire $1,080 payment been charged to expense in the year of payment, Hoosier Hospital's 20X1 expenses would have been overstated and its 20X2 expenses understated.

Prepaid Interest

Assume that Hoosier Hospital obtained a six-month loan of $18,000 from a bank on November 1, 20X1. The hospital issued to the bank a promissory note, paying 8 percent interest in advance for the six-month term of the note. The hospital's transaction entry on November 1 was as follows:

Cash	101	$17,280	
Prepaid interest	109	720	
Bonds payable	250		$18,000
Proceeds of 6-month note issued to bank,			
with 8% interest deducted in advance:			
Face amount of note	$18,000		
Less interest—			
$18,000 × 8% × 6/12 months	720		
Proceeds of note	$17,280		

Interest on the note for a full year would be $1,440 (8 percent of $18,000). The loan, however, is for a six-month period, and only a half-year's interest is prepaid. Interest expense is $120 per month ($720 ÷ 6 months).

At December 31, 20X1, interest expense for November and December has been incurred by the hospital. The necessary adjusting entry at year-end is the following:

Interest expense	608	$ 240	
Prepaid interest	109		$ 240
Adjustment for interest expense on bank			
loan for November and December 20X1:			
$18,000 × 8% × 2 months ÷ 12 months			
= $240			

The remaining $480 ($720 – $240) of prepaid interest is an asset at the end of 20X1. The bank "owes" to the hospital the use of the borrowed money for another four months. This $480 will be charged to interest expense in 20X2.

Summary of Process for Handling Prepaid Expenses

A hospital will likely have other types of prepaid expenses. Whatever the particular expense item, adjustments are made in the manner shown in the preceding illustrations. The procedure is summarized as follows:

1. Assuming the prepayment is debited to a prepaid expense account in the transaction entry:

Prepaid Expense		Expense	
Transaction entry	Adjusting entry	Adjusting entry	

The amount of the adjusting entry is that portion of the prepayment that has expired and should be recorded as expense of the current period.

2. Assuming the prepayment is debited to an expense account in the transaction entry:

Prepaid Expense		Expense	
Adjusting entry		Transaction entry	Adjusting entry

The amount of the adjusting entry is that portion of the prepayment that has not expired and is to be recorded as expense in a future period.

Prepaid expenses are assets because they represent unexpired costs that benefit a future accounting period. They represent benefits, such as insurance protection; use of equipment, or use of money, to be received in the future and consequently should not be charged to expense in the current period.

Accrued Expenses

Accrued expenses are expenses that have been incurred but for which the hospital has not yet paid. Accrued expenses represent the costs of goods and services consumed or used in hospital operations of the current period, but for which the hospital will not make expenditures until some future accounting period. The liability for these future disbursements is called an *accrued liability,* or an *accrued expense payable.* In most cases, the liability is presented among the current liabilities in the balance sheet of the hospital. Examples include accrued interest payable and accrued salary and wages payable (sometimes called *accrued payroll*).

At the end of each accounting period, the trial balance accounts must be scanned and analyzed to determine the need for adjustments for accrued expenses. Once the necessary adjustments are determined, they are journalized and posted to the hospital's ledger.

Accrued Interest

Let us assume that Hoosier Hospital issued $80,000 of 9 percent, 15-year bonds on July 1, 20X1, at face value. The transaction entry was as follows:

Cash	101	$80,000	
Bonds payable	250		$80,000
Proceeds from issuance of $80,000 of			
9%, 15-year bonds at face value			

Assume also that interest on these bonds is payable semiannually on January 1 and July 1 of each year, commencing January 1, 20X2. These semi-annual interest payments therefore will be $3,600 ($80,000 × 9 percent × 6/12 months). At the trial balance date, December 31, 20X1, no interest has yet been paid on these bonds; the first interest payment is due January 1, 20X2.

So, in this situation an expense has been incurred but is unrecorded and unpaid. The required December 31, 20X1, adjusting entry is the following:

Interest expense	608	$ 3,600	
Accrued interest payable	203		$ 3,600
Adjustment for 6 months' interest			
accrued on bonds since July 1, 20X1			

The money borrowed by the hospital through the issuance of the bonds costs the hospital 9 percent per year. Because the hospital had the use of this money for six months (July through December 20X1), the cost of using the money for this half-year period should be recorded as an expense in 20X1. The fact that this expense has not been paid by the hospital has nothing at all to do with the recognition of the expense in the 20X1 account-ing period. Because the interest has not been paid, however, the adjusting entry must establish the liability as accrued interest payable.

On January 1, 20X2, the first semiannual interest payment date, the bond interest is paid. The transaction entry is as follows:

Accrued interest payable	203	$ 3,600	
Cash	101		$ 3,600
Payment of semiannual interest on			
bonds for the 6 months ended			
December 31, 20X1			

In this way, the bond interest applicable to 20X1 is charged to 20X1 expense, although it was not actually paid until 20X2. Had the December 31, 20X1, adjusting entry not been made, 20X1 interest expense would have been understated.

Accrued Salaries and Wages

In Hoosier Hospital's preadjusted trial balance (see Figure 5.1), the salaries and wages expense account (account 601) has a debit balance of $139,600. This is the amount of 20X1 salaries and wages paid to hospital employees in 20X1. But is this the correct amount of salaries and wages expense for 20X1?

For the purpose of illustration, assume that Hoosier Hospital pays all of its employees on the first day of each month for salaries and wages they earned in the preceding month. The $139,600 appearing in the trial balance is, therefore, salaries and wages only for the first 11 months of 20X1. Employees' salaries and wages for December 20X1 have not yet been paid and, consequently, are not included in the salaries and wages expense account balance. These December salaries and wages will be paid January 1, 20X2, but should be recorded as 20X1 expenses. On December 31, 20X1, the hospital employees have earned their December pay. The hospital has received the benefit of their time and efforts during the month. The December payroll is a cost that has been incurred by the hospital, but that cost is unrecorded and unpaid. It is an expired cost that must be recognized as a 20X1 expense, and as of December 31, 20X1, a liability of the hospital to its employees.

Assume that the December 20X1 payroll is determined to be $13,000. (In actual practice, the accrued payroll figure sometimes must be estimated. More will be said about this in a later chapter.) The necessary adjusting entry at December 31, 20X1, is as follows:

Salaries and wages expense	601	$13,000	
Accrued salaries and wages payable	204		$13,000
Adjustment for accrued payroll for the month of December 20X1			

This entry puts salaries and wages into the expense of the period during which they were incurred as hospital expenses. It also establishes a liability for unpaid salaries and wages for inclusion in the hospital's December 31, 20X1, balance sheet.

On January 1, 20X2, the December 20X1 payroll is paid. Assuming that the amount actually disbursed on that date is the same as the amount that was accrued in the preceding adjusting entry, the transaction entry is the following:

Accrued salaries and wages payable	204	$13,000	
Cash	101		$13,000
Payment of December 20X1 accrued salaries and wages			

Thus, the salaries and wages are recorded as expenses of the period in which they are incurred as expenses rather than in the period in which they are paid.

Adjusting Entry for Salaries and Wages

Now, a complication should be introduced. Disregard the previous situation and assume instead that Hoosier Hospital pays its employees every two weeks—that is, every 14 days. Let us say that the last payroll period in 20X1 was the 14-day period ending December 27, 20X1. On the following day, December 28, employees received their paychecks for that 14-day pay period.

What this means is that the trial balance figure for salaries and wages expense of $139,600 represents 361 days of payroll expense (not 365 days). Employees have presumably worked another four days in 20X1 (December 28–31) for which they have not yet been, and will not be, paid until after the end of the next 14-day payroll period (January 10, 20X2). These four days of payroll cost, however, must be recorded as 20X1 expense.

Let us assume that these four days of payroll are computed (perhaps estimated in some way) to be $3,700. The necessary December 31, 20X1, adjusting entry is as follows:

Salaries and wages expense	601	$3,700	
Accrued salary and wages payable	204		$ 3,700
Adjustment for accrued payroll for the			
last 4 days of December 20X1			

Now assume that the actual payroll for the 14-day period ending January 10, 20X2, turns out to be $13,000. When this is paid on January 11, 20X2, the transaction entry is:

Accrued salary and wages payable	204	$3,700	
Salaries and wages expense	601	9,300	
Cash	101		$13,000
Payment of payroll for the 14-			
day period ending January 10, 20X2			

This entry records the payment of two things: (1) the four days of payroll for 20X1 that were recorded previously as a liability and as 20X1 expense and (2) the ten days of payroll for 20X2 that are debited to 20X2 expense. In this way, employees' salaries and wages are recorded as expenses of the period in which they are incurred by the hospital, and not necessarily in the period in which they are paid.

Hospitals, of course, have many types of expense accruals other than those illustrated here. Whatever expense items they might be, they are handled in the manner described for accrued interest and accrued payroll. The required adjusting entry will always be a debit to an expense account and a credit to a liability account. Then, when that liability is paid, the liability account is debited and the cash account credited.

Reversing Entries

In some accounting systems, **reversing entries** are prepared on the first day of each new accounting period. They are called reversing entries because they "reverse" certain previously recorded adjusting entries. The reversing entries are made to avoid certain complications in the accounting routine. This book, however, employs reversing entries only in a small number of cases. One of these relates to adjustments for accrued payroll. Let us examine the reversing procedure in that area.

Reversing Entries for Accrued Payroll

Assume the facts of the preceding illustration: Hoosier Hospital had paid $139,600 of salaries and wages during 20X1, $3,700 of salaries and wages were accrued at year end, and $13,000 of salaries and wages were paid on January 11, 20X2. The (1) 20X1 summary transaction entry, (2) 20X1 year-end adjusting entry, (3) December 31, 20X1, closing entry, (4) January 1, 20X2, reversing entry, and (5) January 11, 20X2, transaction entry are shown in the following list:

(1) Salaries and wages expense	601	$139,600	
Cash	101		$139,600
Payments of salaries and wages during 20X1			
(2) Salaries and wages expense	601	3,700	
Accrued salaries and wages payable	204		3,700
Adjustment for accrued salaries and wages at December 31, 20X			
(3) Revenue and expense summary	301	143,300	
Salaries and wages expense	601		143,300
To close the expense account			
(4) Accrued salaries and wages payable	204	3,700	
Salaries and wages expense	601		3,700
Reversal of December 31, 20X1, adjusting entry			
(5) Salaries and wages expense	601	13,000	
Cash	101		13,000
Payment of salaries and wages on January 11, 20X2			

Notice that the reversing entry (number 4) is the reverse of the December 31, 20X1, adjusting entry (number 2). The reversing entry eliminates the accrued salaries and wages payable account and places a credit balance of $3,700 in the 20X2 salaries and wages expense account. Entry number 5 debits the salaries and wages expense account for $13,000. As a result, the 20X2 salaries and wages expense account winds up with a debit balance of $9,300, the correct amount for the first ten days of 20X2.

Thus, because of the reversing entry, the total amount of salaries and wages paid on January 11, 20X2, can be debited to the expense account. In other words, there is no need to break the debit amount between the expense account and the accrued salaries and wages payable account. This is one of the complications avoided by using reversing entries. If we had not made the reversing entry, the accounting transactions would be as follows:

(1) Salaries and wages expense	601	$139,600	
Cash	101		$139,600
Payments of salaries and wages during 20X1			
(2) Salaries and wages expense	601	3,700	
Accrued salaries and wages payable	204		3,700
Adjustment for accrued salaries and wages at December 31, 20X1			
(3) Revenue and expense summary	301	143,300	
Salaries and wages expense	601		143,300
To close the expense account			
(4) No reversing entry is made.			
(5) Accrued salaries and wages payable	204	3,700	
Salaries and wages expense	601	9,300	
Cash	101		13,000
Payment of salaries and wages on January 11, 20X2			

You should not conclude, however, that all adjusting entries are to be reversed. Some are reversed, and some are not. In this book, the use of reversing entries will be limited to a few illustrations concerning accrued expenses (such as salaries and wages) and accrued revenues (seen in the following chapter).

Questions

Q5.1. What is the purpose of adjusting entries? Distinguish between transaction and adjusting entries.
Q5.2. Describe briefly the matching principle.
Q5.3. Define *prepaid expense*. Give three examples of hospital expense items that may be prepaid.
Q5.4. Define *accrued expense*. Give three examples of hospital expense items that often must be accrued at the end of an accounting period.
Q5.5. Distinguish between prepaid and accrued expenses.
Q5.6. Distinguish among preadjusted trial balance, adjusted trial balance, preclosing trial balance, and postclosing trial balance.
Q5.7. Why are prepaid expenses reported in a balance sheet as assets?
Q5.8. Why are accrued expenses reported in a balance sheet as liabilities?
Q5.9. What is the purpose of reversing entries? Distinguish between adjusting entries and reversing entries.

Exercises

E5.1.   Eston Hospital paid a three-year insurance premium of $1,350 in advance on January 1, 20X1.
Required: What amount should Eston Hospital report as prepaid insurance in its December 31, 20X2, balance sheet?

E5.2.   Eastland Hospital paid a three-year insurance premium in advance on January 1, 20X1. The hospital's adjusted trial balance at December 31, 20X2, included a prepaid insurance account with a balance of $1,480.
Required: What was the amount of the insurance premium paid on January 1, 20X1?

E5.3.   Early Hospital rented certain equipment for use in its business offices on October 1, 20X1, paying one year's rent of $1,800 in advance.
Required: What amount should appear as prepaid rent in Early Hospital's postclosing trial balance at December 31, 20X1?

E5.4.   Edson Hospital obtained a six-month loan of $24,000 from a bank on August 1, 20X1, paying 10 percent interest in advance. The interest was debited to interest expense.
Required: Assuming that adjustments are made annually on December 31 only, prepare the necessary adjusting entry for December 31, 20X1.

E5.5.   Using the data of Exercise 5.4, assume that the August 1, 20X1, transaction entry debited the interest to prepaid expense.
Required: If adjustments are made annually on December 31 only, what is the necessary adjusting entry at December 31, 20X1?

E5.6.   Esterbrook Hospital issued $100,000 of 6 percent, 20-year bonds on July 1, 20X1, at face value. Interest is payable semiannually on January 1 and July 1 of each year, beginning January 1, 20X2.
Required: Assuming that adjustments are made annually on December 31 only, prepare the necessary adjusting entry on December 31, 20X1.

E5.7.   Easy Hospital's preadjusted trial balance at December 31, 20X1, includes a salaries and wages expense account with a debit balance of $805,200. It is determined, however, that employees have earned an additional $38,900 of salaries and wages in 20X1 that have not yet been paid.
Required: Prepare the necessary adjusting entry for December 31, 20X1.

E5.8.   Ernst Hospital's 20X2 statement of operations reports salaries and wages expense of $699,400. The hospital's balance sheets include the following accounts:

> 12/31/X1 Accrued salaries and wages payable $ 41,600
> 12/31/X2 Accrued salaries and wages payable   38,400

Required: What was the amount of salaries and wages actually paid in cash during 20X2?

E5.9.   Extant Hospital paid $355,100 of salaries and wages during 20X2. Its balance sheets reported accrued salary and wages payable and related liabilities as follows:

> 12/31/X2 $28,300
> 12/31/X1   25,700

Required: What amount should be reported as salaries and wages expense in Extant Hospital's 20X2 statement of operations?

E5.10.   Eucher Hospital's 20X2 statement of operations reported insurance expense of $8,000. Its balance sheets reported prepaid insurance as follows:

> 12/31/X1 $ 1,400
> 12/31/X2   1,100

Required: What was the amount actually paid in cash for insurance premiums during 20X2?

E5.11.   Easter Hospital paid $4,600 of rent expense during 20X2. Its balance sheets reported prepaid rent expense as follows:

> 12/31/X1 $ 1,200
> 12/31/X2   900

Required: What amount should be reported as rent expense in Easter Hospital's 20X2 statement of operations?

Problems

P5.1.   Exerto Hospital's preadjusted trial balance on December 31, 20X1, included the following accounts, among others:

Acct. No.		
107	Prepaid insurance	$5,040

108	Prepaid rent	2,100
109	Prepaid interest	1,200
604	Insurance expense	-0-
606	Rent expense	-0-
608	Interest expense	-0-

The hospital paid a three-year insurance premium in advance on January 1, 20X1. On August 1, 20X1, a year's rent was paid in advance. A $20,000, 12 percent loan for six months was obtained from a bank on November 1, 20X1, and the interest was paid in advance by the hospital.

Required: Prepare, in general journal form, the necessary adjusting entries at December 31, 20X1.

P5.2.   Eversure Hospital's preadjusted trial balance at December 31, 20X1, included the following accounts, among others:

Acct.
No.

203	Accrued interest payable	$ -0-
204	Accrued salaries and wages payable	-0-
601	Salaries and wages expense	245,600
608	Interest expense	-0-
250	Bonds payable	120,000

On September 1, 20X1, the hospital issued its $120,000, 8 percent, six-month note to a local bank in connection with a short-term loan. An analysis indicated that employees had earned $33,600 of salaries and wages during 20X1 that had not been paid to them.

Required: Prepare, in general journal form, the necessary adjusting entries at December 31, 20X1.

P5.3.   Exacto Hospital's preadjusted trial balance at December 31, 20X1, included the following accounts, among others:

Acct.
No.

107	Prepaid insurance	$ 5,760
108	Prepaid rent	2,700
109	Prepaid interest	3,600
202	Notes payable	80,000
203	Accrued interest payable	-0-
204	Accrued salaries and wages payable	-0-
250	Bonds payable	400,000
601	Salaries and wages expense	755,200
604	Insurance expense	-0-

| 606 | Rent expense | -0- |
| 608 | Interest expense | -0- |

The following additional information is available:

1. A three-year insurance premium was prepaid on January 1, 20X1.
2. One year's rent was paid in advance on June 1, 20X1.
3. On December 1, 20X1, an $80,000, 9 percent, six-month loan was obtained from a local bank. Interest was prepaid.
4. Unpaid salaries and wages at December 31, 20X1, totaled $68,700.
5. On October 1, 20X1, $400,000 of 6 percent, ten-year bonds were issued at face value. Interest on these bonds is payable annually on October 1, beginning October 1, 20X2.

Required: Prepare, in general journal form, the necessary adjusting entries for December 31, 20X1.

P5.4.   The following accounts appeared in the adjusted trial balance of Evansville Hospital at December 31, 20X1:

Cash	$ 26,300
Accounts receivable	105,900
Inventory	14,700
Prepaid insurance	1,800
Prepaid rent	900
Prepaid interest	500
Buildings and equipment	575,000
Accounts payable	29,700
Bonds payable	125,000
Accrued interest payable	2,300
Accrued salaries and wages payable	9,800
Notes payable	350,000
Hospital net assets	193,600
Routine services revenue	135,000
Ancillary services revenue	75,800
Other operating revenues	30,900
Salaries and wages expense	140,000
Supplies expense	31,000
Utilities expense	29,000
Insurance expense	8,200
Repairs expense	5,400
Rent expense	7,100
Interest expense	4,900
Other expenses	1,400

Required: Prepare, in good form, (1) a balance sheet at December 31, 20X1, and (2) a statement of operations for the year then ended.

P5.5.   Eunice Hospital's preadjusted trial balance at December 31, 20X1, included the following accounts, among others:

Acct. No.		
107	Prepaid insurance	$ 0-
108	Prepaid rent	-0-
109	Prepaid interest	-0-
202	Notes Payable	80,000
203	Accrued interest payable	-0-
204	Accrued salaries and wages payable	-0-
250	Bonds payable	100,000
601	Salaries and wages expense	399,500
604	Insurance expense	5,760
606	Rent expense	2,700
608	Interest expense	4,800

The following additional information is available:

1. A three-year insurance premium was prepaid on January 1, 20X1.
2. One year's rent was paid in advance on June 1, 20X1.
3. On December 1, 20X1, an $80,000, 12 percent, six-month loan was obtained from a local bank; interest was prepaid.
4. Unpaid salaries and wages at December 31, 20X1, amounted to $27,400.
5. On April 1, 20X1, $100,000 of 6 percent, 15-year bonds were issued at face value. Interest on these bonds is payable annually on April 1, beginning April 1, 20X2.

Required: Prepare, in general journal form, the necessary adjusting entries at December 31, 20X1.

DEFERRED AND ACCRUED REVENUES

Thiis chapter introduces some additional adjustments of the Hoosier Hospital's December 31, 20X1, trial balance (see Figure 5.1). These adjustments are of two major types:

1. *Deferred revenues.* Certain revenues have been received in cash but as yet have not been earned by the hospital.
2. *Accrued revenues.* Certain revenues have been earned but as yet have not been received in cash by the hospital.

The adjustments required for these items are similar to those illustrated in the preceding chapter for prepaid and accrued expenses. This chapter, however, concerns revenues, not expenses. The accrual basis objective of the adjustments described here is to give accounting recognition to revenues in the accounting period in which they are earned, regardless of when, if ever, the related cash receipts occur. Although hospital revenues are, for the most part, received in cash in the period earned, a substantial amount of revenues is earned prior to the receipt of cash. Less frequently, certain other revenues may be earned in an accounting period subsequent to the period in which the related cash receipts occur.

Deferred Revenues

Deferred revenues, sometimes called *deferred income, prepaid income,* or *revenues received in advance,* consist of revenue items for which cash has been received but that the hospital has not yet earned. Because of the cash receipt, the hospital must provide certain corresponding goods and services in some future accounting period (or periods). Examples of deferred revenues include rentals received in advance and advance receipts of tuition for educational programs conducted by the hospital. More complicated deferred revenue situations are discussed at later points in this book.

Deferred Rent

Let us assume that Hoosier Hospital rents office space in its building to certain physicians on its medical staff. This practice began on August 1, 20X1, when a year's rent of $4,200 ($350 per month) was received in advance. At that time, Hoosier Hospital made the following transaction entry:

Cash	101	$4,200	
Deferred rental income	205		$4,200
Receipt of a year's rent in advance			
for office space provided for			
staff physicians ($350 per month)			

On August 1, 20X1, then, the hospital has a liability to the physicians to provide office space for their use during the next 12 months. The deferred rental income account reflects that liability. On December 31, 20X1, the hospital has provided the office space for five months (August through December). The hospital therefore has earned $1,750 of rental income ($350 × 5 months). Because this income has not been recorded by the hospital, the following adjusting entry is required:

Deferred rental income	205	$1,750	
Rental income	404		$1,750
Adjustment for 5 months of			
rental income earned from provision			
of office space for physicians			

This entry recognizes the rental income earned in 20X1 and reduces the deferred rental income account to the correct December 31, 20X1, balance of $2,450. In other words, on December 31, 20X1, the hospital has a remaining liability to furnish office space for seven months in 20X2. This liability is measured at $350 per month ($350 × 7 months = $2,450).

Thus, $2,450 of rental income received in 20X1 is deferred to 20X2, the year in which it will be earned by the hospital. Were this not done, the income of 20X1 would be overstated and the 20X2 income understated. The accrual basis of accounting prevents such misstatements.

Adjusting Entries for Rental Space Income also may arise from the rental of space in the hospital as sleeping quarters for interns and residents, or the hospital may own separate buildings that are used as residences for nurses and other personnel. Space in the hospital's lobby and public areas may be rented to private vendors for gift shops and newsstands. A hospital-operated television service also may produce rental income. In any of these cases, adjusting entries may be appropriate at the end of each accounting period.

Deferred Tuition

Assume that Hoosier Hospital operates an educational program, such as a school of nursing or a school for laboratory technologists. Further assume that, on September 1, 20X1, the hospital received $2,160 of fees and tuition for the nine-month school year that ends May 31, 20X2. For this transaction, Hoosier Hospital made the following entry:

Cash	101	$2,160	
Deferred tuition income	206		$2,160
Receipt of tuition ($240 per month) for the			
9-month school year ending May 31, 20X2			

Here again, the hospital has received revenue in advance. The hospital has an obligation to the students in the program to provide educational services during the next nine months. This liability is represented by the credit to the deferred tuition income account. When the tuition is received, the hospital has earned no income.

By the end of 20X1, however, the school presumably has been operating for four months (September through December), and the hospital therefore has earned $960 of tuition income ($240 × 4 months, or 4 months ÷ 9 months × $2,160). The following adjusting entry is required at December 31, 20X1:

Deferred tuition income	206	$ 960	
Tuition income	405		$ 960
Adjustment for tuition income earned in			
20X1 ($240 per month × 4 months)			

This entry gives accounting recognition to the tuition income earned during the current year and defers recognition of the remaining tuition revenue to 20X2. Hoosier Hospital will report $960 of tuition income in its 20X1 statement of operations and $1,200 of deferred tuition income (a current liability) in its December 31, 20X1, balance sheet.

Summary of Accounting Procedures for Deferred Revenues

The accounting procedures for deferred revenues are summarized in the following T-accounts:

1. Assuming the transaction entry credited the cash received to a deferred revenue account:

Revenue		Deferred Revenue	
Adjusting entry		Adjusting entry	Transaction entry

The adjusting entry transfers the amount of revenue earned during the current period from the liability account (deferred revenue) to the revenue account.

2. Assuming the transaction entry credited the cash received to a revenue account:

Revenue		Deferred Revenue	
Adjusting entry	Transaction entry		Adjusting entry

The adjusting entry transfers the amount of unearned revenue from the revenue account to the deferred revenue account.

Thus, the nature and amount of the required adjusting entry depend on the account initially credited in the transaction entry.

Accrued Revenues

Accrued revenues consist of revenue items that the hospital has earned but for which the hospital has not recorded a receivable or collected cash. The hospital, of course, routinely provides goods and services to patients and has a claim against them (or third-party payers) for the value of those goods and services. These claims are recorded as receivables (assets), as previously indicated. In addition, the hospital provides other types of services that produce revenues and require the recognition of related receivables. Examples of these accrued revenue items are accrued interest receivable, accrued rent receivable, and accrued tuition receivable. This discussion illustrates the accrual of interest revenues and receivables.

Let us say that Hoosier Hospital invested $12,000 in 8 percent government bonds on October 1, 20X1. These bonds, purchased at face value, pay interest annually on October 1, commencing October 1, 20X2. The transaction entry was as follows:

Temporary investments	102	$12,000	
Cash	101		$12,000
Purchase of $12,000 (face value) of			
8% government bonds for temporary			
investment			

Perhaps at this time Hoosier Hospital had a cash balance in excess of its then-current needs. In accordance with good business practice, it was decided to invest those funds for a short period of time to obtain interest income. Although the bonds may be ten-year bonds, the hospital intends to hold them only as a temporary or short-term investment. As a result, the investment will be classified as a current asset in Hoosier Hospital's balance sheet.

At December 31, 20X1, Hoosier Hospital has held this investment for three months (October through December). The hospital has earned interest income of $240 ($12,000 × 8 percent × 3/12 months), and the following year-end adjusting entry must be recorded:

Accrued interest receivable	103	$ 240	
Interest income	403		$ 240
Adjustment for 3 months' interest			
earned on temporary investments in			
government bonds			

This entry gives accounting recognition to interest income earned (but not yet received) during 20X1. The interest, however, will be received on the next annual interest payment date, October 1, 20X2. So, the entry makes a debit to the appropriate asset account, accrued interest receivable. In Hoosier Hospital's December 31, 20X1, balance sheet, the accrued interest receivable will be reported as a current asset.

On October 1, 20X2, the hospital will receive in cash a full year's interest, or $960 (8 percent of $12,000), on the bond investment. The following might be the transaction entry at that time:

Cash	101	$960	
Accrued interest receivable	103		$240
Interest income	403		720
Receipt of a year's interest on temporary investment in 8% government bonds, $240 of which was recognized as income in 20X1.			

Recording Income in the Year in Which it Is Earned

Notice that all of the interest income was received in cash in 20X2, but $240 of it was recorded as 20X1 income, and $720 was recognized as 20X2 income. Thus, income is recorded in the year in which it is earned and not necessarily in the year in which it is received in cash.

Hoosier Hospital might have chosen to make a reversing entry on January 1, 20X2. In addition, if Hoosier Hospital prepared monthly financial statements, adjusting entries would have been made monthly. Chapter 9 covers monthly adjustment procedures in detail. So, assuming annual adjustments only, Hoosier Hospital could have made the following reversing entry on January 1, 20X2:

Interest income	403	$240	
Accrued interest receivable	103		$240
Reversal of December 31, 20X1, entry for accrued interest on temporary investment in government bonds			

This entry eliminates the balance in the accrued interest receivable account and places a debit balance in the 20X2 interest income account. Then, when the annual interest is received on the investment on October 1, 20X2, the following transaction entry is made:

Cash	101	$960	
Interest income	403		$ 960
Receipt of a year's interest on temporary investment in 8% government bonds			

When this $960 credit is posted to the interest income account, the account then has the proper $720 balance: the $960 credit posting minus the $240 debit posting from the reversing entry. Compare this transaction entry (assuming a reversing entry was made) with the previously illustrated transaction entry (assuming no reversing entry was made) for October 1, 20X2. Thus, the use of reversing entries tends to simplify subsequent transaction entries.

Summary of Adjustments for Prepayments and Accruals

This chapter has illustrated adjusting entries for deferred and accrued revenues; the preceding chapter illustrated adjustments for prepaid and accrued expenses. Now, let us bring these adjustments together as they would appear in Hoosier Hospital's general journal for 20X1. The adjusting journal entries (AJEs) numbered 1 through 5 in Figure 6.1 were discussed in the preceding chapter; those numbered 6 through 8 were described earlier in this chapter.

Explanation of Adjusting Entries

Entries 1, 2, and 3 are the adjustments arising from the prepayment of expenses during 20X1. In each case, an expense account is debited, and an asset account is credited. This is because we have assumed that the hospital has an accounting policy of debiting prepaid expense accounts in the initial transaction entry. For example, when insurance premiums are paid, a debit is made to prepaid insurance, not to insurance expense.

Adjusting entries 4 and 5 are those necessary to give accounting recognition to accrued expenses (expenses incurred during 20X1 but not yet paid). In each case, the entry debits an expense account and credits a liability account. This is always true for adjustments for accrued expenses.

Entries 6 and 7 are adjusting entries for deferred (prepaid) revenues. Each of these entries debits a liability account and credits a revenue account. This is because we have assumed that it is Hoosier Hospital's accounting policy to credit a deferred revenue account whenever revenue items are received in advance. For example, when rental prepayments are received, a credit is made to the deferred rental income account (account 205), not to the rental income account (account 404).

Entry 8 relates to the accrual of income that was earned during 20X1 but that had not been received in cash by the end of the year. The entry debits an asset account and credits an income account. This is always true of adjustments for accrued revenues.

All of these adjusting entries, of course, are posted in due course to Hoosier Hospital's ledger. When this is accomplished, most of the ledger accounts will have correct balances reflecting accrual basis accounting.

Entry No.	Accounts and Explanations	Acct No.	Dr.	Cr.
1	Insurance expense	604	$ 1,200	
	Prepaid insurance	107		$ 1,200
	Adjustment for part of prepaid premium that expired during 20X1 (Chapter 5)			
2	Rent expense	606	720	
	Prepaid rent	108		720
	Adjustment to record rent expense for May through December 20X1, at $90 per month (Chapter 5)			
3	Interest expense	608	240	
	Prepaid interest	109		240
	Adjustment for interest on bank loan for November and December 20X1 (Chapter 5)			
4	Interest expense	608	3,600	
	Accrued interest payable	203		3,600
	Adjustment for 6 months' interest accrued on bonds since July 1, 20X1 (Chapter 5)			
5	Salaries and wages expense	601	13,000	
	Accrued salaries and wages payable	204		13,000
	Adjustment for accrued payroll for the month of December 20X1 (Chapter 5)			
6	Deferred rental income	205	1,750	
	Rental income	404		1,750
	Adjustment for 5 months of rental income earned from provision of office space for physicians (Chapter 6)			
7	Deferred tuition income	206	960	
	Tuition income	405		960
	Adjustment for tuition income earned in 20X1 (Chapter 6)			
8	Accrued interest receivable	103	240	
	Interest income	403		240
	Adjustment for 3 months' interest on temporary investment in government bonds (Chapter 6)			

FIGURE 6.1

Hoosier Hospital 20X1 Journal (Adjusting Entries)

These eight entries, however, are not all of the adjusting entries normally required at the end of a fiscal year. In the next chapter, two additional types of adjustments are considered. These adjustments relate to revenue deductions and to depreciation.

Questions

Q6.1.   Define *deferred revenue*. Give two examples of deferred revenue.

Q6.2.   Define *accrued revenue*. Give two examples of accrued revenue.

Q6.3.   Why is deferred revenue reported in a balance sheet as a liability?

Q6.4.   Why is accrued revenue reported in a balance sheet as an asset?

Q6.5.   Fodder Hospital received a year's rent in advance on May 1, 20X1. The hospital's December 31, 20X1, balance sheet reported deferred rental income of $580. What was the amount of rent received on May 1, 20X1?

Q6.6.   Ferntown Hospital received $1,800, representing a year's rent in advance, on November 1, 20X1. In the transaction entry, $1,800 was credited to the deferred rental income account. Assuming that adjustments are made annually on December 31 only, what adjusting entry should be made on December 31, 20X1?

Q6.7.   Refer to the data of Question 6.6 but assume that the rental income account was credited for $1,800 in the transaction entry. Assuming that adjustments are made annually on December 31 only, what adjusting entry should be made on December 31, 20X1?

Exercises

E6.1.   Foster Hospital's 20X2 statement of operations reported rental income of $8,200. The hospital's balance sheets reported deferred rental income as follows:

12/31/X1	$1,700
12/31/X2	1,300

Required: What was the amount of rent actually received in cash during 20X1?

E6.2.   Fat Hospital received in cash rental payments of $10,700 during 20X2. Its balance sheets reported deferred rental income as follows:

12/31/X2	$2,600
12/31/X1	1,800

Required: What amount should be reported as rental income in Fat Hospital's 20X2 statement of operations?

E6.3. On September 1, 20X1, Fasby Hospital received $10,620 of fees and tuition for one of its educational programs that has a nine-monthschool year ending May 31, 20X2.
Required: What amount should be reported as deferred tuition income in the hospital's December 31, 20X1, balance sheet?

E6.4. Favor Hospital invested $60,000 in 8 percent government bonds on August 1, 20X1. These bonds, which were purchased at face value, pay interest annually on August 1, commencing August 1, 20X2.
Required: Assuming that adjustments are made annually on December 31 only, prepare the necessary adjusting entry for accrued interest as of December 31, 20X1.

E6.5. Flabby Hospital received interest payments of $8,600 during 20X2. Its balance sheets reported accrued interest receivable as follows:

12/31/X1	$1,100
12/31/X2	1,400

Required: What amount should be reported as interest income in the hospital's 20X2 statement of operations?

Problems

P6.1. Frangipani Hospital's December 31, 20X1, preadjusted trial balance includes the following accounts, among others:

Acct. No.		
102	Temporary investments	$24,000
103	Accrued interest receivable	-0-
205	Deferred rental income	5,400
206	Deferred tuition income	4,320
403	Interest income	-0-
404	Rental income	-0-
405	Tuition income	-0-

The following additional information is available:

1. On September 1, 20X1, the hospital invested $24,000 (face

value) in 8 percent government bonds that pay interest annually on September 1, commencing September 1, 20X2.

2. On June 1, 20X1, the hospital received a year's rent in advance.
3. On September 1, 20X1, the hospital received nine months' tuition in advance for one of its educational programs.

Required: Prepare, in general journal form, the necessary adjusting entries at December 31, 20X1.

P6.2.   Frosty Hospital's December 31, 20X1, preadjusted trial balance includes the following accounts, among others:

Acct. No.		
102	Temporary investments	$30,000
103	Accrued interest receivable	-0-
205	Deferred rental income	-0-
206	Deferred tuition income	-0-
403	Interest income	-0-
404	Rental income	5,400
405	Tuition income	4,320

The following additional information is available:

1. On April 1, 20X1, the hospital invested $30,000 (face value) in 8 percent government bonds that pay interest annually on April 1, commencing April 1, 20X2.
2. On June 1, 20X1, the hospital received a year's rent in advance.
3. On September 1, 20X1, the hospital received nine months' tuition in advance for one of its educational programs.

Required: Prepare, in general journal form, the necessary adjusting entries at December 31, 20X2.

P6.3.   The following is Flapper Hospital's preadjusted trial balance as of December 31, 20X1:

Acct. No.		
101	Cash	$ 34,900
102	Temporary investments	60,000
103	Accrued interest receivable	-0-
104	Accounts receivable	172,000
106	Inventory	15,000
107	Prepaid insurance	6,480
108	Prepaid rent	4,500
109	Prepaid interest	2,400

120/130/140	Land, Buildings, and Equipment		350,020
201	Accounts payable		$ 28,200
202	Notes payable		48,000
203	Accrued interest payable		-0-
204	Accrued salaries and wages payable		-0-
205	Deferred rental income		3,600
206	Deferred tuition income		4,900
250	Bonds payable		200,000
301	Hospital net assets		335,300
302	Revenue and expense summary		-0-
401	Routine services revenue		97,500
402	Ancillary services revenue		58,200
403	Interest income		-0-
404	Rental income		-0-
405	Tuition income		-0-
406	Other operating revenues		19,300
601	Salaries and wages expense	100,000	
602	Supplies expense	25,000	
603	Utilities expense	12,000	
604	Insurance expense	-0-	
605	Repairs expense	9,000	
606	Rent expense	-0-	
608	Interest expense	-0-	
610	Other expenses	3,700	
		$795,000	$795,000

The following additional information is available:

1. On August 1, 20X1, the hospital invested $60,000 (face value) in 8 percent government bonds that pay interest annually on August 1, commencing August 1, 20X2.
2. On January 1, 20X1, a three-year insurance premium was paid in advance.
3. One year's rent was received in advance on March 1, 20X1.
4. One year's rent was paid in advance by the hospital on May 1, 20X1.
5. On November 1, 20X1, the hospital issued its six-month, 10 percent note for $48,000 to a local bank in connection with a short-term loan. The interest was prepaid by the hospital.
6. On October 1, 20X1, the hospital issued $200,000 of 6 percent, ten-year bonds at face value. These bonds pay interest semiannually on October 1 and April 1, commencing April 1, 20X2.
7. Unpaid salaries and wages at December 31, 20X1, amounted to $16,800.

8. On September 1, 20X1, the hospital received nine months' tuition in advance for one of its educational programs.

Required: (1) Enter the preadjusted December 31, 20X1, balances in general ledger accounts. (2) Prepare, in general journal form, the necessary adjusting entries at December 31, 20X1. (3) Post the adjusting entries to the ledger accounts and prepare an adjusted trial balance at December 31, 20X1. (4) Prepare a statement of operations for 20X1 and a balance sheet at December 31, 20X1. (5) Prepare, in general journal form, the necessary closing entries at December 31, 20X1. (6) Post the closing entries to the ledger accounts. (7) Prepare a postclosing trial balance at December 31, 20X1.

DEPRECIATION AND REVENUE DEDUCTIONS

Adjustment procedures for prepaid expenses, accrued expenses, deferred revenues, and accrued revenues were discussed in the preceding two chapters. This chapter describes and illustrates two additional types of adjustments required at the end of the accounting period. The first concerns depreciation of the hospital's plant assets. The second relates to the problem of revenue deductions: contractual adjustments, charity care adjustments, and bad debts. When this chapter is concluded, you will have been introduced to most of the adjusting entries related to hospital accounting.

Depreciation

Hoosier Hospital's December 31, 20X1, trial balance (refer again to Figure 5.1) includes the following account balances to which your attention should now be directed:

Acct. No.		Dr.	Cr.
120	Land	$ 25,000	
130	Buildings	180,000	
131	Accumulated depreciation—buildings		$ -0-
140	Equipment	60,000	
141	Accumulated depreciation—equipment		-0-
607	Depreciation expense	-0-	

Depreciation Recorded Through Adjusting Entries

Asset accounts 120, 130, and 140 are asset accounts whose debit balances reflect the original historical costs of the hospital's plant assets: land, buildings, and equipment used in hospital operations (and not held for investment purposes or for sale in the ordinary course of business). Accounts 131 and 141 are called **contra asset accounts**—that is, negative asset accounts. These accounts reflect the amount of plant assets cost that has been charged to expense (depreciation) in the hospital's statements of operations of the current and prior accounting periods. Expense account 607 reports the amount of depreciation expense for the current period. Depreciation therefore enters the accounting records through adjusting entries that debit depreciation expense and credit the appropriate accumulated depreciation accounts.

Assume, for purposes of illustration, that Hoosier Hospital acquired all of its plant assets in a cash transaction on January 1, 20X1:

Land	120	$ 25,000	
Buildings	130	180,000	
Equipment	140	60,000	
Cash	101		$265,000
Purchase of plant assets for cash			

These plant assets were used throughout 20X1. Because the activities of the year were made possible by (and benefited from) the use of these assets, is it not logical to expect that some part of the cost of the assets should be charged as expense against the revenues of the period?

Nature of Depreciation

Depreciation is an accounting procedure by which the cost (less salvage value, if any) of certain plant assets is allocated to expense over the estimated useful lives of such assets in a systematic and rational manner. The amount of plant asset cost allocated to a particular accounting period is called the **depreciation expense**. A fundamental point to remember is that depreciation is a process of cost allocation, not of valuation. You should understand that depreciation, in the accounting sense, is not a measurement of the loss in the market value of an asset during a given period.

Consider, for example, an item of equipment used in the radiology department of the hospital. This equipment cost, say, $4,000 when acquired on January 1, 20X1. Obviously, the equipment will not last forever; it eventually will wear out and/or become obsolete with time, use, and changes in technology. When the equipment reaches the point at which it is no longer useful to the hospital, it will be discarded (either sold or scrapped) and probably replaced by new equipment. The amount, if any, for which the old equipment can be sold at the end of its useful life is called **salvage value**, also called *residual value* or *scrap value*.

To compute depreciation on this radiology equipment, we must estimate its useful life (usually in years) and its salvage value (if any). These estimates must be made when the equipment is acquired. Hence, they must be based on informed judgment and experienced opinion. (We will investigate this matter more closely in a subsequent chapter.)

So, let us assume that we estimate a useful life of six years and a salvage value of $400 for the equipment. This means that we expect the equipment to be used over a six-year period from the beginning of 20X1 to the end of 20X6, at which time it may sell for $400. Then, subtracting the salvage value from the cost of the equipment, we obtain $3,600 ($4,000 – $400), which is the depreciation base, or depreciable cost. This is the net cost (acquisition cost minus salvage value) to the hospital for the use of the equipment over its six-year life. We can depreciate no more than $3,600.

If we divide the $3,600 depreciable cost by the estimated useful life of six years to determine annual depreciation expense ($3,600 ÷ 6 years), we find that depreciation expense is $600 per year. This method of computing the annual amount of depreciation expense is referred to as **straight-line depreciation**. It is perhaps the most widely used depreciation method. We will examine other depreciation methods in a subsequent chapter.

At the end of 20X1, then, $600 of the cost of the radiology equipment must be recognized as depreciation expense. This is accomplished by the following adjusting entry:

Depreciation expense	607	$ 600
Accumulated depreciation—		
equipment	141	$ 600
Adjustment for depreciation of		
radiology equipment for 20X1		

The 20X1 statement of operations will report $600 of depreciation expense. In the balance sheet at December 31, 20X1, the presentation is the following:

Equipment, at cost	$4,000	
Less accumulated depreciation	600	
Equipment, net		$3,400

Note that accumulated depreciation, the contra asset account, is shown in the balance sheet as a deduction from the asset account. The resulting $3,400 figure is the undepreciated cost of the equipment; it also is referred to as the "book value" of the equipment. It is not necessarily, however, the "market value" of the equipment—that is, it is not the price for which the equipment could be sold by the hospital on December 31, 20X1.

Each year for the next five years, $600 will be recorded as annual depreciation expense. That is, depreciation will accumulate at the rate of $600 per year. In the December 31, 20X3, balance sheet, for example, the presentation will be as follows:

Equipment, at cost	$4,000	
Less accumulated depreciation	1,800	
Equipment, net		$2,200

Here, depreciation has accumulated for three years: 20X1–20X3, to a total of $1,800 ($600 × 3 years). This will continue until the end of 20X6, at which time the equipment will be fully depreciated and, presumably, retired from service by the hospital.

What if the equipment is not retired at the end of 20X6? Suppose the useful life and salvage value estimates turn out to be incorrect. What happens if the equipment is sold prior to 20X6? These are very interesting questions, but we must defer a consideration of the answers to subsequent chapters.

One additional point, however, should be made here. Assume that the equipment mentioned above was acquired on, say, July 1, 20X1. In that case, how much depreciation should be taken on the equipment for 20X1? The answer is a half-year's depreciation, or $300 ($600 ÷ 12 months × 6 months), because the hospital had the use of the equipment for only six months. (The hospital may adopt a different policy with respect to this matter, but we will not discuss it at this time.) Had the equipment been acquired on December 31, 20X1, no depreciation expense would be recorded in 20X1 for this equipment.

Adjusting Entries

Returning now to Hoosier Hospital, let us develop the December 31, 20X1, adjusting entries for depreciation. Land is nondepreciable, but depreciation must be computed and recorded for the hospital's buildings and equipment; buildings and equipment are depreciable assets.

Depreciation of Buildings   The useful life of Hoosier Hospital's buildings is estimated to be 50 years. Salvage value is estimated to be 20 percent of the cost of the buildings, or $36,000 (20 percent of $180,000). The depreciable cost, then, is $144,000 ($180,000 – $36,000), and annual depreciation is $2,880 ($144,000 ÷ 50 years). At December 31, 20X1, the following adjusting entry is required:

Depreciation expense	607	$2,880	
Accumulated			
depreciation—buildings	131		$2,880

Adjustment for 20X1 depreciation
of hospital buildings:

Cost	$180,000
Less salvage value (20%)	36,000
Depreciable cost	$144,000

$144,000 ÷ 50 years = $2,880

If monthly adjustments were made by Hoosier Hospital during 20X1, this entry would be made for $240 ($2,880 ÷ 12 months) at the end of each month.

The $2,880 of depreciation on the buildings will appear among the expenses in Hoosier Hospital's 20X1 statement of operations. In the process of closing the books at the end of the year, the depreciation expense account will be closed. The accumulated depreciation account, however, is not closed; it is presented in the hospital's December 31, 20X1, balance sheet in the manner described earlier. It also is carried forward into 20X2 as one of the opening balances for that year.

Depreciation of Equipment   Assume that the estimated useful life of Hoosier Hospital's equipment is ten years and that the salvage value is 10 percent, or $6,000 (10 percent of

$60,000). The required adjusting entry at December 31, 20X1, is as follows:

		Dr.	Cr.
Depreciation expense	607	$ 5,400	
Accumulated			
depreciation—equipment	141		$5,400

Adjustment for 20X1 depreciation
of hospital equipment:

Cost	$60,000
Less salvage value (10%)	6,000
Depreciable cost	$54,000
$54,000 ÷ 10 years = $5,400	

    In actual practice, the computation of depreciation is complicated by the fact that hospitals own many different types of equipment that have been acquired on different dates and that have different useful lives and salvage values. And, of course, different depreciation methods may be applied to different classes of equipment.

    Several depreciation expense accounts usually are employed in an actual situation. To reduce the amount of detail, however, we are using a single depreciation expense account for depreciation of both buildings and equipment.

Revenue Deductions

Turn your attention now to several other accounts in Hoosier Hospital's December 31, 20X1, trial balance (see Figure 5.1). The relevant accounts are as follows:

Acct. No.		Dr.	Cr.
104	Accounts receivable	$96,600	
105	Allowance for uncollectible accounts		$ -0-
501	Contractual adjustments	19,400	
502	Charity care adjustments	29,200	
609	Bad debt expense	-0-	

    You know, of course, that account 104 reflects the uncollected billings made to patients (or to third-party payers) for hospital services rendered. On December 31, 20X1, then, $96,600 of Hoosier Hospital's 20X1 patient services revenues remain uncollected and in accounts receivable. Account 104 is always debited (and revenues credited) for all services provided at full, established rates for those services, regardless of the financial status or medical classification of the patients served by the hospital. This provides an accounting measurement of the monetary value of the hospital services rendered during the period.

    In fact, hospitals do not always collect their full, established rates for services rendered. There are several reasons for this situation.

Contractual Adjustments

The first reason why hospitals often do not collect their full rates concerns certain third-party contracts. Under these contracts, the hospital has agreed to provide certain services to a particular group of patients at contract rates that are less than the hospital's full rates. The difference generally is not collectible by the hospital from those patients. This uncollectible difference usually is accumulated in another revenue deduction account called contractual adjustments (account 501).

To illustrate, assume that Hoosier Hospital provides $10,000 of services to certain third-party patients under a contract that provides for 90 percent reimbursement to the hospital. The entries are as follows:

Accounts receivable	104	$10,000	
Routine services revenue	401		$6,000
Ancillary services revenue	402		4,000
Services rendered to patients			
Cash	101	9,000	
Contractual adjustments	501	1,000	
Accounts receivable	104		10,000
Collection of third-party accounts at 90%			

The $1,000 of lost revenue (10 percent of $10,000) is debited to the contractual adjustments account that, like charity care adjustments, will be included in the worksheets to the statement of operations as a deduction from gross patient services revenues, but will not appear on statements of operations distributed outside the hospital.

Statement 7 of the HFMA Principles and Practices Board concludes that revenues be reported net of contractual adjustments in general-purpose financial statements (see www.hfma.org). In other words, revenues should be reported at the amount that the third-party payer has an obligation to pay. In this book, we will treat contractual adjustments as revenue deductions for preparing worksheets.

Charity Care Adjustments

The second reason why hospitals fail to collect their revenues is that most hospitals provide services to all who are in need of those services, regardless of the recipients' ability to pay. Hospitals render a considerable volume of services to the financially indigent, either at nominal service rates based on the patient's ability to pay or at no charge whatsoever (see www.aha.org for the American Hospital Association recommendations on this subject). The difference between the hospital's established rates for such services and the amount collected (if any) is called **charity care adjustments**. The amount of charity care provided by the hospital is accumulated and reported as a revenue deduction in the charity care adjustments (account 502). Because this account reflects "lost revenues," it has a debit balance. In compliance with GAAP, which dictate reporting requirements for financial statements distributed external to the hospital, charity care is reported as a note to the financial statements. The note should include the hospital's policy for providing charity care as well as some indication of the amount of charity care provided. This amount may be reported as volume of charity care, cost of charity care, or revenues lost due to charity care. Most hospitals report revenues lost because it is an easier number to obtain, and lost revenues is a larger amount than costs, thus making the hospital appear more charitable.

To illustrate, assume that Hoosier Hospital provides certain ancillary services to a group of charity patients. Established rates for these services total $174, but the hospital receives nothing.

Two entries are necessary:

Accounts receivable	104	$174	
Ancillary services revenue	402		$174
Services rendered to charity patients			
Charity care adjustments	502	174	
Accounts receivable	104		174
Write-off of patients' accounts			
to charity care			

Bad Debt Expense

A third reason why hospitals fail to collect their revenues is that some patients who have the financial ability to pay simply do not pay their hospital bills, just as they may not pay their other bills. If these patients' accounts remain uncollected after the hospital's best collection efforts, they are written off as **bad debts**. Prior to 1990, hospitals treated bad debts as a deduction from revenues. After 1990, GAAP required hospitals to show bad debt as an operating expense based on charges lost because of bad debt (account 609). While reporting charges somewhat exaggerates the impact of bad debt, charges are more uniformly reported than costs in that hospitals use a variety of ways to determine costs associated with services provided.

It is very important not to confuse bad debts with charity care. Bad debts arise from services rendered to patients who are *able but unwilling* to pay; charity care services are provided to patients who are *unable to pay*.

Statement 2 of the HFMA Principles and Practices Board sets forth the differentiation between bad debts and charity care, and the time when the differentiation should be made (see www.hfma.org). Prior to providing services, or as soon thereafter as possible in the case of emergencies, the financial status of patients should be clearly established so as to permit accurate accounting classifications of all patient services transactions.

To illustrate, assume that Hoosier Hospital provides certain ancillary services to a group of patients who later refuse to pay their bills. Established rates for these services total $150, but the hospital receives nothing.

Two entries are necessary:

Accounts receivable	104	$150	
Ancillary services revenue	402		$150
Services rendered to patients			
Bad debt expense	609	150	
Accounts receivable	104		150
Write-off of patients' accounts			
to bad debt			

Making Allowances for Revenue Deductions and Bad Debt Expense

In addition to accounting recognition of charity care adjustments, contractual adjustments, and bad debt expenses during an accounting period, adjusting entries for these revenue deductions also are necessary at the end of the period. These entries consist of estimates of charity care adjustments, contractual adjustments, and bad debt expenses related to services rendered during the period and included in the end-of-period accounts receivable.

This estimated portion of accounts receivable likely to prove uncollectible in the next accounting period is debited to the revenue deduction accounts and credited to the allowance for uncollectible accounts (account 105). This is done to match gross revenues with related revenue deductions and bad debt expense in the same accounting period. It is the same principle described in Chapter 5 as the matching of revenue and expense.

The allowance for uncollectible accounts is a contra asset account. It is presented in the hospital's balance sheet as a deduction from accounts receivable in much the same manner that accumulated depreciation is deducted from the hospital's plant assets. Journal entries relating to allowances for uncollectible accounts are illustrated later in this chapter.

Contractual Allowance   Hoosier Hospital's December 31, 20X1, trial balance includes account 501, contractual adjustments, which has a debit balance of $29,200. All of these revenue deductions were recorded by the hospital in a series of entries, but the following entry summarizes them:

Contractual adjustments	501	$29,200	
Accounts receivables	104		$29,200
Write-off of patients' accounts to			
contractual adjustments			

This entry records the contractual adjustments given accounting recognition during 20X1. At December 31, however, how much of the $96,600 of accounts receivable will prove to be uncollectible by reason of contractual adjustments?

If it is possible to identify the contractual adjustments portion of individual accounts, such amounts should be written off immediately and directly to the contractual adjustments account. This procedure generally is possible in part because the hospital should know the amount of the discount it is contractually obligated to honor and can therefore write the discount off immediately to the contractual adjustments account. This may necessitate an automated contract management system. In cases where the hospital relies on the insurance company to determine the amount of the discount and writes the discount off at time of payment, the hospital may not be collecting the full amount due from the insurance company. Would the insurance company have a vested interest to underpay the hospital? Sometimes it is not possible to write off the accounts immediately and directly, and so an estimate is made of the percentage of accounts receivable likely to prove uncollectible because of contractual adjustments. Let us assume that only $20,000 of year-end accounts receivable are subject to contractual adjustments and that an estimated 12 percent of these balances probably will be uncollected because of such adjustments. The following is the required December 31, 20X1, adjusting entry:

Estimating Contractual Adjustments

Contractual adjustments	501	$2,400	
Allowance for uncollectible accounts	105		$2,400
Adjustment for estimated portion of			
accounts receivable likely to prove			
uncollectible by reason of contractual			
adjustments (12% of $20,000)			

This entry matches the revenue deduction for contractual adjustments with the related revenues recorded during 20X1.

In 20X2, when $1,900 of 20X1 accounts receivable are found to be uncollectible by reason of contractual adjustments, the following entry is made:

Allowance for uncollectible accounts	105	$1,900	
Accounts receivable	104		$1,900
Write-off of a portion of 20X1			
accounts receivable against the			
allowance for uncollectibles			

Had the allowance account not been established by the December 31, 20X1, adjusting entry, the 20X2 write-off above would have been made to revenue deductions (contractual adjustments) of 20X2. This would have produced a mismatching of revenues and revenue deductions.

Charity Care Allowance

Recall that Hoosier Hospital's December 31, 20X1, trial balance includes account 502, charity care adjustments, with a debit balance of $19,400. This indicates that the hospital, in a series of journal entries, gave accounting recognition to $19,400 of charity care rendered during 20X1. In a single summary entry, the following was recorded:

Charity care adjustments	502	$19,400	
Accounts receivable	104		$19,400
Write-off of patients' accounts to charity care			

Prior to this, when the services were provided to charity patients, entries were made to record the revenues and establish the accounts receivable.

Estimating Charity Care Allowance

At year's end, however, there are $96,600 of accounts receivable. How much of this $96,600 will not be collected because of charity care? If it is possible and practicable to identify specific accounts (or portions of specific accounts) as charity, such accounts (or portions of them) should be written off immediately and directly to the charity care adjustments account. This procedure is frequently feasible because charity care patients should be identified before the time of service for all nonemergent treatments and services. If not, as in the case of emergency patients who have not been identified as charity care or, in the case of ongoing treatment to charity care patients, an estimate generally is made of the percentage of accounts receivable likely not to be collected because of being charity care. Assuming this percentage to be 5 percent, the necessary adjusting entry at December 31, 20X1, is recorded as follows:

Charity care adjustments	502	$ 4,830	
Allowance for uncollectible accounts	105		$ 4,830
Allowance established for estimated portion of accounts receivable likely to prove uncollectible because of charity care (5% of $96,600 = $4,830)			

This entry matches the charity care revenue deduction with the related revenues recorded during 20X1. The entry also establishes the allowance account so that the accounts receivable will be reported in the December 31, 20X1, balance sheet at net realizable value, or collectible value.

In 20X2, when it is determined that a 20X1 patient account of, say, $700 is deemed uncollectible by reason of financial indigence, the following entry is made:

Allowance for uncollectible accounts	105	$ 700	
Accounts receivable	104		$ 700
Write-off of 20X1 charity accounts			
to the allowance for uncollectibles			

Had the adjusting entry not been made at the end of 20X1 to establish the allowance account for estimated charity care, the 20X2 write-off would have been debited to the 20X2 charity care (revenue deductions) account. And this would have put the debit to charity care in the wrong year! The charity care was provided in 20X1, not in 20X2.

Bad Debts

A third account, bad debt expense (account 609), appears in the December 31, 20X1, trial balance of Hoosier Hospital. Because this account has no balance, it can be correctly assumed that the hospital has not recognized any bad debts during 20X1. As of December 31, however, the hospital has $96,600 of accounts receivable. How much of these receivables will prove to be uncollectible by reason of bad debts?

Determining Bad Debts

If it can be determined that specific accounts are bad debts on December 31, those particular accounts should be written off immediately and directly to the bad debts account—in other words, debit bad debts and credit accounts receivable. This procedure, however, often is not feasible, particularly with those accounts that have been on the books only a short time and for which additional collection efforts will be made in the future. Thus, an estimate must be made as to the amount of bad debts likely to arise out of the December 31 accounts receivable.

This estimate may be developed as a percentage of accounts receivable or as a percentage of patient services revenues for the period. It also may be determined through the preparation of a so-called aging schedule for the year-end accounts receivable. These methods of estimating bad debts are described fully in a later chapter. Until we consider them in detail, we will estimate bad debts simply as a percentage of year-end accounts receivable, recognizing that this procedure is not always appropriate.

Let us assume, then, that Hoosier Hospital estimates its bad debts at 10 percent of December 31, 20X1, accounts receivable. The required adjusting entry is the following:

Bad debt expense	609	$9,660	
Allowance for uncollectible accounts	105		$9,660
Adjustment for estimated portion of			
accounts receivable likely to prove			
uncollectible by reason of bad debt			
(10% of $96,600 = $9,660)			

This entry puts the revenue bad debt expense in the same year in which the related revenues and accounts receivable arose.

In 20X2, when an individual patient's account of, say, $950 is deemed to be a bad debt and therefore uncollectible, the entry is:

Allowance for uncollectible accounts	105	$ 950	
Accounts receivable	104		$ 950
Write-off of a patient's account			
deemed to be a bad debt			

Had the allowance account not been established at the end of 20X1, the write-off in 20X2 necessarily would have been charged to bad debt expense of 20X2 (the wrong year, in that the related revenues were recognized in 20X1).

Allowance for Uncollectible Accounts

The assumed December 31, 20X1, adjusting entries for contractual adjustments, charity care adjustments, and bad debt expense (and its respective allowance) are summarized as follows:

Contractual adjustments	501	$ 2,400	
Allowance for uncollectible accounts	105		$ 2,400
Adjustment for estimated amount of			
contractual adjustments in year-end			
accounts receivable			
Charity care adjustments	502	4,830	
Allowance for uncollectible accounts	105		4,830
Adjustment for estimated charity services			
in year-end accounts receivable			
Bad debt expense	609	9,660	
Allowance for uncollectible accounts	105		9,660
Adjustment for estimated bad debts			
in year-end accounts receivable			

Although a separate allowance account generally is maintained for each type of revenue deduction and bad debt expense, a single allowance account is used here to reduce the amount of detail.

Taken together, these entries establish a total credit balance of $16,890 ($4,830 + $2,400 + $9,660) in the allowance account. The balance sheet of Hoosier Hospital at December 31, 20X1, therefore, will report the following:

Accounts receivable		$96,600
Less allowance for uncollectible accounts	16,890	
Accounts receivable, net (of allowance)		$79,710

The $79,710 figure is the net realizable value of the hospital's accounts receivable at December 31. It is the amount of the accounts receivable estimated to be collectible in cash in the future (early in 20X2). This balance sheet valuation of accounts receivable is a GAAP.

Summary of Adjustments for Depreciation and Revenue Deductions

In the previous chapter, adjusting journal entries for prepayments and accruals were illustrated (see Figure 6.1). Those adjustments were numbered as entries 1 through 8. Figure 7.1 presents the adjusting entries discussed in this chapter as entries 9 through 13. Entries 9 and 10 are for depreciation expense; entries 11 through 13 are for revenue deductions and bad debt expense. The next chapter pulls together all 13 adjusting entries and prepares the 20X1 financial statements for Hoosier Hospital.

Entry No.	Accounts and Explanations	Acct No.	Dr.	Cr.
9	Depreciation expense	607	$2,880	
	Accumulated depreciation—			
	buildings	131		$2,880
	Adjustment for 20X1 depreciation of hospital buildings			
10	Depreciation expense	607	5,400	
	Accumulated depreciation—			
	equipment	141		5,400
	Adjustment for 20X1 depreciation of hospital equipment			
11	Contractual adjustments	501	2,400	
	Allowance for uncollectible accounts	105		2,400
	Adjustment for estimated contractual adjustments in year-end accounts receivable			
12	Charity care adjustments	502	4,830	
	Allowance for uncollectible accounts	105		4,830
	Adjustment for estimated charity care in year-end accounts receivable			
13	Bad debt expense	609	9,660	
	Allowance for uncollectible accounts	105		9,660
	Adjustment for estimated bad debts in year-end accounts receivable			

FIGURE 7.1

Hoosier Hospital 20X1 Journal (Adjusting Entries)

Questions

Q7.1. What is a contra asset account? Give two examples of such an account.

Q7.2. Define *depreciation* as the term is used in accounting.

Q7.3. For plant assets, what is salvage value? How is the amount of salvage value determined for a particular asset?

Q7.4. How is the estimated useful life of a plant asset determined?

Q7.5. Gordon Hospital purchased a new item of equipment for $15,000 on January 1, 20X1. This equipment has an estimated useful life of ten years and an expected salvage value of 20 percent. Compute the amount of straight-line depreciation for 20X1.

Q7.6. For depreciable plant assets, what is meant by the term "book value"?

Q7.7. Is land a depreciable asset? Explain.

Q7.8. Gravity Hospital purchased a new item of equipment on January 1, 20X1. The equipment has an estimated useful life of ten years and an expected salvage value of 20 percent. Gravity Hospital's December 31, 20X5, balance sheet reports $10,000 of accumulated depreciation on this equipment. What was the cost of the equipment when it was acquired on January 1, 20X1?

Q7.9. Gamma Hospital purchased a new item of equipment for $40,000 on May 1, 20X1. The equipment has an estimated useful life of ten years and an expected salvage value of $4,000. What amount should be reported as accumulated depreciation on this equipment in Gamma Hospital's December 31, 20X2, balance sheet?

Q7.10. Hospitals do not always collect their full, established rates for services rendered. Explain why this situation exists.

Q7.11. Distinguish among contractual adjustments, charity care adjustments, and bad debt expense.

Q7.12. At what amount should patients' accounts receivable be valued in a hospital's balance sheet?

Exercises

E7.1. Garry Hospital provides $1,600 of routine services and $1,400 of ancillary services to a patient under a third-party contract that provides for 85 percent reimbursement to the hospital. The remaining 15 percent is not billable to the patient.
Required: Make general journal entries to record (1) the services rendered to the patient and (2) the collection of the patient's account.

E7.2. Great Hospital has $100,000 of accounts receivable at December 31, 20X1. It is estimated that 9 percent of these accounts will eventually prove to be bad debts and, therefore, uncollectible. During 20X2, $8,300 of the 20X1 accounts receivable are written off as bad debts. *Required*: Make general journal entries to record (1) the estimated bad debts at December 31, 20X1, and (2) the write-off of bad accounts during 20X2.

E7.3.   Goodcare Hospital has $100,000 of accounts receivable at December 31, 20X1. It is estimated that 7 percent of these accounts will be uncollectible by reason of charity care, 10 percent will not be collectible because of contractual adjustments, and 4 percent will prove to be bad debts.
Required: (1) Make the necessary adjusting entries at December 31, 20X1, and (2) indicate how the receivables should be reported in the hospital's balance sheet for December 31, 20X1.

E7.4.   Gracious Hospital purchased the following plant assets on January 1, 20X1:

	Cost	Salvage Value	Estimated Useful Life (Years)
Land	$ 100,000		
Buildings	8,000,000	$1,600,000	40
Equipment	4,500,000	500,000	20

Required: (1) Assuming straight-line depreciation, what is the depreciation expense for 20X4? (2) At what amount, net of accumulated depreciation, would these assets be presented in the balance sheet of the hospital at December 31, 20X6?

E7.5.   Golly Hospital purchased equipment with the following costs:

Purchase Date	Cost	Estimated Useful Life (Years)
1/1/X1	$ 100,000	8
4/1/X1	200,000	10
7/1/X1	300,000	6

Required: All equipment has a 20 percent salvage value. What is depreciation expense for 20X1?

Problems

P7.1.   Goodness Hospital's general ledger contains the following unadjusted account balances, among others, at December 31, 20X1:

Acct. No.		
104	Accounts receivable	$ 850,000
105	Allowance for uncollectible accounts	-0-
120	Land	25,000
130	Buildings	3,000,000
131	Accumulated depreciation—buildings	-0-
140	Equipment	1,800,000
141	Accumulated depreciation—equipment	-0-
501	Contractual adjustments	-0-
502	Charity care adjustments	-0-
607	Depreciation expense	-0-
609	Bad debt expense	-0-

The following additional information is available:

1. Of the December 31, 20X1, accounts receivable, it is estimated that 15 percent will prove to be uncollectible due to these factors:

   Contractual adjustments, 6%
   Charity care adjustments, 4%
   Bad debt expense, 5%

2. The hospital building, which was acquired on January 1, 20X1, has an estimated useful life of 40 years and an expected salvage value of $200,000.

3. Equipment, which cost $1,500,000, was acquired on January 1, 20X1. Additional equipment was acquired on July 1, 20X1, for $300,000. All equipment has a 20 percent salvage value and an estimated useful life of ten years.

Required: Prepare, in general journal form, all necessary adjusting entries at December 31, 20X1.

P7.2. Certain of the accounts in Gateway Hospital's preadjusted trial balance at December 31, 20X6, are as follows:

Acct. No.		
102	Temporary investments	$ 60,000
103	Accrued interest receivable	-0-
104	Accounts receivable	940,000
105	Allowance for uncollectible accounts	3,000
107	Prepaid insurance	1,800
120	Land	50,000
130	Buildings	4,000,000

131	Accumulated depreciation—buildings	450,000
140	Equipment	1,900,000
141	Accumulated depreciation—equipment	750,000
203	Accrued interest payable	-0-
205	Deferred rental income	3,000
250	Bonds payable	100,000
403	Interest income	2,875
404	Rental income	1,780
501	Contractual adjustments	71,300
502	Charity care adjustments	56,290
604	Insurance expense	11,450
607	Depreciation expense	-0-
608	Interest expense	9,230
609	Bad debt expense	-0-

The following additional information is available:

1. The hospital's temporary investments consist of $60,000 (face value) of 8 percent bonds that were acquired on October 1, 20X7. These bonds pay interest annually on October 1, commencing October 1, 20X7.

2. Account 105 is used only for estimated bad debts; charity care adjustments and contractual adjustments are charged directly to accounts 502 and 501, respectively. The $3,000 credit balance in account 105 here represents the excess of estimated bad debts at December 31, 20X5, over the actual bad debts written off during 20X6. It is estimated that all of the December 31, 20X6, accounts receivable are collectible except for 5 percent that probably will prove to be bad debts.

3. Account 107 includes a three-year insurance premium paid in advance on June 1, 20X6.

4. The hospital building, which was acquired on January 1, 20X1, has an estimated useful life of 40 years and an expected 10 percent salvage value.

5. All the equipment was acquired on January 1, 20X1. It has an estimated useful life of 12 years and a $100,000 salvage value.

6. Account 202 represents the face amount of a 12 percent, six-month bank loan obtained by the hospital on November 1, 20X6. Interest on the note was not prepaid.

7. Account 205 represents a year's rent received in advance on March 1, 20X6.

Required: Prepare, in general journal form, the necessary adjusting entries for December 31, 20X6.

P7.3.   Gaterburg Hospital's general ledger contains the following unadjusted account balances, among others, for December 31, 20X5:

Acct. No.		
104	Accounts receivable	$120,000
105	Allowance for uncollectible accounts	-0-
120	Land	15,000
130	Buildings	900,000
131	Accumulated depreciation—buildings	80,000
140	Equipment	450,000
141	Accumulated depreciation—equipment	120,000
501	Contractual adjustments	-0-
502	Charity care adjustments	-0-
607	Depreciation expense	-0-
609	Bad debt expense	-0-

The following additional information is available:

1. Of the December 31, 20X5, accounts receivable, it is estimated that 17 percent will prove to be uncollectible due to the following:
   a. Contractual adjustments, 7 percent
   b. Charity care adjustments, 6 percent
   c. Bad debt expense, 4 percent
2. The hospital building was acquired on January 1, 20X1. It has an estimated useful life of 40 years and an estimated salvage value of $100,000.
3. On January 1, 20X1, the hospital acquired $400,000 of equipment having an estimated useful life of 12 years and an estimated salvage value of 10 percent. Additional equipment, costing $50,000 and acquired on May 1, 20X5, has an estimated useful life of eight years and an estimated salvage value of $2,000.

Required: (1) Prepare, in general journal form, the necessary adjusting entries at December 31, 20X5. (2) Indicate the manner in which receivables should be presented in the hospital's December 31, 20X5, balance sheet. (3) Indicate the presentation of plant assets in the hospital's December 31, 20X5, balance sheet.

ACCOUNTING CYCLE SUMMARY

Chapter 5 began an illustration explaining the 20X1 financial activities of the hypothetical Hoosier Hospital. That illustration was continued in Chapters 6 and 7. Now we want to summarize quickly the discussion in those chapters and proceed to complete the accounting cycle for Hoosier Hospital. A summary of all of the procedures involved in the cycle is presented in Figure 8.1. This diagram is quite similar to the one presented for the annual accounting cycle in Chapter 4 (see Figure 4.8). Here, however, we have included the adjustment process.

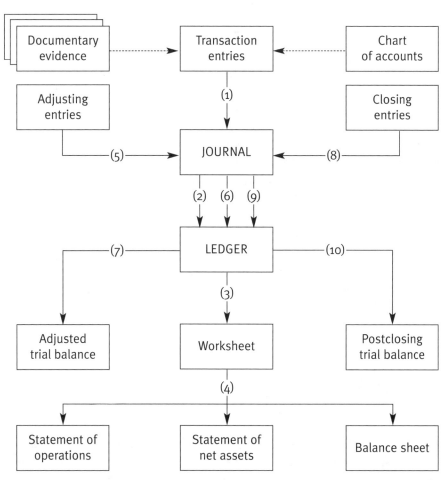

FIGURE 8.1
Summary of Accounting Procedure

Journalizing and Posting Transaction Entries

Recall that Hoosier Hospital opened on January 1, 20X1. Over the course of the year, thousands of business transactions were completed with patients, third-party payers, suppliers, employees, and others. As these transactions occurred, documentary evidence was used as a basis for the development of transaction entries. These entries were journalized in the hospital's 20X1 journal (step 1 in Figure 8.1) to provide a chronological record of the increase and decrease effects of the transactions on the accounting classifications set forth in the hospital's chart of accounts. At the end of the year, the transaction entries were posted from the journal to the ledger (step 2 in Figure 8.1), and the year-end balance of each account was determined. These balances then were arranged in a preadjusted trial balance and entered on a worksheet (step 3 in Figure 8.1). The previously illustrated trial balance is repeated here as Figure 8.2.

Expansion of the Worksheet

Instead of preparing a separate preadjusted trial balance, we could enter the trial balance directly on the worksheet, as shown in Figure 8.3. This worksheet is used to develop the necessary adjusting entries. Each of the trial balance accounts is carefully scrutinized to determine the need for an adjustment of its balance. As these adjustments are determined, they are entered in the adjustments column of the worksheet (but not in the journal at this time). When all of the adjustments have been made, the adjusted balances of the accounts are extended into the columns for adjusted balances on the worksheet.

Completing the Worksheet

The worksheet then is completed by the extension of the adjusted balances into the appropriate statement columns. In footing the statement columns, the excess of revenues over expenses for the year and the hospital's year-end net assets balance are determined. Naturally, the various columns of the worksheet must balance.

Financial Statements

The next procedure in the accounting cycle (step 4 in Figure 8.1) is the preparation of the financial statements (statement of operations, statement of net assets, and balance sheet) for 20X1 for Hoosier Hospital. These statements are prepared directly from the information contained in the worksheet.

FIGURE 8.2

Hoosier
Hospital
Preadjusted
Trial Balance,
December 31,
20X1

Acct. No.	Account Titles	Dr.	Cr.
101	Cash	$ 38,300	
102	Temporary investments	12,000	
103	Accrued interest receivable	-0-	
104	Accounts receivable	96,600	
105	Allowance for uncollectible accounts		$ -0-
106	Inventory	10,500	
107	Prepaid insurance	3,600	
108	Prepaid rent	1,080	
109	Prepaid interest	720	
120	Land	25,000	
130	Buildings	180,000	
131	Accumulated depreciation—buildings		-0-
140	Equipment	60,000	
141	Accumulated depreciation—equipment		-0-
201	Accounts payable		29,840
202	Notes payable		18,000
203	Accrued interest payable		-0-
204	Accrued salaries and wages payable		-0-
205	Deferred rental income		4,200
206	Deferred tuition income		2,160
250	Bonds payable		80,000
301	Hospital net assets		225,000
302	Revenue and expense summary		-0-
401	Routine services revenue		151,300
402	Ancillary services revenue		137,400
403	Interest income		-0-
404	Rental income		-0-
405	Tuition income		-0-
406	Other operating revenues		27,100
501	Contractual adjustments	29,200	
502	Charity care adjustments	19,400	
601	Salaries and wages expense	139,600	
602	Supplies expense	28,600	
603	Utilities expense	14,400	
604	Insurance expense	-0-	
605	Repairs expense	8,300	
606	Rent expense	-0-	
607	Depreciation expense	-0-	
608	Interest expense	-0-	
609	Bad debt expense	-0-	
610	Other expenses	7,700	
	Totals	$675,000	$675,000

FIGURE 8.3 Hoosier Hospital Worksheet to Develop Financial Statements, Year Ended December 31, 20X1

Acct. No.	Account Titles	Preadjusted Trial Balance 12/31/x1 Dr.	Cr.	12/31/x1 Adjustments Dr.	Cr.	Adjusted Trial Balance Dr.	Cr.	20x1 Income Statement Dr.	Cr.	20x1 Equity Statement Dr.	Cr.	12/31/x1 Balance Sheet Dr.	Cr.
101	Cash	38,300				38,300						38,300	
102	Temporary investments	12,000				12,000						12,000	
103	Accrued interest receivable			(8) 240		240						240	
104	Accounts receivable	96,600				96,600						96,600	
105	Allowance for uncollectible accounts				(11) 4,830 (12) 2,400 (13) 9,660			16,890					16,890
106	Inventory	10,500				10,500						10,500	
107	Prepaid insurance	3,600			(1) 1,200	2,400						2,400	
108	Prepaid rent	1,080			(2) 720	360						360	
109	Prepaid interest	720			(3) 240	480						480	
120	Land	25,000				25,000						25,000	
130	Buildings	180,000				180,000						180,000	
131	Accumulated depreciation—buildings				(9) 2,880		2,880						2,880
140	Equipment	60,000				60,000						60,000	
141	Accumulated depreciation—Equipment				(10) 5,400		5,400						5,400
201	Accounts payable		29,840				29,840						29,840
202	Notes payable		18,000				18,000						18,000
203	Accrued interest payable				(4) 3,600		3,600						3,600
204	Accrued salaries and wages payable				(5) 13,000		13,000						13,000
205	Deferred rental income		4,200	(6) 1,750			2,450						2,450
206	Deferred tuition income		2,160	(7) 960			1,200						1,200
250	Bonds payable		80,000				80,000						80,000
301	Hospital net assets		225,000				225,000				225,000		
302	Revenue and expense summary												

Continued

FIGURE 8.3 (CONTINUED) Hoosier Hospital Worksheet to Develop Financial Statements, Year Ended December 31, 20X1

Acct. No.	Account Titles	Preadjusted Trial Balance 12/31/x1 Dr.	Cr.	12/31/x1 Adjustments Dr.	Cr.	Adjusted Trial Balance Dr.	Cr.	20x1 Income Statement Dr.	Cr.	20x1 Equity Statement Dr.	Cr.	12/31/x1 Balance Sheet Dr.	Cr.
401	Routine services revenue		151,300				151,300		151,300				
402	Ancillary services revenue		137,400				137,400		137,400				
403	Interest income				(8) 240		240		240				
404	Rental income				(6) 1,750		1,750		1,750				
405	Tuition income				(7) 960		960		960				
406	Other operating revenues		27,100				27,100		27,100				
501	Contractual adjustments	29,200		(11) 2,400		31,600		31,600					
502	Charity care adjustments	19,400		(12) 4,830		24,230		24,230					
601	Salaries and wages expense	139,600		(5) 13,000		152,600		152,600					
602	Supplies expense	28,600				28,600		28,600					
603	Utilities expense	14,400				14,400		14,400					
604	Insurance expense			(1) 1,200		1,200		1,200					
605	Repairs expense	8,300				8,300		8,300					
606	Rent expense			(2) 720		720		720					
607	Depreciation expense			(9) 2,880 (10) 5,400		8,280		8,280					
608	Interest expense			(3) 240 (4) 3,600		3,840		3,840					
609	Bad debt expense			(13) 9,660		9,660		9,660					
610	Other expenses	7,700				7,700		7,700					
	Totals	675,000	675,000	46,880	46,880	717,010	717,010	291,130	318,750				
	Net income for the year							27,620			27,620		
	Totals							318,750	318,750	-0-	252,620		
	Hospital net assets, December 31, 20x1									252,620		425,880	252,620
	Totals									252,620	252,620	425,880	425,880

FIGURE 8.4

Hoosier Hospital Statement of Operations, Year Ended December 31, 20X1

Gross patient services revenues:		
Routine services	$151,300	
Ancillary services	37,400	
Gross patient services revenues		$288,700
Less revenue deductions:		
Contractual adjustments	21,800	
Charity care adjustments	34,030	
Total revenue deductions		55,830
Net patient services revenues		232,870
Other operating revenues:		
Rent	1,750	
Tuition	960	
Other	27,100	
Total other operating revenues		29,810
Total operating revenues		262,680
Less operating expenses:		
Salaries and wages	152,600	
Supplies	28,600	
Utilities	14,400	
Insurance	1,200	
Repairs	8,300	
Rent	720	
Depreciation	8,280	
Interest	3,840	
Bad debt	9,660	
Other	7,700	
Total operating expenses		235,300
Operating income		27,380
Nonoperating income (interest)		240
Excess of revenue over expenses for the year		$ 27,620

FIGURE 8.5

Hoosier Hospital Statement of Hospital Net Assets, Year Ended December 31, 20X1

Hospital net assets, January 1	$225,000
Excess of revenues over expenses for 20X1	27,620
Hospital net assets, December 31	$252,620

FIGURE 8.6

Hoosier
Hospital
Balance Sheet,
December 31,
20X1

Assets

Cash		$ 38,300
Temporary investments		12,000
Accrued interest receivable		240
Accounts receivable	$96,600	
Allowance for uncollectible accounts	16,890	
Accounts receivable, net of allowances		79,710
Inventory		10,500
Prepaid insurance		2,400
Prepaid rent		360
Prepaid interest		480
Total current assets		143,990
Land		25,000
Buildings	$180,000	
Accumulated depreciation—buildings	2,880	
Buildings, net of depreciation		177,120
Equipment	60,000	
Accumulated depreciation—equipment	5,400	
Equipment, net of depreciation		54,600
Total long-term assets		256,720
Total assets		$400,710

Liabilities and Net Assets

Accounts payable	$29,840	
Notes payable	18,000	
Accrued interest payable	3,600	
Accrued salaries and wages	13,000	
Deferred rental income	2,450	
Deferred tuition income	1,200	
Total current liabilities		$ 68,090
Bonds payable		80,000
Total liabilities		148,090
Hospital net assets		252,620
Total liabilities and net assets		$400,710

Preparing the Financial Statements

Figure 8.4 illustrates Hoosier Hospital's 20X1 statement of operations;
Figure 8.5, the statement of hospital net assets; and Figure 8.6, the balance
sheet. Because these statements are somewhat more sophisticated than the
ones previously illustrated, you should give them careful study.

Entry No.	Accounts and Explanations	Acct No.	Dr.	Cr.
1	Insurance expense	604	$ 1,200	
	Prepaid insurance	107		$ 1,200
	Adjustment for portion of prepaid premium that expired during 20X1 (see Chapter 5)			
2	Rent expense	606	720	
	Prepaid rent	108		720
	Adjustment to record rent expense for May through December 20X1, at $90 per month (see Chapter 5)			
3	Interest expense	608	240	
	Prepaid interest	109		240
	Adjustment for interest on bank loan for November and December 20X1 (see Chapter 5)			
4	Interest expense	608	3,600	
	Accrued interest payable	203		3,600
	Adjustment for 6 months' interest accrued on bonds since July 1, 20X1 (see Chapter 5)			
5	Salaries and wages expense	601	13,000	
	Accrued salaries and wages payable	204		13,000
	Adjustment for accrued payroll for the month of December 20X1 (see Chapter 5)			
6	Deferred rental income	205	1,750	
	Rental income	404		1,750
	Adjustment for 5 months of rental income earned from provision of office space for physicians (see Chapter 6)			
7	Deferred tuition income	206	960	
	Tuition income	405		960
	Adjustment for tuition income earned in 20X1 (see Chapter 6)			
8	Accrued interest receivable	103	240	
	Interest income	403		240
	Adjustment for 3 months' interest on temporary investment in government bonds (see Chapter 6)			

Continued

Entry No.	Accounts and Explanations	Acct No.	Dr.	Cr.
9	Depreciation expense	607	2,880	
	Accumulated depreciation— buildings	131		2,880
	Adjustment for 20X1 depreciation of hospital building (see Chapter 7)			
10	Depreciation expense	607	5,400	
	Accumulated depreciation— equipment	141		5,400
	Adjustment for 20X1 depreciation of hospital equipment (see Chapter 7)			
11	Contractual adjustments	501	2,400	
	Allowance for uncollectible accounts	105		2,400
	Adjustment for estimated contractual adjustments in year-end accounts receivable (see Chapter 7)			
12	Charity care adjustments	502	4,830	
	Allowance for uncollectible accounts	105		4,830
	Adjustment for estimated charity care in year-end accounts receivable (see Chapter 7)			
13	Bad debt expense	609	9,660	
	Allowance for uncollectible accounts	105		9,660
	Adjustment for estimated bad debts in year-end accounts receivable (see Chapter 7)			

FIGURE 8.7 (CONTINUED) Hoosier Hospital 20X1 Journal (Adjusting Entries)

Journalizing and Posting Adjusting Entries

After the financial statements are distributed to Hoosier Hospital's management, governing board, and other interested parties, the accountant returns to the journal to journalize the adjusting entries for the year (step 5 in Figure 8.1). This is illustrated in Figure 8.7.

Once they are journalized, the adjusting entries are posted to the ledger (step 6 in Figure 8.1). The postings of these entries to Hoosier Hospital's ledger accounts are shown in Figure 8.8. There, the unadjusted balances in the ledger accounts are unlabeled, and the adjusted balances are encircled. Keep in mind as you examine Figure 8.8 that the postings of adjusting entries are numbered 1 through 13. You may wish to trace each of these postings from the journal (see Figure 8.7).

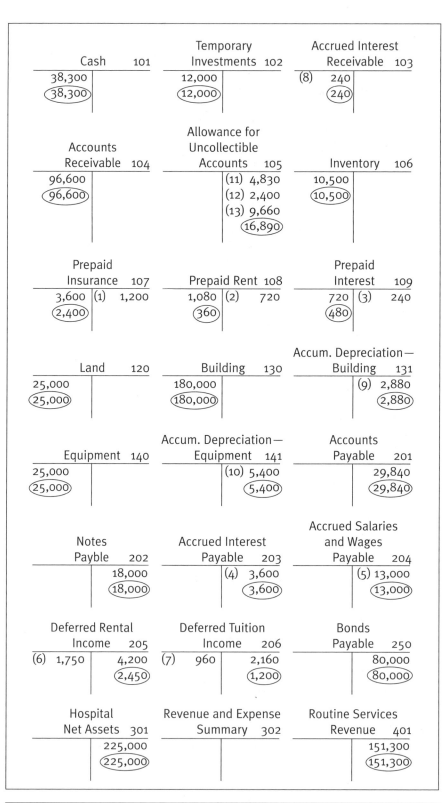

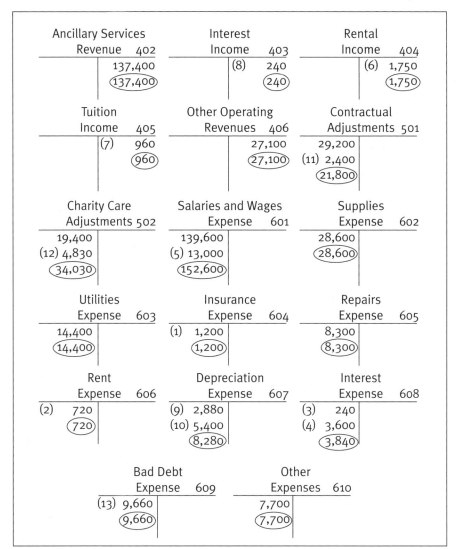

FIGURE 8.8
(Continued)
Hoosier
Hospital 20X1
Ledger (With
Adjusting
Entries)

Preparing an Adjusted Trial Balance

After the adjusting entries are posted and adjusted balances are obtained in the ledger accounts, the adjusted balances may be arranged in an adjusted trial balance (step 7 in Figure 8.1). Hoosier Hospital's adjusted trial balance is not illustrated here because an adjusted trial balance appears on the worksheet in Figure 8.2.

Journalizing and Posting Closing Entries

The next procedure in the accounting cycle is the preparation of closing entries. The entries are recorded in the journal (step 8 in Figure 8.1) as

FIGURE 8.9

Hoosier
Hospital 20X1
Journal
(Closing
Entries)

Entry No.	Accounts and Explanations	Acct No.	Dr.	Cr.
14	Routine services revenue	401	$151,300	
	Ancillary services revenue	402	137,400	
	Interest income	403	240	
	Rental income	404	1,750	
	Tuition income	405	960	
	Other operating revenues	406	27,100	
	Revenue and expense summary	302		$318,750
	To close revenue accounts			
15	Revenue and expense summary	302	55,830	
	Contractual adjustments	501		21,800
	Charity care adjustments	502		34,030
	To close revenue deduction accounts			
16	Revenue and expense summary	302	235,300	
	Salaries and wages expense	601		152,600
	Supplies expense	602		28,600
	Utilities expense	603		14,400
	Insurance expense	604		1,200
	Repairs expense	605		8,300
	Rent expense	606		720
	Depreciation expense	607		8,280
	Interest expense	608		3,840
	Bad debt expense	609		9,660
	Other expenses	610		7,700
	To close expense accounts			
17	Revenue and expense summary	302	27,620	
	Hospital net assets	301		27,620
	To close revenue and expense summary account and add excess of revenues over expenses to net assets			

shown in Figure 8.9. Notice that the closing entries are numbered 14 through 17. In addition to the closing of revenue and expense accounts, the revenue deduction accounts also must be closed, as indicated in entry 15.

Posting Closing Entries to the Ledger

The closing entries are now posted to the ledger (step 9 in Figure 8.1), as illustrated in Figure 8.10. When this is completed, the revenue, revenue deduction, and expense accounts are double-ruled to indicate that those accounts are closed.

Cash 101	Temporary Investments 102	Accrued Interest Receivable 103
38,300	12,000	(8) 240
(38,300)	(12,000)	(240)

Accounts Receivable 104	Allowance for Uncollectible Accounts 105	Inventory 106
96,600	(11) 4,830	10,500
(96,600)	(12) 2,400	(10,500)
	(13) 9,660	
	(16,890)	

Prepaid Insurance 107	Prepaid Rent 108	Prepaid Interest 109
3,600 | (1) 1,200	1,080 | (2) 720	720 | (3) 240
(2,400)	(360)	(480)

Land 120	Buildings 130	Accum. Depreciation— Buildings 131
25,000	180,000	(9) 2,880
(25,000)	(180,000)	(2,880)

Equipment 140	Accum. Depreciation— Equipment 141	Accounts Payable 201
60,000	(10) 5,400	29,840
(60,000)	(5,400)	(29,840)

Notes Payble 202	Accrued Interest Payable 203	Accrued Salaries and Wages Payable 204
18,000	(4) 3,600	(5) 13,000
(18,000)	(3,600)	(13,000)

Deferred Rental Income 205	Deferred Tuition Income 206	Bonds Payable 250
(6) 1,750 | 4,200	(7) 960 | 2,160	80,000
(2,450)	(1,200)	(80,000)

Hospital Net Assets 301	Revenue and Expense Summary 302	Routine Services Revenue 401
225,000	(15) 65,490 | (14) 318,750	(14) 151,300 | 151,300
(17) 27,620	(16) 225,640	
(252,620)	(17) 27,620	

FIGURE 8.10

Hoosier Hospital 20X1 Ledger (With Closing Entries)

Continued

FIGURE 8.10
(CONTINUED)
Hoosier
Hospital 20X1
Ledger
(With Closing
Entries)

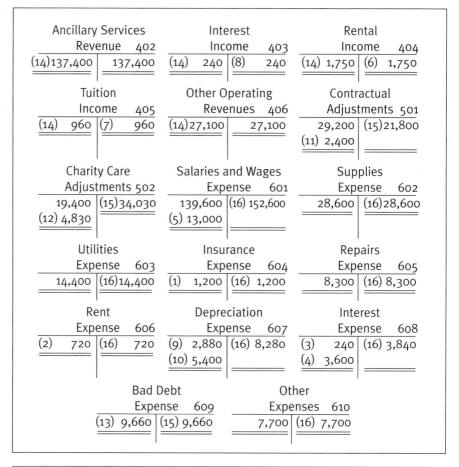

Preparing a Postclosing Trial Balance

The last step in the accounting cycle is the preparation of a postclosing trial balance (step 10 in Figure 8.1). The December 31, 20X1, postclosing trial balance for Hoosier Hospital is illustrated in Figure 8.11. Note that the remaining balances are those for asset, liability, and net assets accounts only. It is with these balances that Hoosier Hospital will begin the new year, 20X2. On January 1, 20X2, a new accounting cycle commences.

Questions

Q8.1. List and describe briefly each of the ten major steps in a complete accounting cycle.

Q8.2. "Annual financial statements cannot be prepared until the books are closed for the year." Do you agree or disagree? Explain your answer.

Q8.3. The following is a random listing of accounting procedures. Indicate the normal sequence in which these procedures are performed.

FIGURE 8.11

Hoosier Hospital Postclosing Trial Balance, December 31, 20X1

Acct. No.	Accounts and Titles	Dr.	Cr.
101	Cash	$ 38,300	
102	Temporary investments	12,000	
103	Accrued interest receivable	240	
104	Accounts receivable	96,600	
105	Allowance for uncollectible accounts		$ 16,890
106	Inventory	10,500	
107	Prepaid insurance	2,400	
108	Prepaid rent	360	
109	Prepaid interest	480	
120	Land	25,000	
130	Buildings	180,000	
131	Accumulated depreciation—buildings		2,880
140	Equipment	60,000	
141	Accumulated depreciation—equipment		5,400
201	Accounts payable		29,840
202	Notes payable		18,000
203	Accrued interest payable		3,600
204	Accrued salaries and wages payable		13,000
205	Deferred rental income		2,450
206	Deferred tuition income		1,200
250	Bonds payable		80,000
301	Hospital net assets		252,620
	Totals	$425,880	$425,880

a. Prepare financial statements.

b. Journalize closing entries.

c. Post adjusting entries to the ledger.

d. Prepare the general worksheet.

e. Journalize transaction entries.

f. Post closing entries to the ledger.

g. Prepare adjusted trial balance.

h. Post transaction entries to the ledger.

i. Prepare postclosing trial balance.

j. Journalize adjusting entries.

Q8.4. Garden Hospital paid a three-year insurance premium of $3,600 in advance on January 1, 20X1, debiting the $3,600 to the prepaid account. At the end of the year, the necessary adjusting entry was not made, and the omission was not discovered. What effect would this error have on total assets, total liabilities, and hospital net assets, as reported in the hospital's balance sheet for December 31, 20X1?

Q8.5. Goshen Hospital paid an account payable of $4,500 during December 20X1. In the transaction entry, however, the debit was made to supplies expense. The error was not discovered until after the financial statements for 20X1 were prepared. What effect would this error have on total assets, total liabilities, and hospital net assets, as reported in the hospital's December 31, 20X1, balance sheet?

Q8.6. Gibson Hospital received $2,300 in payment of a patient's account receivable on December 27, 20X1. In the transaction entry, however, the credit was made erroneously to routine service revenues. The error was not discovered until after the financial statements for 20X1 were prepared. What effect would this error have on total assets, total liabilities, and hospital net assets, as reported in the hospital's December 31, 20X1, balance sheet?

Exercises

E8.1. Getwell Hospital provides you with the following information:

	12/31/X2	12/31/X1
Accrued interest receivable	$4,100	$3,900
Prepaid interest	6,400	5,700
Accrued interest payable	3,200	3,600
Deferred interest income	4,800	5,300

In 20X2, the hospital received $38,000 of interest in cash and paid $54,000 of interest.

Required: What should be reported in the hospital's 20X2 statement of operations as (1) interest expense and (2) interest income?

E8.2. Goodwill Hospital provides you with the following information from its 20X2 general ledger:

Revenue and Expense
Summary   302

899,204	964,382
65,178	

Required: Assuming the hospital net assets at December 31, 20X1, were $516,894, what were the hospital net assets at December 31, 20X2?

E8.3. Goodhope Hospital provides you with the following information:

	12/31/X2	12/31/X1
Deferred rental income	$8,000	$7,500

Prepaid rent	7,400	8,200
Accrued rent receivable	6,300	6,200
Accrued rent payable	5,100	5,900

The hospital's 20X2 statement of operations reports rental income of $40,000 and rental expense of $60,000.

Required: (1) What was the amount of rent received in cash during 20X2? (2) What was the amount of rent paid in cash during 20X2?

E8.4.   Goodcare Hospital follows an accounting policy under which all income received in cash is credited to income, and all expense paid in cash is debited to expense. At the end of each month, adjusting entries are made for prepayments and accruals. The prepayments and accruals at the end of January 20X2 were as follows:

Prepaid expenses	$4,000
Prepaid income	3,000
Accrued expenses	6,000
Accrued income	5,000

Required: If the necessary adjusting entries are not made on January 31, 20X2, by what amount would the January excess of revenues over expenses be overstated (or understated) for (1) prepaid expenses, (2) prepaid income, (3) accrued expenses, and (4) accrued income?

Problems

P8.1.   Given here is the preadjusted trial balance of Greatville Hospital at December 31, 20X1, the end of the hospital's current fiscal year:

Acct. No.		Dr.	Cr.
101	Cash	$ 31,600	
102	Temporary investments	15,000	
103	Accrued interest receivable	-0-	
104	Accounts receivable	102,400	
105	Allowance for uncollectible accounts		$ -0-
106	Inventory	11,600	
107	Prepaid insurance	1,980	
108	Prepaid rent	2,100	
109	Prepaid interest	1,200	
120	Land	22,000	
130	Buildings	175,000	

131	Accumulated depreciation—buildings		-0-
140	Equipment	80,000	
141	Accumulated depreciation—equipment		-0-
201	Accounts payable		31,300
202	Notes payable		20,000
203	Accrued interest payable		-0-
204	Accrued salaries and wages payable		-0-
205	Deferred rental income		1,680
206	Deferred tuition income		1,215
250	Bonds payable		100,000
301	Hospital net assets		207,085
302	Revenue and expense summary		-0-
401	Routine services revenue		169,300
402	Ancillary services revenue		128,700
403	Interest income		-0-
404	Rental income		-0-
405	Tuition income		-0-
406	Other operating revenues		29,800
501	Contractual adjustments	20,300	
502	Charity care adjustments	28,200	
601	Salaries and wages expense	141,200	
602	Supplies expense	27,300	
603	Utilities expense	15,100	
604	Insurance expense	-0-	
605	Repairs expense	7,600	
606	Rent expense	-0-	
607	Depreciation expense	-0-	
608	Interest expense	-0-	
609	Bad debt expense	-0-	
610	Other expenses	6,500	
	Totals	$689,080	$689,080

The following additional information is available:

1. The temporary investment consists of $15,000 (face value) of 8 percent bonds acquired by the hospital on October 1, 20X1. These bonds pay interest annually on October 1, commencing October 1, 20X2.

2. Of the December 31, 20X1, accounts receivable, it is estimated that 12 percent will eventually prove uncollectible by reason of (1) contractual adjustments, 5 percent; (2) charity care, 4 percent; and (3) bad debts, 3 percent.

3. A three-year insurance premium of $1,980 was paid in advance by the hospital on January 1, 20X1.

4. The hospital prepaid a year's rent of $2,100 on June 1, 20X1.
5. On November 1, 20X1, the hospital borrowed $20,000 from a bank by issuing a six-month, 12 percent note. Interest on the note was prepaid.
6. The hospital building, which was acquired on January 1, 20X1, has an estimated useful life of 40 years and a salvage value of $15,000.
7. The equipment, which was acquired on January 1, 20X1, has an estimated useful life of eight years and a 10 percent salvage value.
8. On April 1, 20X1, the hospital issued $100,000 of 15-year, 6 percent bonds at face value. These bonds pay interest annually on April 1, commencing April 1, 20X2.
9. Unpaid salaries and wages at December 31, 20X1, totaled $15,600.
10. The hospital received one year's rent of $1,680 in advance on March 1, 20X1.
11. On September 1, 20X1, the hospital received nine months' tuition in advance in connection with one of its educational programs.

Required: (1) Prepare a worksheet to develop financial statements in the manner illustrated in Figure 8.3. (2) Prepare, in good form, a complete set of financial statements for 20X1.

P8.2. Certain of the adjusted balances in the ledger of Gatorberg Hospital at December 31, 20X1, the end of the hospital's current fiscal year, are provided here:

Acct. No.		
301	Hospital net assets	$275,000
302	Revenue and expense summary	-0-
401	Routine services revenue	159,700
402	Ancillary services revenue	101,800
403	Interest income	2,600
404	Rental income	1,900
405	Tuition income	1,500
406	Other operating revenues	29,800
501	Contractual adjustments	42,300
502	Charity care adjustments	31,700
601	Salaries and wages expense	145,900
602	Supplies expense	21,500
603	Utilities expense	12,300

604	Insurance expense	2,300
605	Repairs expense	4,100
606	Rent expense	2,800
607	Depreciation expense	9,400
608	Interest expense	1,400
609	Bad debt expense	11,600
610	Other expenses	7,200

Required: (1) Prepare, in general journal form, the necessary closing entries for the year ended December 31, 20X1. (2) Prepare, in good form, the 20X1 statement of operations for Gatorberg Hospital.

P8.3. The following is the preadjusted trial balance of Grandtown Hospital at December 31, 20X1, the end of the hospital's current fiscal year:

Acct. No.		Dr.	Cr.
101	Cash	$ 37,500	
102	Temporary investments	30,000	
103	Accrued interest receivable	-0-	
104	Accounts receivable	120,000	
105	Allowance for uncollectible accounts		$ -0-
106	Inventory	14,000	
107	Prepaid insurance	3,600	
120	Land	25,000	
130	Buildings	250,000	
131	Accumulated depreciation—buildings		-0-
140	Equipment	140,000	
141	Accumulated depreciation—equipment		-0-
201	Accounts payable		37,400
203	Accrued interest payable		-0-
204	Accrued salaries and wages payable		-0-
205	Deferred rental income		2,700
250	Bonds payable		150,000
301	Hospital net assets		395,700
302	Revenue and expense summary		-0-
401	Routine services revenue		171,200
402	Ancillary services revenue		110,300
403	Interest income		-0-
404	Rental income		-0-
406	Other operating revenues		23,500
501	Contractual adjustments	22,700	
502	Charity care adjustments	31,100	
601	Salaries and wages expense	155,600	

602	Supplies expense	33,100	
603	Utilities expense	14,900	
604	Insurance expense	-0-	
605	Repairs expense	6,400	
607	Depreciation expense	-0-	
608	Interest expense	4,500	
609	Bad debt expense	-0-	
610	Other expenses	2,400	
	Totals	$890,800	$890,800

The following additional information is available:

1. The temporary investment consists of $30,000 (face value) of 8 percent bonds acquired by the hospital on November 1, 20X1. These bonds pay interest annually on November 1, commencing on November 1, 20X2.
2. Of the December 31, 20X1, accounts receivable, it is estimated that 14 percent will eventually prove uncollectible by reason of (1) charity care, 7 percent; (2) contractual adjustments, 4 percent; and (3) bad debts, 3 percent.
3. A two-year insurance premium of $3,600 was paid in advance by the hospital on January 1, 20X1.
4. The hospital building, which was acquired on January 1, 20X1, has an estimated useful life of 50 years and a 20 percent salvage value.
5. The equipment, which was acquired on January 1, 20X1, has an estimated useful life of 12 years and a $20,000 salvage value.
6. On January 1, 20X1, the hospital issued $150,000 of 20-year, 6 percent bonds at face value. These bonds pay interest semiannually on January 1 and July 1, commencing July 1, 20X1.
7. Unpaid salaries and wages at December 31, 20X1, amounted to $12,300.
8. The hospital received one year's rent of $2,700 in advance on June 1, 20X1.

Required: (1) Prepare a worksheet to develop financial statements in the manner illustrated in Figure 8.3. (2) Prepare, in good form, a complete set of financial statements for 20X1. (3) Prepare, in general journal form, the necessary adjusting entries at December 31, 20X1, for the year then ended. (4) Prepare, in general journal form, the necessary closing entries on December 31, 20X1, for the year then ended.

DEVELOPMENT OF INTERIM FINANCIAL STATEMENTS

U p to now, this book has dealt with the accounting process in annual terms: annual posting of transaction entries and annual financial statements. This chapter examines the procedures of accounting from a monthly point of view. The preparation of monthly adjusting entries and the development of a set of interim financial statements is the major objective. As mentioned earlier, interim financial statements are those prepared during the course of a hospital's fiscal year. The illustration presented in this chapter consists of preparation of a statement of operations for the month of September 20X1 and for the nine months ending September 30, 20X1. In addition, a September 30, 20X1, balance sheet will be prepared.

Interim financial statements are essential to the effective management of hospitals. Important managerial decisions are made during the course of a fiscal year that require the kinds of information provided by monthly statements of operations and balance sheets. In addition, many other types of accounting reports may be prepared weekly or daily (a cash report, for example). Certain of these special reports are illustrated later in this book. For now, you are concerned only with the routine statements of operations and balance sheets prepared at the end of each month.

Monthly Trial Balances

Assume that a hypothetical Hiowa Hospital began its corporate existence on January 1, 20X1. Financial statements were prepared for 20X1 and 20X2, and the hospital is now in its third year of operations, 20X3. The 20X3 transactions have been journalized and posted through September 30. Monthly adjusting entries have been journalized and posted through August 31, and monthly financial statements have been prepared at the end of each month, January through August 20X3. It is now time to prepare financial statements for September 20X3 and for the nine months ended September 30, 20X3.

Hiowa Hospital's trial balances at August 31 and September 30, 20X3, are presented in Figure 9.1. Notice that the August 31 trial balance is an adjusted trial balance. It includes the adjusted balances, as of August 31, of all of the hospital's accounts. The net assets balance is, of course, the opening

Acct. No.	Accounts and Titles	Adjusted Trial Balance 8/31/X3 Dr.	Adjusted Trial Balance 8/31/X3 Cr.	Unadjusted Trial Balance 9/30/X3 Dr.	Unadjusted Trial Balance 9/30/X3 Cr.
101	Cash	$ 30,900		$ 33,200	
103	Accrued interest receivable	800		800	
104	Accounts receivable	84,000		87,100	
105	Allowance for uncollectible accounts		$ 8,400		$ 8,400
106	Inventory	9,800		11,300	
107	Prepaid insurance	2,400		2,400	
110	Long-term investments	60,000		60,000	
120	Land	23,000		23,000	
130	Buildings	187,500		187,500	
131	Accumulated depreciation—buildings		20,000		20,000
201	Accounts payable		18,200		19,400
203	Accrued interest payable		5,500		5,500
204	Accrued salaries and wages payable		4,600		-0-
205	Deferred rental income		980		980
250	Bonds payable		100,000		100,000
301	Hospital net assets		219,420		219,420
302	Revenue and expense summary		-0-		-0-
401	Routine services revenue		164,000		187,300
402	Ancillary services revenue		96,100		106,800
403	Interest income		800		800
404	Rental income		700		700
406	Other operating revenues		46,300		52,200
501	Contractual adjustments	27,000		31,800	
601	Salaries and wages expense	160,000		176,400	
602	Supplies expense	24,000		26,800	
603	Utilities expense	16,000		18,100	
604	Insurance expense	1,200		1,200	
607	Depreciation expense	5,000		5,000	
608	Interest expense	4,000		4,000	
609	Bad debt expense	11,400		11,400	
610	Other expenses	38,000		41,500	
	Totals	$685,000	$685,000	$721,500	$721,500

(December 31, 20X2) net assets balance because the books of the hospital have not been closed since December 31, 20X2.

This trial balance includes an eight-month accumulation of revenues, revenue deductions, and expense balances, adjusted through August 31, 20X3. In short, these are the figures used in Hiowa Hospital's August 31 balance sheet and in its statement of operations for the eight months ended August 31, 20X3. These statements are illustrated in Figures 9.2 and 9.3.

FIGURE 9.2
Hiowa Hospital
Statement of
Operations,
Eight Months
Ended August
31, 20X3

Gross patient services revenues:		
Routine services	$164,000	
Ancillary services	96,100	
Gross patient services revenue		$260,100
Less revenue deductions:		
Contractual adjustments	27,000	
Total revenue deductions		27,000
Net patient services revenues		233,100
Other operating revenues:		
Rent	700	
Other	46,300	
Total other operating revenues		47,000
Total operating revenues		280,100
Less operating expenses:		
Salaries and wages	160,000	
Supplies	24,000	
Utilities	16,000	
Insurance	1,200	
Depreciation	5,000	
Interest	4,000	
Bad debts	11,400	
Other	38,000	
Total operating expenses		259,600
Operating income		20,500
Nonoperating income (interest)		800
Excess of revenues over expenses		$ 21,300

(The statement of operations for the month of August 20X3 is not illustrated, although we assume the statement was prepared.)

Developing the Adjusting Entries for September

Carefully note that Hiowa Hospital's trial balance for September 30, 20X3, is an *unadjusted* trial balance. The figures in this trial balance are those in the August 31 trial balance together with the effects of the September transactions of the hospital. In other words, this trial balance includes the unadjusted asset

FIGURE 9.3

Hiowa Hospital
Balance Sheet,
August 31,
20X3

Assets		
Cash		$ 30,900
Accrued interest receivable		800
Accounts receivable	$84,000	
Allowance for uncollectible accounts	8,400	
Accounts receivable, net of allowances		75,600
Inventory		9,800
Prepaid insurance		2,400
Total current assets		$ 119,500
Long-term investments		60,000
Land		23,000
Buildings	187,500	
Accumulated depreciation—buildings	20,000	
Buildings, net of depreciation		167,500
Total long-term assets		250,500
Total assets		$370,000
Liabilities and Net Assets		
Accounts payable	$18,200	
Accrued interest payable	5,500	
Accrued salaries and wages payable	4,600	
Deferred rental income	980	
Total current liabilities		29,280
Bonds payable (6% bonds payable, due 20X8)		100,000
Total liabilities		129,280
Hospital net assets, January 31*	219,420	
Excess of revenues over expenses for		
8 months ended August 31	21,300	
Hospital net assets, August 31		240,720
Total liabilities and net assets		$370,000

*Change in net asset balance shown within balance sheet in lieu of separate statement of hospital net assets

and liability balances as of September 30; the hospital net assets balance as of December 31, 20X2; and the unadjusted revenue, revenue deduction, and expense balances at September 30, 20X3. So, before financial statements can be prepared for September and for the nine months ended September 30, the September adjusting entries must be developed.

You will have noticed that Hiowa Hospital's account titles and numbers are somewhat different from those used earlier in the Hoosier Hospital illustration. Some of these differences arise from an effort to simplify the illustration (a single account for depreciable plant assets, for example). Other changes were made to introduce new accounts and procedures. Although there is a degree of uniformity in charts of accounts from one hospital to another, there also may be considerable differences because of variations in size, organizational structure, and range of services, among other factors.

Accrued Interest Receivable

Hiowa Hospital's September 30 trial balance includes $60,000 of long-term investments (account 110). This consists of $60,000 (face value) of 8 percent, ten-year corporate bonds purchased by the hospital at face value on July 1, 20X3. These bonds pay interest semiannually on July 1 and January 1, beginning on January 1, 20X4. The semiannual interest payments to the hospital will be $2,400 ($60,000 × 8 percent × 6/12 months). Thus, Hiowa Hospital is earning interest income of $400 per month ($2,400 ÷ 6 months) on these bonds.

On July 31 and August 31, Hiowa Hospital made an adjusting entry to accrue the monthly interest income as follows:

Accrued interest receivable	103	$400	
Interest income	403		$400
Monthly adjustment for accrual of			
monthly interest income on corporate			
bonds held as long-term investments			

Because this entry was made on July 31 and on August 31, Hiowa Hospital's August 31 trial balance includes $800 of accrued interest receivable and $800 of interest income. The September 30 (unadjusted) trial balance, of course, includes the same figures because the September 30 adjustment has not yet been made, so the entry just shown must be repeated at September 30. This will be September 30, 20X3, adjusting entry (1). Notice that it has been entered on the worksheet in Figure 9.4. Later, the adjustment will be entered in Hiowa Hospital's journal.

The same adjusting entry will be made on October 31, November 30, and December 31 to produce a year-end balance of $2,400 in the accrued interest receivable account. Then, when the interest is received in cash on January 1, 20X4, a transaction entry will be made to debit cash and credit the accrued interest receivable account. As a result, the bond interest income is recognized monthly as it is earned, rather than at the time it is received in cash.

Recognizing Interest Income as it Is Earned

Bad Debts

At the end of each month since the year began, Hiowa Hospital has been making an adjusting entry to maintain a balance in its allowance for uncollectible accounts (account 105) equal to 10 percent of month-end accounts

FIGURE 9.4 Hiowa Hospital Worksheet to Develop Financial Statements, Nine Months Ended September 30, 20X3

Acct. No.	Account Title	Unadjusted Trial Balance, 9/30/X3 Dr.	Cr.	9/30/X3 Adjustments Dr.	Cr.	Adjusted Trial Balance, 9/30/X3 Dr.	Cr.	Statement of Operations Dr.	Cr.	Statement of Net Assets Dr.	Cr.	Balance Sheet Dr.	Cr.
101	Cash	33,200				33,200						33,200	
103	Accrued interest receivable	800		(1) 400		1,200						1,200	
104	Accounts receivable	87,100				87,100						87,100	
105	Allowance for uncollectible accounts		8,400		(2) 310		8,710						8,710
106	Inventory	11,300				11,300						11,300	
107	Prepaid insurance	2,400			(3) 150	2,250						2,250	
110	Long-term investments	60,000				60,000						60,000	
120	Land	23,000				23,000						23,000	
130	Buildings	187,500				187,500						187,500	
131	Accumulated depreciation—buildings		20,000		(4) 625		20,625						20,625
201	Accounts payable		19,400				19,400						19,400
203	Accrued interest payable		5,500		(7) 500		6,000						6,000
204	Accrued salaries and wages payable		-0-		(5) 3,100		3,100						3,100
205	Deferred rental income		980	(6) 140			840						840
250	Bonds payable		100,000				100,000						100,00
301	Hospital net assets		219,420				219,420				219,420		
302	Revenue and expense summary		-0-										
401	Routine services revenue		187,300				187,300		187,300				
402	Ancillary services revenue		106,800				106,800		106,800				
403	Interest income		800	(1) 400			1,200		1,200				
404	Rental income		700	(6) 140			840		840				
406	Other operating revenues		52,200				52,200		52,200				
501	Contractual adjustments	26,000				26,000		26,000					
502	Charity care adjustments	5,800				5,800		5,800					
601	Salaries and wages expense	176,400		(5) 3,100		179,500		179,500					
602	Supplies expense	26,800				26,800		26,800					
603	Utilities expense	18,100				18,100		18,100					
604	Insurance expense	1,200		(3) 150		1,350		1,350					
607	Depreciation expense	5,000		(4) 625		5,625		5,625					
608	Interest expense	4,000		(7) 500		4,500		4,500					
609	Bad debt expense	11,400		(2) 310		11,710		11,710					
610	Other expenses	41,500				41,500		41,500					
	Totals	721,500	721,500	5,225	5,225	726,435	726,435	320,885	348,340				
	Net income for 9 months ended 9/30/X3							27,455			27,455		
	Totals							348,340	348,340	-0-	246,875	246,875	
	Hospital net assets, 9/30/X3									246,875			246,875
										246,875	246,875	405,550	405,550

receivable. This is an accounting policy that assumes that 10 percent of the accounts receivable balance will prove to be bad debts. As mentioned before, there are other methods of accounting for bad debts, but this is the method we will use for our present purposes.

As specific accounts are determined to be worthless, the accounts are written off by a debit to the allowance for uncollectible accounts. To illustrate, let us assume that the account had a credit balance of $6,000 to start the 20X3 year. At the end of each month from January through August, an adjusting entry has been made to adjust the account credit balance to 10 percent of receivables. A summary of the eight entries follows as a single entry: **Write-off of Uncollectible Accounts**

Bad debt expense	609	$11,400	
Allowance for uncollectible accounts	105		$11,400
Adjustments of allowance account to 10%			
of month-end receivables			

We assumed, however, that the year began with a $6,000 credit balance in the account. The eight adjusting entries added $11,400 to the account, so why is the August 31 balance only $8,400? It might appear to you that the August 31 balance should be $17,400 ($6,000 + $11,400).

In an unspecified number of journal entries during the first eight months of 20X3, Hiowa Hospital has written off $9,000 of worthless accounts. A summary of these entries is shown here as a single entry:

Allowance for uncollectible accounts	105	$ 9,000	
Accounts receivable	104		$ 9,000
Write-off of uncollectible receivables			
during first eight months of 20X3			

Thus, between January 1 and August 31, the allowance for uncollectible accounts (which began with a $6,000 credit balance) has been credited with a total of $11,400 and debited for a total of $9,000. The August 31 balance of the account therefore is $8,400 (that is, $6,000 + $11,400 − $9,000). The August 31 debit balance of the bad debts account is of course the amount recorded during the first eight months of 20X3, or $11,400 (see the September 30 trial balance in Figure 9.4).

The balances in the accounts for bad debt expense and the allowance for uncollectible accounts have not changed since August 31. This is because the September 30 adjusting entry has not yet been made and because we assume that no accounts have been written off during September. The required September 30 adjusting entry is as follows:

Bad debt expense	609	$ 310	
Allowance for uncollectible accounts	105		$ 310

Adjustment to increase allowance account
to 10% of September 30, 20X3,
accounts receivable:

Allowance balance, 9/30	$8,400
Desired balance (10% of $87,100)	8,710
Required increase	$ 310

This gives the allowance for uncollectible accounts a credit balance of $8,710, which is the desired 10 percent of September 30 receivables. This is entry (2) on the worksheet illustrated in Figure 9.4.

Prepaid Insurance

Assume a single comprehensive insurance policy on which Hiowa Hospital paid a two-year premium of $3,600 in advance on January 1, 20X3. This means that insurance expense is $150 per month ($3,600 ÷ 24 months). Assuming that the payment of the premium was recorded as a debit to prepaid insurance (account 107), the following adjusting entry has been made at the end of each of the eight months starting January 31:

Insurance expense	604	$ 150	
Prepaid insurance	107		$ 150
Adjustment for monthly expiration			
of prepaid insurance premium			

Because this entry has been made eight times, the trial balance for August 31 shows $1,200 of insurance expense and $2,400 of prepaid insurance ($3,600 – $1,200). This adjustment is repeated on September 30 as entry (3) in Figure 9.4.

Depreciation

Hiowa Hospital purchased all of its depreciable assets on January 1, 20X1, for $187,500. Let us say that these assets (buildings) have a composite useful life of 25 years, but no salvage value is expected. This means that depreciation expense on a straight-line basis is $7,500 annually ($187,500 ÷ 25 years), or $625 per month ($7,500 ÷ 12 months). So, Hiowa Hospital has been making the following monthly adjusting entry:

Depreciation expense	607	$625	
Accumulated depreciation—			
buildings	131		$625
Adjustment for monthly depreciation			

Thus, the September 30 trial balance shows $5,000 ($625 × 8 months) of depreciation expense. The accumulated depreciation balance, however, includes all the depreciation recorded since the assets were acquired: depreciation for 12 months in 20X1, 12 months in 20X2, and eight months in 20X3. This is a total of 32 months, or $20,000 ($625 × 32 months) of accumulated depreciation at September 30, 20X3.

This depreciation adjustment also must be made at September 30. This is entry (4) in Figure 9.4. The entry will be repeated every month until the assets are sold or otherwise retired from use by the hospital.

Repeating the Depreciation Adjustment Each Month

Accrued Salaries and Wages Payable

On August 31, Hiowa Hospital obviously made an adjusting entry for $4,600 of accrued salaries and wages (refer to the August 31 trial balance in Figure 9.1, account 204). That entry charged $4,600 of salaries and wages to expense and credited $4,600 to the accrued liability account. When these salaries and wages were paid in early September, the liability was eliminated. This is why no balance appears in the accrued salaries and wages payable account in the September 30 trial balance.

Now assume that, during the latter part of September, Hiowa Hospital employees earned $3,100 of salaries and wages that have not yet been paid. The required September 30, 20X3, adjusting entry is as follows:

Salaries and wages expense	601	$3,100	
Accrued salaries and			
wages payable	204		$3,100
Adjustment for accrued payroll at			
September 30, 20X3			

This entry appears on the worksheet in Figure 9.4 as entry (5).

As explained in Chapter 5, reversing entries sometimes are employed in connection with certain adjustments relating to accrued expenses. Hiowa Hospital, for example, might have made a September 1 reversing entry for the $4,600 adjustment of August 31. Similarly, the $3,100 adjustment just shown may be reversed on October 1. Whether or not reversing entries are made, however, the interim statements are not affected; the adjusted figures will be the same.

Use of Reversing Entries

Deferred Rental Income

Assume that a private enterprise began operating a gift shop in the hospital on April 1, 20X3. At that time, Hiowa Hospital received one year's rent ($1,680) in advance. The hospital's rental income, then, is $140 per month ($1,680 ÷ 12 months). Assuming that the $1,680 was credited to deferred rental income (account 205) at the time it was received, the hospital has been making a monthly adjustment of $140 to rental income (account 404) for five months (April through August). The monthly adjusting entry has been as follows:

Deferred rental income	205	$140	
Rental income	404		$140
Adjustment to record rental income			
earned during the month			

Because this entry has been made five times, the September 30 trial balance shows a balance of $700 in the rental income account. The deferred rental income balance, for the same reason, is $980 ($1,680 − $700).

Now, at September 30, the same adjusting entry is required again. Figure 9.4 includes this rental income adjustment as entry (6).

Accrued Interest Payable

Hiowa Hospital issued $100,000 of 6 percent, 12-year bonds at face value on October 1, 20X2. These bonds pay interest annually on October 1, commencing October 1, 20X3. At the end of each month, starting October 31, 20X2, Hiowa Hospital has been making the following adjusting entry for the monthly accrual of interest expense on these bonds:

Interest expense	608	$500	
Accrued interest payable	203		$500
Adjustment for monthly accrual of			
interest on bonds payable:			
$100,000 × 6% × 1/12 months = $500			

This entry has been made 11 times (October 20X2 through August 20X3) to produce a September 30 trial balance figure of $5,500 in accrued interest payable. However, the September 30 balance of the interest expense account is only $4,000 because the remaining $1,500 of interest was charged to expense in 20X2. That $1,500 was interest expense for October, November, and December of 20X2, and the interest expense account balance was eliminated from the hospital's ledger by a December 31, 20X2, closing entry.

This $500 adjustment for interest expense must be made again at September 30, 20X3. This adjustment appears in Figure 9.4 as entry (7).

This completes all of the September 30, 20X3, adjustments required for Hiowa Hospital. The worksheet (see Figure 9.4) for the first nine months of 20X3 is now completed, and a set of interim financial statements can be prepared.

Interim Statements

Based on the information assembled on the worksheet (see Figure 9.4), an interim statement of operations for the nine months ended September 30, 20X3, along with a statement of operations for the month of September 20X3, can be prepared. Figure 9.5 shows the interim statement of operations. The dollar amounts for the September statement of operations are obtained simply

	Month Ended 9/30/X3	Nine Months Ended 9/30/X3
Gross patient services revenues:		
Inpatient services	$23,300	$187,300
Outpatient services	10,700	106,800
Total gross patient services revenues	34,000	294,100
Revenue deductions:		
Contractual adjustments	4,000	26,000
Charity care adjustments	800	5,800
Total revenue deductions	4,800	31,800
Net patient services revenues	29,200	262,300
Other operating revenues:		
Rent	140	840
Other	5,900	52,200
Total other operating revenues	6,040	53,040
Total operating revenues	35,240	315,340
Operating expenses:		
Salaries and wages	19,500	179,500
Supplies	2,800	26,800
Utilities	2,100	18,100
Insurance	150	1,350
Depreciation	625	5,625
Interest	500	4,500
Bad debts	310	11,710
Other Expenses	3,500	41,500
Total operating expenses	29,485	289,085
Operating income	5,755	26,255
Nonoperating income (interest)	400	1,200
Excess of revenues over expenses	$ 6,155	$ 27,455

FIGURE 9.5

Hiowa Hospital Statements of Operations, Month of September 20X3, and the Nine Months Ended September 30, 20X3

by subtracting the eight-month statement of operations figures from the nine-month statement of operations figures. To obtain the salaries and wages expense for September, for example, the $160,000 expense figure in the statement of operations for the eight months ended August 31 (see Figure 9.2) is subtracted from the $179,500 expense figure in the statement of operations for the nine months ended September 30, 20X3. In actual practice, the monthly amounts are obtained by summarizing the transactions of each month alone, thus providing an automatic verification of the change in year-to-date totals.

Providing for Comparative Data

Figure 9.6 presents Hiowa Hospital's September 30, 20X3, balance sheet, with the necessary figures taken from the worksheet (see Figure 9.4). The

FIGURE 9.6

Hiowa Hospital
Balance Sheets,
September 30
and August 31,
20X3

	9/30/X3	8/31/X3
Assets		
Cash	$ 33,200	$ 30,900
Accrued interest receivable	1,200	800
Accounts receivable, net of allowances	78,390	75,600
($8,710 at Sept. 30 and $8,400 at Aug. 31)		
Inventory	11,300	9,800
Prepaid insurance	2,250	2,400
Total current assets	126,340	119,500
Long-term investments	60,000	60,000
Land	23,000	23,000
Buildings	166,875	167,500
(net of accumulated depreciation of $20,625		
at Sept. 30 and $20,000 at Aug. 31)		
Total long-term assets	249,875	250,500
Total assets	$376,215	$370,000
Liabilities and Net Assets		
Accounts payable	$ 19,400	$ 18,200
Accrued salaries and wages	3,100	4,600
Accrued interest	6,000	5,500
Deferred rental income	840	980
Total current liabilities	29,340	29,280
Bonds payable	100,000	100,000
Total liabilities	129,340	129,280
Hospital net assets, January 1	219,420	19,420
Excess of revenues over expenses:		
For 9 months ended September 30	27,455	
For 8 months ended August 31		21,300
Hospital net assets	246,875	240,720
Total liabilities and net assets	$376,215	$370,000

August 31 balance sheet also is included so that comparative financial data are reported. Income and other statements, of course, also can be presented in comparative form. Later in this book, we will get into the managerial analysis and interpretation of comparative financial statements.

Journalizing and Posting Adjusting Entries

After the interim financial statements have been prepared, the accountant returns to the journal and records the September 30, 20X3, adjusting entries

Entry No.	Accounts and Explanations	Acct. No.	Dr.	Cr.
1	Accrued interest receivable	103	$ 400	
	Interest income	403		$ 400
	Adjustment for accrual of monthly interest income on corporate bonds held as long-term investments			
2	Bad debt expense	609	310	
	Allowance for uncollectible accounts	105		310
	Adjustment to increase allowance account to 10% of month-end receivables			
3	Insurance expense	604	150	
	Prepaid insurance	107		150
	Adjustment for monthly expiration of prepaid insurance premium			
4	Depreciation expense	607	625	
	Accumulated depreciation	131		625
	Adjustment for monthly depreciation			
5	Salaries and wages expense	601	3,100	
	Accrued salaries and wages payable	204		3,100
	Adjustment for accrued payroll			
6	Deferred rental income	205	140	
	Rental income	404		140
	Adjustment to record rental income earned during the month			
7	Interest expense	608	500	
	Accrued interest payable	203		500
	Adjustment for monthly accrual of interest on 6% bonds payable			

FIGURE 9.7

Hiowa Hospital 20X3 Journal (September 30 Adjusting Entries)

as shown in Figure 9.7. These journal entries then are posted to the ledger accounts (not shown here). When the postings are completed, Hiowa Hospital's ledger account balances will agree with the figures in the adjusted trial balance columns of the worksheet. During the following month (October 20X3), the procedures previously described for September are repeated. As a final point, notice that the books are not closed in the interim accounting process; the books are closed annually on the last day of the fiscal year.

Questions

Q9.1. What are interim financial statements?

Q9.2. Why are interim financial statements prepared?

Q9.3. Hart Hospital's long-term investments consist of $90,000 of 8 percent, 15-year bonds purchased by the hospital at face value on January 1, 20X1. These bonds pay interest semiannually on January 1 and July 1. Hart Hospital's accounting period is the calendar year. What amounts should be reported in the hospital's adjusted trial balance at November 30, 20X1, for interest income and accrued interest receivable?

Q9.4. Hello Hospital, whose accounting period is the calendar year, began 20X1 with a $10,000 credit balance in its allowance for uncollectible accounts. At the end of each month of the year, an adjusting entry is made to adjust the allowance account credit balance to 10 percent of receivables. Also at the end of each month of the year, an entry is made to write off accounts receivable deemed to be uncollectible. Indicate the presentation of receivables in Hello Hospital's balance sheet at March 31, 20X1, given the following data:

	January	February	March
Receivables—			
patient services at end of month	$128,000	$151,000	$147,000
Accounts written off at end of month	8,000	11,000	15,000

Q9.5. On January 1, 20X1, Hope Hospital paid a three-year insurance premium of $6,480 in advance. This premium payment was recorded as a debit to prepaid insurance. What amount should be reported as prepaid insurance in the hospital's preadjusted trial balance at August 31, 20X1? What amount should be reported as insurance expense in the hospital's statement of operations for the nine months ended September 30, 20X1? What amount should be reported as prepaid insurance in the hospital's balance sheet at October 31, 20X1?

Q9.6. Happy Hospital paid $145,700 of salaries and wages during the month of May 20X1. The hospital's balance sheets reported accrued salaries and wages as follows:

April 30, 20X1	$31,200
May 31, 20X1	37,800

What amount should be reported as salaries and wages expense in the hospital's statement of operations for the month ended May 31, 20X1?

Q9.7. If a hospital prepares interim financial statements, how often must adjusting entries be made? How often must closing entries be made?

Q9.8. A private enterprise began operating a gift shop in Hope Hospital on May 1, 20X1. At that time, the hospital received a year's rent ($3,000) in advance. The $3,000 was credited to deferred rental income. Assuming that the hospital prepares monthly statements, make the necessary adjusting entry at September 30, 20X1.

Q9.9. Hillside Hospital issued $300,000 of 6 percent, 15-year bonds at face value on April 1, 20X1. These bonds pay interest semiannually on April 1 and October 1, commencing October 1, 20X1. The hospital's fiscal year ends December 31. What amounts should be reported in the hospital's adjusted trial balance at November 30, 20X1, for bond interest expense and accrued bond interest payable?

Q9.10. Harmless Hospital purchased all its depreciable equipment on January 1, 20X1, for $800,000. This equipment has an estimated useful life of 12 years and an estimated salvage value of 10 percent. The hospital's fiscal year ends on December 31. What amounts should be reported in the hospital's preadjusted trial balance at May 31, 20X3, for depreciation expense and accumulated depreciation?

Exercises

E9.1. Hype Hospital provides you with the following information:

	10/31/X1	11/30/X1
Prepaid rent expense	$1,000	$2,000
Accrued rent receivable	3,000	4,000
Deferred rental income	5,000	6,000
Accrued rent payable	7,000	8,000

During November, $40,000 of rent was paid and $50,000 of rent was received in cash.

Required: What should the November 20X1 statement of operations report as rent expense and rental income?

E9.2. Hipp Hospital provides you with the following information:

	10/31/X2	11/30/X2
Accrued interest receivable	$4,100	$3,900
Prepaid interest	6,400	5,700
Accrued interest payable	3,200	3,600
Deferred interest income	4,800	5,300

The hospital's November statement of operations reports $25,000 of interest income and $30,000 of interest expense.

Required: (1) What was the amount of interest received in cash during November? (2) What was the amount of interest paid in cash during November?

E9.3.   Helping Hospital provides you with the following accounts drawn from its adjusted general ledger at October 31, 20X1:

Accounts Receivable		Allowance for Uncollectible Accounts	
240,000	450,000	9,500	24,000
500,000	9,500		13,550

The hospital's fiscal year ends September 30. Uncollectible accounts are estimated at 10 percent of accounts receivable.
Required: Identify each of the dollar amounts in each of these ledger accounts.

E9.4.   Highest Hospital provides you with the following accounts drawn from its adjusted general ledger at October 31, 20X1:

Inventory		Accounts Payable	
55,000	100,000	110,000	60,000
95,000			95,000

The hospital's fiscal year ends September 30.
Required: Identify each of the dollar amounts in each of these ledger accounts.

Problems

P9.1.   Hohum Hospital's adjusted trial balance at March 31, 20X6, and its unadjusted trial balance at April 30, 20X6, are shown here:

Acct. No.		Adjusted Trial Balance March 31, 20X6 Dr.	Cr.	Unadjusted Trial Balance April 30, 20X6 Dr.	Cr.
101	Cash	$30,300		$25,400	
103	Accrued interest receivable	1,800		1,800	
104	Accounts receivable	80,000		86,000	
105	Allowance for uncollectible accounts		$ 8,000		$ 1,400
106	Inventory	11,000		10,300	
107	Prepaid insurance	3,675		3,675	
110	Long-term investments	90,000		90,000	

		Debit	Credit	Debit	Credit
120	Land	15,000		15,000	
130	Buildings	400,000		400,000	
131	Accumulated depreciation—buildings		63,000		63,000
201	Accounts payable		21,600		23,900
203	Accrued interest payable		2,400		2,400
204	Accrued salaries and wages payable		4,700		-0-
205	Deferred rental income		2,340		2,340
250	Bonds payable		160,000		160,000
301	Hospital net assets		355,235		355,235
302	Revenue and expense summary		-0-		-0-
401	Routine services revenue		81,400		115,200
402	Ancillary services revenue		56,100		72,900
403	Interest income		1,800		1,800
404	Rental income		780		780
406	Other operating revenues		12,120		16,020
501	Contractual adjustments		11,500		14,900
601	Salaries and wages expense	90,600		120,300	
602	Supplies expense	15,100		21,700	
603	Utilities expense	10,200		14,500	
604	Insurance expense	525		525	
607	Depreciation expense	3,000		3,000	
608	Interest expense	2,400		2,400	
609	Bad debt expense	3,300		3,300	
610	Other expenses	1,075		2,175	
	Totals	$769,475	$769,475	$814,975	$814,975

The hospital's fiscal year ends December 31. Additional information is available as follows:

1. Long-term investments consist of $90,000 (face value) of 8 percent, ten-year bonds purchased by the hospital on January 1, 20X6. The bonds pay interest semiannually on January 1 and July 1, commencing July 1, 20X6.
2. A two-year insurance premium of $4,200 was paid in advance on January 1, 20X1.
3. Depreciable plant assets, all of which were acquired on January 1, 20X1, have an estimated useful life of 30 years and a 10 percent salvage value.
4. On January 1, 20X6, the hospital issued $160,000 of 6 percent, 15-year bonds at face value. These bonds pay interest annually on January 1, commencing January 1, 20X7.

5. A year's rent of $3,120 was received in advance on January 1, 20X6.

6. At the end of each month, the allowance for bad debts is adjusted to a credit balance equal to 10 percent of month-end accounts receivable.

7. Unpaid salaries and wages at April 30, 20X6, totaled $3,400.

Required: (1) Prepare a worksheet to develop financial statements for the four months ended April 30, 20X6, in the manner illustrated in Figure 9.4. (2) Prepare, in good form, a statement of operations for the month of April 20X6 and for the four months then ended, in the manner illustrated in Figure 9.5. (3) Prepare, in good form, balance sheets at April 30 and March 31, 20X6, in the manner illustrated in Figure 9.6. (4) Prepare, in general journal form, all necessary adjusting entries for the month ended April 30, 20X6.

P9.2.   Highcare Hospital's adjusted trial balance at May 31, 20X4, and its unadjusted trial balance at June 30, 20X4, are shown here (the hospital's fiscal year ends December 31):

Acct. No.		Adjusted Trial Balance May 31, 20X4 Dr.	Cr.	Unadjusted Trial Balance June 30, 20X4 Dr.	Cr.
101	Cash	$38,400		$ 16,640	
103	Accrued interest receivable	800		800	
104	Accounts receivable	95,000		106,500	
105	Allowance for uncollectible accounts		$ 7,600		$300
106	Inventory	10,800		12,300	
107	Prepaid insurance	3,420		3,420	
110	Long-term investments	60,000		75,000	
120	Land	14,000		14,000	
130	Buildings	480,000		480,000	
131	Accumulated depreciation—buildings		82,250		82,250
201	Accounts payable		19,700		24,100
204	Accrued salaries and wages payable		3,900		-0-
203	Accrued interest payable		2,000		2,000
205	Deferred rental income		2,160		2,160
250	Bonds payable		200,000		200,000
301	Hospital net assets		356,810		356,810
302	Revenue and expense summary		-0-		-0-

401	Routine services revenue		100,200		128,700
402	Ancillary services revenue		78,400		93,500
403	Interest income		800		800
404	Rental income		720		720
406	Other operating revenues		12,880		15,100
501	Contractual adjustments	12,600		15,700	
601	Salaries and wages expense	101,400		122,300	
602	Supplies expense	16,100		19,800	
603	Utilities expense	11,200		13,900	
604	Insurance expense	900		900	
607	Depreciation expense	10,250		10,250	
608	Interest expense	5,000		5,000	
609	Bad debt expense	2,900		2,900	
610	Other expenses	4,650		7,030	
	Totals	$867,420	$867,420	$906,440	$906,440

The following additional information is available:

1. Long-term investments consist of $60,000 (face value) of 8 percent, 15-year bonds purchased by the hospital on April 1, 20X4, with interest payable annually on April 1, and $15,000 (face value) of 8 percent, ten-year bonds purchased by the hospital on June 1, 20X4, with interest payable annually on June 1.
2. A two-year insurance premium was paid in advance on January 1, 20X4.
3. On January 1, 20X1, the hospital purchased $450,000 of depreciable plant assets having an estimated useful life of 15 years and an estimated salvage value of 20 percent. On May 1, 20X4, the hospital purchased additional depreciable plant assets at a cost of $30,000 (estimated useful life of eight years and a 20 percent salvage value).
4. A year's rent was received in advance on March 1, 20X4.
5. On April 1, 20X2, the hospital issued $200,000 of 6 percent, ten-year bonds at face value. These bonds pay interest semiannually on April 1 and October 1.
6. At the end of each month, the allowance for bad debts is adjusted to a credit balance equal to 8 percent of month-end accounts receivable.
7. Unpaid salaries and wages at June 30, 20X4, totaled $4,100.

Required: (1) Prepare a worksheet to develop financial statements for the six months ended June 30, 20X4, in the manner illustrated in Figure 9.4. (2) Prepare, in good form, statements of operations for the month of June, 20X4, and for the six months then ended, in the manner illustrated in Figure 9.5. (3) Prepare, in good form, balance sheets at June 30 and May 31, 20X4, in the manner illustrated in Figure 9.6. (4) Prepare, in general journal form, all necessary adjusting entries for the month ended June 30, 20X4.

EXPANSION OF THE CHART OF ACCOUNTS

Illustrations in the preceding chapters were based on a highly simplified chart of accounts suitable to an introductory discussion of the fundamentals of bookkeeping. Having accomplished this, we now must expand the chart of accounts to permit the introduction of more realistic accounting techniques and procedures. The expanded chart of accounts developed in this chapter will serve as a basis for the discussion in the next four chapters, but additional refinements will be made at appropriate points throughout the remainder of this book. By the end of your study of this textbook, you will have been exposed to a substantially complete chart of accounts such as you might find in actual practice in a hospital. It is important to note that the chart of accounts presented in this chapter is for teaching purposes. Hospitals actually use a different chart of accounts, which best reflects not only their size and their tax status but also how they are organized as evidenced by their organizational chart.

Balance Sheet Accounts

The chart of balance sheet accounts employed by Hartful Hospital is shown in Figure 10.1. You are already acquainted with many of the accounts, but a number of changes and additions require brief explanations. A more thorough discussion of these accounts will appear in subsequent chapters. Segregation of the balance sheet accounts into self-balancing groups as required by net assets accounting is deferred to Chapter 15. The accounts described in the present chapter relate only to the general (unrestricted) net assets groups.

Asset Accounts
In this numerical coding system, the hospital's asset accounts are those numbered in the 10000 series. Any account having a "1" as the initial digit of its number is an asset account. When net assets accounting (discussed in Chapter 15) is employed, the second digit is used to specify the net assets group in which the asset is located.

The net assets designators are the second digits 0, 1, or 2. The third and fourth digits of the account number specify the primary subclassification of assets. Consider, as an example, account 10110 as follows:

General Net Assets Designators

<table>
<tr><td>Digit
Position</td><td></td><td></td><td></td></tr>
<tr><td>First</td><td>1</td><td>=</td><td>Asset</td></tr>
<tr><td>Second</td><td>0</td><td>=</td><td>Unrestricted net assets group</td></tr>
<tr><td>Third</td><td>1</td><td>=</td><td>Cash</td></tr>
<tr><td>Fourth</td><td>1</td><td>=</td><td>General checking account</td></tr>
<tr><td>Fifth</td><td>0</td><td>=</td><td>Unspecified</td></tr>
</table>

Meaning of the Third and Fourth Digits

In other words, all 101 accounts are cash accounts; the fourth digit indicates the type of cash account. Similarly, all 104 accounts are accounts for patient account receivables; the fourth digit is used to indicate whether the receivables relate to in-house or discharged inpatients or outpatients.

Uses of the Fifth and Sixth Digits

This chart of accounts also provides for the use of a fifth and even a sixth digit, depending on individual hospital requirements, for a secondary subclassification of asset accounts. You need not be concerned, however, with this additional detail provided by the sixth digit. Our discussion is limited, at this point, to the five-digit primary account number. Beginning in the next chapter, however, all asset account numbers will have six digits to be consistent with the six-digit revenue and expense account numbers.

Notice that there are two cash checking accounts. Account 10110 is Hartful Hospital's general checking account, into which all cash receipts are deposited. All hospital disbursements, other than employees' individual payroll checks, are made by checks drawn against this account. Account 10120 is used only for payroll checks, and will be discussed in Chapter 13.

Hartful Hospital employs three accounts for receivables from patients. As services are rendered to inpatients, account 10410 is debited; it is credited when payments are received from patients prior to their discharge from the hospital. The account also is credited (and account 10420 debited) for the unpaid balances of patients' accounts at the time of discharge. All subsequent collections on these accounts are credited to account 10420. Account 10430 is debited for services provided to outpatients and is credited for all collections received on outpatients' accounts. These accounts for receivables are general ledger control accounts; they show the total amount due collectively from patients in each of the three classifications.

Information as to the amounts due from individual patients is developed and maintained in separate subsidiary ledgers to be illustrated subsequently in Chapter 12. At frequent intervals, the sum of the individual account balances in each subsidiary ledger will need to be reconciled to the balance reflected by the related general ledger control account.

Uncollectible Accounts

Also notice that the chart provides for a classification of the allowance for uncollectible accounts into three separate accounts according to the nature or type of

Assets
  Current Assets
  10100   Cash
          10110   Cash—general checking account
          10120   Cash—payroll checking account
          10130   Petty cash fund
  10200   Temporary investments
  10300   Accrued interest receivable
  10400   Accounts receivable
          10410   Inpatient receivables—in-house
          10420   Inpatient receivables—discharged
          10430   Outpatient receivables
  10500   Allowance for uncollectible accounts
          10510   Allowance for uncollectible accounts—bad debts
          10520   Allowance for uncollectible accounts—contractuals
          10530   Allowance for uncollectible accounts—charity service
  10600   Inventory
  10700   Prepaid insurance
  10800   Prepaid rent
  10900   Prepaid interest
  11000   Long-term investments
  12000   Land
  13000   Buildings
          13100   Accumulated depreciation—buildings
  14000   Equipment
          14100   Accumulated depreciation—equipment

Liabilities
  Current Liabilities
  20100   Accounts payable
  20200   Notes payable
  20300   Accrued interest payable
  20400   Accrued salaries and wages payable
          20410   FIT withheld
          20420   FICA withheld and accrued
  20500   Deferred rental income
  20600   Deferred tuition income

  Noncurrent Liabilities
  25000   Bonds payable

  Net Assets
  30100   Hospital net assets
          30110   Unrestricted net assets
          30120   Temporarily restricted net assets
          30130   Permanently restricted net assets
  30200   Revenue and expense summary

FIGURE 10.1

Hartful
Hospital Chart
of Balance
Sheet Accounts

the corresponding revenue deductions. Account 10530, for example, will reflect the amount of receivables estimated to be uncollectible by reason of charity service that has been rendered to financially indigent patients. Similar allowance accounts are maintained for estimated contractual adjustments and for estimated bad debts. All of these accounts, although listed in the asset classification, will carry credit balances. They are contra asset accounts. Detailed consideration is given to these accounts in Chapters 12 and 16.

In view of the explanations previously provided in this book, it is not necessary at this time to comment further on the remaining asset accounts. You will find additional coverage of these accounts in later chapters. Account 10600 (inventory), for example, will be attended to in Chapter 17, and the accounts for land, buildings, and equipment will be treated fully in Chapter 18. Discussions of other asset accounts not included in Figure 10.1 will also be provided at appropriate points in subsequent chapters.

Liability and Net Assets Accounts

The liability and net assets accounts are numbered in the 20000 and 30000 series, respectively. The liability accounts are numbered 20000 through 25000; the net assets accounts are numbered 30100 through 30200. As was true for the asset accounts, fifth and sixth digits are available for a secondary subclassification of the liability and net assets accounts whenever additional detail is required by the individual hospital. The present discussion, however, is confined to the five-digit primary account numbers. But, beginning with the next chapter, all liability and net assets account numbers will consist of six digits to be consistent with the six-digit revenue and expense account numbers.

Most of Hartful Hospital's liability and net assets accounts have been discussed earlier. The two accounts you have not previously encountered are 20410 and 20420: the payroll tax accounts. The nature and use of these accounts will be described fully in Chapters 13 and 17, and you need not be concerned with them now. Of course, hospitals typically maintain liability and net assets accounts that are not included in Figure 10.1; we shall add these accounts to our discussion at suitable times.

Statement of Operations Accounts

Hartful Hospital's organizational structure is presented in condensed form in Figure 10.2. Notice that the hospital activity is organized into five basic divisions, each having an administrative office. The managing officer of each division often has the title of director (director of nursing services, for example) or vice president (vice president for administrative services, for example). These divisional managers report to the hospital's chief executive officer (president or administrator), to whom they are responsible for the activities organized within their particular divisions.

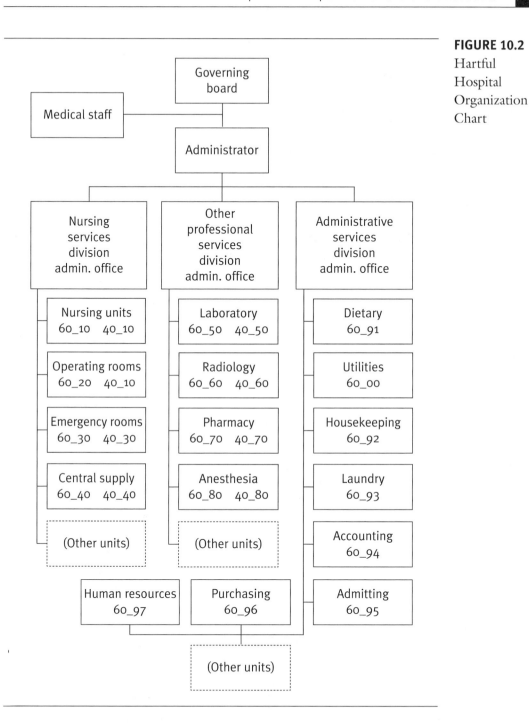

FIGURE 10.2

Hartful
Hospital
Organization
Chart

Figure 10.2 provides a representative sample of the types of services (or departments) included in each division. It is not feasible in this book to deal with a larger number of organizational units. Moreover, you should be aware that a single "box" in the sample organizational chart may represent two or more separately organized units. "Nursing units," for example, may be organized somewhat as follows:

- Medical and surgical acute care
- Pediatric, acute care
- Psychiatric, acute
- Obstetric, acute
- Newborn nursery, acute
- Intensive care
- Cardiac care
- Other

The significance of this, in terms of the design of the chart of accounts, is that a separate revenue and expense account must be provided for each nursing care unit. Only by accumulating and reporting revenues and expenses by individual organizational units can a financial evaluation of the performance of each unit be made by the hospital's management.

Typical Hospital Accounting Units

As another example, consider the box labeled "accounting." This function may be organized into several different units:

- General accounting
- Budgets and costs
- Payroll accounting
- Tax accounting
- Accounts payable
- Patient accounting
- Other

Although there are no revenues directly associated with these units, the expenses of each unit should be separately accumulated in the accounts. In the interest of brevity and for teaching purposes, however, this does not appear in our Hartful Hospital illustrations.

In addition to recognizing that the illustrative organization chart in Figure 10.2 is greatly condensed, you also should not regard the chart as indicative of how all hospitals are, or should be, organized. No two hospitals are exactly alike; hospitals differ in size, range of services, management philosophy, and other important ways. These differences have an effect on the manner in which hospitals are organized. What may be a sound organizational pattern for one hospital may not be satisfactory for another.

Responsibility Accounting

The important point to recognize is that, regardless of how a particular hospital is organized, the hospital's statement of operations accounts should be designed to conform to that hospital's organizational structure. The basic principle of **responsibility accounting** is that each organizational unit (division, department, or section) of the hospital is a responsibility center, performing an activity or function, and headed by an individual responsible for attaining its mission. Each of these individuals is a decision maker who has a significant degree of authority over the amounts of resources used in his or her center. Because all centers incur expenses, every center is an expense (or cost) center. Some centers also generate revenues through the provision of patient services for which a specific charge is made; these centers also are referred to as **revenue centers**. Housekeeping, for example, is an expense center but not a revenue center; radiology, however, is both an expense center and a revenue center.

Under responsibility accounting, the revenue and expense accounts are classified in a manner that permits revenues to be recorded according to the centers responsible for generating them and expenses to be recorded according to the centers responsible for their incurrence. Each center is charged only for those expenses that can be directly associated with the activities of that center, however, and over which the center manager has decision-making authority. All other expenses, as you will soon see, are recorded in a special "unassigned" expense classification.

Hartful Hospital's chart of statement of operations accounts appears in condensed form in Figure 10.3 on page 193. Observe here that the classification of the statement of operations accounts conforms to Hartful Hospital's organizational pattern. This necessary relationship between a hospital's organizational structure and its chart of accounts is indicated by the placement of revenue and expense account numbers in the corresponding boxes in the organizational chart as shown in Figure 10.2. As you can see, each of the organizational units has its own expense and (where applicable) revenue accounts. Each center is charged with the expenses it incurs and is credited with the revenues (if any) it generates. In this way, relevant expense and revenue data can be developed for the purpose of measuring and evaluating the performance of each center and its manager or supervisor. GAAP format treats bad debt expense as an operating expense usually placed in the unassigned expense category.

Revenue Accounts

In this numerical coding system, the first digit of revenue accounts is 4. When the first digit of a revenue account number is 4, the second digit indicates the fund, and the third, fourth, and fifth digits provide a classification of revenue by specific organizational units. Account number 40120, for example, designates the following:

Digit
Position

First   4 = Revenues

Second   0 = Operating fund
Third   1 = Inpatient services revenue
Fourth   2 = Operating room
Fifth   0 = Unspecified

In other words, 120 is the numerical code for the operating room department or function. Similarly, 150 is the code for laboratory, 270 is the designation for pharmacy, and so on.

When a particular service is organized into several subordinate units, as is often true of the laboratory department, the account numbering system provides for a numbering scheme such as the following:

Account No.	Subordinate Units
151	Chemistry
152	Hematology
153	Histology
154	Autopsy
155	Immunology
156	Blood bank

Even when the laboratory is a single organizational unit, this series of accounts may be used to obtain a classification of laboratory revenues by type of service or examination.

As another example of the use of the third, fourth, and fifth digits for revenue accounts, observe the following account classifications for the types of revenues derived from acute care nursing units:

Account No.	Subordinate Units
111	Medical and surgical, unit 1
112	Medical and surgical, unit 2
113	Medical and surgical, unit 6
114	Pediatric, unit 1
115	Pediatric, unit 2
116	Psychiatric unit
117	Obstetric unit
118	Newborn nursery

Although our Hartful Hospital illustration will not include this much detail, it is important to keep in mind that detailed revenue information of this kind is essential in actual practice.

When the first digit of a revenue or revenue deduction account is 4 or 5, the second digit refers to the fund type; third, fourth, and fifth digits are used mainly to classify the revenue or revenue deduction by type.

FIGURE 10.3

Hartful
Hospital Chart
of Statement
of Operations
Accounts

Revenues

Nursing Services
40110   Nursing units
40120   Operating room
40130   Emergency room
40140   Central supply
———   Other accounts, as necessary

Ancillary Services
40150   Laboratory
40160   Radiology
40170   Pharmacy
40180   Anesthesiology
———   Other accounts, as necessary
40300   Interest income
40400   Rental income
40500   Tuition income
40600   Other operating revenues
     40610   Cafeteria
     40620   Parking
———   Other accounts, as necessary
40700   Premium revenue
40800   Nonoperating revenues
     40810   Unrestricted contributions
     40820   Interest income
———   Other accounts, as necessary
50000   Deductions from revenues
     50010   Contractual adjustments
     50020   Charity care adjustments

Expenses
60100   Salaries and wages expense
     60110   Nursing units
     60120   Operating room
     60130   Emergency room
     60140   Central supply
     60150   Laboratory
     60160   Radiology
     60170   Pharmacy
     60180   Anesthesiology
     60190   Administrative services
          60191   Dietary
          60192   Housekeeping
          60193   Laundry
          60194   Accounting
          60195   Admitting
          60196   Purchasing
          60197   Human resources
          60198   Health information management

Continued

FIGURE 10.3
CONTINUED
Hartful
Hospital Chart
of Statement
of Operations
Accounts

– – –	Other accounts, as necessary
60200	Supplies expense

	60210	Nursing units
	60220	Operating room
	60230	Emergency Room
	60240	Central supply
	60250	Laboratory
	60260	Radiology
	60270	Pharmacy
	60280	Anesthesiology
	60290	Administrative services

		60291	Dietary
		60292	Housekeeping
		60293	Laundry
		60294	Accounting
		60295	Admitting
		60296	Purchasing
		60297	Human resources
		60298	Health information management

– – –	Other accounts, as necessary
60300	Utilities expense
60400	Insurance expense
60500	Repairs expense
60600	Rent expense
60700	Depreciation expense
60800	Interest expense
60900	Bad debt expense
61000	Other expenses

Sixth Digit to Classify Patient Services Revenues

This chart of accounts also calls for the use of a sixth digit in connection with revenue accounts in the 40000 series. This sixth digit is employed to classify these patient services revenues by type of patient. The patient classifications may be handled as follows:

Sixth Digit	Subordinate Units
0	Inpatient, acute
1	Inpatient, long-term
2	Outpatient, emergency
3	Outpatient, referred
4	Outpatient, clinic
5	Day care
6	Home health care
7	
8	Other classifications
9	

A seventh digit may be used to subclassify further revenues in whatever manner may be desired by the individual hospital. Presumably, this classification could be related to the financial status of the patient (source of payment), the type of hospital accommodation (private or semiprivate), and so on.

Finally, many charts of accounts also provide for eighth, ninth, and possibly tenth digits to be used as a three-digit suffix to classify revenues by functional units for purposes of uniform reporting. For our present purposes, you should only be concerned with the four-digit revenue account numbers that are seen in Hartful Hospital's chart of accounts.

Three-Digit Suffix to Classify Revenues by Functional Units

Expense Accounts

In this chart of accounts, the first digit of the expense accounts is a 6. When the first digit of an expense account number is 6, the second indicates the fund, and the third, fourth, and fifth digits provide a classification of expense by organizational units. Account number 60120, for example, designates the following:

Digit Position			
First	6	=	Expenses
Second	0	=	Operating fund
Third	1	=	Salaries and wages expense
Fourth	2	=	Operating room
Fifth	0	=	Unspecified

As noted earlier in the discussion of revenue accounts, 120 is the numerical code for the operating room department or function. Thus, operating room revenue is account 40120; operating room expense is account 60120. A similar procedure is followed for all other organized units that incur expenses and generate revenues.

In situations in which a particular service is organized into several subordinate units, as is often true of the laboratory department, the account numbering system for expense accounts parallels that of the revenue accounts in a scheme such as the one in the following:

Expense Account No.		Revenue Account No.
60151	Chemistry	40151
60152	Hematology	40152
60153	Histology	40153
60154	Autopsy	40154
60155	Immunology	40155
60156	Blood bank	40156

As another example of the use of the third, fourth, and fifth digits as codes for the various organizational units, observe the following account classifications for expenses and revenues related to the acute care nursing units:

Expense Account No.		Revenue Account No.
60111	Medical and surgical, unit 1	40111
60112	Medical and surgical, unit 2	40112
60113	Medical and surgical, unit 6	40113
60114	Pediatric, unit 1	40114
60115	Pediatric, unit 2	40115
60116	Psychiatric unit	40116
60117	Obstetric unit	40117
60118	Newborn nursery	40118

The Hartful Hospital illustrations presented in later chapters do not include this much detail, but you should keep in mind that detailed expense information of this kind is required in actual practice.

When the first digit of an expense account number is 6, the second digit is the fund designation, and the third, fourth, and fifth digits are used to classify the expense by various departments or by natural classifications.

Sixth and Seventh Digits for Natural Classifications

For expense accounts not classified by natural classification, this chart of accounts provides sixth and seventh digits that can be used as indicators for the natural classification of expenses in each organizational unit of the hospital.

Within each of the preceding major categories, detailed classifications should be maintained to indicate job classifications, kinds of benefits, types of fees, types of supplies, and so on. A sufficient number of digits is available to permit such breakdowns in each category.

Handling Unassigned Expenses

Several accounts are provided for Hartful Hospital's unassigned expenses. These expenses are general in nature and, in the regular accounting routine, are not charged or assigned to specific departmental expense centers. The reason for this is that, for the most part, these expenses are not controllable by individual department managers and supervisors. In the periodic cost-finding procedure, however, the unassigned expenses are allocated to the various expense centers to determine the full costs of providing departmental services. Cost-finding (cost accounting) procedures will not be dealt with in this book.

Chapter 11 incorporates Hartful Hospital's chart of accounts into a journal and ledger system. It is important, therefore, to master the materials presented in this chapter before you move on to the next chapter. Detailed applications of Hartful Hospital's chart of accounts also are encountered in Chapters 12, 13, and 14.

Questions

Q10.1. What is your understanding of the term *responsibility accounting*?

Q10.2. What is a responsibility center? Give an example.

Q10.3. Distinguish between an expense center and a revenue center. Give an example of each.

Q10.4. What are unassigned expenses? Give four examples.

Q10.5. Why do you think professional associations like the Healthcare Financial Management Association publishes model charts of accounts?

Q10.6. The chart of accounts contains an account numbered 40130 and 60130. Explain briefly what each digit of these account numbers mean.

Q10.7. The following account appeared in the ledger of Hartful Hospital on May 31, 20X3:

Account Number	20100	
5/31 $49,351	5/1	$46,877
	5/31	52,308
		49,834

Briefly identify each of the figures in the account.

Q10.8. The expanded chart of accounts contains an account numbered 40110. Explain briefly what the digits of this account number mean.

Q10.9. In connection with revenue accounts in the 40000 series, the chart of accounts provides for the use of a fifth digit. For what purpose is this fifth digit employed?

Q10.10. In the chart of accounts, the first digit of expense account numbers is 6. Briefly explain the meaning of this initial digit.

Q10.11. The chart of accounts contains an account numbered 60170. Explain briefly what the digits of this account number mean.

Q10.12. In connection with expense accounts in the 60000 series, the chart of accounts provides for the use of fifth and sometimes sixth digits. For what purpose are these fifth and sixth digits employed?

Q10.13. In the chart of accounts, the first digit of revenue account numbers is 4. Briefly explain the meaning of this initial digit.

Q10.14. In the account numbering system set forth in the chart of accounts, how can you distinguish between a liability account number and a hospital net assets account number?

11

SPECIAL JOURNALS AND LEDGERS

In the preceding chapters, all transactions were recorded in one journal: the general journal. All postings of these transaction entries were made to one ledger: the general ledger. Charges to patients for services rendered were debited to a single accounts receivable account; purchases of supplies on account from suppliers were credited to a single accounts payable account. We rather conveniently ignored the need for maintaining a continuous record of the amounts due from each patient or due to each supplier.

These procedures were followed in earlier chapters only to simplify the introductory explanation of the accounting process. In actual practice, using a single journal and ledger is not feasible. The necessity for keeping receivables records for individual patients and records of payables according to individual creditors cannot be avoided. In this chapter, and in the next three, you will have an opportunity to study a multijournal, multiledger system as it is maintained manually (in handwritten or typewritten form). The system overcomes the inefficiency of the single journal and ledger procedure, and it provides the detailed information required for hospital receivables and payables.

The illustrated system assumes that the accounting records are maintained manually. This assumption is made only for pedagogical reasons. All hospitals, including smaller ones, have electronic accounting systems because the volume of transactions prohibits the use of methods that are entirely manual. But your time is not wasted in a study of the manual system illustrated here, because in essence all systems fulfill the same functions.

Overview of the System

The system of special journals and ledgers described in this chapter and explored in detail in the next three chapters includes

- A general journal,
- Six special journals,
- A general ledger, and
- Two special (subsidiary) ledgers.

The five-digit numerical coding scheme for the accounts involved in this system was outlined in the previous chapter.

FIGURE 11.1 Hartful Hospital Journal and Ledger System

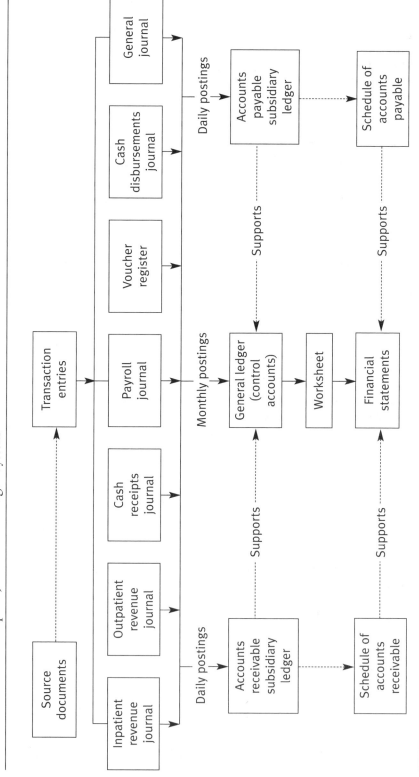

Recording Transactions

Figure 11.1 summarizes the flow of transaction data through the system. As transactions occur, documentary evidences—charge tickets, purchase orders, cash receipt slips, bank deposit slips, and other business papers—are accumulated. These source documents serve as a basis for transaction entries in the journal system. A separate journal is maintained for each major type of transaction. The cash receipts journal, for example, records all of the hospital's cash receipt transactions, the cash disbursements journal is used to record all cash disbursements, and so on. This permits a division and specialization of labor within the accounting function. In a large organization, for example, a different accounting employee may be assigned to each journal. Therefore, transactions are likely to be recorded in a more accurate and efficient manner than would be possible using only one journal.

Thus, as daily transactions are completed, they are recorded by transaction entries in the appropriate journal. These entries accumulate in the journals day by day over a period of a month. At the end of each month, the accumulated entries in each special journal are totaled, and the totals are posted to the hospital's general ledger; individual daily entries are not posted to the general ledger accounts. For example, daily entries are made in the cash receipts journal to record debits to cash. These numerous individual debits are totaled at the end of the month, and only the total is posted to the general ledger cash account. This greatly reduces the number of individual postings to be made to the general ledger accounts and eliminates much of the detail that the general ledger otherwise would contain.

Accounts Receivable and Accounts Payable Subsidiary Ledgers

Certain daily postings, however, are made to the subsidiary ledgers. Two of the subsidiary ledgers maintained by Hartful Hospital are identified in Figure 11.1. One of these is the **accounts receivable subsidiary ledger**, sometimes referred to simply as the *patients' ledger* or *receivables ledger*. It consists of a ledger account for each patient. These accounts receive daily debit postings from the revenue journal, and daily credit postings come from the cash receipts journal. (Occasional debit and credit postings also may arise from certain transaction entries made in the general journal.) In this way, a continuous daily balance is maintained in each patient's account.

The total of these individual balances is reconciled monthly against the balances of the accounts receivable "control" accounts (accounts 10410, 10420, and 10430) in the general ledger. In addition, a schedule of individual subsidiary ledger balances can be prepared in support of the total of accounts receivable as reported in the month-end balance sheet. These procedures will be described more fully in Chapter 12.

The other subsidiary ledger seen in Figure 11.1 is the **accounts payable subsidiary ledger**, often called simply the *payables ledger*. This ledger consists of a separate ledger account for each supplier of goods and services purchased by the hospital. These accounts receive daily credit postings from the voucher register and daily debit postings from the cash disbursements journal. In this way, a continuous daily balance is maintained in each supplier's account. The total of the individual subsidiary ledger balances is reconciled monthly with the accounts payable control account (20100) in the general ledger. A schedule of these subsidiary ledger balances can be prepared at the end of each month to support the accounts payable total reported in the month-end balance sheet. These procedures will be described more fully in Chapter 14.

Payroll Ledger

Another subsidiary ledger maintained by Hartful Hospital is the payroll subsidiary ledger, which reflects the employees' individual earnings records. This ledger is used in connection with the payroll journal and is discussed at length in Chapter 13. Subsidiary ledgers for inventories and plant assets are described and illustrated at subsequent points in this book.

Journal System

Hartful Hospital's journal system is based on the following seven classifications of the business transactions of the hospital:

1. Charges to inpatients for services rendered
2. Charges to outpatients for services rendered
3. Cash receipts
4. Purchases of supplies and services
5. Payroll
6. Cash disbursements
7. All other transactions

In the system described here, as noted earlier, a separate journal is maintained for each of these seven major types of transactions.

Inpatient Revenue Journal

The inpatient revenue journal, illustrated in Figure 11.2, is used only to record those transactions that result in charges to inpatients for hospital services provided to them. No other type of transaction should be recorded in this journal, nor should inpatient revenue transactions be recorded in any of the other journals. As hospital services are rendered to inpatients, source documents—census reports and charge tickets, for example—are prepared. Copies of these documents are sent to the hospital accounting offices, where they are turned over to the employee who maintains the inpatient revenue journal. This person uses the source documents as the

FIGURE 11.2 Inpatient Revenue Journal

20X1 Date	(✓)	Inpatient Receivables Dr.	Nursing Services Revenue Credits						Other Professional Services Revenue Credits					Sundry Debits and Credits		
			Nursing Units	Operating Rooms	Emergency Rooms	Central Supply	Other Units	Other Units	Laboratory	Radiology	Pharmacy	Anesthesia	Other Units	Account Numbers	Dr.	Cr.
		Debit	Credit	Credit	Credit	Credit	Credit	Credit	Credit	Credit	Credit	Credit	Credit			
		10410	40110	40120	40130	40140			40150	40160	40170	40180				
Totals																

basis for daily journal entries that debit patients' accounts receivable and credit the various patient services revenue accounts. The details of this procedure are provided in Chapter 12.

Posting Totals to General Ledger

These daily entries in the inpatient revenue journal are not posted to the hospital's general ledger. Instead, at the end of the month, each column of the journal is totaled, and the totals (except for the sundry debits and credits columns) are posted to the general ledger accounts indicated. Entries in the sundry columns must be individually posted, but entries in these columns will not be frequent or numerous.

Daily postings, however, are made to the accounts receivable subsidiary ledger. These postings consist of debits to individual patients' accounts for the services rendered to them each day. Naturally, steps must be taken to ensure that the total of these debit postings for each day equals the total debit to accounts receivable entered in the journal for that day. Again, you will find the details of this posting procedure explained in Chapter 12.

Outpatient Revenue Journal

The outpatient revenue journal, illustrated in Figure 11.3, is used only to record transactions that result in charges to outpatients for hospital services provided to them. No outpatient revenue transactions should be recorded in any of the other journals, nor should any other type of transaction be recorded in this journal. We will assume, for our present purposes, that all services rendered to outpatients at Hartful Hospital are passed through the outpatient receivables account (10430). This procedure is followed even though payment may be received from outpatients at the time services are rendered to them. The alternative procedure, followed when outpatient services can be provided on a cash basis, is to bypass the receivables account and debit cash directly (crediting the appropriate outpatient revenue accounts). This alternative procedure generally should be discouraged, however, because it tends to weaken internal control over outpatient revenues and cash receipts and contradicts accrual accounting principles.

As hospital services are rendered to outpatients, source documents (charge tickets) are prepared in the service-rendering departments. (These departments do not receive cash; outpatients pay for the services at a centralized cash-receiving station as they enter or leave the hospital, or they are billed for the services after the fact.) The departments enter the charge tickets in outpatient services logs or reports. Copies of the logs, along with copies of the related charge tickets, are routed to the hospital's accounting offices, where they are turned over to the accounting employee who is responsible for maintaining the outpatient revenue journal. These documents are used as the basis for debiting outpatient receivables and crediting the appropriate revenue accounts.

FIGURE 11.3 Outpatient Revenue Journal

20X1 Date (✓)	Outpatient Receivables Dr.	Nursing Services Revenue Credits				Other Professional Services Revenue Credits						Sundry Debits and Credits		
		Operating Rooms	Emergency Rooms	Central Supply	Other Units	Laboratory	Radiology	Pharmacy	Anesthesia	Other Units		Account Numbers	Dr.	Cr.
Totals	Debit 10430	Credit 40220	Credit 40230	Credit 40240	Credit	Credit 40250	Credit 40260	Credit 40270	Credit 40280	Credit				

FIGURE 11.4 Cash Receipts Journal

20X1 Date	Cash Receipt Slip Nos.	Cash Dr.	Revenue Deduction Debits — Contractual Adjustments	Charity Care Adjustments	Other	Accounts Receivable Credits — Inpatients In-house	Discharged	Outpatients	Other Credits — Cafeteria Sales	Parking	Sundry Debits and Credits — Account Numbers	Dr.	Cr.
Totals		Debit 10110	Debit 50010	Debit 50020	Debit	Credit 10410	Credit 10420	Credit 10430	Credit 40610	Credit 40620			

At the end of the month, the journal columns are footed, and the totals are posted to the general ledger. Daily postings of charges to outpatients are made to the accounts receivable subsidiary ledger. You will see the details of the process of journalizing and posting outpatient revenue transactions in Chapter 12. The procedure is much the same as for inpatient revenues.

Cash Receipts Journal

Hartful Hospital's cash receipts journal is illustrated in Figure 11.4. It is used to record all cash receipts from whatever source. As was noted earlier, the hospital has a centralized cashiering location. As cash is received, either by mail or over the counter, a cash receipt slip is prepared for each item. All cash receipts are deposited intact daily. Copies of the bank deposit slips, along with copies of the related cash receipt slips, are sent to the hospital's accounting offices each day. Here, the employee in charge of the cash receipts journal uses the source documents to record debits to cash and credits to the receivables accounts.

The journal columns are footed at the end of each month, and the totals are posted to the indicated general ledger accounts. Daily postings are made to the accounts receivable ledger to give individual patients credit for the payments received from them or on their behalf from their third-party sponsors. Details of the procedure of journalizing and posting of cash receipts appear in Chapter 12. We also will examine internal control principles and practices with respect to hospital revenues and cash receipts.

Payroll Journal

The payroll journal employed by Hartful Hospital is illustrated in Figure 11.5. This journal is used to record the salaries and wages earned by hospital employees during each pay period. As you can see, the journal provides columns for the recording of gross pay, payroll taxes and other withholdings, and the net payroll. The necessary data for the payroll journal entries are compiled from information provided by departmental time reports, personnel department records, time clock cards, and other source documents, as will be explained in detail in Chapter 13.

Once the net payroll (assume a figure of $116,492) is determined and credited to the accrued salaries and wages payable account (20400), individual paychecks are written and issued to hospital employees. The checks are drawn against the hospital's cash—payroll checking account (10120), but no entry is made to credit that account. Instead, the amount of the net (accrued) payroll is vouchered through the accounts payable account in the voucher register as follows:

Accrued salaries and wages payable	20400	$116,492	
Accounts payable	20100		$116,492

FIGURE 11.5 Payroll Journal

19X1 Date	Department	Check Numbers	Gross Payroll		Deductions from Payroll Credits				Accrued Payroll Cr.
			Account Numbers	Amount Dr.	FIT Withheld	FICA Withheld	Other	Total	
Totals					Credit 20410	Credit 20420			Credit 20400

The debit closes the accrued employee compensation and related liabilities account (which previously was established with a credit from the payroll journal) and sets up the amount of the net payroll as an account payable.

Then, a single check is written against the cash—general checking account (10110) and recorded in the cash disbursements journal as follows:

Drawing the Payroll Funds

Accounts payable	20100	$116,492	
Cash—general checking account	10110		$116,492

Thus, the cash—payroll checking account is never debited or credited, nor does it ever have a ledger balance (other than perhaps a nominal balance). The $116,492 check drawn on the general checking account, of course, is deposited to the payroll checking account at the hospital's bank. When the individual paychecks are cashed by employees, the payroll checking account is automatically cleared to a zero balance. This procedure removes the large volume of paychecks from the general checking account, thereby facilitating the reconciliation of that account with the monthly bank statement. Another illustration of these procedures will be provided in Chapter 14.

All postings from the payroll journal are made on a monthly basis. Hartful Hospital, however, does maintain (as required by law) an employees' individual earnings record, which in effect is a subsidiary payroll ledger. We will examine this record in Chapter 13.

Voucher Register

Hartful Hospital follows an accounting policy that requires that all disbursements be vouchered through accounts payable. In other words, an entry such as the following is prohibited by the system:

Supplies expense—dietary	60291	$1,387	
Cash—general checking account	10110		$1,387

This disbursement or any other disbursement requires the preparation of a document known as a voucher. The vouchering of proposed disbursements includes the auditing of invoices and the securing of authorizations. Once an item is vouchered and approved for payment, the voucher register entry is as follows:

Supplies expense—dietary	60291	$1,387	
Accounts payable	20100		$1,387

Thus, before a check is written, an investigation is made of the proposed disbursement, and (if approved) a credit is made to a liability account (accounts payable). When the check is written, an entry is made in the cash disbursements journal, as follows:

| Accounts payable | 20100 | $1,387 | |
| Cash—general checking account | 10110 | | $1,387 |

This procedure, known as a **voucher system**, provides a high order of accounting control over hospital disbursements. A major portion of Chapter 14 will be devoted to a description of the voucher system employed by Hartful Hospital.

Entering Vouchers   Figure 11.6 illustrates Hartful Hospital's **voucher register**, which also may be called an *accounts payable journal* or *purchases journal*. As invoices and bills are received by the hospital, they are vouchered (processed for payment) by accounting employees. The vouchers, along with the underlying documents (purchase orders and receiving reports, for example), are turned over to the person who maintains the voucher register. This person enters the vouchers in the register, recording debits to the various accounts indicated by the column headings. In each case, the credit is to accounts payable.

At the end of the month, the column totals are posted to the general ledger accounts. Daily postings are made to the accounts payable subsidiary ledger to maintain a daily record of the amounts due to individual hospital creditors. This procedure is described more fully in Chapter 14.

Cash Disbursements Journal

Hartful Hospital's *cash disbursements journal* is illustrated in Figure 11.7. This journal, which also is known as a *cash payments journal* or *check register*, is used to record all hospital disbursements for whatever purpose. Vouchered items, as they become due for payment, are sent to the hospital's disbursing officer— that is, the individual who has authority to sign checks drawn on the hospital's checking account. This person, if satisfied as to the propriety of the disbursements, signs the related checks and has them mailed to the appropriate parties. The paid voucher, along with attached underlying documents, is returned to the accounting office, where the person in charge of the cash disbursements journal records the disbursements by debits to accounts payable and credits to cash. The paid vouchers are then placed in a file that should be retained for the period of time specified. Chapter 14 illustrates these procedures in more detail.

Posting the Cash Disbursements   Monthly postings are made to the general ledger of the column totals in the cash disbursements journal. Daily debit postings are made to the accounts payable subsidiary ledger.

General Journal

The general journal used by Hartful Hospital is shown in Figure 11.8. You are already well acquainted with this journal. It is important that you now understand, however, that the general journal is used sparingly in a multijournal

FIGURE 11.6 Voucher Register

| 20X1 Date | Accounts Payable Credits | | Payroll-Related Debits | | | Nursing Services/Expense Debits | | | | | Other Professional Services Expense Debits | | | | |
		(✓)	Accrued Payroll	FIT Withheld	FICA W/H & Accrued	Nursing Units	Operating Rooms	Emergency Rooms	Central Supply	Laboratory	Radiology	Pharmacy	Anesthesia
Totals													
	Credit 20100		Debit 20400	Debit 20410	Debit 20420	Debit 60210	Debit 60220	Debit 60230	Debit 60240	Debit 60250	Debit 60260	Debit 60270	Debit 60280

Continued

FIGURE 11.6 (CONTINUED) Voucher Register

General Services Expense Debits			Fiscal Services Expense Debits		Administrative Services Expense Debits		Sundry Debits and Credits		
Dietary	Utilities	House-keeping	Laundry	Accounting	Admitting	Purchasing	Human Resources	Account Numbers	Dr.	Cr.
Debit 60291	Debit 60300	Debit 60292	Debit 60293	Debit 60294	Debit 60295	Debit 60296	Debit 60297			

FIGURE 11.7

Cash
Disbursements
Journal

20X1 Date	Description	Check Numbers	Cash Cr.	Accounts Payable Dr.	Dr.	Sundry Debits and Credits		
						Account Numbers	Dr.	Cr.
	Totals							
			Credit	Debit	Debit			
			10110	20100				

FIGURE 11.8

General Journal

20X1 Date	Accounts and Explanations	Account Numbers	Dr.	Cr.

system. In Hartful Hospital's system, the general journal is used only to record those transactions for which a special journal has not been provided. It will be used mainly for adjusting and closing entries. Most transaction entries will be recorded in the six specialized journals.

Ledger System

If Hartful Hospital maintained only a general ledger, that ledger would have to contain a separate account for each patient and each hospital creditor. As you can imagine, such a ledger would be immense, cumbersome, and unmanageable. For this reason, the individual accounts for hospital patients and creditors are removed from the general ledger and are established as subsidiary ledgers.

The general ledger, however, does contain control accounts for patient receivables and accounts payable.

Balancing Subsidiary Ledgers

As mentioned several times in the preceding discussion, the general ledger control accounts are posted monthly for the *accumulated totals* provided by the special journals; the subsidiary ledgers, however, are posted daily in the *individual amounts* of transactions. This requires that the subsidiary ledgers be balanced against, and reconciled with, the month-end balances of the related general ledger control accounts. This is an extremely important feature of a hospital's overall internal control system, as you will see in the chapters to follow.

Questions

Q11.1. What are the advantages of maintaining several special journals rather than a single general journal?

Q11.2. Distinguish between the general ledger and a subsidiary ledger. Name three types of subsidiary ledgers.

Q11.3. What is the purpose of having sundry debits and credits columns in a special journal? Describe the posting procedure for the amounts entered in these columns.

Q11.4. State two advantages of maintaining control accounts in the general ledger of a hospital.

Q11.5. How would you determine that a special journal balances?

Q11.6. "Whenever a debit posting is made to a general ledger control account, one or more credit postings of the same aggregate total must be posted to the related subsidiary ledger." Do you agree or disagree? Explain your answer.

Q11.7. Why must transactions be posted to the subsidiary ledgers more frequently than to the general ledger?

Q11.8. Hartful Hospital employs the seven journals indicated in Figure 11.1. Indicate the name of the journal in which each of the following types of transactions would be recorded:
a. Charges for services rendered to outpatients
b. Purchase of supplies on account
c. Payments made on accounts payable
d. Charges for services rendered to inpatients
e. Issuance of payroll checks to employees
f. Cash collections received on patients' accounts
g. Cash purchases of supplies
h. Sale of long-term investments for cash
i. Purchase of new equipment on account
j. Receipt of interest income from temporary investments

Q11.9. Describe briefly the posting procedure for the revenue journal and the cash receipts journal.

Q11.10. An inpatient charge ticket for $60 was correctly recorded in the inpatient revenue journal, but the patient's account in the accounts receivable subsidiary ledger was incorrectly debited for only $6. How will this error be discovered?

Q11.11. Describe briefly the posting procedure for the payroll journal, voucher register, and cash disbursements journal.

Q11.12. An invoice for the purchase of $150 of supplies was correctly recorded in the voucher register, but the supplier's account in the accounts payable subsidiary ledger was incorrectly credited for $510. How will this error be discovered?

Q11.13. Hartful Hospital provides many outpatient services on a cash basis. In such cases, would it be appropriate to bypass the outpatient revenue journal and record the transaction directly in the cash receipts journal only to debit cash and credit outpatient revenue? Explain your answer.

Q11.14. What is the purpose of the check (✓) column in the inpatient revenue journal?

Q11.15. Describe briefly the use of the cash—payroll checking account (10120).

Q11.16. In the accounting system described in this chapter, is an entry such as the following possible?

Supplies expense—laboratory	60250	$259	
Cash—general checking account	10110		$259
To record cash purchase of supplies for the laboratory department			

Explain your answer.

Q11.17. The following is a list of general ledger accounts. For each account, name the journals from which debit and credit postings normally would be received.

  a. Inpatient services revenue—pharmacy
  b. Outpatient receivables
  c. Inpatient receivables—in-house
  d. Other operating revenues—cafeteria
  e. Notes payable

Q11.18. The following is a list of general ledger accounts. For each account, name the journals from which debit and credit postings normally would be received.

  a. Cash—general checking account
  b. Supplies expense—pharmacy
  c. Salaries and wages expense—pharmacy
  d. Equipment
  e. Accounts payable

Q11.19. The following is a list of general ledger accounts. For each account, name the journals from which debit and credit postings normally would be received.

  a. Operating room revenues
  b. Notes payable
  c. Unrestricted contributions
  d. Deductions from revenues—charity care adjustments
  e. Accrued salaries and wages payable

Q11.20. The following is a list of general ledger accounts. For each account, name the journals from which debit and credit postings normally would be received.

  a. Prepaid insurance
  b. Temporary investments
  c. Allowance for uncollectible accounts
  d. Land
  e. Hospital net assets

12

REVENUES, RECEIVABLES, AND CASH RECEIPTS

This chapter explains the basic procedures involved in recording revenues, receivables, and cash receipts. The discussion and illustrations relate to our hypothetical Hartful Hospital, whose chart of accounts was outlined in Chapter 10 and whose journal and ledger system was introduced in Chapter 11. Although the procedures here are similar to those found in actual practice, you should recognize that there is no ideal system that is completely applicable to all hospitals. You should not assume, therefore, that the procedures followed by Hartful Hospital are precisely identical to those of any particular real-world hospital. The discussion will, however, give you an excellent understanding of the accounting requirements as well as an insight into certain methods that have been developed to meet those requirements. These observations also apply to the materials of Chapters 13 and 14.

Recording Inpatient Revenues

The greatest share of hospital revenues generally is derived from the services rendered to inpatients. These services are of two major types: (1) the daily room, board, and routine nursing services; and (2) the other professional, or ancillary, services. The accounting objective is to make a prompt and accurate record, on the accrual basis and at the hospital's established rates, of all services rendered, regardless of the amounts (if any) the hospital expects to collect for those services. As a matter of fact, hospitals usually collect less than their full, established service rates, usually because of contracts that the hospitals have entered into with third-party insurance-type payers (e.g., Medicare, Medicaid, managed care organizations), but this has no effect on the amount of revenue to be recorded when services are rendered to patients. Any differences between gross revenues (measured at established rates) and collectible revenues are recorded as revenue deductions. This procedure permits a monetary measurement of earned revenues, "lost" revenues, and collectible revenues.

Daily Inpatient Services

As a person enters the hospital as an inpatient, several different forms are completed. An illustration of one of these forms is presented in Figure 12.1.

FIGURE 12.1 Inpatient Ledger Card

Hartful Hospital

37

LAST   FIRST   M.I.   MAIDEN

Patient
Street
City & State
Sex & Age   Birthdate
Adm. Date   Time
I.D. No.   State
Eff. Date   Ins. Paid Thru
Group No.   Kind or
Father's Name   Benefit Code
Nearest Rel.
Resp. Party
Employer
Attn. Phy.
Prev. Adm. Yr.
Adm. Diagnosis

Hosp. No.
Phone
Mar. Status
Birthplace
Soc. Sec. No.
Ins. or His. No.

Race
Mother's Maiden Name
Relation
Relation
Occupation
Religion
Pastor
Baby Birthdate

Date	Room No.	Beds	Rate	Days
				Total Days
				Basic / Suppl.

BlueCross Case No.

Complete Final Diagnosis

A ☐ Discharged   B ☐ Still Hospitalized   C ☐ Expired

Discharge Date & Time
Occupation
Address
Address
Address
Church   Address

M ☐   F ☐

MED ☐   SUR ☐   PED ☐   OB ☐   EMERG ☐   URG ☐   ELEC ☐

Service Charges

	Supplies (2)	X-Ray (3)	Lab-Path (4)	Drugs (5)	Nursery (6)	Room, Food & Nursing (7)
Miscellaneous Service						
Code	Amount	(1)				
Total Charges						

Credits

Date		Cash Unless Coded		Balance
		Amount	Code	

Summary of Billing

	Supplies	X-Ray	Lab-Path	Drugs	Nursery	Room, Food & Nursing
Total	Credits	Balance				

Basic
Suppl.
Patient's Portion

Patient's Portion

LEDGER COPY

It is a multipart form, one part of which is sent to the accounting office, where it serves as the patient's individual subsidiary ledger card. It is important that information obtained in the admitting process allows for proper classification of the patient (and the related revenues and receivables) according to demographic and insurance status, medical category, and so forth.

During the period of stay, the inpatient's ledger card is charged for the services provided, and the appropriate revenue accounts will be credited. The accounting and control systems must provide detailed written evidence of all hospital services provided as well as documentation of the attending physician's authorizations. This evidence appears in the patient's medical charts, which are maintained at the nursing stations, and in supporting source documents that are kept in the accounting department. As you will see shortly, the ledger card will be credited for payments received from or on behalf of the patient. And, in many cases, noncash credits for charity and contractual adjustments may be made to the ledger card. On the patient's discharge, the medical documents are filed in the medical records department; the financial documents are retained in the accounting department for billing and collection purposes.

Uses of the Inpatient's Ledger Card

A major portion of the charges to inpatients arises from the provision of room, board, and normal nursing services. These services sometimes are referred to as **routine services** or *daily patient services.* In any event, these charges are compiled from information obtained from the daily census report. Forms and procedures differ, but the determination of charges and revenues for daily patient services basically is a matter of multiplying occupied rooms (beds) by established daily charges for those accommodations. In the Hartful Hospital system, a "day-rate service sheet" is used as a combination of census report and revenue-charge summary. This form, shown in Figure 12.2, consists of a preprinted listing of each room and bed in the hospital. It is classified by nursing unit, including an indication of the daily charge for each type of accommodation.

Determining Charges for Daily Services

The sheet is pretotaled for 100 percent occupancy. As a part of the midnight census, a line is drawn through the listing of each unoccupied bed. The total revenue represented by these unoccupied accommodations is computed and deducted from the 100 percent occupancy figures. This produces the gross earned revenues for the day as well as the charge to each patient's ledger card. The objective is to secure a high degree of assurance that the census of patients is accurate, that debits are made to patients' accounts, and that credits are made to revenue accounts in the correct amounts for all daily services provided.

Other (Professional) Ancillary Services

A physician must order most services rendered to patients. Such orders are written in the patient's chart by attending physicians and prescribe all necessary

FIGURE 12.2 Daily Report of Day-Rate Service

FORM 842 DAILY REPORT OF DAY RATE SERVICE
PHYSICIAN'S RECORD CO., BERWYN, ILLINOIS • PRINTED IN U.S.A.
PENN-WAY HOSPITAL ACCOUNTING SYSTEM

INSTRUCTIONS:

Occupancy Total: This reperesents the total amount of day-rate service charges to patients for the day and is the sum of the

Deductions: Total amount resulting from either unoccupied beds or changes in the number of beds in rooms.

Additions: Total amount due to additional beds being placed in rooms or changes for a part of a day.

BedComplement Total: Total amount based on 100% occupancy of all available beds.

Bed Complement Total and Additions Minus Deductions

FIGURE 12.3

Requisiton-Charge Ticket

LABORATORY	Walk ☐	Check If Patient Is Leaving Today ....m. ☐	N 99999
	Chair ☐	*If this is a CREDIT, check here and also circle amount ☐	
	Bed ☐		

Patient's Name _____ Room No. _____

If OUT-Patient Address _____ Age _____

Requested by Dr. _____ Date _____ 20____

Adm.	Repeat	EXAMINATION OR TEST REQUESTED	CHARGE*
		Blood Count–Complete ☐R.B.C.☐W.B.C.☐Hb.☐Diff.	
		Urinalysis–Voided☐Catheterized☐Time Collected____.M.	
		Kahn☐ Kline☐Kolmer☐Mazzini☐Wassermann☐ _____	
		Special Tests, etc. (Specify) _____	

Medical, etc.☐Surgical☐Operation Scheduled for–Date____ 20__ Time____.M.

Remarks_____ Signed_____

1. **Please Send 1st and 2nd Copies to Laboratory**   **Number Checked off on Control Sheet** ☐   **Posted to Patient's Account** ☐

patient services. Nurses or other nursing station personnel (acting under the nurses' supervision) requisition the services so prescribed. To obtain adequate accounting control over the charges and revenues arising from these services, therefore, the full cooperation of all nursing personnel is essential.

Preparing and Processing Requisition-Charge Tickets

As various ancillary services are required for patients, nursing station personnel prepare requisition-charge tickets, such as the one illustrated in Figure 12.3. A separate set of tickets may be used for each type of service. Each ticket may be prenumbered, and charge tickets for each service may be of different colors to aid with identification and sorting.

The charge tickets often are prepared in triplicate. The original and duplicate copies go to the professional department that renders the service; the triplicate copy remains at the nursing station. The ticket gives the professional department the authority to render the prescribed service. Periodically during each day, the original copies of the charge tickets are collected from the professional departments and are taken to the hospital's accounting offices; the duplicates remain with the professional department. The charge tickets are usually priced either in the professional departments or in the accounting office.

Each day, an accounting employee sorts the charge tickets by color (department). Each color group is then totaled to determine the day's revenue for each departmental service. The same tickets are sorted according to individual patient so that appropriate charges can be made to the appropriate patient's ledger card. Naturally, a reconciliation must be made to ascertain whether the total debits to the ledger cards equal the total of all tickets, and whether the total credits to the various revenue accounts equal the total of all tickets. In some systems, a worksheet is prepared to summarize the charge tickets and make the necessary daily reconciliations.

Inpatient Revenue Journal

Whatever the data collection system, daily journal entries must be made to record debits to the inpatient receivables control accounts and credits to the various revenue accounts. We will assume that Hartful Hospital uses the day-rate service sheet and requisition charge tickets to generate the necessary data. These data are journalized in the inpatient revenue journal as indicated in Figure 12.4. This is merely a sample entry to illustrate the manner in which a day's inpatient revenues may be recorded. A similar entry is made each day of the month. You will have to imagine that all 31 lines of the journal are filled. Assume that the 31 daily entries add to the column totals shown in the journal.

Summarizing Charges It is assumed here that a daily worksheet summary of the day-rate service sheet and all charge tickets is prepared in the accounting office. The total of the day-rate service sheet and the total of the charge tickets together make up the total $14,645 debit to inpatient receivables—in-house (10410) for May 5, 20X1. Similarly, an analysis of the day-rate service sheet and of the charge tickets provides the totals credited to each revenue center account for the same day. Each day's entry should be cross-footed to check whether the total of credits equals the amount of the debit to inpatient receivables.

Thus, a daily summary of charges and revenues is entered on a single line of the journal. When this procedure is followed, an indication of charge ticket numbers in the journal is not feasible. This requires the retention of the worksheet or other form on which the summary totals were determined, as well as retention of the day-rate service sheets and charge tickets in appropriate files. In this way the necessary "audit trails" (paperwork proofs) are provided for the hospital's internal and external auditors. In other words, the system must facilitate the auditors' tracing of journal entries to source documents and must provide safeguards against either the omission of transactions or the recording of the same transaction more than once. An alternative would be to journalize the charge tickets individually, but this often is not feasible in a manual system because of the large number of charge tickets issued each day.

Notice the sundry debit and credit columns on the far right side of the journal. These columns are provided for occasional debits or credits that may

20X1 Date		(✓)	Inpatient Receivables Dr.	Nursing Services Revenue Credits					
				Nursing Unit	Operating Room	Emergency Room	Central Supply	Other Units	Other Units
5	5	✓	14,645	6,250	900	450	1,100		
	Totals		453,995	187,500	26,100	14,400	34,100		
			Debit	Credit	Credit	Credit	Credit	Credit	Credit
			10410	40110	40120	40130	40140		

Continued

FIGURE 12.4

Inpatient Revenue Journal

FIGURE 12.4
(Continued)
Inpatient
Revenue
Journal

Other Professional Services Revenue Credits					Sundry Debits and Credits		
Laboratory	Radiology	Pharmacy	Anesthesia	Other Units	Account Numbers	Dr.	Cr.
1,820	2,135	1,040	950				
56,420	88,835	24,960	21,680				
Credit 40150	Credit 40160	Credit 40170	Credit 40180	Credit			

be required but for which appropriate separate columns have not been included in the journal. The journal should be designed so that the use of these sundry columns will rarely be necessary.

As these daily summaries of charges and revenues are entered in the journal, daily postings of charges are made to the inpatients' subsidiary ledger cards on the basis of the information provided by the day-rate service sheet and the individual charge tickets sorted according to patient name, hospital number, or room number. The total of these debit postings, of course, must equal the total debited to inpatient receivables in the journal. When this equality has been established, a check mark (✓) is placed in the journal column provided beside the date.

No daily postings are made to the general ledger accounts. At month's end, however, the various columns of the journal are totaled and cross-footed to ensure that the total of the debit columns equals the total of the credit columns. Each column total is then posted to the appropriate general ledger account as indicated at the foot of each column.

As noted earlier, the Hartful Hospital procedure is a manual system; it is described here in simplified terms to illustrate certain principles more easily. Today all hospitals, large and small, use computers due to the great volume of account activity.

Recording Outpatient Revenues

Charges and revenues for departmental services to outpatients also may be determined in much the same way as was described for inpatient revenue accounting. A charge ticket is originated, either at a centralized outpatient reception desk or in the professional departments providing the outpatient services. In some cases, personnel of the service-rendering department in daily services logs summarize the outpatient charge tickets. The accounting department, on a daily basis, collects a copy of this log, along with copies of related charge tickets. On the basis of these documents, a daily summary of outpatient charges and revenues is prepared and entered on a single line of the outpatient revenue journal, as illustrated in Figure 12.5 for May 5, 20X1. The worksheet on which this summary was developed, the logs, and the charge tickets should be retained to provide an appropriate audit trail.

Daily postings are made of charges to outpatient subsidiary ledger cards. Again, a special column (✓) is provided in the journal to indicate that the individual debit postings to the ledger cards equal the total debited to the outpatient receivables column in the journal. At month's end, the various columns are totaled, and the totals are posted to the general ledger accounts. Entries in the sundry columns, however, must be posted individually.

FIGURE 12.5 Outpatient Revenue Journal

20X1 Date	(✓)	Outpatient Receivable Dr.	Nursing Services Revenue Credits				Other Professional Services Revenue Credits					Sundry Debits and Credits		
			Operating Room	Emergency Room	Central Supply	Other Units	Laboratory	Radiology	Pharmacy	Anesthesia	Other Units	Account Numbers	Dr.	Cr.
5 5	✓	2,160	1,500	4,800	290		470	510	210	50				
Totals		64,800	3,900	9,000	5,700		17,040	21,630	5,880	1,650				
		Debit 10430	Credit 40220	Credit 40230	Credit 40240	Credit	Credit 40250	Credit 40260	Credit 40270	Credit 40280	Credit			

FIGURE 12.6
Cash Receipt Slip

CASH RECEIPT

GENERAL COMMUNITY HOSPITAL
STREET ADDRESS
CITY, STATE, ZIP CODE

No. 10351

Patient's Name ______________________________

Room No...

$...

Received the Sum of ______________________ **and** ______ **Dollars**
100

Cash ☐ **Check** ☐ **Money Order** ☐

GENERAL COMMUNITY HOSPITAL

Date **20**

By

THANK YOU

Recording Cash Receipts

An immediate written record should be made of all cash receipts. In many hospital accounting systems, this record is generated through the preparation of a cash receipt slip, such as the one illustrated in Figure 12.6. Cash receipts are of two types: mail receipts and over-the-counter receipts. Two employees may be assigned responsibility for opening incoming mail. Working together, they extract the cash items from the mail and list these items on a mail remittance report. One copy of the report is sent directly to the accounting department, one copy (with the cash items) goes to cashiering, and one copy is retained by the mail openers.

Distributing Cash Receipt Slips

On receipt of the cash items from the incoming mail, the cashier issues a cash receipt slip for the total amount. One copy is given to the mail openers, one copy is sent to the accounting department, and one copy is retained by the cashier. For counter receipts, the cashier prepares individual cash receipt slips, again in triplicate. One copy is given to the patient, one copy is sent to the accounting department as a medium for postings to the patients' ledger, and one copy is filed permanently in numerical sequence. All cash items, both mail and counter receipts, should be carefully controlled and should be deposited daily and intact. Cash disbursements should never be made from cash receipts. A copy of the bank deposit slip is routed to the accounting office.

At the end of each day, the cash receipt slips are summarized and entered in the cash receipts journal. An accounting employee compares the

FIGURE 12.7 Cash Receipts Journal

20X1 Date	Cash Receipt Slip Nos.	Cash Dr.	Revenue Deduction Credits			Accounts Receivable Credits			Other Credits		Sundry Debits and Credits		
			Contractual Adjustments	Charity Care Adjustments	Other	Inpatients In-house	Inpatients Discharged	Outpatients	Cafeteria Sales	Parking	Account Numbers	Dr.	Cr.
5 5	443-657	13,815	1,040	480		1,420	11,350	1,930	560	75			
Totals		477,500	31,600	14,400		43,020	401,850	57,900	18,480	2,250			
		Debit 10110	Debit 50010	Debit 50020	Debit	Credit 10410	Credit 10420	Credit 10430	Credit 50010	Credit 50020			

cash receipt slips with the mail remittance report and with the duplicate bank deposit slip. The cash receipt slips, sorted by patient name, and the mail remittance report can be used to make the necessary credit postings to the individual patient's ledger card.

Hartful Hospital's cash receipts journal is illustrated in Figure 12.7. A sample entry for May 5, 20X1, has been included to indicate how the daily cash receipt transactions are recorded. If cash receipt slips are issued in several different numerical series concurrently, an indication of cash receipt slip numbers in the journal may not be practicable. When this is the case, either the slips must be journalized individually or a worksheet summary must be developed to provide an adequate audit trail.

The posting of entries from the cash receipts journal is the same as for the revenue journals. Daily postings are made to the patients' ledger; monthly postings of column totals are made to the general ledger.

Debits to Revenue Deduction Accounts

Notice that the cash receipts journal includes columns for debits to the revenue deduction accounts. To describe how these columns are used, assume a discharged patient with an account balance of $1,250. On May 5, 20X1, $1,000 is received by the hospital from the patient's third-party sponsor in full payment of the account. The entry to be made by the hospital is as follows:

Cash	10100	$1,000	
Contractual adjustments	50010	250	
Inpatient receivables—discharged	10420		$1,250

It is assumed here that the $250 difference between the patient's hospital bill and the amount reimbursed by the third party is not, under the terms of the contract, recoverable from the patient.

Thus, in Hartful Hospital's system, debits are made to the revenue deduction accounts as patients' accounts are paid. Here, the cash receipts journal is designed to provide columns for those debits. In other systems, however, a separate receivables adjustments and allowances journal, or revenue deductions journal, is employed to account for these items. But whatever the procedure may be, it is essential that all noncash credits to receivables be authorized and approved by a responsible hospital official who has no access to the hospital's cash receipts and receivables records. This is necessary to protect against a theft of cash receipts that may be covered up by unwarranted write-offs of accounts receivable balances that were really paid.

The method used by Hartful Hospital in accounting for revenue deductions is satisfactory as an accounting routine. Care must be taken, however, to make sure that revenue deductions are recognized on the accrual basis. The deductions must be recognized in the same period as the related revenues. To accomplish this, an adjusting entry is required at the end of each period for which a balance sheet and statement of operations are prepared. To illustrate the procedure for contractual adjustments, let us assume that a hospital had $3.6 million revenues in 20X1 and that $600,000 of this total remains in accounts receivable at December 31, 20X1. In collecting the $3 million of accounts receivable during the year, assume that contractual adjustments totaling $150,000 were recorded. In other words, contractual adjustments averaged about 5 percent of receivables.

Adjusting Entry for Year-End Receivables

This means that the year-end accounts receivable probably include $30,000 (5 percent of $600,000) of unrecognized contractual adjustments. This $30,000 must be recognized as revenue deductions in 20X1, the year in which the related revenues are recorded. The required December 31, 20X1, adjusting entry is the following:

Contractual adjustments	50010	$ 30,000	
Allowance for uncollectible accounts —contractuals	10520		$30,000

When the $600,000 of accounts receivable are collected in 20X2, the actual contractual adjustments on these accounts are recorded in accordance with the routine described for Hartful Hospital, without regard to the adjusting entry. A reversing entry (the reverse of the above adjusting entry) can be made by the hospital on January 1, 20X2, to avoid recording the same contractual adjustments twice (in 20X1 and 20X2). Or, if one prefers, the adjusting entry at the end of the first monthly reporting period in 20X2 can simply adjust to the appropriate balance at that time in the allowance for uncollectible accounts—contractuals.

A similar procedure can be followed for revenue deductions arising from the provision of charity care. The treatment of bad debts, however, is generally somewhat different, and we will defer a discussion of this point to Chapter 16.

Reconciling Control Accounts and Subsidiary Records

As you have seen, Hartful Hospital maintains three receivables control accounts in its general ledger. These accounts (with assumed May 1, 20X1, balances) are as follows:

Acct. No.		
10410	Inpatient receivables—in-house	$110,000
10420	Inpatient receivables—discharged	800,000
10430	Outpatient receivables	16,000

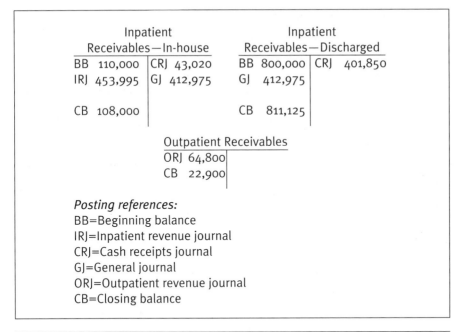

FIGURE 12.8
Month-End
General Ledger
Postings

Hartful Hospital also maintains a separate patients' subsidiary ledger for each of these control accounts. Let us assume that the total of the individual debit balances in each subsidiary ledger at May 1, 20X1, agrees with the debit balance of the related general ledger control account at May 1, 20X1.

Month-End Postings to General Ledger

During the month of May, as entries were made in the revenue and cash receipt journals, daily postings of charges and credits were made to the patients' subsidiary ledgers. Month-end postings of journal column totals were made to the control accounts in the general ledger, as illustrated in Figure 12.8.

All of the postings in this illustration are drawn from the journals shown previously in this chapter, except for postings from the general journal. Not mentioned earlier is the fact that as inpatients are discharged, Hartful Hospital makes entries in the general journal to transfer the unpaid account balances from the in-house to the discharged classification of receivables. That is, during May, patients whose unpaid balances together totaled $412,975 were discharged from the hospital.

Now, after the month-end postings are made as indicated in the T-accounts in Figure 12.8, we have a May 31, 20X1, balance in each of the three receivables control accounts. The individual ledger card balances in each of the three subsidiary ledgers are totaled. In the absence of accounting errors, the total of the in-house inpatient receivables ledger should be $108,000. Similarly, the discharged inpatient receivables ledger cards should total $811,125, and the outpatient ledger cards should total $22,900.

Investigating Discrepancies

Whenever a subsidiary ledger does not reconcile with the corresponding control account, the situation should be thoroughly investigated, and the reasons for the discrepancy identified. Considering the importance of recording hospital receivables accurately and the availability of efficient data processing equipment, there simply is no excuse for a failure to make regular monthly reconciliations of accounts receivable controls and subsidiary ledgers.

You now have seen the Hartful Hospital accounting system as related to its revenue and cash receipt transactions. The next chapter deals with the payroll accounting procedures of the hospital.

Questions

Q12.1. State the basic objective of accounting for services rendered to inpatients and outpatients.

Q12.2. Describe briefly how the amounts to be charged to inpatients for services rendered to them generally are determined.

Q12.3. Describe briefly how the amounts to be charged to outpatients for services rendered to them generally are determined.

Q12.4. How often should postings be made from the inpatient and outpatient revenue journals? Explain your answer.

Q12.5. Describe briefly how the daily amounts to be debited to cash and credited to patients' accounts receivable generally are determined.

Q12.6. How often should postings be made from the cash receipts journal? Explain your answer.

Q12.7. Lyst Hospital's general ledger contained the following receivables control account balances at October 31:

Inpatient receivables—in-house	$ 57,000
Inpatient receivables—discharged	216,000
Outpatient receivables	19,000

The inpatient receivables column in the November inpatient revenue journal totaled $98,000, and the outpatients receivables column of the November outpatient revenue journal totaled $34,000. The receivables columns of the November cash receipts journal provided the following totals:

Inpatient receivables—in-house	$ 11,400
Inpatient receivables—discharged	107,600
Outpatient receivables	32,300

The November general journal contained a number of entries that transferred a total of $101,900 in inpatient receivables from the in-house account to the discharged account. If you prepared adding machine tape totals of the individual patients' ledger card balances at November 30, what total would you expect to find in each of the following subsidiary ledgers?

a. Inpatient receivables—in-house

b. Inpatient receivables—discharged

c. Outpatient receivables

Q12.8. Inpatient Joe Lane received the following services on November 7, 20X1:

Daily patient services (room and board)	$125
Operating room	750
Central supply	124
Laboratory	116
Pharmacy	79
Anesthesia	225
Telephone (long-distance calls)	34

Explain how you would enter this information in the journal and ledger system described in this chapter.

Q12.9. On October 12, 20X1, Loud Hospital borrowed $50,000 from a local bank by issuance of a 120-day, 9 percent note. Explain how you would enter this transaction in the hospital's cash receipts journal.

Q12.10. Lana Lowe, when admitted to Lawson Hospital, was classified as a charity care patient. Lana was admitted on June 1 and was discharged from the hospital on June 8. Services rendered to her during this period totaled $3,672 at the hospital's established rates. What entries should be made by Lawson Hospital to record the services rendered to Lana and to give recognition to the fact that nothing will be collected for those services? Indicate the names of the journals in which these entries will be made.

Q12.11. What are some of the basic features of a good system of internal control over revenues and cash receipts?

Q12.12. Lamp Hospital's daily patient service (routine service) charge is $85 per day for a semiprivate accommodation. On August 29, 20X1, daily patient service charges were correctly entered in the inpatient revenue journal but, in posting to the receivables subsidiary ledger, one patient's account was inadvertently charged for only $58. How might this error be detected?

PAYROLL ACCOUNTING PROCEDURES

The discussion presented in this chapter deals with some of the basic accounting principles and practices relating to the hospital payroll. You may be aware that employee compensation accounts for more than 50 percent of the operating expenses of most hospitals. That the majority of expense is related to employee compensation, however, should not be surprising in view of the following factors:

- The hospital is largely a personal-service, labor-intensive business that generally requires five to six employees per inpatient.
- The hospital necessarily must employ many highly skilled specialists and professional people who command relatively high salaries.
- The nature and importance of healthcare services is such that high-quality, adequately paid personnel should be employed.
- Competition from industrial and commercial businesses for such personnel has led to an increased general level of compensation.

Like any other business, the hospital also is subject to minimum wage laws, a variety of payroll taxes, and other governmental regulations that have added significant amounts to employee compensation costs. In addition, the unionization of hospital workers and the emergence of employee pension plans are two relatively recent developments that have had a major impact on salaries, wages, and other employee benefits.

It seems clear, therefore, that particular emphasis must be given in hospitals to personnel management and labor cost control. Among other things, this emphasis requires the development of accurate and reliable information about payroll and payroll-related costs through sound accounting methods and practices. This chapter continues the Hartful Hospital illustration and provides an opportunity to study some of the procedures hospital accounting departments follow for employee compensation costs.

Compilation of Gross Payrolls

Hartful Hospital, like most hospitals, maintains a centralized human resources department, whose basic functions include recruitment and orientation of new employees and maintenance of permanent personnel records. In addition to the many records that must be kept for tax purposes, the human resources department keeps a complete, up-to-date employment history or service file for all employees. The centralization of these functions and records localizes responsibility, promotes efficiency, and facilitates control over the size, quality, productivity, and cost of the hospital labor force.

Mechanisms for Recording Employee Hours

The human resources department, in cooperation with the accounting department of the hospital, should develop and administer a clear-cut procedure for recording and reporting the time worked by all employees. Some hospitals use electronic time and attendance systems. Others use time clocks for this purpose, while still others use manually prepared time reports or time cards, such as the one illustrated in Figure 13.1. In any case, the department head or supervisor signs (electronically or manually) and approves the time records before they are sent to the accounting department for processing.

It is essential for time records to be complete and accurate in recording attendance and hours worked. The records should also fully comply with the provisions of the Internal Revenue Service Code, Fair Labor Standards Act, and other laws imposing various requirements on employers. Time records also should be designed to facilitate the computation of the payroll and the development of the necessary labor statistics. Analyses of the payroll in terms of hours as well as dollars are extremely important to financial management in hospitals.

Compiling the gross payroll is not particularly difficult. Accounting employees independent of the timekeeping function examine all time cards for hourly employees to determine that the records have been properly executed and approved and that the hours worked by each employee have been correctly computed. Hours must then be multiplied by authorized rates of pay. If overtime hours have been worked, a separate calculation is required. Employee benefits such as paid vacations, paid holidays, and sick leave also affect computation of gross earnings.

Example of Overtime Computation

Assume that a particular employee is paid $6 per hour for a regular workweek of 40 hours. This employee's gross earnings for a week during which he or she worked 48 hours ordinarily would be $288 ($6 × 48 hours). The Fair Labor Standards Act (popularly known as the Wages and Hours Law) provides not only for a minimum hourly wage but also requires that time and a half be paid for hours in excess of 40 hours worked in a given week. The computation of the employee's earnings for the 48-hour week therefore becomes the following:

Regular workweek ($6 × 40 hours)	$240
Overtime ($6 × 8 hours)	48
Overtime premium ($3 × 8 hours)	24
Gross earnings	$312

FIGURE 13.1

Employee Time
Record

	DATES*	ON	OFF	Hrs.	ON	OFF	Hrs.	ON	OFF	Hrs.	TOTAL HOURS	Employees DO NOT WRITE IN THIS SPACE		
	1 16											TOTAL ☐ Hours ☐ Days		
	2 17											Rate per ☐ Hour ☐ Day		
	3 18											Total Cash Compensation		
	4 19											Other Compensation		
	5 20													
	6 21													
	7 22											TOTAL EARNINGS		
	8 23											Deductions		
	9 24											Withholding Tax		
	10 25													
	11 26													
	12 27													
	13 28													
	14 29											TOTAL DEDUCTIONS		
	15 30													
	31											AMOUNT OF CHECK		

Name _____ Month _____ 20___

Emp. No. or Dept. _____ Floor_____ Position _____

*Cross out Column of Dates that Does Not Apply

CODE: A—Absent, deduction   S—Sick, deduction   SUPERVISOR
     AN—Absent, no deduction   Ⓢ Sick, no deduction
     V—Vacation, no deduction

Time and Salary Computation

Application of the provisions of the Wages and Hours Law to the compensation of hospital employees is substantially more involved than indicated here, but we cannot pursue the matter further in this book. It is important to note, however, that good payroll accounting practice provides for the separate recording of overtime compensation because such information is useful in evaluating the utilization of personnel by department heads.

For salaried employees, the gross pay per period is a fixed amount that, once determined, does not vary until the salary is changed. All changes in salaries or in hourly rates should enter into the calculation of gross pay only when such changes are authorized in writing by the human resources department. The payroll clerk should not act on verbal orders. The time records kept for salaried personnel also should be properly executed, approved, and signed by department heads or supervisors.

Payroll Deductions

Payroll accounting is complicated greatly by the various deductions or withholdings that must be made from employees' gross earnings so as to determine the amounts in which paychecks should be produced. Many withholding deductions are required by legislation enacted by federal, state, and local governments, which impose a number of taxes on salaries and wages paid to hospital personnel. Other withholding items arise in connection with group insurance, retirement plan, and savings plan agreements with employees. Some of these deductions are described here.

Income Taxes

The federal income tax program has operated on a pay-as-you-go basis for many years. This payment system requires employers to withhold from employees' salaries and wages an amount approximating the income tax on those earnings. The amount, computed from tax withholding tables furnished by the government, varies according to the amount of taxable wages, length of the payroll period, employee's marital status, and number of dependents (exemptions) claimed by the employee.

Tax Remittances and Reports

The income tax amounts so withheld by the hospital must be remitted to the government at times specified by law. For most hospitals, remittance must often be made within a few days following each pay period. This is accomplished by deposit of the withheld amounts in an authorized government depository (bank). In addition, a quarterly report must be filed to provide a summary of all wages paid and taxes withheld during each quarter. Rather severe penalties and interest charges are imposed on employers who fail to withhold taxes and deposit taxes, or who fail to file payroll tax returns in the prescribed manner and at the specified time.

Most states and some large cities also levy income taxes. In such cases, hospitals often must withhold these taxes. Amounts withheld, as determined by formulas or tables, are remitted periodically to the governmental units in accordance with the particular laws.

FICA (Social Security) Taxes

The Federal Insurance Contributions Act (FICA), popularly known as Social Security, provides for a tax on employees' earnings to finance a federal program of old-age, survivors', disability, and healthcare benefits for workers and their families. Hospitals and their employees were at first exempt from this law when it was originally enacted in 1935, but the basic law has been amended many times to extend its coverage and to increase the tax rate, amount of earnings subject to tax, and benefits provided. The 1965 amendment included enactment of the Federal Hospital Insurance Program, widely known as Medicare.

As is true of income tax, the FICA tax must be withheld by the hospital from taxable wage payments to employees. The 1935 act provided for a 1 percent tax on the first $3,000 of wages paid to each employee in any one year, but subsequent amendments to the law have increased both the tax rate and the base earnings (maximum annual earnings subject to tax). As of 2005, the Old Age, Survivor, and Disability Insurance (OASDI) portion of the FICA tax is 6.2 percent of the first $90,000 of taxable wages paid to each employee. The Medicare portion of the FICA tax is 1.45 percent of taxable wages paid to each employee, with no maximum limit. In other words, the maximum annual tax is $5,580 per employee earning $90,000 for the OASDI portion, as well as $1,305 for the Medicare portion plus an additional 1.45 percent of all wages over $90,000. This amount may be increased in the future by increasing the tax rate, base earnings, or both.

Employer's Matching FICA Payment

So, FICA taxes are withheld from employees' earnings just as are income taxes. Provisions of the FICA tax legislation, however, also require an equal contribution by the hospital. The employer must "match" the amount of FICA tax withheld from employees' wages. Thus, a tax is imposed on the hospital. To put it another way, the 2005 FICA tax was 12.4 percent on total wages up to $90,000; half was withheld from employees' earnings and half was paid by the hospital employer. Both the employer's and the employee's FICA taxes are remitted to the U.S. government at the same time as and together with the federal income tax (FIT) withholdings. In addition, the 2005 Medicare tax was 2.9 percent on total wages with no limit.

Example of Hospital's Withholding Entries

Entries for the withholding of FIT and FICA, and for the accrual of the hospital's share of FICA, are illustrated later in this chapter for Hartful Hospital, but a simpler example might be useful at this point. Assume that a single employee earns a salary of $2,000 per month, all of which is subject to tax. Assume a 15 percent federal income tax rate, a 12.4 percent FICA tax rate, and a 2.9 percent Medicare tax rate. Monthly entries with respect to this particular employee are as follows:

Salaries and wages expense	$2,000	
FICA withheld and accrued		$ 124
FIT withheld and accrued		300
Medicare withheld and accrued		29
Accrued payroll liability		1,547
Accrual of payroll and withholding of related taxes		
Accrued payroll liability	1,547	
Cash		1,547
Issuance of paycheck		
Employee benefits (expense)	153	
FICA withheld and accrued		124
Medicare withheld and accrued		29
Accrual of hospital's share of FICA and Medicare		

FICA withheld and accrued	248	
Medicare withheld and accrued	58	
FIT withheld	300	
Cash		606
Remittance of payroll taxes		
withheld and accrued		

You should recognize that the matching FICA (OASDI and Medicare) tax imposed on the hospital represents a significant expense. There also is the rather considerable clerical expense involved in computing and recording the withholdings, preparing the many payroll tax reports, and keeping the detailed payroll records required by these laws.

Other Deductions

In addition to the compulsory tax withholdings, a variety of other items may be withheld from salary and wage payments to employees. These withholding categories usually require the written consent of the employee. Other deductions include

- Government savings bonds or other employee savings plan;
- Premiums for health, accident, hospital, and life insurance;
- Union membership dues;
- Employee retirement plans; and
- Employee contributions to United Way, or other charities.

At specified intervals, the hospital must summarize these withholdings in appropriate reports and remit the amounts withheld to the proper agencies.

Recording the Payroll

On the basis of time cards, time reports, and other source documents that have been collected from the various departments, the payroll clerk is able to compute the gross pay of each employee for the pay period involved. The payroll tax deductions then are calculated for each employee by the application of tax rates and the use of tax tables. Other deductions are determined on the basis of written agreements and authorizations obtained from employees. A final step is the subtraction of total deductions from gross pay to arrive at net pay for each employee. All of these data then are entered on the face of the time card or other record for each employee.

Sample Payroll Check and Stub

Next, a payroll check is prepared for each employee in the net pay amount indicated on the employee's time card. A sample payroll check is illustrated in Figure 13.2. Notice that the upper portion is a stub that provides, for the

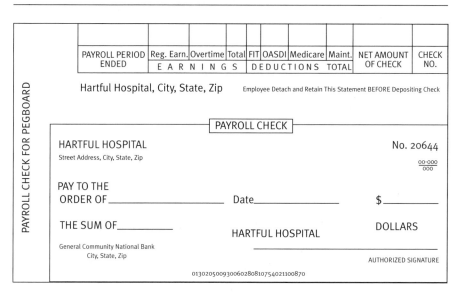

FIGURE 13.2
Employee
Payroll Check

employee's personal records, complete information as to gross earnings, deductions, and net pay.

Recording Totals in the Payroll Journal

The individual time records, sorted by department, are now summarized to obtain departmental totals for gross pay, deductions, and net pay. These totals then are entered in the payroll journal, as indicated in Figure 13.3. (An alternative procedure is to list each employee's name and data in the journal individually, but this procedure may not be feasible.) The illustrative entry includes FIT and FICA withholdings assumed to be 20 percent and 6 percent, respectively. We also assume, for simplicity, that Hartful Hospital pays all of its employees once each month. The column totals shown in the journal therefore are totals for May 20X1. If the hospital paid its employees every two weeks or twice each month, a separate journal page would be used for each pay period.

Recording Matching Payments in the General Journal

As indicated in the payroll journal, May payroll withholdings were $58,400 for FIT and $17,520 for FICA taxes (For simplicity, we will assume that FICA represents the OASDI and Medicare accounts). The hospital's matching share of FICA taxes for the month is recorded in the general journal on May 31, 20X1 by the following entry:

Employee benefits—FICA	61100	$17,520	
FICA withheld and accrued	20420		$17,520
Accrual of hospital's share of			
FICA taxes on May payroll			

FIGURE 13.3 Payroll Journal

20X1 Date		Department	Check Numbers	Gross Payroll		Deductions from Payroll Credits				Accrued Payroll Cr.
				Account Numbers	Amount Dr.	FIT Withheld	FICA Withheld	Other	Total	
5	31	Nursing services:								
		Nursing units		60110	191,400	38,280	11,484		49,764	141,636
		Operating rooms		60120	8,200	1,640	492		2,132	6,068
		Emergency rooms		60130	6,400	1,280	384		1,664	4,736
		Central supply		60140	7,700	1,540	462		2002	5,698
		Other professional services:								
		Laboratory		60150	8,200	1,640	492		2,132	6,068
		Radiology		60160	7,700	1,540	462		2002	5,698
		Pharmacy		60170	4,900	980	294		1,274	3,626
		Anesthesia		60180	5,500	1,100	330		1,430	4,070
		Dietary		60191	9,400	1,880	564		2,444	6,956
		Housekeeping		60192	7,500	1,500	450		1,950	5,550
		Laundry		60193	6,800	1,360	408		1,768	5,032
		Accounting		60194	6,700	1,340	402		1,742	4,958
		Admitting		60195	5,300	1,060	318		1,378	3,922
		Purchasing		60196	3,900	780	234		1,014	2,886
		Human resources		60197	4,100	820	246		1,066	3,034
		Health information management		60198	8,300	1,660	448		2,158	6,142
		Totals			292,000	58,400	17,520		75,920	216,080
					Debit	Credit	Credit	Credit	Credit	Credit
						20410	20420			20400

Notice that the May net payroll of $216,080 is not credited to cash (even though the payroll checks have already been written) but to accrued salaries and wages payable (20400). As you will see in the next chapter, a single voucher is prepared in this amount and is entered in the hospital's voucher register as follows:

Accrued salaries and wages payable	20400	$216,080	
Accounts payable	20100		$216,080
Voucher for May payroll			

Entering Accrued Employee Compensation and Related Liabilities in the Cash Disbursements Journal

Immediately following this, a check for $216,080 is drawn against the general checking account and is entered in the cash disbursements journal as follows:

Accounts payable	20100	$216,080	
Cash—general checking account	10120		$216,080
Issuance of check for May payroll			

This check is deposited in the hospital's payroll checking account, but no entry is made in the payroll checking account to record the deposit. The individual payroll checks, you remember, were drawn on the payroll checking account, but no entry was made to that account for those checks. When the payroll checks are cashed by employees, the payroll checking account automatically clears to the zero or imprest balance maintained in the account. This procedure removes a large volume of paychecks from the general checking account and simplifies reconciliation of the payroll checking account.

Posting Departmental Totals

Each departmental total in the gross pay column is posted at the end of the month to the general ledger salaries and wages expense accounts indicated. Other postings to the general ledger are of column totals. In addition to those in the general ledger, postings also must be made to the employees' individual earnings records that often take the form illustrated in Figure 13.4. This detailed record, which is required by tax laws and regulations, is in effect a subsidiary ledger supporting the departmental salaries and wages expense accounts.

The information in this subsidiary ledger is quite useful for preparing various quarterly and annual tax reports and other employment information forms.

Safeguarding Payroll Funds

The employees responsible for compilation of payrolls should neither sign nor distribute payroll checks. Once prepared, the unsigned checks should be examined by the disbursing authority, who should be satisfied as to their

FIGURE 13.4

Employee's
Individual
Earnings
Record

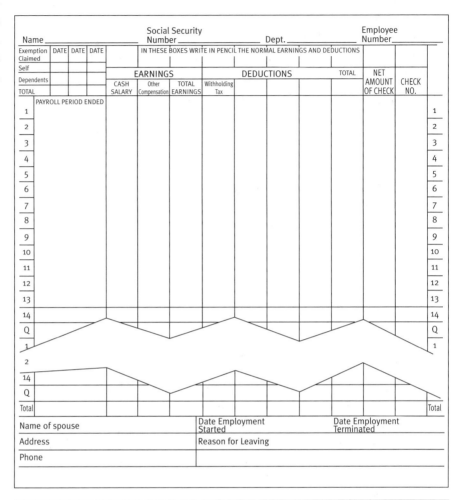

accuracy and authenticity. This may involve a check of certain computations on a sample basis and a comparison of payees and pay rates with independently controlled personnel records. (In many instances, these procedures are performed by the hospital's internal auditors.) Care particularly must be given to avoiding the following:

- Inclusion of nonexistent persons on the payroll of a department
- Issuance of any checks to former employees whose names have not been removed from the payroll
- Payment of incorrect rates of pay
- Payment for overtime hours when none were worked

If a mechanical check signer is employed, its use should be strictly controlled.

The distribution of payroll checks should be centralized, and procedures should be employed to ensure that employees receiving checks are properly identified. The method of distributing checks, as well as the person who distributes checks, should be changed occasionally. Unclaimed paychecks should not be returned to the payroll accounting unit but should be investigated and retained for a reasonable period of time by a person who is independent of the payroll functions. Checks that remain unclaimed beyond this period should be fully investigated for cause.

Donated Services

Hospitals sometimes receive services donated by various organizations whose members work without monetary compensation in certain areas of hospital activity. Donated services such as these should properly be recorded at fair market value only when (1) the donor and hospital have the equivalent of an employer-employee relationship, and (2) there is an objective basis for determining the amounts that might otherwise have been paid for such services. When these requirements are met, the determined amounts should be recorded as operating expenses with an offsetting credit to nonoperating revenues. The necessary entry (amount assumed) in general journal form is indicated as follows:

Salaries and wages expense—donated services	$28,400	
Nonoperating revenues— donated services		$28,400
To record fair market value of services donated to the hospital		

Services of a nonessential nature provided by guilds, auxiliaries, and similar organizations generally should not be recorded in the accounts.

Payroll-Related Costs

In addition to the basic earnings of hourly and salaried employees, a number of other related cost elements enter into hospital labor cost considerations. These elements include the previously discussed overtime earnings, vacation, holiday pay, sick pay, and the OASDI and Medicare taxes imposed on hospitals. Some other elements include unemployment taxes, workers compensation insurance, employee life and hospitalization insurance premiums, and pension plan costs. The total of these and other employee benefits constitutes a very substantial cost to the hospital (often 30 percent or more of total employee compensation).

Vacation Pay

After a specified period of employment, hospital employees generally are entitled to an annual vacation with full pay. Assuming a two-week vacation each year, employees in effect are paid for 50 weeks of work over a 52-week period. The reality of the situation is that the vacation pay is earned by employees, and is incurred as a cost by the hospital, during the 50 working weeks. It is incorrect, therefore, to defer recognition of vacation pay as an expense until it is actually paid. Instead, vacation pay should be charged to expense in the periods during which the employee earns it.

Example of Recording Vacation Pay Expense   To illustrate the necessary entries, let us assume that a hospital has 200 employees, each of whom earns $500 per week and is entitled to a two-week vacation each year. The proper weekly payroll entry for this group (disregarding withholdings) is as follows:

Salaries and wages expense	$104,000	
Cash		$100,000
Accrued vacation pay liability		4,000
Accrual of weekly payroll, including		
earned vacation pay		

In other words, each employee earns $1,000 ($500 × 2 weeks) of vacation pay over the 50 weeks of work, or $20 per week. This means that $4,000 ($20 × 200 employees) should be charged to expense weekly with a corresponding accrual of the vacation pay liability. When vacations are taken, the liability account is debited and cash is credited.

Unemployment Taxes

In addition to FICA taxes, hospitals may also be subject to federal and state tax laws dealing with unemployment compensation. The gross federal unemployment tax (FUTA) is at this writing (2005) 6.2 percent of the first $7,000 of taxable wages paid to each employee during a given year, but a maximum 5.4 percent credit may be allowed for participation in a state unemployment tax (SUTA) program. Thus, the net federal tax is currently 0.8 percent. State tax laws vary, but we will assume a 5.4 percent rate.

In any event, the hospital must accrue these taxes on each payroll by making an entry such as the following (assuming a $100,000 payroll):

Employee benefits — FUTA		
(0.8% of $100,000)	$ 800	
Employee benefits — SUTA		
(5.4% of $100,000)	5,400	
FUTA taxes payable		$ 800
SUTA taxes payable		5,400
Accrual of payroll tax expenses		

Notice that in this case, these taxes are charged to the employee benefits account under the unassigned expense classification rather than to departmental expense centers. An employer may choose to charge these directly to individual departments or to an unassigned expense classification. This is a decision based upon preference. If charged to an unassigned account, these expenses should be allocated to departmental expense centers in the cost-finding procedure at the end of the year.

FUTA and SUTA Charged to Employee Benefits Account

Observe that the unemployment taxes are paid by the hospital; these taxes are not withheld from employees' wages. Periodically, as required by law, the hospital must submit unemployment tax reports and remit the taxes to the appropriate governmental agency.

Other Cost Elements

States have workers compensation laws that provide various benefits to disabled workers. In some cases, a tax is imposed on the employer, but more often the state laws establish standard benefits and allow hospitals to provide for such benefits through the purchase of appropriate insurance from a commercial insurance company. The premiums paid by the hospital are charged to expense (employee benefits).

Life, health, accident, disability, dental, and hospitalization insurance plans often are established on a group basis by hospitals on behalf of their employees. Participation in these group programs generally is voluntary, but the hospital frequently pays a substantial portion of the premiums as an employee benefit. Such payments by the hospital naturally are chargeable to expense in the employee benefits classification.

Increasing attention recently has been given to the establishment of pension and retirement plans for hospital employees. All or most of the costs of such programs frequently are paid by the hospital. A discussion of the rather complex accounting procedures involved, however, is beyond the scope of this book.

This concludes the discussion of payroll accounting. Having studied this and the materials on revenues and cash receipts in the preceding chapter, we can now begin our examination of Hartful Hospital's procedures for non-labor expenses, accounts payable, and cash disbursements.

Questions

Q13.1.   Give four reasons why employee compensation generally comprises more than 50 percent of total operating expenses in hospitals.

Q13.2.   An employee of Mount Hospital is paid $8.80 per hour for a normal workweek of 40 hours. During a given week, this employee worked a total of 50 hours. Compute the employee's earnings for that week, assuming time and a half for overtime work.

Q13.3.   What is the current FICA (OASDI and Medicare) tax rate? What is the maximum annual amount of FICA tax that is paid by an employee?

Q13.4.   An employee of Monroe Hospital earns a salary of $4,000 per month, payable on the first day of the following month. Assume that the federal income tax withholding is 20 percent and that the FICA tax is 7 percent. With respect to this one employee, make the following necessary entries:

a. Record the employee's gross earnings, tax deductions, and net pay for January 20X1.

b. Accrue the hospital's share of FICA taxes as of January 31, 20X1.

c. Record issuance of the paycheck on February 1, 20X1.

d. Record remittance of January payroll taxes to the government.

Q13.5.   Other than taxes, list five types of withholding deductions that often are made from hospital employees' paychecks.

Q13.6.   Describe briefly the general procedures followed in computing the gross payroll in a hospital for a given pay period.

Q13.7.   How should hospital accountants record donated services?

Q13.8.   The fair market value of donated services received by Madison Hospital during April 20X1 was $31,400. Make the necessary entry at April 30, 20X1, to record these donated services.

Q13.9.   Briefly describe the basic features of a good internal control system for a hospital payroll.

Q13.10.   Lucky Hospital has 450 employees, each of whom earns $800 per week and is entitled to a two-week vacation each year. Disregarding withholding deductions, make the proper weekly payroll entry for this group of employees. Twenty of these employees take their vacations during the first two weeks of June. Make the necessary entry to record the paychecks issued to these 20 employees for the vacation period.

Q13.11.   Liston Hospital's gross payroll for January 20X1 is $250,000. Assuming a 0.5 percent federal unemployment tax rate and a 2.5 percent state unemployment tax rate, make the necessary entry to accrue the hospital's unemployment tax expense for January 20X1.

Q13.12.   As a part of the regular accounting routine, should unemployment taxes and the hospital's share of FICA taxes be charged to departmental cost center accounts? Explain your answer.

Q13.13.   Explain briefly how state workers compensation laws affect the hospital's payroll accounting.

Q13.14.   Describe briefly the operation of an imprest payroll checking account. What are the advantages of such a system?

Q13.15. An employee of Lefferson Hospital is paid $10 per hour for a regular workweek of 40 hours. During a particular week, this employee worked 48 hours. Assume that the FICA tax is 8 percent and that 20 percent of the employee's gross pay is withheld for federal income taxes. Assume also that the federal unemployment tax is 2 percent and that the state unemployment tax is 5 percent. Make all necessary entries for this week.

Q13.16. Lason Hospital's payroll for the month ended May 31, 20X1, is summarized as follows:

- Gross payroll, $462,000
- FIT withheld, 20 percent
- FICA withheld, 8 percent
- FUTA rate, 2 percent
- SUTA rate, 4 percent

Indicate how the May payroll would be entered in the journal and ledger systems described in Chapter 13.

Q13.17. What specific information would you expect to find on an employee's individual earnings record?

Q13.18. An employee of Loppup Hospital earns a salary of $1,000 per month, payable on the first day of the following month. Assume the following tax rates:

- FIT, 20 percent
- FICA, 8 percent
- FUTA, 2 percent
- SUTA, 5 percent

For this employee, make all necessary entries to record the March 20X1 payroll and related matters. Indicate the journal in which each entry should be made.

14

EXPENSES, PAYABLES, AND CASH DISBURSEMENTS

In accounting for hospital expenses, considerable attention naturally is given to salaries, wages, and employee benefits. These costs added together typically represent more than 50 percent of total operating expenses. The remaining expenses, however, require the same careful attention by hospital accountants. Very substantial amounts are expended each year for supplies, utilities, other purchased services, insurance, interest, and other items. Effective management of these nonlabor costs requires the use of sound accounting procedures.

This chapter examines Hartful Hospital's accounting system as it relates to these expenses, along with the corresponding liabilities and cash disbursements. The discussion touches briefly on the purchasing and receiving functions, two of the major components of good supply chain management, describing the voucher system and illustrating the use of the voucher register and the cash disbursements journal. In the last part of this chapter, you will also see a summary of postings from all of Hartful Hospital's journals to the general ledger accounts. This is provided in an effort to tie together the materials of Chapters 10 through 14.

Purchasing

Procurement of supplies and services is a function of major importance in hospitals. It cuts across all departmental lines and accounts for a significant percentage of the hospital's annual expenditures. The purchasing responsibility consists basically of acquiring required supplies and services of the appropriate quality, in the proper quantities, at the times needed, and at reasonable costs. Ideally, the purchasing function is centralized and performed by an organized purchasing department headed by an experienced purchasing agent. This tends to minimize waste and duplication through standardization of buying and using many of the supply items required in the provision of hospital services. Limited authority to purchase certain products and services, however, sometimes must be given to selected department heads. In smaller hospitals, administrative personnel may do the buying personally or may carefully supervise and coordinate it.

Initiating Purchases with the Purchase Requisition

To set the wheels of purchasing in motion, the purchasing department must be made aware of the need to purchase. In the manual process, this may be accomplished through the preparation of a purchase requisition form, such as the one illustrated in Figure 14.1. An inventory storekeeper or department manager generally fills out this form. A copy of the purchase requisition is sent to the purchasing department to inform that department of the items to be purchased; a duplicate copy is retained in a file as evidence that the request was made.

The purchasing department, noting that the purchase requisition is properly authorized, makes appropriate choices of quantity, price, and vendor, in accordance with prescribed administrative policies. A purchase order, one form of which is presented in Figure 14.2, is then prepared to acquire the supplies or services desired. The purchase order generally is a multipart form with several copies, distributed as follows:

1. One copy of the purchase order is sent to the accounting department for subsequent use in invoice audit and approval for payment. The information also is useful in the budgeting of cash disbursements.
2. A second copy is sent to the requisitioning department and/or store-keeper as notification that the order has been placed. The originator of the purchase will match this copy with the retained copy of the purchase requisition to make sure that the purchasing department received and acted on all requisitions.
3. Two copies are sent to the vendor company. One copy is for the vendor's own use; the other is signed and returned to the hospital's purchasing department as an acknowledgment of the order and the vendor's intent to fill it.
4. In some systems, another copy of the purchase order is routed to the hospital's receiving department (or to the inventory storeroom, where the storekeeper performs the receiving function). This copy, however, generally should not provide information about quantities ordered.
5. A final copy is retained by the purchasing department in an unfilled orders file, which is carefully monitored to avoid delays in the acquisition of desired supplies and services.

When the vendor returns the acknowledgment copy of the purchase order to indicate its acceptance of the order on the terms specified, the purchasing department will match this document with the copy of the purchase order in the unfilled orders file. The document will be retained in this file and is monitored until the purchasing department is notified of the receipt of the items purchased. An acknowledged purchase order constitutes a legal contract with the supplier, and all required information (including quantities, accurate description, price, and terms) therefore must be carefully indicated.

FIGURE 14.1

Sample of a
Purchase
Requisition

HARTFUL HOSPITAL
PURCHASE REQUISITION   PURCHASE ORDER NO. _____

DEPARTMENT_____ DATE _____ 20_____

FLOOR OR DIVISION _____ DATE REQUIRED_____ 20_____

TO ELIMINATE DELAY KINDLY FURNISH COMPLETE DESCRIPTION OF ARTICLE				
QUANTITY	UNIT	DESCRIPTION OF ARTICLE	(State fully what item is to be used for)	UNIT PRICE

REQUESTED BY

APPROVED BY

SEND ORIGINAL TO PURCHASING AGENT. DUPLICATE IS RETAINED BY STORE ROOM CLERK OR DEPARTMENT HEAD.

There is an interesting sidelight to the above-described manual process. In the 21st century, many hospitals have been able to automate these processes, and many have effectively gone paperless. All parts of the process that starts with the purchase requisition and will ultimately end with payment for the goods or services are performed inside the information technology systems of the hospital, distributor and manufacturer, group purchasing organization (GPO), and their banks. For purposes of this book, we will provide the manual processes with the understanding that many organizations have now automated all of the processing and reporting functions of the supply chain.

Receiving

On receipt of purchased supplies from vendors, the hospital's receiving department manager has the responsibility for counting, weighing, or otherwise measuring the quantities of goods received. The quality and condition of the goods are also checked. As a result of this process, a receiving report, such as the one shown in Figure 14.3, is prepared. (In some systems, the packing slip, bill of lading, or a copy of the purchase order may serve this purpose.) After the incoming shipment has been examined in this way, the goods are moved into the hospital storerooms (or directed to the appropriate

FIGURE 14.2
Sample of a
Purchase Order

PURCHASE ORDER	HARTFUL HOSPITAL	NO. 49793
	ADDRESS	
	CITY–STATE–ZIP CODE	THIS ORDER NUMBER MUST APPEAR ON ALL CORRESPON- DENCE, INVOICES, PACKAGES, AND SHIPPING PAPERS

TO

DATE _____ 20___
DEPT. _____
SHIP VIA _____
F.O.B. _____
TERMS_____
DELIVERY
REQUIRED _____

QUANTITY	DESCRIPTION	PRICE	PER UNIT	AMOUNT

BY _____

department). Supplies placed in the hospital's general storerooms remain there, under the storekeeper's control, until issued from the inventory for use in various service departments.

Preparing a Receiving Report

The receiving report is prepared as a record of the quantity of goods actually received. A copy of the receiving report is sent to the purchasing department, where it is used to clear the related purchase order from the unfilled-orders file. A second copy is routed to the accounting department to be used in subsequent invoice processing and approval for payment. Another copy follows the goods into the storeroom, and the receiving department may retain a final copy as a work record.

Recording Purchases

In due course, the vendor bills the hospital for the items purchased. When it arrives in the incoming mail, the invoice, which should be addressed to the accounts payable department, should be sent directly from the mailroom to the

FIGURE 14.3

Sample of a Receiving Report

HARTFUL HOSPITAL		
RECEIVING REPORT		

NO. _____

DATE _____ 20___

RECEIVED FROM _____

ADDRESS _____

PURCHASE ORDER NO. _____

QUANTITY	UNIT	DESCRIPTION OF ARTICLE

RECEIVED_____

accounts payable department. In this department, the three documents relating to the purchase—the purchase order, the receiving report, and the vendor's bill or invoice—are then matched. This comparison is made to ascertain the correctness of prices, quantities, invoice extensions (quantities × unit prices), and other matters. This is commonly known as the three-way match.

Preparing the Voucher/Check and Voucher Package

In the voucher system employed by Hartful Hospital, a combination voucher/check is now prepared in duplicate and is attached to the other three documents to form what is called a voucher package, as illustrated in Figure 14.4. The package is turned over to the accounting employee responsible for maintaining the hospital's voucher register.

Entering Information in the Voucher Register

On the basis of the information contained in the approved voucher packages, the transactions are entered in the voucher register, as shown in Figure 14.5. Once these entries are made, the voucher packages are placed in a file of unpaid vouchers, where they are retained until their respective due dates. This file functions as the accounts payable subsidiary ledger in some accounting

FIGURE 14.4

Components of
the Voucher
Package

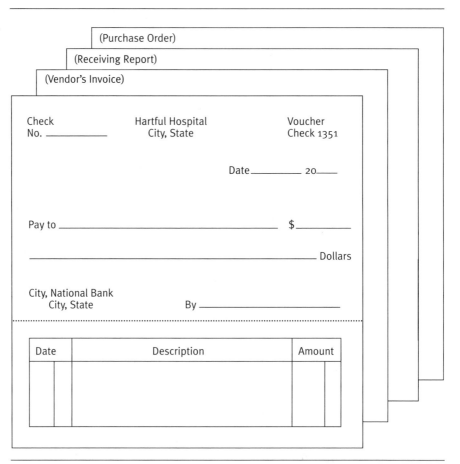

(Purchase Order)

(Receiving Report)

(Vendor's Invoice)

| Check No. _____ | Hartful Hospital City, State | Voucher Check 1351 |

Date _____ 20 _____

Pay to _____ $ _____

_____ Dollars

City, National Bank
City, State   By _____

Date	Description	Amount

systems. In other systems, postings are made to individual vendor or supplier accounts in much the same manner as described earlier for accounts receivable. In any case, the subsidiary record for accounts payable should be reconciled regularly with the control account for accounts payable in the general ledger.

Examine the sample entries in Figure 14.5's voucher register. On May 1, 20X1, for example, you see the entry to record a $450 voucher for the purchase of certain pharmaceuticals. This required a debit to supplies expense—pharmacy (60270) and a credit to accounts payable (20100). The entry indicates how individual vouchers are journalized in the register. As an alternative, all the vouchers issued on a given day may be summarized and entered on a single line of the register, as illustrated by the entry of May 2, 20X1. The sample entry of May 10, 20X1, relates to the purchase of an item of depreciable equipment. This entry demonstrates the use of the sundry debit and credit columns, and emphasizes the fact that all disbursements (no matter what the purpose) must be vouchered through accounts payable.

Notice also the voucher register entries of May 31, 20X1. Vouchering of the May payroll requires the preparation of (1) a voucher in the

FIGURE 14.5 The Voucher Register

20X1 Date		Account Payable Cr.	(✓)	Payroll-Related Debits			Nursing Services Expense Debits				Other Professional Services Expense Debits			
				Accrued Payroll	FIT Withheld	FICA W/H & Accrued	Nursing Units	Operating Room	Emergency Room	Central Supply	Laboratory	Radiology	Pharmacy	Anesthesia
5	1	450											450	
	2	4,690									1,820	1,400		
	10	16,000	✓											
	31	227,080	✓	227,080										
	31	81,440	✓		48,400	33,040								
Totals		429,328		227,080	48,400	33,040	23,120	4,600	3,900	9,800	4,100	4,700	7,460	2,200
		Credit		Debit	Debit	Debit	Debit	Debit	Debit	Debit	Debit	Debit	Debit	Debit
		20100		20400	20410	20420	60210	60220	60230	60240	60250	60260	60270	60280

Continued

FIGURE 14.5 (CONTINUED) Voucher Register

| | Administrative Services Expense Debits | | | | | | | Sundry Debits and Credits | | |
Dietary	House-keeping	Laundry	Accounting	Admitting	Purchasing	Human Resources	Account Numbers	Dr.	Cr.
410								16,000	
21,500	3,800	4,300	7,008	6,100	1,020	1,200	16,000		
Debit 60291	Debit 60292	Debit 60293	Debit 60294	Debit 60295	Debit 60296	Debit 60297			

amount of $216,080 to record the amount to be transferred from the general checking account to the payroll checking account and (2) a voucher for $93,444 to record the liability to governmental agencies for payroll taxes withheld and accrued. Later, you will see entries in the cash disbursements journal to record payment of these vouchers. The following shows the payroll journal and general journal entries. Note that various departmental account numbers for salaries and wages expenses would appear in the account number column.

Payroll Journal

Salaries and wages expense	60100	$292,000	
FIT withheld	20410		$ 8,400
FICA withheld and accrued	20420		17,520
Accrued salaries and			
wages payable	20400		216,080
To record May payroll			

General Journal

Employee benefits—FICA	61100	$ 17,520	
FICA withheld and accrued	20420		$ 17,520
To record hospital's share of			
FICA taxes on May payroll			

Recording Cash Disbursements

Just prior to their due dates, the approved voucher packages are removed from the file for unpaid vouchers and are sent to the hospital's treasurer or other disbursing authority. These voucher packages, with the unsigned check included, may be examined by the disbursing officer to confirm the propriety of the disbursements proposed. When the officer is satisfied, he or she signs the checks and mails them directly to the vendor. (Signed checks should not be returned to the accounting department for mailing.) All documents in the voucher packages then are indelibly stamped or perforated "PAID" to prevent their reuse in support of another disbursement. The packages then are returned to the accounting department to the person responsible for the cash disbursements journal. This employee now records the paid vouchers in this journal, as illustrated in Figure 14.6. After these entries are made, the voucher packages marked as paid are placed in a file for paid vouchers; here they are kept for the period specified by the hospital's record retention policies.

Observe the illustrative entries in the journal. Check number 2275, for example, was issued on May 9, 20X1, in payment of the $450 voucher seen earlier in the voucher register. Because a 2 percent discount was deducted and credited to the purchase discounts earned account, the check was written for

FIGURE 14.6 Cash Disbursements Journal

20x1 Date	Description	Check Numbers	Cash Cr.	Purchases Discounts Cr.	Accounts Payable Dr.	Dr.	Sundry Debits and Credits Acount Numbers	Dr.	Cr.
5 9	Central Pharmaceutical Co.	2275	441	9	450				
31	Payroll Checking Account	2690	227,080		227,080				
31	Internal Revenue Service	2691	81,440		81,440				
	Totals		451,295	2,309	453,604				
			Credit	Credit	Debit	Debit			
			10110	40630	20100				

only $441. On May 31, 20X1, check number 2690 was issued to transfer the amount of the net payroll for May from the general checking account to the payroll checking account. Check number 2691 was written for the remittance of May payroll taxes withheld and accrued. (All checks issued on a given day may be summarized and entered on a single line of the journal, rather then journalizing each individual check.)

Summary of Procedures for Recording Transactions

To summarize the Hartful Hospital illustration in the last five chapters, let us examine the general ledger postings from all journals and present the hospital's financial statements for the five months ended May 31, 20X1. The revenue and cash receipts journals were shown in Chapter 12, the payroll journal was illustrated in Chapter 13, and the voucher register and cash disbursements journal were provided in this chapter. Now, in Figure 14.7, Hartful Hospital's general journal for May is reproduced to indicate the adjusting entries that were necessary at the end of the month.

Tracing the Postings for Hartful Hospital
It is suggested that you trace all the postings from each of Hartful Hospital's journals to the general ledger accounts provided in Figure 14.8. The posting references are as follows:

Posting Reference	
BB	Balance, May 1, 20X1 (assumed)
IRJ	Inpatient revenue journal (Chapter 12)
ORJ	Outpatient revenue journal (Chapter 12)
CRJ	Cash receipts journal (Chapter 12)
PJ	Payroll journal (Chapter 13)
VR	Voucher register (Chapter 14)
CDJ	Cash disbursements journal (Chapter 14)
GJ	General journal (Chapter 14)
CB	Balance, May 31, 20X1

After all postings are made from the journals, a trial balance (not shown here) is taken of the general ledger account balances at May 31, 20X1. Let us assume that this trial balance indicates the necessary equality of debit and credit balances.

Financial Statements and Supporting Schedules
Using the May 31, 20X1, general ledger balances, we present Hartful Hospital's statement of operations for the five months ended May 31, 20X1, in

FIGURE 14.7

General Journal

20X1 Date		Accounts and Explanations	Account Numbers	Dr.	Cr.
5	31	Inpatient receivables—discharged	10420	412,975	
		Inpatient receivable—in-house	10410		412,975
		To transfer unpaid account			
		balances from in-house to			
		discharged receivables			
	31	Accrued interest receivable	10300	1,350	
		Interest income	40300		1,350
		To accrue interest earned in May			
	31	Bad debt expense	60900	3,700	
		Contractual adjustments	50010	11,400	
		Charity care adjustments	50020	6,600	
		Allowance for uncollectible			
		accounts:			
		Bad debts	10510		3,700
		Contractuals	10520		11,400
		Charity service	10530		6,600
		To adjust allowance accounts to			
		correct balances			
	31	Insurance expense	60400	1,800	
		Prepaid insurance	10700		1,800
		To adjust for expiration of			
		insurance premiums			
	31	Depreciation expense	60700	28,000	
		Accumulated depreciation—			
		buildings	13100		13,000
		Accumulated depreciation—			
		equipment	14100		15,000
		To record depreciation expense			
		for May			
	31	Employee benefits	61100	16,520	
		FICA withheld and accrued	20420		16,520
		To accrue hospital's share of FICA			
		taxes on May payroll			
	31	Interest expense	60800	14,700	
		Accrued interest payable	20300		14,700
		To accrue interest expense for May			
	31	Deferred rental income	20500	1,800	
		Rental income	40400		1,800
		To record rental income earned			
		in May			

Cash—General Checking Account 10110	
BB 180,000	CDJ 451,295
CFJ 447,500	

Cash—Payroll Checking Account 10120	

Petty Cash Fund 10130	
BB 500	

Temporary Investments 10200	
BB 150,000	

Accrued Interest Receivable 10300	
BB 5,400	
GJ 1,350	

Inpatient Receivables— In-house 10410	
BB 110,000	CRJ 43,020
IRJ 453,995	GJ 412,975

Inpatient Receivables— Discharged 10420	
BB 800,000	CRJ 401,850
GJ 412,975	

Outpatient Receivables 10430	
BB 16,000	CRJ 57,900
ORJ 64,800	

Allowance for Bad Debts 10510	
	BB 11,000
	GJ 3,700

Allowance for Contractuals 10520	
	BB 56,000
	GJ 11,400

Allowance for Charity Service 10530	
	BB 28,000
	GJ 6,600

Inventory 10600	
BB 5,000,000	

Prepaid Income 10700	
BB 14,000	GJ 1,800

Land 12000	
BB 175,000	

Buildings 13000	
BB 5,000,000	

Accumulated Depreciation— Buildings 13100	
	BB 1,200,000
	GJ 13,000

Equipment 14000	
BB 3,000,000	
VR 16,000	

Accumulated Depreciation— Equipment 14100	
	BB 900,000
	GJ 15,000

Accounts Payable 20100	
CDJ 453,604	BB 65,000
	VR 458,600

Notes Payable 20200	
	BB 80,000

Accrued Interest Payable 20300	
	BB 18,300
	GJ 14,700

Accrued Salaries and Wages Payable 20400	
VR 227,080	PJ 227,080

FIT Withheld 20410	
VR 48,400	PJ 48,400

FICA Withheld and Accrued 20420	
VR 33,040	PJ 16,520
	GJ 16,520

FIGURE 14.8
General
Ledger

Continued

FIGURE 14.8 (Continued)
General Ledger

Deferred Rental Income 20500	
GJ 1,800	BB 9,600

Bonds Payable 25000	
	BB 2,400,000

Hospital Net Assets 30100	
	BB 4,559,240

Revenue and Expense Summary 30200	

Nursing Units— IP Revenues 40110	
	BB 896,500
	IRJ 187,500

Operating Room— IP Revenues 40120	
	BB 104,400
	IRJ 26,100

Emergency Room— IP Revenues 40130	
	BB 57,600
	IRJ 14,400

Central Supply—IP Revenues 40140	
	BB 136,400
	IRJ 34,100

Laboratory— IP Revenues 40150	
	BB 225,680
	IRJ 56,420

Radiology— IP Revenues 40160	
	BB 355,340
	IRJ 88,835

Pharmacy—IP Revenues 40170	
	BB 99,840
	IRJ 24,960

Anesthesia—IP Revenues 40180	
	BB 86,720
	IRJ 21,680

Operating Room—OP Revenues 40220	
	BB 15,600
	ORJ 3,900

Emergency Room—OP Revenues 40230	
	BB 36,100
	ORJ 9,000

Central Supply— OP Revenues 40240	
	BB 22,800
	ORJ 5,700

Laboratory—OP Revenues 40250	
	BB 68,160
	IRJ 17,040

Radiology—OP Revenues 40260	
	BB 86,520
	ORJ 21,630

Pharmacy—OP Revenues 40270	
	BB 23,520
	ORJ 5,880

Interest Income 40300	
	BB 5,400
	GJ 1,350

Purchase Discounts 40630	
	BB 9,240
	CDJ 2,309

Revenue Deductions— Contractual Adjustments 50010	
BB 126,400	
CRJ 31,600	
GJ 11,400	

Revenue Deductions— Charity Care 50020	
BB 67,600	
CRJ 14,400	
GJ 6,600	

Nursing Units S&W 60110	
BB 645,600	
VR 161,400	

Operating Room— S&W 60120	
BB 32,800	
PJ 8,200	

Continued

FIGURE 14.8
(CONTINUED)
General Ledger

Emergency Room— S&W 60130	
BB 25,600	
PJ 6,400	

Central Supply S&W 60140	
BB 30,800	
PJ 7,700	

Laboratory S&W 60150	
BB 32,800	
PJ 8,200	

Radiology S&W 60160	
BB 31,800	
PJ 7,700	

Pharmacy S&W 60170	
BB 19,600	
PJ 4,900	

Anesthesia S&W 60180	
BB 23,000	
PJ 5,500	

General Services Admin. Office S&W 60190	
BB 7,900	
PJ 2,000	

Dietary S&W 60191	
BB 37,600	
PJ 9,400	

Housekeeping S&W 60192	
BB 29,100	
PJ 7,500	

Laundry S&W 60193	
BB 15,300	
VR 4,300	

Accounting S&W 60194	
BB 26,800	
PJ 6,700	

Admitting S&W 60195	
BB 21,200	
PJ 5,300	

Purchasing S&W 60196	
BB 15,600	
VR 3,900	

Human Resources S&W 60197	
BB 16,400	
PJ 4,100	

Nursing Units S&E 60210	
BB 92,480	
PJ 23,120	

Operating Room S&E 60220	
BB 18,400	
VR 4,600	

Emergency Room S&E 60230	
BB 39,200	
VR 9,800	

Central Supply S&E 60240	
BB 39,200	
VR 9,800	

Laboratory S&E 60250	
BB 16,400	
VR 4,100	

Radiology S&E 60260	
BB 17,800	
VR 4,700	

Pharmacy S&E 60270	
BB 29,800	
VR 7,460	

Anesthesia S&E 60280	
BB 8,700	
VR 2,200	

General Services Admin. Office S&E 60290	
BB 5,200	
VR 1,300	

Dietary S&E 60291	
BB 86,000	
VR 21,500	

Continued

FIGURE 14.8
(CONTINUED)
General Ledger

Housekeeping			Laundry			Accounting		
	S&E	60292		S&E	60293		S&E	60294
BB 15,200			BB 15,300			BB 31,300		
VR 3,800			VR 4,300			VR 7,008		

Admitting			Purchasing			Human Resources		
	S&E	60295		S&E	60296		S&E	60298
BB 24,500			BB 4,100			BB 4,700		
VR 6,100			VR 1,020			VR 1,200		

Utilities			Insurance			Depreciation		
	S&W	60300		Expense	60400		Expense	60700
BB 24,800			BB 5,900			BB 112,000		
PJ 6,200			GJ 1,800			GJ 28,000		

Interest			Bad Debt			Employee		
	Expense	60800		Expense	60900		Benefits	61100
BB 48,700			BB 12,600			BB 66,300		
GJ 14,700			GJ 3,700			GJ 16,520		

Figure 14.9. Notice that certain totals contained in this statement are supported by a schedule of gross revenues from services to patients (Figure 14.10) and a schedule of operating expenses (Figure 14.11). You should examine this statement and accompanying schedules to acquaint yourself with both their format and content. You also will find it useful to trace some of the statement figures back to the general ledger accounts.

Figure 14.12 presents Hartful Hospital's balance sheet for May 31, 20X1. Carefully examine the format and content of this statement; also, try to trace some of the balance sheet figures back to the general ledger accounts. It is very important for you to have a good understanding of the flow of financial data from the journals, through the ledgers, and into the hospital's financial statements.

Questions

Q14.1. What is the purpose of a purchase requisition? Who prepares it? How many copies are usually made? To whom are the copies sent, and why?

Q14.2. What is the purpose of a purchase order? Who prepares it? How many copies are usually made? To whom are the copies sent, and why?

Gross patient services revenues:		
Routine services		$1,550,100
Ancillary services		1,190,475
Gross patient services revenues (Schedule A)		2,740,575
Less revenue deductions:		
Contractual adjustments	$169,400	
Charity care adjustments	88,600	
Total revenue deductions		258,000
Net patient services revenues		2,482,575
Other operating revenues:		
Cafeteria sales	102,400	
Rental income	6,600	
Purchase discounts earned	11,549	
Total other operating revenues		120,549
Total operating revenues		2,603,124
Less operating expenses:		
Nursing services	1,150,050	
Ancillary services	321,708	
Administrative services (including $140,000 of depreciation and $63,400 of interest)	955,022	
Bad debts	16,300	
Total operating expenses (Schedule B)		2,443,080
Operating income		160,044
Nonoperating income:		
Unrestricted contributions	13,150	
Interest income	6,750	
Total nonoperating income		19,900
Excess of revenues over expenses		$ 179,944

FIGURE 14.9
Hartful Hospital Statement of Operations, Five Months Ended May 31, 20X1

FIGURE 14.10
Hartful Hospital
Gross Patient
Services
Revenues,
Five Months
Ended May 31,
20X1

	Schedule A		
	Inpatients	Outpatients	Total
Routine services:			
Nursing units	$1,084,000		$1,084,000
Operating room	130,500	$ 19,500	150,000
Emergency room	72,000	45,100	117,100
Central supply	170,500	28,500	199,000
Total routine services revenues	1,457,000	93,100	1,550,100
Ancillary services:			
Laboratory	282,100	85,200	367,300
Radiology	444,175	108,150	552,325
Pharmacy	124,800	29,400	154,200
Anesthesiology	108,400	8,250	116,650
Total ancillary services	959,475	231,000	1,190,475
Totals	$2,416,475	$324,100	$2,740,575

Q14.3. Describe briefly the purchasing function in hospitals.

Q14.4. Describe briefly the receiving function in hospitals.

Q14.5. What is the purpose of a receiving report? Who prepares it? How many copies are usually made? To whom are the copies sent, and why?

Q14.6. What documents generally are included in a voucher package?

Q14.7. Describe the voucher system as a means of internal control over cash disbursements by hospitals.

Q14.8. On September 6, 20X1, Newton Hospital purchased $2,500 of dietary supplies on account, terms 2/10, n/30. In other words, if the account is paid within ten days after the invoice date, a 2 percent discount is given to the hospital. Otherwise, the full invoice amount ($2,500) is due and payable within 30 days following the invoice date. The invoice from the supplier is paid on September 15, 20X1. Indicate, in detail, how these transactions should be recorded in the hospital's voucher register, cash disbursements journal, accounts payable subsidiary ledger, and general ledger.

Q14.9. How often should postings be made from the voucher journal and the cash disbursements journal? Explain why the frequency is needed.

Q14.10. Nearby Hospital purchased a new item of equipment for $45,000 on May 27, 20X1. The supplier's invoice was paid on June 10, 20X1. Indicate how these transactions should be recorded in the voucher register, cash disbursements journal, and general ledger of the hospital.

	Schedule B		
	Salaries and Wages	Other Expenses	Total
Routine services:			
Nursing units	$ 820,950	$ 126,100	$ 947,050
Operating room	41,000	23,000	64,000
Emergency room	32,000	19,500	51,500
Central supply	38,500	49,000	87,500
Total routine services expense	932,450	217,600	1,150,050
Ancillary services:			
Laboratory services	60,000	29,000	89,000
Radiology	39,500	22,500	62,000
Pharmacy	24,500	37,260	61,760
Anesthesiology	89,500	19,448	108,948
Total ancillary services expense	213,500	108,208	321,708
Administrative services:			
Dietary	47,000	107,500	154,500
Housekeeping	36,600	19,000	55,600
Laundry	34,000	19,600	53,600
Accounting	43,400	44,808	88,208
Admitting	26,500	30,600	57,100
Purchasing	19,500	5,120	24,620
Human resources	20,500	5,900	26,400
Health information management	25,850	19,500	45,350
Other administrative services	31,700	17,700	49,400
Utilities	31,000	70,624	101,624
Insurance		7,700	7,700
Repair expense		4,700	4,700
Depreciation		140,000	140,000
Interest		63,400	63,400
Employee taxes and benefits		82,820	82,820
Total administrative services expense	316,050	638,972	955,022
Bad debt expense		16,300	16,300
Total operating expenses	$1,462,000	$981,080	$2,443,080

FIGURE 14.11

Hartful Hospital Operating Expenses, Five Months Ended May 31, 20X1

FIGURE 14.12

Hartful Hospital
Balance Sheet,
May 31, 20X1

Assets

Current assets:

Cash		$ 176,755
Temporary investments		150,000
Accrued interest receivable		6,750
Accounts receivable	942,025	
Less allowance for uncollectible accounts	116,700	825,325
Inventory		96,000
Prepaid expenses		12,200
Total current assets		$1,267,030

Property, plant, and equipment:

Land	175,000	
Buildings	5,000,000	
Equipment	3,016,000	
Total	8,191,000	
Less accumulated depreciation	2,128,000	
Net property, plant, and equipment		6,063,000
Total assets		$7,330,030

Liabilities and Net Assets

Current liabilities:

Accounts payable	$ 69,996	
Notes payable	80,000	
Accrued interest payable	33,000	
Deferred rental income	7,800	
Total current liabilities		$ 190,796
Bonds payable		2,400,000
Total liabilities		2,590,796
Hospital net assets, January 1, 20X1	4,559,240	
Excess of revenues over expenses for 5 months ended May 31, 20X1	179,994	
Hospital net assets, May 31, 20X1		4,739,234
Total liabilities and hospital net assets		$7,330,030

PRINCIPLES OF FUND ACCOUNTING

Prior to the issuance of Statement of Financial Accounting Standards (SFAS) No. 117 by the Financial Accounting Standards Board (FASB) and the *1996 AICPA Accounting and Auditing Guide for Health Care Organizations*, the not-for-profit industry used "fund accounting" for purposes of internal recordkeeping and managerial control. These funds were established to maintain control over the revenue received from patients and third parties for healthcare services provided by the hospital, as well as the receipt of contributions, donations, gifts, grants, and endowment resources. Each fund consisted of a self-balancing group of accounts comprised of assets, liabilities, and net assets.

Still, SFAS No. 117, issued in the early 1990s, concluded that although some not-for-profit organizations may choose to classify assets and liabilities into fund groups, information about these groupings is not necessarily a part of general-purpose external financial reporting. Although SFAS No. 117 does not preclude the use of fund accounting for internal purposes, each of the individual internal funds must now be classified into one or more of the following three broad classes of net assets:

1. **Unrestricted net assets** are generated out of operating activities (similar to retained earnings in a for-profit business enterprise).
2. **Temporarily restricted net assets** are restricted by donors and are used for specific purposes once restrictions are set. These restrictions are usually met with the passage of time.
3. **Permanently restricted net assets** are also restricted by donors and are used for specific purposes. However, these restrictions do not expire and cannot be removed.

Certain of these funded resources might be available, at the discretion of the governing board, for the financing of the regular day-to-day operating activities of the hospital. Let us assume, for example, that a person gives Hartful Hospital $25,000 in cash and says to the hospital, "Use this money however you wish!" There is no stipulation or restriction by the donor about the specific purpose for which the money is to be used. In cases such as this, regardless of the amount involved, the resources are classified as unrestricted net assets. Although the receipt of such resources must be recorded by the hospital as nonoperating revenue (40810, unrestricted contributions), the resources may be used to acquire plant assets, to pay operating expenses, or for any other purpose determined by the governing board.

Other contributed resources received by hospitals, however, may be restricted by donors to specific uses and purposes, such as constructing new hospital buildings, purchasing new equipment, or financing hospital charity work, research, and educational activities. Such resources are not available for any purpose other than that specified by the donor. Let us assume, for example, that an individual gives Hartful Hospital $25,000 in cash and says to the hospital, "Use this money to purchase new equipment for your radiology department." In all such cases, regardless of the amount involved, the resources are classified as **restricted resources** and will be considered either temporarily or permanently restricted, depending on the donor's wishes.

There is both a legal and a moral obligation on the part of the hospital to comply fully with donors' restrictions and stipulations. Failing to observe the stated wishes of donors or not providing a proper accounting for the use or disposition of donor-restricted resources may give rise to very serious legal penalties.

Aside from the legal obligation to fulfill donors' requirements, there is also an administrative or managerial need to maintain in the accounting records a careful distinction between unrestricted and restricted resources. A hospital's managers, in making their financing and investing decisions, must have information regarding which resources are available for any general operating purpose and which resources are limited to particular donor-restricted purposes. Otherwise, unauthorized and even illegal use might be made of donated resources. Furthermore, donors often require from the hospital a periodic accounting for the use of the donated resources.

This internal system of accounting for funds (now called net assets accounting) has evolved in response to these stewardship (fiduciary) accountability requirements. It is the objective of this chapter to give you an opportunity to learn the basic principles of the fund accounting system. Because many not-for-profit hospitals employ fund accounting procedures, the materials in this chapter deserve your attention. The discussion, however, will be at an introductory level.

Nature of Fund Accounting

You will recall from the previous section that SFAS No. 117 does not preclude the use of fund accounting for internal purposes, but that each of the individual internal funds must now be classified into one of the three broad classes of net assets. Thus, this book will now discuss some of the aspects of fund accounting that will then lead to the further net assets classification.

Assets	$8,500				
Liabilities	2,500				
Net assets	6,000				
Total liabilities and net assets	$8,500				

FIGURE 15.1
Community
Hospital
Balance Sheet,
September 30,
20X1

	Unrestricted Fund	Restricted Funds			Total All Funds
		Fund A	Fund B	Fund C	
Assets	$4,000	$1,000	$2,000	$1,500	$8,500
Liabilities	1,900	200	400	-0-	2,500
Hospital net assets	2,100	800	1,600	1,500	6,000
Total liabilities and net assets	$4,000	$1,000	$2,000	$1,500	$8,500

FIGURE 15.2
Community
Hospital
Balance Sheet,
September 30,
20X1

Fund accounting may be defined as a system of accounting in which the resources (and related obligations) of a hospital are segregated in the accounting records into self-balancing sets of accounts (funds) for the purpose of carrying on specific activities or attaining particular objectives in accordance with legal and other restrictions. The hospital itself is the primary accounting entity. In a fund accounting system, however, this primary entity is broken down into a number of subordinate accounting entities funds.

In view of this rather complex definition, perhaps your understanding of fund accounting will be enhanced if you consider a simple example. Take a moment to examine Figure 15.1, a consolidated balance sheet for an assumed Community Hospital.

This balance sheet could be quite misleading about the financial position of Community Hospital, however, if there were donor or other externally imposed restrictions on the hospital's use of certain of its assets. Assuming there are such restrictions, a revised balance sheet is shown in Figure 15.2 as it would appear in accordance with the principles of fund accounting and net assets reporting.

Reporting Resources Available to Pay Particular Liabilities

Clearly, this revised balance sheet provides a much different impression of Community Hospital's financial position. We see that of the $8,500 of assets, only $4,000 is unrestricted and available for general operating purposes. These are the only assets that can be used to pay the $1,900 of liabilities reported in the unrestricted fund. The other $4,500 of hospital net assets are restricted by donors to particular uses, whatever they may be. So, the column in Figure 15.2 that totals all funds really has no particular significance to the hospital's creditors. It is included only to indicate the relationship between Figures 15.1 and 15.2.

Thus, in fund accounting and net assets reporting, assets and related liabilities are segregated in the hospital's accounts and reports into unrestricted and restricted funds, depending on the absence or presence of donor or other externally imposed restrictions. In this context, net assets do not mean cash, but simply a self-balancing group of related accounts. Notice that net assets, both unrestricted and restricted, consist of equal debits (assets) and credits (liabilities and net assets). This equality is maintained throughout all operations in the fund and net assets accounting process.

Maximum of One Unrestricted Fund

Observe that Community Hospital has a single unrestricted fund account. In fund accounting and net assets reporting, there is one (and only one) unrestricted fund. On the other hand, the hospital has three restricted funds. Restricted resources, as you will shortly see, are classified according to the three major types of restrictions that are externally imposed on donated resources.

Restrictions from External Sources Only

An extremely important point to recognize here is that the term *restricted* should be used only to refer to resources that are *externally restricted*. That is, when we speak of restricted funds, we are referring to a self-balancing set of accounts containing resources whose use has been restricted by persons or other entities external to the hospital. The hospital's governing board, by its actions, can designate certain assets to particular uses, but the board does not have the power to restrict their use in terms of the hospital's legal relationships with its creditors.

Restricted Funds Versus Board-Designated Assets

The board can make whatever designations it wishes for internal management purposes, but if donors do not restrict the use of resources they contribute to the hospital, the board cannot do it for the donors. Moreover, what the board can do, it can undo. So, this text does not refer to "board-restricted funds." When the board earmarks certain assets for a specific purpose, the term **board-designated assets** describes the situation. Assets that are so designated, however, are unrestricted assets and must be reported as a part of the hospital's unrestricted fund.

Note that many hospitals have established separately incorporated foundations. A foundation seeks and receives donations on behalf of the hospital. Eventually, the donated resources are transferred from the foundation to the hospital, but an in-depth discussion of this topic is beyond the scope of this book.

Types of Funds

Fund accounting and net assets reporting, as it is employed by hospitals, uses three major categories of net assets: unrestricted, temporarily restricted, and permanently restricted. There is only one unrestricted fund, but restricted funds, whether temporarily or permanently restricted, may be classified into three major types: (1) specific-purpose funds, (2) plant replacement and expansion funds, and (3) endowment funds. For purposes of this book, we will assume that many hospitals still prefer to use internal designated funds for control purposes. Thus, we will briefly examine the nature and content of each of these types of funds and then describe their general placement with the three net assets categories on the balance sheet.

Unrestricted Fund

An **unrestricted fund** (sometimes called a *general fund*) may be maintained by hospitals. In all cases, an unrestricted or general fund will be included as an unrestricted net asset on the balance sheet. This fund includes all hospital resources, with related obligations, that are not restricted by any external authority or donor. All of the resources of this fund are available for general operating activities at the discretion of the hospital's governing board. In addition, the accounts of the unrestricted fund include all the revenues and expenses to be reported in the hospital's statement of operations.

Think back to the extended Hartful Hospital illustration of the last five chapters; all of the accounts were unrestricted fund accounts, which were then classified as unrestricted net assets. The chart of accounts presented in Chapter 10 is, except for a few accounts to be added in this and later chapters, a chart of accounts for Hartful Hospital's unrestricted net assets.

Restricted Funds

Some hospitals receive substantial amounts of resources by donation. If donors attach no strings, such resources are recorded as unrestricted net assets regardless of any action that might be taken by the hospital's governing board. It must be presumed that if the donor wished to restrict the use of the resources, the donor would do so at the time of donation. If the donors make no such restrictions, the governing board cannot do it for the donors because such board actions would not be proper or legally binding.

A majority of donated resources, however, are restricted in some way by donors. These resources are of three major types:

1. Resources restricted for specific operating purposes
2. Resources restricted for acquisition of plant assets
3. Resources restricted as endowments

These resources are recorded in three types of restricted funds:

1. Specific-purpose fund
2. Plant replacement and expansion fund
3. Endowment fund

All restricted fund accounts have assets, liabilities, and/or net assets or net assets accounts only. There are no revenue or expense accounts for the restricted funds, although it can be argued that the use of such accounts would be logical and useful.

Specific-Purpose Funds Resources that are restricted by donors for purposes other than plant assets acquisitions or endowments are recorded in a specific-purpose fund. Assume, for example, that Hartful Hospital receives $25,000 in cash from a donor who restricts the use of the resources to a specific purpose, such as charity service, research activities, or educational programs conducted by the hospital. The specific-purpose fund entry uses the following general format:

Cash	17110	$25,000	
Donated resources received	27131		$25,000
Receipt of resources donor-restricted			
to educational programs			

Depending upon the donor's wishes and directions as stipulated in the donation document, these specific-purpose funds will be either permanently or temporarily restricted. Once recorded for their specific purpose and their designation as temporarily or permanently restricted, these resources remain restricted funds until such time as the specified purposes are completed by appropriate activity in the unrestricted fund, such as rendering charity service to indigent patients, performing research work, or providing educational programs.

As expenditures are made for the donor-specified purposes by the unrestricted fund, periodic transfers of the previously restricted resources are made to the unrestricted fund from the appropriate specific-purpose fund. Assuming that the $25,000 is transferred to the unrestricted fund to finance educational programs, the necessary entries are as follows:

Specific-Purpose Fund			
Transfers to unrestricted fund	27141	$25,000	
Cash	17110		$25,000
Transfer of resources to			
unrestricted fund to finance			
educational programs			

Unrestricted Fund

Cash	10110	$25,000	
Transfers from restricted funds for for educational programs	40640		$25,000
Resources received from specific-purpose fund to finance educational programs			

Notice that the account (40640) credited in the unrestricted fund is a revenue account in the "other operating revenues" category. Because expenditures for educational programs are recorded as unrestricted fund expenses, this credit accomplishes an appropriate matching of revenues and expenses. Similar procedures would be followed for transfers related to charity service and research activities.

Until transfers such as these are made, however, the resources of the specific-purpose funds should be prudently invested. Income and gains on these investments should be credited to the proper specific-purpose fund accounts. At the end of each fiscal year, these accounts should be closed to the specific-purpose fund balance, which will then be reported in the appropriate temporarily or permanently restricted net assets on the balance sheet.

Cash and other restricted resources received from donors and other external authorities for the acquisition of plant assets are included in the plant replacement and expansion fund. Assume, for example, that a donor gives the hospital $80,000 for the purchase of a new item of radiological equipment. The entry in a plant replacement and expansion fund is as follows: **Plant Replacement and Expansion Funds**

Cash	16110	$80,000	
Donated resources received	26131		$80,000
Receipt of resources donor-restricted to purchase of plant assets			

Until the equipment is purchased using the resources of the unrestricted fund, this $80,000 remains in the plant replacement and expansion fund. The $80,000 should be placed in some form of income-producing investment. Income and gains on such investments should be credited to accounts 27132 and 27133. At the end of the year, these accounts (along with accounts 26121, 26124, 26131, and 26141) are closed to the plant replacement and expansion fund balance account (26100).

When the equipment is purchased by the unrestricted fund, $80,000 (plus any net investment income) is transferred to the unrestricted fund. The entries to record the transfer are the following:

Plant Replacement and Expansion Fund

Transfers to unrestricted fund	26141	$80,000	
Cash	16110		$80,000
Transfer of resources to unrestricted fund to finance purchase of equipment for radiology department			

Unrestricted Fund

Cash	10110	$80,000	
Transfers from plant replacement and expansion fund	29122		$80,000
Receipt of resources from plant replacement and expansion fund to finance purchase of equipment			

The credit in the unrestricted fund is made to a temporary unrestricted fund balance account, not a revenue account. Plant assets, including those that are purchased with previously restricted resources, are not recorded in the plant replacement and expansion fund but in the unrestricted fund.

In some instances, a hospital receives promises to give from donors to contribute money for future purchases of plant assets. The receipt of such promises to give should be recorded in the plant replacement and expansion fund as follows:

Pledges receivable	16400	$40,000	
Allowance for uncollectible pledges	16500		$ 4,000
Donated resources received	26131		36,000
Receipt of promises to give (estimated to be 90% collectible) donor-restricted to the acquisition of plant assets			

A similar procedure is followed for the receipt of promises to give relating to other funds. Figure 15.3 indicates the relevant accounts used in the other funds.

Another important point concerns the procedure to be followed when plant assets are donated in kind to a hospital. Assume, for example, that a donor gives the hospital an item of equipment having a fair market value of $80,000 (rather than giving the hospital $80,000 with which to purchase the equipment). Where this occurs, no entry is made in the plant replacement and expansion fund. Instead, the following entry is made in the unrestricted fund:

Equipment	14000	$80,000	
Value of donated plant assets	29130		$80,000
Receipt of donated equipment at fair market value			

	Account Numbers			
	Plant Replacement and Expansion Fund	Specific-Purpose Fund	Endowment Fund	Unrestricted Fund
Assets				
Cash—general checking account	16110	17110	18110	
Temporary investments	16200	17200	18200	
Accrued income receivable	16300	17300	18300	
Pledges receivable	16400	17400	18400	19400
Allowance for uncollectible pledges	16500	17500	18500	19500
Due from unrestricted fund	16910	17910	18910	
Due from plant P&E fund		17920	18920	19920
Due from specific-purpose fund	16930		18930	19930
Due from endowment fund	16940	17940		19940
Other assets	16950	17950	18950	19950
Liabilities and Fund Balance				
Due to unrestricted fund	26810	27810	28810	
Due to plant P&E fund		27820	28820	29820
Due to specific-purpose fund	26830		28830	29830
Due to endowment fund	26840	27840		29840
Fund balance	26100	27100	28100	
Transfers from unrestricted fund	26121			
Transfers from plant P&E fund				29122
Transfers from specific purpose fund				a
Transfers from endowment fund	26124	27124		a
Donated resources received	26131	27131	28131	
Investment income	26132	27132		
Investment gains and losses	26133	27133	28133	
Transfers to unrestricted fund	26141	27141		
Transfers to plant P&E fund				29142

[a]See text discussion later in this chapter

FIGURE 15.3

Hartful Hospital Chart of Accounts— Restricted Funds Including Additional Unrestricted Fund Accounts

The account credited is not a revenue account but a temporary unrestricted fund balance account. A donation of plant assets in kind is assumed to be a contribution to the permanent capital of the hospital and is not reported as revenue in the statement of operations.

Endowment Funds

Endowments consist of contributed resources that, by donor restriction, are not to be expended but are to be held intact for the production of income. By their very definition, endowment funds are almost always classified as permanently restricted net assets. Assume, for example, that Hartful Hospital receives $100,000 from a donor who specifies that the money is to be invested in securities and held as an endowment of the hospital. The endowment fund entries are as follows:

Cash	18110	$100,000	
Donated resources received	28131		$100,000
Receipt of resources to be held			
as an endowment			

Investments	18200	$100,000	
Cash	18110		$100,000
To record the investment of			
endowment funds received			

At the year's end, account 28131 (along with account 28133) is closed to the endowment fund balance account (28100).

Income from investments of endowment funds may be donor- restricted or immediately available for general operating purposes. If the income is restricted by the donor to specific operating purposes, for example, this income should not be recorded in the endowment fund but should be recorded directly in the appropriate specific-purpose fund as follows (amount is assumed):

Cash	17110	$ 7,500	
Transfers from endowment fund	27124		$ 7,500
Receipt of income earned on			
endowment fund investments and			
donor-restricted for specific operating			
purposes			

If the income is donor restricted to the acquisition of plant assets, the income should be recorded directly in the plant replacement and expansion fund through accounts 16110 and 26124 in the manner illustrated earlier.

On the other hand, the income earned on endowment fund investments may not be donor restricted in any way. In these cases, the income should be recorded directly in the unrestricted fund as follows:

Cash	10110	$7,500	
Unrestricted income from			
endowment fund	40830		$7,500
Receipt of unrestricted income from			
endowment fund investments			

Notice that the credit in the unrestricted fund is to a revenue account to be reported as nonoperating revenues in the hospital's statement of operations.

Thus, investment income on endowment funds is directly recorded in a fund other than the endowment fund. It is not correct to record the income initially in the endowment fund and later to transfer it to another fund. Gains and losses on endowment fund investments, however, generally are recorded in the endowment fund (28133) on the theory that gains and losses follow the endowment fund principal rather than the endowment fund income.

Questions

Q15.1. Distinguish between unrestricted and restricted resources.

Q15.2. Define *fund accounting*. Why is fund accounting a useful system of accounting for many hospitals?

Q15.3. What is a "board-designated fund"? Explain why the resources of funds of this kind are not classified as restricted resources.

Q15.4. Offside Hospital received donations of an item of medical equipment having a fair market value of $100,000 and $100,000 cash restricted by the donor to the purchase of medical equipment. How should each of these donations be accounted for when received? Explain why the treatment differs.

Q15.5. Only Hospital received a $300,000 cash donation that is restricted by the donor. In what fund do you think this $300,000 should be recorded?

Q15.6. Only Hospital received a $300,000 cash donation that was not restricted by the donor in any manner. The governing board of the hospital, however, voted to restrict this $300,000 to the purchase of plant assets. In what fund should this donation be recorded? Explain your answer.

Q15.7. When should resources be transferred from the specific-purpose funds to the unrestricted fund?

Q15.8. When should resources be transferred from the plant replacement and expansion funds to the unrestricted fund of the hospital?

Q15.9. When, if ever, should resources be transferred from the unrestricted fund to the plant replacement and expansion funds? When, if ever, should resources be transferred from the endowment funds to the unrestricted fund?

Q15.10. If investments held in a restricted fund are sold at a gain, in what fund should the gain be recorded?

Q15.11. In what fund should unrestricted investment income earned on endowment fund investments be recorded?

Q15.12. In the context of fund accounting, what does the word *fund* mean?

Q15.13. List, and describe briefly, each of the funds used in hospital accounting.

Q15.14. During 20X1, Open Hospital's unrestricted fund received $18,000 cash from its specific-purpose funds. Of this total, $13,000 was for charity service and $5,000 for research activities. How should the $18,000 be recorded in the accounts of the unrestricted fund?

QUICK ASSETS

The **quick assets** of a hospital consist of cash and those other assets (temporary investments and receivables) that can be quickly and directly converted into cash. This chapter discusses certain of the accounting problems and procedures related to such assets. Although cash, marketable securities, and receivables may appear in any fund, most of the materials of this chapter relate to the quick assets of the unrestricted fund. You should understand, however, that the accounting methods and practices described here are generally applicable to the quick assets found in the restricted funds.

Cash

Cash may be defined as consisting of actual money and other immediately available resources or credit instruments generally accepted as media of exchange and used as money equivalents. This includes coin and paper currency, demand deposits in banks, checks, and money orders. Postage stamps, however, are supplies, not cash. Postdated checks and IOUs from employees are properly treated as receivables. The very essence of cash is its availability as a medium of exchange.

Considerable attention is given to cash accounting because of its rather obvious value as the means of financing hospital activities. Cash also is the asset likely to be most susceptible to fraudulent misappropriation by employees and others. Finally, it should be recognized that, because of the large volume of cash transactions hospitals complete, the incidence of honest errors can be quite high unless appropriate accounting procedures and internal controls are observed.

Bank Reconciliations

The bank reconciliation (illustrated in Figure 16.1) should be regarded as one of the more important accounting and internal control procedures. It aids in the prevention and detection of fraud, the discovery of errors in accounting records, and the determination of the accuracy of the bank statement. Bank statements, of course, should be delivered unopened to the person who is to perform the reconciliation, and they should remain in that person's control until the reconciliation is completed. Reconciliations should be supervised by the hospital controller and should be performed by someone who does not handle cash or cash records.

	Books		Bank	
	Dr.	Cr.	Dr.	Cr.
Balances, 11/30	$182,062			168,934
Deposits in transit, 11/30:				
Date Amount				
11/29 21,604				
11/30 18,217				
Total				39,821
Checks outstanding, 11/30:				
Date Number Amount				
10/19 4529 1,361				
10/27 4326 412				
11/10 4533 89				
11/30 4517 145				
Total			$19,655	
Bank service charges for November		$ 37		
NSF checks returned by bank:				
Robert M. Patient check dated 11/14; deposited 11/17		519		
William L. Patient check dated 11/20; deposited 11/21		909		
Collection of treasury bills by bank		25,000		
Bank errors:				
Deposit of 11/27 omitted from bank statement				16,400
Check of Othercity Hospital erroneously charged against Homecity account				187
Book errors:				
Check #4649 for $234, dated 11/15, erroneously journalized as $324	90			
Totals	207,152	1,465	19,655	225,342
Offsets		1,465		19,655
Adjusted balances, 11/30	205,687			205,687

A bank reconciliation is primarily a matter of adjusting two incorrect cash balances (the ledger balance and the bank statement balance) to a correct amount representing the actual amount of cash over which the hospital has control—that is, the cash balance to be reported in the balance sheet. Ordinarily, the book balance will be incorrect, for the following two reasons:

1. Items may have been properly subtracted from the bank statement balance, but not from the book balance (for example, bank service charges and patients' checks deposited by the hospital that prove to be uncollectible). This is reconciled by deducting the appropriate items from the book balance.

2. Items may have been properly added to the bank statement balance, but not to the book balance (for example, collections of items by the bank on behalf of the hospital). This is reconciled by adding the appropriate items to the book balance.

On the other hand, the bank statement balance normally will be incorrect for the following two reasons:

1. Items may have been properly added to the book balance, but not to the bank balance (for example, hospital deposits in transit at the bank statement date). This is reconciled by adding the appropriate items to the bank statement balance.
2. Items may have been properly subtracted from the book balance, but not from the bank balance (for example, checks issued and outstanding at the bank statement date). This is reconciled by deducting the appropriate items from the bank statement balance.

In addition, both the book and bank statement balances may not be correct because of errors made by the hospital and the bank. Banks do make errors!

To illustrate the bank reconciliation procedure, assume that the general checking account of Homecity Hospital has a November 30, 20X1, general ledger balance of $182,062. A few days following the end of the month, the hospital receives the November bank statement that reports a November 30, 20X1, balance of only $168,934. Neither of these figures should be reported as the cash balance in the hospital's month-end balance sheet. The two figures must be reconciled to an adjusted (correct) balance. This is accomplished through a reconciliation of the book and bank balances in the manner shown in Figure 16.1.

The reconciliation begins with the entry of the November 30 balances in the respective book and bank columns. The $182,062 book balance is obtained from the general ledger (10110); the $168,934 bank balance is found on the November bank statement. Typically, it is to be hoped, the book balance is a debit balance while the bank balance normally is a credit balance (from the bank's point of view, the hospital's balance is a liability of the bank). If the account is overdrawn, of course, the book balance will be a credit, and the bank balance will be a debit.

The next step is to list the deposits in transit at November 30. A deposit in transit is a deposit made by the hospital (usually on the last day or so of the month) that does not appear on the bank statement for that month. At some banks, there may be a lag or delay of a day or so in recording customer's deposits, particularly where the customer makes deposits after banking hours through 24-hour banking stations and night depository systems. Deposits in transit may be identified by a comparison of deposits as shown on the bank statement with entries in the cash receipts journal.

Deposits as Debits to Hospital and Credits on Bank Statements

If the hospital deposits all receipts daily and intact (as it should), daily debits to cash in the journal will be the same amounts as the daily bank deposits. If a deposit was listed as in transit on the prior month's reconciliation, the person making the reconciliation also should ascertain that the deposit appears on the current month's bank statement. (Note that deposits are debits on the hospital's books but appear as credits on the bank statement because, from the bank's point of view, the hospital's cash balance is a liability.)

Note in the figure that Homecity Hospital has two deposits in transit on November 30 that total $39,821. This amount has been included in the hospital's November receipts per books but does not appear as deposits on the November bank statement. To reconcile, therefore, the $39,821 is credited (added) to the bank balance in the reconciliation. As a part of the December 31, 20X1, reconciliation process, the person preparing it should make sure that this $39,821 appears as deposits on the December bank statement.

Checks Compared to Last Month's Reconciliation and Journal

Next, the checks outstanding at November 30 are listed by date, number, and amount on the reconciliation. When the November bank statement is received, the checks included with the statement are arranged in numerical order and are compared (1) with the listing of checks outstanding on the prior month's (October) reconciliation and (2) with the hospital's cash disbursements journal and payroll journal entries of the current month. An investigation should be made of checks that remain outstanding from the prior month's reconciliation to determine whether payment should be stopped on such checks. And, perhaps on a sample basis, the endorsements on canceled checks might be examined for possible irregularities.

As of November 30, Homecity Hospital had a total of $19,655 of outstanding checks. These are checks that were written and included in the hospital's disbursements but that had not yet been presented to the hospital's bank for payment. The bank has no knowledge of this "float" and consequently did not reduce the hospital's checking account balance for those checks. This situation arises because payees sometimes hold the hospital's checks for a few days before cashing them, because delays occur in the postal system and time is required for checks to clear the banking system. In any event, the outstanding checks are debited to (deducted from) the bank balance in the reconciliation because the hospital no longer has control of the amount of money represented by such items. The person who prepares the December 31 reconciliation should determine whether these $19,655 of outstanding checks clear the bank in December.

Debit Memos

The November bank statement includes a number of debit and credit memos that specify certain special items that have been charged or credited by the bank to the hospital's account. One of the debit memos indicates that the bank service charge for November was $37. This has been deducted by the bank in arriving at the hospital's November 30 balance, but the $37 has not yet been recorded in the hospital's November disbursements. The bank service charges are credited to the books column of the reconciliation.

Two other debit memos are for **NSF (not sufficient funds)** checks that were received from patients, recorded as cash receipts, and deposited by the hospital during November. Unfortunately, those patients did not have sufficient funds in their checking accounts to cover these checks. These checks appeared as deposits (November 17 and 21) on the bank statement but, when their NSF status was determined, the bank subsequently charged them back against the hospital's account. So, to reconcile, the $1,428 total of bad checks must be credited to the book balance in the reconciliation. These defaulting patients should immediately be contacted to work out a plan to make these checks good. The writing of bad checks is a serious matter, and steps should be taken by the hospital to recover those amounts.

Credit Memos

The November bank statement also includes a credit memo representing the collection by the bank of $25,000 of treasury bills for the hospital. These bills, which are issued by the U.S. Treasury Department, were being held as temporary investments by the hospital. They matured late in November and were turned over to the bank for collection from the government. (A part of the November service charge includes the fee charged by the bank for this collection service.) The $25,000 appearing on the bank statement as a deposit must be debited to the books column of the reconciliation.

Comparisons made of the bank statement with the hospital's cash records uncovered certain errors made by the bank during November as well as an error made by the hospital's accounting personnel during the month. One of the bank errors was an omission from the bank statement of a $16,400 deposit that was made by the hospital on November 27. Apparently, the bank credited this deposit in error to another customer's account. In order to reconcile, the omitted deposit must be credited to the bank columns of the reconciliation. The bank also made an error in charging one of Othercity Hospital's checks for $187 against Homecity Hospital's account. This is reconciled by a credit to the bank columns.

The error made by Homecity Hospital was in journalizing check number 4649, written for $234 in payment of an account payable, in the incorrect amount of $324. This caused an understatement of $90 ($324 – $234) in the month-end ledger cash balance. To reconcile, the $90 must be added back to the book balance.

Totaling the Columns

After all necessary adjustments have been determined, each of the columns of the reconciliation is totaled. Then, the books credit column total is offset against the books debit column total, and the bank debit column total is offset against the bank credit column total. This provides the adjusted (correct) cash balance at November 30, or $205,687. This is the cash balance that should be reported in Homecity Hospital's balance sheet at November 30, 20X1. But, because the general ledger account has a $182,062 balance, the following adjusting entry is required in the hospital's general journal:

Cash—general checking account	$23,625	
Accounts receivable—patients	1,428	
Supplies expense—		
administrative services	37	
Temporary investments		$25,000
Accounts payable		90
Adjustment of accounts per		
November 30, 20X1, bank reconciliation		

The debit of $23,625 increases the general ledger cash balance to $205,687, the debit of $1,428 charges the bad checks back to the patients' accounts, and the $37 debit records the bank service charges as November expenses. The credit of $25,000 eliminates the treasury bills from the temporary investments account, and the credit of $90 corrects the error in accounts payable (when check number 4649 was entered in the cash disbursements journal, $90 too much was debited to the accounts payable account). Notice that no entry is necessary for deposits in transit, outstanding checks, or bank errors. The deposits in transit and the outstanding checks have already been recorded in the hospital's accounts; the bank errors will be called to the bank's attention so that they may be corrected by the bank in its December statement.

Retention of Bank Reconciliations

The bank reconciliation is an important document; it should not be destroyed. All reconciliations should be retained in appropriate files for review by the hospital's internal and external auditors.

Sometimes bank reconciliations are accomplished by adjusting the bank balance into agreement with the ledger balance (previously adjusted to a correct figure). Although this method will produce a reconciliation and is employed by some auditors, the procedure illustrated in Figure 16.1 is described here for pedagogical reasons, and because it always produces the proper balance sheet figure for cash and organizes all the necessary adjustments in one place—that is, in the books debit and credit columns. Other reconciliation methods may not necessarily provide these two advantages.

As noted in Chapter 14, the use of a special payroll checking account greatly facilitates the bank reconciliation process. The special payroll account allows the large volume of payroll checks to be removed from the general checking account reconciliation. The payroll checking account ordinarily will require no reconciliation, because it tends to reconcile itself to a zero, or imprest, balance. This is true because the deposit of the net payroll amount in the account is exactly offset by the total of the individual payroll checks clearing the account. To encourage employees to deposit their payroll checks promptly, payroll checks may be printed to read "void if not presented for payment within 30 days." Other special checking accounts may be established, if useful, for other frequently recurring disbursements, such as payroll taxes, equipment purchases, and interest payments on the hospital's long-term debt (bonds payable, for example).

Imprest Cash Funds

A hospital should not keep unnecessary cash on hand. All cash receipts should be deposited daily and intact; disbursements should never be made directly from cash receipts. As a general rule, disbursements should be made only by checks that are properly authorized and supported by appropriate vouchers. Any violations of these basic control principles are open invitations to confusion, error, and fraud.

As a practical matter, however, provision usually must be made for the keeping of cash funds in limited amounts from which cash disbursements can be made for items for which the writing of checks is not feasible. For this reason, hospitals often must maintain several so-called petty cash funds, change funds, and check cashing funds. The need for such funds should be evaluated regularly so that their number and size will be neither excessive nor inadequate. All such funds should be accounted for on an imprest basis; that is, each fund should be established in a fixed amount that is replenished periodically when that amount has been exhausted. Responsibility for each imprest (fixed amount) fund should be assigned to a specific employee who, as the fund custodian, has sole control over it.

To illustrate the accounting procedures for petty cash funds, assume that Homecity Hospital decides to establish such a fund in the imprest amount of $750. Accordingly, a check for this amount is drawn payable to the appointed petty cash custodian who cashes the check and places the money for safekeeping in a locked petty cash drawer or box. The entries are as follows:

Petty Cash Funds

Voucher Register

Petty cash fund	$750	
Accounts payable		$750
Voucher to establish petty		
cash fund of $750		

Cash Disbursements Journal

Accounts payable	$750	
Cash—general checking account		$750
Check issued to establish an imprest		
petty cash fund of $750		

Petty Cash
Documentation

Disbursements from the fund are made only by the petty cash custodian, and then only in return for signed receipts, petty cash slips or vouchers, and other supporting documents. A typical petty cash disbursement form is illustrated in Figure 16.2. As cash is paid out of the fund, these forms are completed and retained in the petty cash drawer or box.

When the fund is found to be nearly exhausted, and routinely at the end of each month, a reimbursement check may be drawn to replenish the fund to its imprest amount. Assume that the contents of the petty cash box at month end are as follows:

Coin and currency	$ 87
Petty cash disbursement slips	635
IOU from employee	25
Total	$747

The coin and currency in the box, of course, were determined by actual count. The disbursement slips are removed from the box, totaled, and summarized according to the accounts to be debited for the expenditures. This summary analysis can be entered on the back of specially printed petty cash disbursements envelopes, such as the one shown in Figure 16.3. When the summary is completed, the cash disbursement slips are placed in the envelope and become a part of the voucher package for the check to be drawn to replenish the petty cash fund.

For simplicity, let us assume that the petty cash disbursements of $635 are chargeable only to the accounting department ($415) and the laboratory department ($220). The necessary entries to replenish the fund are as follows:

Voucher Register

Supplies expense—accounting	$415	
Supplies expense—laboratory	220	
Accounts receivable—employees	25	
Cash over and short	3	
Accounts payable		$663
Voucher for check to replenish the		
petty cash fund to the imprest amount		

Cash Disbursements Journal

Accounts payable	$663	
Cash—general checking account		$663
Check issued to replenish the petty cash fund		
to the imprest amount		

Notice that the employee's $25 IOU is debited to accounts receivable—employees. This represents an improper use of the petty cash fund, and the custodian should be instructed not to allow employees to borrow from

PETTY CASH DISBURSEMENT

NO. ______________ DATE ______________ 20____

$ ______________

TO ______________

Amount ______________ DOLLARS

For ______________

____

Account Number ______________

Approved By ______________ Received Payment ______________

FIGURE 16.2 Petty Cash Disbursement Slip

the fund. Note also that the $3 shortage in the fund is debited to a special cash over and short account that is treated as either a miscellaneous expense or miscellaneous income account, depending on its balance at the end of the reporting period.

The $663 check is drawn payable to the petty cash custodian who cashes it and places the money in the petty cash box. This $663, plus the $87 remaining in the fund at the time of reimbursement, brings the petty cash drawer up to a total of $750 again. These replenishments are made as often as the fund is depleted, or at least at the end of each monthly reporting period.

Debits and Credits to Petty Cash

It should be recognized that nowhere in the reimbursement process is the petty cash account debited or credited. This is done only when the imprest amount of the fund is increased or decreased. If reimbursements are required often enough to be bothersome, the imprest amount of the fund might be considered inadequate. Assume, for example, that it is decided to increase the above fund to $1,000. A check therefore is drawn for $250 and is debited to the petty cash account. On the other hand, if reimbursements are infrequent, this may be an indication that the imprest amount is excessive. Suppose, for

FIGURE 16.3 Petty Cash Disbursements Summary

PETTY CASH SUMMARY

No.____________

APPROVED BY ________________ DATE ____________ 20____

AUDITED BY ________________ PAID BY CHECK No.____________

DATE	PETTY CASH VOUCHER NO.	TOTAL	DISTRIBUTION									
											MISCELLANEOUS	
											ACCOUNT	AMOUNT

example, that a decision is made to reduce the $750 fund to an imprest amount of $400. In this case, one would remove $350 of currency from the petty cash box and deposit it in the hospital's general checking account, crediting the petty cash account.

Hospitals often establish change funds in nominal amounts at cash-receiving locations for the purpose of providing change to patients, employees, and visitors. These funds should be balanced daily to the total of recorded cash receipts plus the imprest amount of the change fund. In depositing cash receipts, over and short variations are considered to be in the day's receipts and not in the change fund that is retained in its imprest amount.

Other Imprest Funds

Although hospital policy ordinarily should be that of not cashing any personal or payroll checks for anyone, check-cashing funds often are established as a convenience to employees. Where such check-cashing funds are necessary, they should be maintained on an imprest basis. The custodian of such funds should be independent of all payroll functions.

Internal Cash Controls

Internal cash controls are essential in the hospital's business offices and at all other locations where cash is received or disbursed. These safeguards must be built into the accounting system if hospital cash resources are to be accurately recorded and adequately protected from error and misappropriation. A description of many of these controls and the related accounting procedures for the processing of cash receipts and disbursements has been provided in previous chapters, particularly in Chapters 12 and 14. It would now be useful to provide a listing of some of the basic principles typically incorporated into internal cash control systems:

- All hospital employees who handle or have access to cash should be adequately bonded.
- Petty cash and change funds should be limited in number and should be established in minimum imprest amounts.
- Bank accounts should be reconciled regularly by persons other than those who handle cash receipts, sign checks, or maintain the cash journals and records.
- There must be a distinct segregation of duties between cash handling and cash accounting (for example, persons who handle incoming cash should not have control of the accounts receivable records).
- All cash record forms—checks, bank deposit tickets, cash receipt slips, and petty cash vouchers—should be prenumbered and accounted for by numerical sequence whenever this is feasible.
- Definite responsibility for cash-handling functions and for custody of cash funds should be assigned to specific employees.

- The fewest possible employees should be given access to cash.
- The work of business office personnel should be made complementary so that an error made by one automatically will be discovered by another.
- Physical protection should be provided through the use of vaults, bank facilities, cashiers' cages, locked cash drawers, and similar devices.
- Definite procedures should be established in writing for the handling of all cash transactions.
- Office procedures should be so arranged that misappropriations are unlikely to go undetected without the collusion of two or more employees.
- Internal audits and surprise cash counts should be made by a responsible employee at irregular intervals.

Although this listing is not by any means complete, it is indicative of some of the procedures to be observed in a sound internal control system.

Temporary Investments

Temporary investments are investments that can be quickly and directly converted into cash. Temporarily excessive cash balances should always be invested by the hospital in bank savings accounts, certificates of deposit, U.S. treasury bills, or in some other type of income-producing asset. The investment objectives should be safety, marketability, and a reasonable rate of return. These temporary or short-term investments may appear in the hospital's restricted funds as well as in its unrestricted fund, although long-term investments are more commonly found in the endowment funds and in the plant expansion and replacement funds.

Example of Accounting Procedures for Temporary Investments
To illustrate the accounting procedures for temporary investments in bonds (sometimes referred to as **marketable debt securities**), assume that Homecity Hospital's cash budget indicates that $40,000 of cash should be available for investment for about four months. Accordingly, on October 1, 20X1, the hospital purchases $40,000 of corporate bonds at face value.

These 6 percent bonds pay interest semiannually on November 1 and May 1 (3 percent each interest payment date). Assuming this is an investment of the hospital's unrestricted fund, the entries for 20X1 are shown in Figure 16.4.

The voucher register entry records the investment at cost, which is the quoted price paid for the securities plus brokerage fees and all other acquisition costs. It is assumed here that the quoted price was 100 percent of face, or par, value and that acquisition costs totaled $65. For accounting purposes, then, the cost of this investment was $40,065. Had these securities been

FIGURE 16.4

Entries for
Temporary
Investments

Voucher Register

10/1	Temporary investments	$40,065	
	Accrued interest receivable	1,000	
	Accounts payable		$41,065
	Purchase of temporary investments		
	as follows:		

Purchase price (face value)	$40,000	
Acquisition costs	65	
Total cost	40,065	
Accrued interest:	1,000	
$40,000 \times 6\% \times 5/12$	———	
Total disbursement	$41,065	

Cash Disbursements Journal

10/1	Accounts payable	$41,065	
	Cash—general checking account		$41,065
	Check issued for purchase of		
	temporary investments		

General Journal

10/31	Accrued interest receivable	$200	
	Interest income		$ 200
	Accrual of interest income earned		
	on temporary investments in October:		
	$40,000 \times 6\% \times 1/12$		

Cash Receipts Journal

11/1	Cash—general checking account	$ 1,200	
	Accrued interest receivable		$ 1,200
	Receipt of semiannual interest		
	on temporary investments:		
	$40,000 \times 6\% \times 6/12$		

General Journal

11/30	Accrued interest receivable	$ 200	
	Interest income		$ 200
	Accrual of interest income earned on		
	temporary investments in November		

General Journal

12/31	Accrued interest receivable	$ 200	
	Interest income		$ 200
	Accrual of interest income		
	earned on temporary investments		
	in December		

quoted at, say, 98 percent, the price paid for them would have been $39,200 (98 percent of $40,000), and the cost of the investment would have been recorded as $39,265 ($39,200 + $65).

Because these bonds were acquired between interest payment dates, the seller must be paid the accrued interest on the bonds since the last interest payment date—that is, from May 1 to October 1 (five months' accrued interest). This $1,000 is not charged to expense but to accrued interest receivable because it will be recovered by the hospital on November 1, when the bond issuer pays six months' interest to bondholders. Accrued interest settlements always are made in this manner between investors who trade in bonds. It would not be feasible for the bond issuer to attempt to make these adjustments. Instead, the issuer always pays six months' interest on each interest payment date regardless of the length of time the investor has held the bonds.

On October 31, and at the end of each subsequent monthly reporting period so long as Homecity Hospital holds these bonds, a general journal adjusting entry is required to record the accrued interest income on the investment. The amount of this entry is an approximation of interest for one month; precise computations to exact days or cents can be made but are not necessary in recording most accruals of this type. Note that the October 31 entry increases the balance of the accrued interest receivable account to $1,200—that is, the amount of the semiannual interest received the following day (November 1).

On December 31, the interest income account has a balance of $600, which is reported in Homecity Hospital's 20X1 statement of operations as nonoperating revenue. The $400 of accrued interest receivable will be reported in the hospital's year-end balance sheet as a current asset. The December 31, 20X1, balance sheet also will report the investment at its cost of $40,065.

Suppose, however, that the December 31 quoted market price of these bonds has risen to 102 percent ($40,800), or has fallen to 97 percent ($38,800). Should the carrying value of the investment be adjusted (written up or down) to current market value? Under current GAAP, temporary investments in bonds usually are carried in the accounts and in the balance sheet at their original acquisition cost with market value indicated parenthetically or by footnote. Some accountants argue, however, that such investments should be valued at the lower of cost or market value; others believe that such investments should be reported at market value, whether this is higher or lower than cost. We shall use the cost valuation.

To complete this illustration, let us assume that these investments are sold by the hospital at 102.5 percent and accrued interest on January 1, 20X2, with brokerage fees and other expenses of sale amounting to $76. The cash receipts journal entry is as follows:

Cash—general checking account		$41,324	
Accrued interest receivable			$ 400
Temporary investments			40,065
Gain on sale of temporary investments			859
Sale of temporary investments as follows:			
Sale price (102.5% of $40,000)	$ 41,000		
Less brokerage fees	76		
Net proceeds from sale	$40,924		
Add accrued interest:			
$40,000 × 6% × 2/12 months	400		
Total cash received	$ 41,324		

The credit to accrued interest receivable is necessary to eliminate the balance of that account as established by the income accruals at the end of November and December 20X1. A gain of $859 is realized on the sale; it is computed as the difference between the net proceeds ($40,924) and the cost of the investment ($40,065). This gain will be reported in the 20X2 statement of operations of the hospital among the nonoperating revenues.

Similar procedures are followed in accounting for temporary investments in bonds by the hospital's restricted funds. The accounting procedures for long-term investments in bonds, however, are somewhat different. This matter is pursued at length in Chapter 19.

Short-term investments in corporate stocks usually are reported at the lower of aggregate cost or market.

Receivables

The term **receivables**, as employed in hospital accounting, refers to the realizable cash value of the hospital's legal claim against its patients, third-party payers, and others. Such receivables arise primarily from the provision of healthcare services to patients on a credit basis. In effect, the hospital exchanges its services, including goods and supplies, for the patient's and/or the third party's promise to pay for such services in the future. It is an economic exchange measured in terms of the hospital's full established rates regardless of expectations about future collectibility.

The resulting revenues and related receivables are recorded on the accrual basis in the time period in which the associated healthcare services are provided. Because there is usually a considerable time lag between the provision of services and the receipt of payment for those services, this practice gives rise to substantial amounts of accounts and notes receivable in the balance sheet.

Receivables may also exist in relatively small amounts from transactions that are only indirectly related to the provision of services to patients.

Included in this category are accruals for various miscellaneous items such as interest and rental income earned but not miscellaneous items such as interest and rental income earned but not yet received in cash, advances to employees, tuition charges receivable from students, and donors' pledges receivable. Full and separate disclosure should be made in the hospital balance sheet of all material amounts of these miscellaneous receivables.

Much of the accounting procedure relating to receivables was dealt with in earlier chapters. Here, the discussion is confined to the balance sheet valuation of receivables, accounting for notes receivable, and internal controls for receivables.

Valuation of Receivables

Receivables should be reported in the hospital balance sheet at their net realizable value. In other words, the gross amount of receivables recorded at established service rates in the accounts should be reduced to the net amount that can be reasonably estimated to be actually collectible in cash. Appropriate estimates, as described later, should be made of the amounts uncollectible because of bad debts, contractual adjustments, charity service, and other factors. Such estimates are treated as reductions of gross receivables in the balance sheet by the use of the allowance for uncollectible accounts. These amounts, other than bad debts, should also be included as "revenue deductions" in the statement of operations of the period in which the receivables arose. The treatment for bad debts on the statement of operations changed in the early 1990s. The provision for bad debt (now known as bad debt expense) is included as an operating expense on the statement of operations. These procedures are required to secure a proper balance sheet valuation of the receivables as well as to properly match revenues and revenue deductions on an accrual basis.

Bad Debts

It is reasonable to expect that a certain amount of receivables arising from services provided to self-responsible patients will prove to be uncollectible. Uncollectible amounts also may arise from the uninsured portion of the accounts of patients covered by BlueCross or other third-party payers. At the time of admission, or as soon thereafter as practicable, the financial status of each patient should be determined so that uncollectible amounts can be properly classified and distinguished as arising from bad debts, contractual adjustments, or charity service. After adequate collection efforts have been expended to the point at which additional expenditures cannot be justified on the basis of prospective benefits, amounts still remaining uncollected should be treated as bad debts.

Estimating Bad Debts At the end of each reporting period, an estimate must be made of the amount of receivables that ultimately will prove to be bad debts. This is necessary to prevent an overstatement of assets (receivables) in the balance sheet and to provide for a proper matching of revenues and revenue deductions in the statement of operations of the period in which the receivables originated. It is a procedure required under the accrual basis of accounting.

To illustrate, let us assume that 20X1 is the initial year of operations for Homecity Hospital. During this year, the hospital provided $3.6 million of services to patients and collected $3 million of this amount. At the end of the year, then, accounts receivable total $600,000. Also assume that operating expenses for the year are $3.5 million and that there were no charity patients or contractual adjustments. If nothing is done to consider the possibility of bad debts, the hospital's year-end balance sheet will include $600,000 of accounts receivable among the assets, and the 20X1 statement of operations will report an excess of revenues over expenses of $100,000 ($3.6 million – $3.5 million).

In the first several months of 20X2, $564,000 of the 20X1 accounts receivable are collected. The remaining sum of $36,000 (after diligent efforts to collect it) is deemed to be uncollectible, or bad debts. An entry is made to write off these receivables and charge the $36,000 to the 20X2 bad debt expense account. Observe, however, that the receivables and the related revenues were recorded in 20X1.

This procedure obviously places the bad debts in the wrong year. The $36,000 of bad debts should have been given accounting recognition as a bad debt expense in 20X1—the year in which the related revenue was recorded. This means that the excess of revenues over expenses for 20X1 was overstated by $36,000. In addition, there was a $36,000 overstatement of assets (accounts receivable) in the December 31, 20X1, balance sheet. The receivables should have been stated in that balance sheet at net realizable cash value, or $564,000 ($600,000 – $36,000).

Three Methods of Estimating Bad Debts

The difficulty, of course, is that it is impossible to predict precisely which individual accounts will prove to be bad debts. It also is impossible to determine precisely the total dollar amount of accounts that will prove to be uncollectible in the future; no one has perfect foresight. Nevertheless, a reasonable estimate can, and should, be made so that the degree of misstatement in the financial statements will be minimized. There are three methods by which bad debts may be estimated for accrual basis accounting purposes:

Method 1: Application of a percentage, based on past experience, to the balance of accounts receivable at the end of the reporting period

Method 2: Application of a percentage, based on past experience, to the total of charges to patients' accounts during the reporting period

Method 3:   Determination through an analysis of individual accounts in the patients' ledger, taking into account the length of time each account has remained unpaid ("aging the accounts receivable")

As a matter of actual practice, hospitals often employ all three methods, comparing the results of each so as to arrive at the most accurate estimate of probable bad debts.

The percentage used in these methods often is an average percentage based on several prior years' experience and tempered by expectations of conditions that might exist in the future collection period. Computations of these percentages, of course, are based only on the self-responsible portions of patients' accounts receivable, because billings to third parties are generally collectible in full. In the following example, we assume that an average of about 60 percent of the hospital's charges are billed to third-party payers, leaving 40 percent payable by patients themselves.

Using Method 1   Let us return to the end of 20X1 and attempt to estimate the amount of bad debts likely to arise in 20X2 from the $600,000 of accounts receivable. If we use the first method noted and assume that the estimated bad debts percentage is 12 percent, bad debts will be estimated at $28,800 as follows:

Accounts receivable, 12/31/X1	$ 600,000
Less third-party portion (60%)	360,000
Self-responsible portion	240,000
Percentage of bad debts (12%)	.12
Estimated bad debts	$ 28,800

Using Method 2   However, if we use the second method and assume that the estimated bad percentage is 2.4 percent of revenues, bad debts will be estimated at $34,560 as follows:

Charges to patients—20X1	$3,600,000
Less third-party portion (60%)	2,160,000
Self-pay portion	1,440,000
Percentage of bad debts (2.4%)	.024
Estimated bad debts	$ 34,560

You should not assume from this example that method 2 will always provide a larger estimate than method 1, or that it will produce the most accurate estimate. It can be argued that method 2 may be statistically superior to method 1 because of the larger base (charges rather than receivables) used. Under either method, the critical factor is the soundness of assumptions and judgments underlying the determination of the bad debts percentage.

The aging procedure (method 3) is likely to provide the most accurate esti- *Using Method 3* mate of bad debts. It also is the most managerially useful method in that it requires a detailed, account-by-account examination of patients' receivables. The procedure involves the classification of account balances into "age" groups, depending on the number of days that have elapsed since the date of discharge, as illustrated in Figure 16.5. (In some cases, the aging may be made on the basis of time elapsed since the date of the last payment received on the account. Our illustration merely provides a DLP—date of last payment—column to indicate this information when it is desired.)

As you can see in the aging schedule, a total is obtained for each age group. For example, $90,000 of receivables are in-house accounts, $50,000 of receivables are 1–30 days old, $40,000 are 31–60 days old, $30,000 are 61–90 days old, and so on. Appropriate percentages based on past experience are then applied to these totals to obtain an estimate of total probable bad debts. As you might expect, the percentage used increases with the age of the accounts. The older the account, the less likely it is to be collected.

Using the bad debt estimate provided by the aging schedule, the required adjusting entry at the end of 20X1 is as follows:

Bad debt expense	$ 36,300	
Allowance for uncollectible		
accounts—bad debts		$ 36,300
Required provision for bad debts		
per accounts receivable aging schedule		

Thus, the 20X1 statement of operations will include the $36,300 of estimated bad debts as an expense of the year. And the balance sheet at December 31, 20X1, will present the receivables as follows:

Accounts receivable	$600,000	
Less allowance for uncollectible		
accounts—bad debts	36,300	$563,700

In this way, the accounts receivable are reduced to net realizable value for balance sheet presentation purposes.

Let us now assume that, during 20X2, $564,000 of these accounts are collected by the hospital. The hospital credit manager concludes that the remaining $36,000 of accounts are definitely uncollectible. The summary entries are the following:

Cash Receipts Journal		
Cash—general checking account	$564,000	
Accounts receivable		$564,000
Collections on 20X1 accounts		
receivable during 20X2		

FIGURE 16.5 Accounts Receivable Aging Schedule, December 31, 20X1

| Patient Name | Account Balance | Third-Party Portion | Total | In-house | Self-Responsible Portion — Elapsed Days Since Discharge | | | | | DLP | Remarks |
					1–30	31–60	61–90	91–180	Over 180		
Able, Marcus C.	1,420	690	730	730							
Active, James R.	2,466	1,314	1,152		1,152						
Adams, Mary P.	608		608						608		
Agar, Thomas J.	1,190		1,190				1,190				
Akron, Louise M.	782		782			782					
Allen, Richard Q.	532		532					532			
Ammons, Peter C.	808	355	453	453							
Etc.											
Totals	600,000	360,000	240,000	90,000	50,000	40,000	30,000	20,000	10,000		
Bad debt percentages				.05	.08	.12	.20	.40	.90		
Estimaged bad debts			6,300	4,500	4,000	4,800	6,000	8,000	9,000		

General Journal

Allowance for uncollectible accounts—bad debts	$36,000	
Accounts receivable		$ 36,000
Write-off of accounts receivable		
deemed to be bad debts		

The specific 20X1 accounts written off during 20X2 are removed or otherwise eliminated from the active section of the patients' subsidiary ledger. The ledger cards and related records are placed in an inactive file and are retained under the control of a responsible employee who does not have any access to incoming cash receipts. This is designed to prevent the theft of subsequent cash collections on previously written-off accounts. Where such recoveries are made, the credit should be made to the allowance account or to a special account titled "recoveries of accounts written off."

To complete this illustration, assume that Homecity Hospital's accounts receivable at the end of 20X2 total $685,000. Bad debts are estimated at $41,000, determined in the manner previously described for the end of 20X1. The required adjusting entry for bad debts at December 31, 20X2, is as follows:

General Journal

Bad debt expense		$40,700	
Allowance for uncollectible		
accounts—bad debts		$ 40,700
Required provision for bad debts:		
Required allowance		
account balance (credit)	$ 41,000	
Present allowance		
account balance (credit)	300	
Required adjustment	$40,700	

Recall that bad debts were estimated in the amount of $36,300 at the end of 20X1, but actual write-offs during 20X2 were only $36,000. This means that the allowance account is left with a $300 credit balance at December 31, 20X2. Because a credit balance of $41,000 is required (based on an aging schedule) at the end of 20X2, the adjustment is made for only $40,700. On the other hand, if 20X2 write-offs had been $38,000, the allowance account would have had a December 31, 20X2, debit balance of $1,700. In that case, the above entry would have been made for $42,700 ($41,000 + $1,700) to obtain the desired $41,000 credit balance in the allowance account.

The same procedure is followed when bad debts are estimated as a percentage of year-end receivables (method 1). When bad debts are estimated as a percentage of charges (method 2), however, the estimated amount of bad debts is simply debited to bad debt expense and credited to the allowance for uncollectible accounts. In other words, when method 1 or method 3 is employed, the result is the required balance in the allowance for uncollectible accounts at the end of the reporting period. The allowance account is adjusted to that balance. When method 2 is used, however, the result is the amount to be debited to bad debt expense and credited to the allowance account.

Contractual Adjustments

Under contractual agreements with third-party payers, hospitals often receive less than their full rates and are sometimes prohibited from collecting the difference from patients who are covered by the contract. In such cases, the amount of these differences—called **contractual adjustments**—included in end-of-period receivables must be determined. This may be done by a direct analysis of individual accounts or on a percentage basis developed either from a sample of the accounts or from past experience. The procedure is similar to that for estimating bad debts.

Estimating Contractual Adjustments To illustrate, recall (from Figure 16.5) that the third-party portion of Homecity Hospital's December 31, 20X1, receivables was $360,000, measured in terms of the hospital's full service rates. Earlier, it was assumed that the third-party payers paid 100 percent of such rates; now let us assume that the hospital is reimbursed on the average at only 95 percent of such rates. If this 5 percent difference is not billable to the patients involved, the following adjusting entry is required at December 31, 20X1:

General Journal

Deductions from revenues—contractual adjustments	$ 18,000	
Allowance for uncollectible accounts—contractuals		$ 18,000
Required provision for estimated contractual adjustments included in year-end receivables:		
5% of $360,000 = $18,000		

Including the previously determined estimate of bad debts, the December 31, 20X2, balance sheet presentation of receivables is the following:

Accounts receivable	$600,000	
Less allowance for uncollectible accounts—bad debts	36,300	
Less allowance for uncollectible accounts—contractuals	18,000	$545,700

The 20X1 statement of operations, of course, will include the $18,000 of estimated contractual adjustments as a deduction from the patient services revenues of the year. Where the precise amounts of contractual adjustments can be determined, they may be credited directly to accounts receivable rather than to the allowance account.

Assume now that payments received on these accounts from third-party payers in 20X2 amount to $341,000. The necessary entries are summarized in a single cash receipts journal entry as follows:

Cash Receipts Journal

Cash—general checking account	$341,000	
Deductions for revenues—		
contractual adjustments	19,000	
Accounts receivable		$360,000
Receipt of payments for third-party		
portion of 12/31/X1 receivables		

Notice that the $19,000 debit is made here to revenue deductions and not to the allowance account because of the assumed design of the cash receipts journal (see the cash receipts journal illustrated in Figure 11.4).

So, at the end of 20X2, the allowance for uncollectible accounts for contractual adjustments remains with the $18,000 credit balance established at the end of 20X1. If the amount of contractual adjustments at December 31, 20X2, is estimated at $19,500, the required adjusting entry is as follows:

General Journal

Deductions from revenue—			
contractual adjustments		$ 1,500	
Allowance for uncollectible			
accounts—contractuals			$ 1,500
Required provision for			
contractual adjustments			
at 12/31/X2:			
Required allowance	$19,500		
Present balance of			
allowance account	18,000		
Required adjustment	$ 1,500		

On the other hand, if the $19,000 were debited to the allowance account in this cash receipts journal entry, the December 31, 20X2, adjustment would be made in the amount of $20,500 ($19,500 plus the debit balance of $1,000 in the allowance account). Either procedure is acceptable.

The preceding illustrations for bad debts and contractual adjustments were presented in annual terms for ease of exposition. You must understand, however, that these adjustments are made monthly in actual practice. This is necessary to make the monthly financial statements more accurate and useful for internal management purposes.

Charity Service

As indicated in previous chapters (see particularly Chapter 7), uncollectible receivables arising from the provision of charity service to patients may be accounted for using an allowance account in the manner described here for contractual adjustments. This method may be used where the amount of charity service in receivables is determined by estimate rather than by specific identification. In many cases, however, such amounts are readily determinable, and the use of the allowance account method is not necessary. Instead, charity service is recorded by direct credits to the receivables account.

Accounting for Notes Receivable

It is not uncommon for hospitals to accept interest-bearing promissory notes from patients who, faced with a substantial hospital bill, require an extended period of time to accumulate the resources with which to pay their accounts. To illustrate the accounting procedures, assume that a patient gives Homecity Hospital an 8 percent, 90-day promissory note on March 1, 20X1, in settlement of a $9,000 account with the hospital. The total interest on this note is $180 ($9,000 × 8 percent × [90 days ÷ 360 days]), or $2 per day. It should be recognized as earned income by the hospital through monthly accruals, as shown in Figure 16.6. Elapsed days between any two dates are computed by counting the first day or the last day, but not both; in other words, the number of days between March 1 and March 31 is 30.

It is assumed here that the note in question is a **term note receivable**—that is, that the face amount of the note and all interest is payable in a single sum on the maturity date of the note (May 30, 20X1).

Should the patient fail to pay the note at maturity, the debit of $9,180 is made to dishonored notes receivable rather than to cash. The failure of the patient to honor the note, however, in no way changes the fact that interest income of $180 was earned. If further collection efforts are unsuccessful, the $9,180 is written off as a bad debt.

Notes Receivable Used as a Source of Funds

To illustrate how patients' notes receivable may be used as a source of funds by the hospital, let us backtrack to March 31. Assume that the first two entries in Figure 16.6 have already been made and that the hospital discounts the note receivable at a local bank. Assuming that the bank discount rate is 12 percent, the entry to record the discounting of the note is as follows:

FIGURE 16.6

Accounting for

Notes Receivable

General Journal

3/1	Notes receivable	$9,000	
	Accounts receivable		$9,000
	Receipt of 8%, 90-day note receivable in		
	settlement of patient's account		

3/31 Accrued interest receivable $ 60
      Interest income $ 60
    Interest income earned in March:
    $9,000 × 8% × 1/12 = $60

4/30 Accrued interest receivable $ 60
      Interest income $ 60
    Interest income earned in April:
    $9,000 × 8% × 1/12 = $60

Cash Receipts Journal

5/30 Cash—general checking account $9,180
      Interest income $ 60
      Accrued interest receivable   120
      Notes receivable   9,000
    Collection of note receivable and accrued interest

Cash Receipts Journal

3/31 Cash—general checking account $8,996
    Interest expense   64
      Accrued interest receivable $ 60
      Notes receivable discounted   9,000
    Discounting of a $9,000 note
    receivable at 12% at local bank

    The maturity value of this note is $9,180, and there are 60 days remaining before that maturity date. The discount charged by the bank (rounded to the nearest dollar) therefore is $184 ($9,180 × 12 percent × [60 days ÷ 360 days]). The proceeds of the note to the hospital are $8,996 ($9,180 – $184)—that is, on March 31 the bank gives the hospital $8,996 for the patient's note. The hospital gives up the right to receive the $9,180 maturity value of the note. The maturity value will be collected by the bank.

    Notice here the credit to notes receivable discounted. This is a contingent liability account. So, assuming that the note was discounted "with recourse" (as is usual), the hospital is obligated to pay the bank $9,180 at the maturity date of the note if the patient does not. This account is presented in the hospital's balance sheet as a direct deduction from notes receivable in the assets section.

No other entries related to this note are made by the hospital until the May 30 maturity date. Following are the two sets of entries to be made on May 30 by the hospital, assuming (1) that the patient pays the bank and (2) that the patient does not pay the bank:

(1) General Journal

Notes receivable discounted	$9,000	
Notes receivable		$9,000
Payment by patient of discounted note receivable		

(2) Voucher Register

Notes receivable discounted	$9,000	
Notes receivable dishonored	9,195	
Notes receivable		$9,000
Accounts payable		9,195
Voucher for payment of discounted note receivable		
dishonored by patient		

Cash Disbursements Journal

Accounts payable	$9,195	
Cash—general checking account		$9,195
Check issued to pay bank for		
dishonored note receivable discounted		

Protest Fee for Dishonored Discounted Notes

When a discounted note is dishonored, the bank generally makes a charge often called a protest fee. In this case, the fee was $15, making the total payment to the bank $9,195 ($9,000 + $180 + $15). Notice that the face amount of the note, the interest, and the protest fee is charged back to the patient by the debit to notes receivable dishonored. If collection efforts are not fruitful, the $9,195 is written off as a bad debt.

Internal Control

Various internal control principles and procedures have been discussed in earlier chapters, particularly in Chapter 12, where you observed that the control of receivables and the control of revenues are closely linked. Thus, let us limit this discussion to a few general observations about the internal control of hospital receivables.

Initiating Receivables Control in the Admitting Process

Receivables control begins in the admitting/registration process, where complete and accurate information must be secured so that an initial determination can be made of each patient's financial status and unnecessary delays may be avoided in subsequent billing and collection efforts. Once patients are admitted, the system should be such as to provide a high degree of assurance that all billable services rendered are promptly and accurately charged to patients' accounts. Unrecorded revenues are unlikely to be charged; if not charged, they will not be billed; and, if not billed, they will not be collected. Having complete and accurate charges to patients' accounts, the objective becomes that of maximum collection of such charges at the earliest practicable time.

Separating Billing and Collections Responsibilities

The billing function usually should be performed by someone other than those who maintain the patients' subsidiary ledger records or the cashiers. Sound procedures should be followed (as described in Chapter 12) as collections are received to ensure that patients' accounts are promptly and accurately credited. Noncash credits made to accounts receivable deserve particular attention, as such credits may be used to hide errors and defalcations.

Reconciling Ledgers with Control Accounts

Finally, the regular reconciliation of subsidiary ledgers with receivables control accounts must be recognized as an essential internal control practice.

Questions

Q16.1. What are "quick assets"?

Q16.2. Define *cash*. Are postage stamps, postdated checks, and employee IOUs properly includable in "cash"? If not, how should such items be classified in the balance sheet?

Q16.3. For what reasons are bank reconciliations prepared? By whom should bank reconciliations be prepared?

Q16.4. Explain how you would determine the appropriate imprest amount with which to establish a petty cash fund.

Q16.5. Under what circumstances is the petty cash account debited or credited?

Q16.6. List ten of the most important basic principles typically incorporated into internal cash control systems.

Q16.7. Name three methods by which bad debts may be estimated for accrual basis accounting purposes. Which method is best?

Q16.8. Describe briefly some of the procedures that should be observed to maintain effective internal control over receivables.

Q16.9. Identify and explain the nature of three deductions that may be made to arrive at a balance sheet valuation for accounts receivable.

Q16.10. Define the term *temporary investments*. List some common types of temporary investments available to hospitals.

Q16.11. Purr Hospital's general ledger cash in bank account has a balance of

$213,597 as of November 30. The November bank statement, however, shows a balance of $244,129 at the same date. List four types of factors that may cause such a difference and give an example of each.

Q16.12. Briefly describe the imprest system for operating a petty cash fund and state the principal advantages of the imprest system from the standpoint of internal control.

Exercises

E16.1. Pike Hospital's bank statement shows a March 31 balance of $4,200. An analysis discloses that $1,500 of checks are outstanding and that there is a deposit in transit of $900 at March 31. Bank service charges for March were $25 and an NSF check of $175 was charged against the hospital's account by the bank on March 28. The hospital had deposited this patient's check on March 19. The hospital made a deposit of $400 on March 21 that does not appear on the March bank statement, and the bank admitted its error when contacted about it. On March 25, one of the hospital's bookkeepers journalized a properly drawn $50 check (issued in payment of a supplier's invoice) as $500. *Required*: (1) What amount should the hospital report as cash in bank in its March 31 balance sheet? (2) What adjusting entry should the hospital make on March 31?

E16.2. Pack Hospital maintains a petty cash fund in the imprest amount of $275. The fund is reimbursed at a time when the contents of the petty cash box are as follows:

Petty cash vouchers	$131
Employee's personal check made payable to Pack Hospital	25
IOU from another employee	10
Coin and currency	106

Here petty cash vouchers include a voucher for a $50 purchase of postage stamps. Unused stamps having a face value of $19 remain in the petty cash box.
Required: In the entry to record the reimbursement of the petty cash fund, what amount should be credited to the petty cash account?

E16.3. Pick Hospital provides you with the following 20X1 information:

Accounts receivable, 1/1	$ 45,000
Charges to patients' accounts	639,200
Cash collections on patients' accounts	634,200

Accounts written off as bad debts	4,690
Collection of accounts previously written off as bad debts	350
Allowance for bad debts, 1/1	5,400

The hospital's aging schedule indicates that $6,000 of the 12/31/X1 accounts receivable will prove uncollectible.

Required: What amount should the hospital's 20X1 statement of operations report as bad debt expense?

E16.4. Pink Hospital maintains an allowance for bad debts as a contra account to receivables from patients. On December 31, 20X1, the allowance account had a credit balance of $2,000. Each month, the hospital accrues bad debts equal to 1 percent of charges to patients' accounts. Charges to patients' accounts during 20X2 amounted to $500,000. During 20X2, accounts receivable totaling $8,000 were written off as bad debts. An aging of receivables at December 31, 20X1 indicates that $10,000 of December 31, 20X1 receivables are likely to prove to be bad debts.

Required: By what amount should bad debt expense previously accrued during 20X2 be increased on December 31, 20X1?

E16.5. Poke Hospital provides you with the following data relating to October activity in its checking account with a local bank:

	Per Books	Per Bank
Balances, 9/30	$11,863	$12,310
October receipts	51,422	50,827
October disbursements	48,705	49,107
Balance, 10/31	14,580	14,030

Deposits in transit:
9/30	$139
10/31	?

Checks outstanding:
9/30	$586
10/31	?

Bank service charges for October, $14
NSF check of patient returned with October bank statement, $108

In reconciling the account, you discover two errors: (1) one of the hospital's accountants journalized a $620 check, issued in payment of an account payable, as $260, and (2) the bank charged the hospital for a $150 check drawn by another of the bank's depositors.

Required: What amount should be reported as cash in bank in the hospital's October 31 balance sheet?

Problems

P16.1.   On June 1, Pixie Hospital established a petty cash fund in the imprest amount of $500. On June 14, the contents of the petty cash fund were as follows when the fund was reimbursed:

Coin and currency	$221
Petty cash expense vouchers	216
IOU from employee	10
Check of another employee made payable to Pixie Hospital	50

On June 16, the imprest amount of the petty cash fund was reduced to $300.

Required: (1) Prepare the necessary entries in general journal form at June 1, 14, and 16. (2) Why do you think the imprest amount of the petty cash fund was reduced on June 16?

P16.2.   Plato Hospital decided to establish a petty cash fund on May 1 in the imprest amount of $750. The following transactions relating to the fund took place during May:

1. The fund was established on May 1.
2. The fund was replenished on May 15 at a time when the contents of the fund were as follows:

Currency and coin	$ 42
Expense vouchers	681
Employee IOU	25

3. On May 16, it was decided to increase the imprest amount of the fund to $1,000.
4. The fund was replenished on May 31 at a time when the contents of the fund were as follows:

Currency and coin	$173
Expense vouchers	837

Required: (1) Prepare general journal entries to record all the petty cash transactions for May. (2) Assuming that the petty cash fund was not reimbursed on May 31, prepare the necessary May 31 adjusting entry.

P16.3.   Painless Hospital's general ledger cash in bank account reports a balance of $346,920 as of October 31. An examination of the October bank statement in comparison with the cash records of the hospital, however, discloses the following information:

1. The October 31 balance per bank statement was $465,900.
2. A deposit in transit at October 31 was for $12,800.
3. Checks outstanding at October 31 totaled $89,300.
4. A patient's NSF $5,100 check was returned by the bank with the October statement.
5. Bank service charges for October were $120.
6. The bank inadvertently credited another of its depositors for Painless Hospital's October 26 bank deposit of $10,600.
7. Matured temporary investments of $50,000, plus interest of $2,000, were collected and credited by the bank to the hospital's checking account on October 29.
8. A hospital employee journalized a properly drawn check for $700 as $7,000 on October 11 in settlement of an account payable.

Required: (1) Prepare a bank reconciliation at October 31 for Painless Hospital. (2) Prepare the necessary adjusting entry at October 31.

P16.4. Parkway Hospital's comparison of its cash records with its March bank statement provides the following information:

	Per Books	Per Bank
1. Balances, 2/28	$14,755	$15,862
Receipts	15,431	17,495
Disbursements	13,744	16,087
Balances, 3/31	16,442	17,270

2. Deposits in transit totaled $1,375 at February 28 and $946 at March 31. Checks outstanding were $2,482 at February 28 and $1,949 at March 31.
3. Bank service charges on the March bank statement were $16.
4. An NSF $479 check of a Parkway Hospital patient was returned by the bank with the March statement.
5. On March 30, the bank collected a Parkway Hospital patient's note to the hospital of $2,000 plus $40 interest. The bank credited the hospital for collection of the note and debited the hospital $7 for the service provided.
6. A hospital bookkeeper on March 12 journalized a $487 deposit as $847. This was a collection on a patient's account.
7. On March 22, the bank charged the hospital's account with a $300 check of another of the bank's depositors. The bank has stated that this mistake would be corrected on the April bank statement.
8. On March 27, one of the hospital's bookkeepers journalized a $10 check as $100. This check was issued in settlement of an account payable.

9. On March 29, the bank failed to give the hospital credit for a $1,055 deposit of that date. When notified of the error on April 4, the bank made a correction, to appear on the April bank statement.

Required: (1) Prepare a bank reconciliation at February 28. (2) Prepare a bank reconciliation at March 31. (3) Prepare the required March 31 adjusting entry.

P16.5.   According to its books, Peerless Hospital has a cash balance of $438,104 at June 30. The June bank statement, however, reports a June 30 balance of $486,681. An investigation produces the following information:

1. The bank credited, in error, Peerless Hospital for a deposit of $28,417 made by Peerless Hospital on June 22.
2. Bank service charges for June amounted to $27.
3. Outstanding checks at June 30 were $107,092.
4. A deposit of $39,865 was in transit at June 30.
5. The June bank statement shows a credit of $10,600 (including $600 interest) representing the proceeds of a patient's note collected for the hospital by the bank.
6. The bank returned patients' checks marked "not sufficient funds" in the amount of $2,606.
7. Check number 1791 issued in payment of an account payable of $200 was recorded in error by a hospital bookkeeper as $2,000 even though the check was drawn in the correct $200 amount.

Required: (1) Prepare a bank reconciliation at June 30. (2) Prepare the necessary adjusting journal entry at June 30.

P16.6.   Parson Hospital purchased $60,000 of U.S. government bonds at face value and accrued interest on September 1, 20X1. These 8 percent bonds pay interest semiannually on April 1 and October 1. Brokerage and other acquisition costs totaled $94. The bonds mature on April 1, 20X6, but the hospital intends to hold these securities as short-term investments in its unrestricted fund. On January 1, 20X2, the bonds are sold by the hospital at 103 percent and accrued interest, with brokerage fees and other expenses of sale amounting to $105. The hospital closes its books annually on December 31.
Required: (1) Prepare, in general journal form, all necessary entries for 20X1 in connection with this investment. (2) Indicate how all matters relating to this investment should be presented in the hospital's 20X1 financial statements. (3) Prepare the necessary entry, in general journal form, to record the sale of the bonds on January 1, 20X2.

P16.7. Potter Hospital purchased $75,000 of corporate bonds at face value and accrued interest on August 1, 20X1, with brokerage and other acquisition costs amounting to $88. These 6 percent bonds pay interest semiannually on June 1 and December 1, and mature on June 1, 20X5. The hospital intends to hold these bonds as a temporary investment of its unrestricted fund. On January 1, 20X2, the bonds are sold by the hospital at 98 percent and accrued interest, with brokerage fees and other expenses of sale amounting to $73. Potter Hospital closes its books annually on December 31. *Required*: (1) Prepare, in general journal form, all necessary entries for 20X1 with respect to this investment. (2) Indicate how all matters relating to this investment should be presented in the hospital's 20X1 financial statements. (3) Prepare the necessary entry, in general journal form, to record the sale of the bonds on January 1, 20X2.

P16.8. A patient gave Peppy Hospital a 9 percent, 90-day promissory note on November 1, 20X1, in settlement of a $12,000 account with the hospital. The hospital closes its books annually on December 31. *Required*: (1) Prepare, in general journal form, all necessary entries with respect to this note for 20X1 and 20X2. (2) Indicate how all matters relating to this note should be presented in the hospital's 20X1 financial statements.

P16.9. A patient gave Popover Hospital a 6 percent, 180-day promissory note on October 1, 20X1, in settlement of an $8,000 account with the hospital. The hospital discounted this note on November 1, 20X1, at a local bank whose discount rate is 9 percent. The hospital closes its books annually on December 31. *Required*: (1) Prepare, in general journal form, all necessary entries with respect to this note for 20X1 and 20X2. (2) Indicate how all matters relating to this note should be presented in the hospital's 20X1 financial statements. (3) Prepare, in general journal form, the necessary entry at the maturity date of the note, assuming that the note is dishonored by the patient and the bank makes a protest fee charge of $22.

P16.10. Packer Hospital has $760,000 of accounts receivable as of December 31, 20X1. An aging schedule is prepared that indicates that bad debts should be estimated in the amount of $58,000. Before adjustment, however, the allowance for bad debts account has a December 31, 20X1, credit balance of $3,700. During 20X2, $64,800 of the 20X1 accounts receivable are written off as bad debts; the remainder of the accounts are collected. On December 31, 20X2, Packer Hospital has $827,000 of accounts receivable, and an aging schedule is prepared that indicates that bad debts should be estimated in the amount of $71,000.

Required: (1) Make the necessary entry at December 31, 20X1, to record the required provision for bad debts. (2) Make the necessary summary entry to record the write off of uncollectible accounts in 20X2. (3) Make the necessary entry as of December 31, 20X2, to record the required provision for bad debts. (4) Indicate the presentation of receivables in the hospital's December 31, 20X2, balance sheet.

P16.11. During 20X1, Pirate Hospital charged patients' accounts for a total of $3,500,000. Its general ledger at December 31, 20X1 (the end of the fiscal year), shows the following balances:

Patients' accounts receivable	$425,000	Dr.
Allowance for uncollectible accounts—bad debts	4,300	Cr.

Required: Prepare the necessary adjusting entries for estimated bad debts assuming that the bad debts (1) are estimated at 1 percent of charges, (2) are estimated at 6 percent of receivables, and (3) are based on an aging of the receivables and are estimated at $31,900.

P16.12. Parker Hospital's adjusted trial balance at December 31, 20X1, included the following accounts:

Accounts receivable—patients	$500,000	Dr.
Allowance for uncollectible accounts:		
Bad debts	40,000	Cr.
Contractuals	50,000	Cr.
Charity service	20,000	Cr.

In 20X2, with respect to the 20X1 accounts receivable, write-offs were made as follows: bad debts, $37,400; contractual adjustments, $51,700; and charity service, $19,200. The remainder of the 20X1 receivables were collected. Parker Hospital's accounts receivable at December 31, 20X2, were $600,000. Estimated uncollectible accounts at that date were bad debts, 9 percent; contractual adjustments, 11 percent; and charity service, 1 percent.

Required: Prepare the receivables section of the hospital's balance sheet as of December 31, 20X2, and present all necessary computations of the amounts included in the presentation.

17

INVENTORIES AND CURRENT LIABILITIES

The first part of this chapter is concerned with accounting procedures pertaining to the acquisition, usage, and valuation of hospital inventories. Besides drugs and pharmaceuticals shelved in the pharmacy, the inventories in a hospital include the foodstuffs located in dietary storerooms and numerous other items ranging from the cleaning supplies used in housekeeping to laboratory chemicals and radiological film. Although the inventory of the hospital may not be of substantial size relative to other assets, the annual usage of supplies is a significant cost element. Supply costs may represent as much as 15 percent of total operating expenses. And, like cash, much of the inventory is highly susceptible to theft. It also should be recognized that the cost of maintaining an inventory—purchasing, receiving, storing, issuing, and insuring—is substantial. Finally, it is necessary for accounting purposes that proper determinations be made of the costs of supplies used and of the costs of supplies remaining unused in the hospital inventory. Therefore, the accountant should not underestimate the importance of adequate accounting and internal control procedures with respect to inventories.

The second part of this chapter pulls together some of the previously discussed materials dealing with current liabilities. Certain other related matters not covered before are also introduced from the context of a balance sheet. The balance sheet classification of current liabilities, as you know, includes a wide variety of debts representing goods and services purchased on account, borrowings from banks, accruals for payrolls, payroll-related obligations, interest, and various other obligations. In fact, all cash disbursements made by the hospital ordinarily must pass through current liability accounts of one kind or another. These accounts consequently deserve a considerable amount of accounting and managerial attention.

Inventories

The operations of a hospital enterprise require the purchase and use (or sale) of a variety of goods and supplies. The purchasing and receiving functions were discussed in Chapter 14, and now we turn to the problems of determining (1) the costs of supplies used (the debits to supplies expense accounts) and (2) the costs of supplies unused and on hand (the valuation of the inventory) for balance sheet purposes. These determinations require an inventory accounting system and the adoption of an inventory valuation method.

Most hospitals employ two different inventory accounting systems concurrently. Certain types of supplies are accounted for by the periodic inventory system; others are concurrently maintained on a perpetual inventory basis. To illustrate the two systems, assume that we have the following information for a particular supply item that we shall refer to as Item X:

			Units	Unit Cost
April	1	Inventory	100	$6
	15	Purchase	400	$6
	20	Usage	350	$6

The month begins with $600 (that is, 100 units at $6 per unit) in the inventory account. What entry is made on April 15 when 400 additional units are purchased? What entry should be made on April 20 to record the usage of 350 units? By what procedure is the inventory at April 30 determined? The last two questions would be much more difficult to answer if the April 15 purchase were made at a unit cost other than $6, but we defer this complication to a later point.

Periodic Inventory System

Under the periodic inventory system, no day-to-day record of supplies in inventory is maintained in the accounting records. As supplies are purchased, they may be charged either to inventory (the asset account) or directly to expense. Assuming the latter, the April 15 entry is as follows:

Supplies expense	60200	$2,400	
Accounts payable	20100		$2,400
Purchase of supplies:			
$6 × 400 units = $2,400			

Generally, the debit is made to a supplies expense account only if the department that will use the supplies is known. Otherwise, the debit is made to an inventory account.

Debit to Expense at Time of Purchase, Not at Time of Use   Whether the above debit is made to supplies expense or to inventory, no entry is made on April 20 when 350 units of these supplies are used in departmental activities. At the end of April, then, the accounts would appear as follows:

Inventory	Supply Expense
600	$2,400

The inventory account shows the inventory balance at April 1, not April 30. The supplies expense account indicates the cost of supplies purchased, not the cost of supplies used. Both account balances are incorrect.

So, at April 30, either a physical inventory (actual count) must be taken or an estimate must be made of the number of units in the month-end inventory. In the absence of error or theft, this quantity will be found to be 150 units (100 units + 400 units − 350 units). Cost prices then are assigned to these units, and the account balances are adjusted accordingly:

Inventory	10600	$300	
Supplies expense	60200		$300
Increase in inventory and corresponding			
reduction in supplies expense			

This entry adjusts the inventory to the proper April 30 balance of $900 ($6 × 150 units) and reduces the supplies expense account balance to $2,100 ($6 × 350 units).

If we assume that the April 15 purchase of 400 units was debited to inventory rather than to supplies expense, the necessary April 30 adjusting entry is as follows:

Supplies expense	60200	$2,100	
Inventory	10600		$2,100
Cost of supplies used during April:			
$6 x 350 units = $2,100			

So, regardless of the debit made in the April 15 entry, we end April with $900 in inventory and $2,100 in supplies expense.

The periodic inventory system has the advantage of simplicity; it is clerically inexpensive. Because monthly physical inventory counts usually are not practical (and accurate monthly inventory estimates may not be available), however, the account balances may be somewhat distorted until actual counts and appropriate adjustments can be made. The degree of misstatement usually is not serious for interim reporting purposes, but physical inventories must be taken at least once each year, generally at the end of the fiscal period. The major disadvantage of the periodic inventory system is that the accounting records do not provide a means for control. The physical inventory indicates what the inventory is, of course, but the accounting records do not indicate what the inventory should be. Significant shortages therefore may go undetected.

Perpetual Inventory System

Under the perpetual inventory system, records are maintained to provide a continuous record of supplies purchased, used, and on hand. Supplies accounted for on this basis are always charged to inventory accounts when purchased. The necessary April 15 entry is as follows:

Inventory	10600	$2,400	
Accounts payable	20100		$2,400
Purchase of 400 units of supplies			
at $6 per unit			

An entry is also made in subsidiary inventory ledger records to reflect this inventory acquisition, increasing the inventory balance to 500 units having a total cost of $3,000 (the April 1 inventory of 100 units at $6 each plus the April 15 purchase of 400 units at $6 each). Perpetual inventory ledger cards, such as the one illustrated in Figure 17.1, may be used, or inventory subsidiary records may be maintained by computer. Whatever the means employed, a continuous record is maintained of the units (with unit costs) received, issued, and remaining on hand.

Perpetual Inventory System Forms As the supplies are required by departments for use in day-to-day activities, stores requisition forms (see Figure 17.2) are executed. The forms provide a record of the quantities and costs of supplies used by the various departments of the hospital. Copies of these forms are routed to the accounting department, where they serve as the basis for entries debiting the supplies expense accounts and crediting the inventory accounts. The April 20 entry, for example, is as follows:

Supplies expense	60200	$2,100	
Inventory	10600		$2,100
Requisition from inventory of			
350 units of supplies that cost			
$6 per unit			

An entry also is made in the subsidiary ledger records to reflect a reduction of 350 units in the inventory, thus lowering the inventory balance to 150 units of this supply item. These subsidiary ledger records may be kept in terms of quantities only, unit costs only, or in both quantities and costs, as illustrated in Figure 17.1.

Adjusting the Perpetual Inventory Accounts At least once each year, a physical inventory is taken and the perpetual records are adjusted, if necessary, to reflect the actual count. The main point is that the perpetual inventory ledger, in the absence of accounting errors, indicates precisely what the inventory should be at any time.

Advantages and Disadvantages of Perpetual Inventory System The choice of inventory system depends mainly on the characteristics of particular supply items. If the dollar value of annual usage is substantial, if the supplies have a high unit cost and are susceptible to theft, or if the supplies are directly billable to patients, then the perpetual inventory system is often desirable. The perpetual system provides continuous control over the inventory,

FIGURE 17.1

Perpetual
Inventory
Ledger Card

| LOCATION _____ ITEM _____ STOCK NO. _____ |
| DESCRIPTION _____ UNIT _____ |

1 VENDOR		3 VENDOR		DATE	MAXIMUM	MINIMUM
2		4				

ORDERED				RECEIVED				ISSUED				BALANCE ON HAND		
DATE 20__	ORDER NO.	VENDOR NO.	QUANTITY	DATE 20__	ORDER NO.	QUANTITY	PRICE	AMOUNT	DATE 20__	ORDER NO.	QUANTITY	PRICE	AMOUNT	QUANTITY	PRICE	AMOUNT

because information is immediately available as to inventory levels. Purchasing is facilitated, the adequacy of supplies on hand is more likely, and shortages are readily identified. Perpetual records also are useful for maintaining adequate insurance coverage and for documentation of losses. Because it is a costly system to administer, however, careful studies should be made to determine whether the benefits derived from perpetual records exceed the costs of installing and maintaining them.

Inventory Valuation Methods

The preceding example assumed a single unit cost of supplies. In actual practice, however, supplies typically are purchased during a given time period at different unit costs. A problem therefore arises in determining which unit costs relate to the supply items that have been used during the period and which apply to the units remaining in inventory at the end of the period. These determinations are important because of their direct effect on the hospital's reported operating expenses and excess of revenues over expenses, as well as on the balance sheet valuation of the end-of-period inventory.

As a basis for subsequent illustrations, let us assume the following data concerning a particular supply item:

FIGURE 17.2

Stores
(Inventory)
Requisition
Form

STORES REQUISITION						

REQUISITION NO. _____

DEPARTMENT_____ DATE _____ 20____

FLOOR OR DIVISION _____ DATE REQUIRED_____ 20____

QUANTITY		DESCRIPTION OF SUPPLIES NEEDED	TO BE USED IF PERPETUAL INVENTORIES ARE KEPT			
WANTED	DELIVERED		PRICE	PER	AMOUNT	ACCT. NO.

REQUESTED BY
_____

APPROVED BY
_____

SEND ORIGINAL TO STORE ROOM CLERK. DUPLICATE IS RETAINED BY DEPARTMENT HEAD.

			Units	Cost Unit	Cost Total
May	1	Inventory	200	$2.00	$ 400
	5	Purchase	400	2.50	1,000
	10	Usage	300		
	15	Purchase	500	3.00	1,500
	20	Usage	600		
	25	Purchase	100	3.50	350
					$3,250

The month begins with an inventory of 200 units that cost $2 each. During the month of May, a total of 1,000 more units were purchased at steadily increasing prices, and, because 900 units were used during the month, the May 31 inventory consists of 300 units. In this illustration, the total cost of the opening inventory and purchases is $3,250. What part of this total cost is the cost of supplies used during the month? What part should be assigned to the 300 units remaining in the month-end inventory? There are several different possible answers to these questions, depending on the inventory valuation method that is adopted by the hospital.

Specific Identification

It may be feasible to make a specific identification of unit purchase costs with individual items of inventory. Where the inventory items are packaged or are in containers of some kind, the packages or cartons may be crayon-marked or tagged in some manner to show actual unit costs. Then, as items are issued from inventory to departments, the stores requisition forms can be completed to indicate the specifically identified unit costs. When the annual physical inventory is taken, the marked containers will provide the necessary unit figures for the costing of the units in the inventory. Figure 17.3 illustrates the type of form sometimes used to take the physical inventory and to assign costs to the units counted.

The specific identification method, however, is generally impractical, if not impossible, to apply. This is because of the multiplicity of products in hospital inventories and because the marking of unit costs on each item either is not feasible or is too labor-costly. It therefore is necessary to turn to some assumed flow of inventory units or costs. Some generally accepted assumptions are (1) weighted-average; (2) first-in, first-out; and (3) last-in, first-out. Different assumptions may be made for different classifications of inventory; the same assumption need not be applied to all supply items in the inventory.

Weighted-Average Costing

Weighted-average costing assumes that the units issued from inventory are drawn more or less equally from each acquisition of supplies. It is not necessary, however, that the actual physical flow of the units in inventory correspond with this assumption.

If the periodic inventory system is employed, a weighted average cost for the month of May would be computed as indicated in Figure 17.4. This computation, which is made at the end of the month, indicates that the weighted-average cost per unit was $2.71 (rounded to the nearest cent). The May 31 inventory is therefore valued at $813 ($2.71 × 300 units). This leaves $2,437 ($3,250 − $813) as the cost of supplies used during the month.

Computing the Weighted-Average Cost

The necessary May 31 journal entry, assuming that the month's purchases were debited to the inventory account, is as follows:

Supplies expense	60200	$2,437	
Inventory	10600		$2,437
Cost of supplies used during May,			
under the weighted-average cost			
method (periodic inventory system)			

The credit in this entry reduces the inventory account balance from $3,250 ($400 + $1,000 + $1,500 + $350) to $813. Had purchases been debited to supplies expense, the month-end adjustment would have been a debit to inventory and a credit to supplies expense for $413.

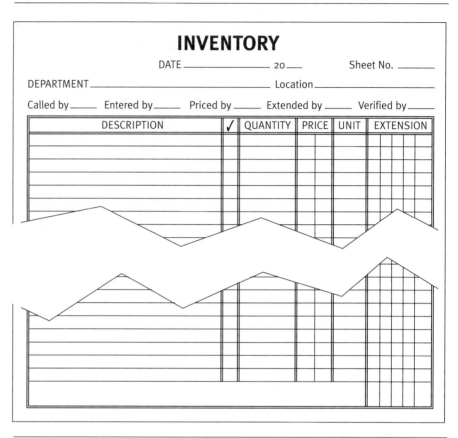

May	1	Inventory	$2.00	×	200 units	=	$ 400
	5	Purchase	$2.50	×	400 units	=	1,000
	15	Purchase	$3.00	×	500 units	=	1,500
	25	Purchase	$3.50	×	100 units	=	350
		Totals			1,200		$3,250

Weighted-average cost ($3,250 ÷ 1,200 units)   = $ 2.71

Computing the Moving Weighted-Average Cost

If the perpetual inventory system is employed but the cost of units issued is recorded only at the end of each month or other convenient period, the computation of the weighted-average cost can be the same as shown in Figure 17.4. On the other hand, it may be desirable to compute and record costs as supplies are issued from the inventory. This requires the computation of a new weighted-average cost after each purchase of supplies at a unit cost different from the current average cost of the inventory. In other words, a "moving" weighted-average cost is computed. Figure 17.5 shows how this computation might appear on an inventory ledger card.

	Purchases				Issues				Balance		
			Cost				Cost				Cost
Date	Units	Unit	Total		Units	Unit	Total		Units	Unit	Total
May 1									200	$2.00	$ 400
5	400	$2.50	$1,000						600	2.33	1,400
10					300	$2.33	$ 700		300	2.33	700
15	500	3.00	1,500						800	2.75	2,200
20					600	2.75	1,650		200	2.75	550
25	100	3.50	350						300	3.00	900
					Cost of supplies used		$2,350				

FIGURE 17.5

Computation of Weighted-Average Cost Perpetual Inventory System

Thus, a new weighted-average cost is determined after each additional purchase. After the purchase of May 5, for instance, the recomputed average cost is $2.33, determined by a division of $1,400 by 600 units. As a result, the cost of supplies used is computed to be $2,350 (compared to $2,437 under the periodic inventory system), and the ending inventory is $900 (compared to $813 under the periodic inventory system).

First-In, First-Out Costing

The first-in, first-out (FIFO) costing method assumes that the supplies issued from inventory are pulled from the oldest stock. This means that the remaining units in inventory are valued in terms of the most recently incurred costs (last-in, still-here, or LISH). The assumption appears logical in that some effort usually is made to issue the oldest stock first. Nevertheless, the actual physical flow of the units need not conform with the underlying FIFO assumption for this method to be acceptable.

If the periodic inventory system is used, the 300-unit inventory at May 31 would be valued as follows:

100 units × $3.50 = $350 (most recent purchase)
200 units × $3.00 =   600 (from next most recent purchase)
300 units $950 May 31 inventory valuation

Because the ending inventory is composed of the most recently incurred costs, the cost assigned to supplies used during the month is $2,300 ($3,250 − $950), the "oldest" costs.

If the perpetual inventory system is used in conjunction with FIFO costing, the same results as noted above are obtained. The procedure is illustrated in Figure 17.6 as it might appear on a subsidiary inventory ledger card. This allows the cost of supplies used to be determined at the time of issuance from inventory rather than only at the end of the month or year.

Determining Costs at Time of Inventory Issuance

FIGURE 17.6

Computation of FIFO Cost Perpetual Inventory System

	Purchases			Issues			Balance		
Date	Units	Cost Unit	Total	Units	Cost Unit	Total	Units	Cost Unit	Total
May 1							200	$2.00	$400
5	400	$2.50	$1,000				200	2.00	400
							400	2.50	1,000
10				200	$2.00	$ 400			
				100	2.50	250	300	2.50	750
15	500	3.00	1,500				300	2.50	750
							500	3.00	1,500
20				300	2.50	750			
				300	3.00	900	200	3.00	600
25	100	3.50	350				200	3.00	900
							100	3.50	350
				Cost of supplies used		$2,300			

Last-In, First-Out Costing

The last-in, first-out (LIFO) method of inventory valuation assumes that the supplies issued from inventory are drawn from the *most recently purchased stock*; the units are charged out of inventory at the most recently incurred costs. This means that the ending inventory will be stated in terms of the earliest (oldest) costs experienced (first-in, still-here, or FISH). It may be somewhat difficult to imagine a hospital supplies situation in which there would actually be a LIFO flow of physical units, but you must remember that the physical flow need not conform to the LIFO assumption for the use of the method to be acceptable. The LIFO procedure is really based on an assumed flow of costs rather than of units.

If the periodic inventory system is used, the physical inventory of 300 units at May 31 would have a cost computed as follows:

200 units × $2.00 = $400 (earliest costs; May 1 inventory)
100 units × $2.50 = 250 (next earliest costs; May 5 purchase)
300                   $650 May 31 inventory valuation

Because the May 31 inventory is composed of the earliest costs incurred, the cost of supplies issued during the month consists of the most recently incurred costs, or $2,600 ($3,250 − $650). Again, although it is unlikely that the oldest physical units comprise the inventory at May 31, the LIFO method's validity does not depend on the actual physical flow of the units of inventory.

	Purchases			Issues			Balance		
		Cost			Cost			Cost	
Date	Units	Unit	Total	Units	Unit	Total	Units	Unit	Total
May 1							200	$2.00	$ 400
5	400	$2.50	$1,000				200	2.00	400
							400	2.50	1,000
10				300	$2.50	$750	200	2.00	400
							100	2.50	250
15	500	3.00	1,500				200	2.00	400
							100	2.50	250
							500	3.00	1,500
20				500	3.00	1,500			
				100	2.50	250	200	2.00	400
25	100	3.50	350				200	2.00	400
							100	3.50	350
		Cost of supplies used				$2,500			

FIGURE 17.7
Computation of LIFO Cost Perpetual Inventory System

Results Differ with LIFO Under Perpetual and Periodic Systems

If the perpetual inventory system is employed in conjunction with the LIFO method, the required procedure is illustrated in Figure 17.7 as it may appear on a subsidiary inventory ledger card. As indicated, the perpetual LIFO cost of supplies used is $2,500 and the May 31 inventory is $750 ($400 + $350), while the periodic LIFO figures were $2,600 and $650. It should be noted that the periodic and perpetual inventory systems ordinarily do not produce the same results when the LIFO method is employed; they do produce the same results, however, when the FIFO method is used.

Conclusions About Costing Methods

The hospital management has a choice among the inventory costing methods in most instances. Which method should be adopted? The method should, of course, be theoretically sound and clerically feasible. Consideration also should be given to the probable effect of the method on the reported results of operations and financial position. The implications of each method for third-party cost reimbursement contracts and tax status (for for-profit healthcare organizations) also may be important.

Figure 17.8 summarizes the results obtained by the use of FIFO, LIFO, and weighted-average costing (the three most widely used methods), assuming the perpetual inventory system. This illustration reveals that, in a period of rising prices, the LIFO method produces the highest operating expenses and the lowest inventory valuation. FIFO produces the opposite results. Weighted-average costing will provide results somewhere between those obtained from FIFO and LIFO.

FIGURE 17.8

Inventory
System

	Costing Method		
	FIFO	Average	LIFO
Inventory, 5/1	$ 400	$ 400	$ 400
Purchases	2,850	2,850	2,850
Total	3,250	3,250	3,250
Less inventory, 5/31	950	900	750
Cost of supplies used in May	$2,300	$2,350	$2,500

Internal Control

Internal controls over the purchase and receipt of supplies for inventory were discussed in Chapter 14. Once supplies are acquired, the initial internal control objective is largely that of protecting the inventory items from theft, damage, waste, and obsolescence, as they remain in storage and then are consumed in hospital operations. A major requirement is the assignment of responsibility to specific employees for management of inventories at each location in the hospital. The number of such locations should be minimized so that centralized control may be better achieved.

The storage areas should be kept clean, adequately lighted, and locked, with access limited strictly to authorized employees. Supplies should be released from the storerooms only on presentation of properly executed inventory requisition forms. Listings of approved authorization signatures should be issued by administration and reviewed periodically. Maximum-minimum controls (often called par levels) should be devised that permit inventories to be maintained in amounts that are neither inadequate nor excessive. Where perpetual inventory records are kept, these records should be reconciled with physical inventories taken at least annually.

Current Liabilities

The traditional working definition of **current liabilities** commonly employed identifies them as obligations that mature and normally will be paid within approximately one year from the balance sheet date. Included in the current liability classification are notes payable, accounts payable, current maturities of long-term debt, accrued liabilities for expenses and other items, and deferred revenues.

Notes Payable

Notes payable are obligations in the form of promissory notes issued to trade creditors for the purchase of goods and services, to banks for loans of a short-term character, and to other organizations. Whereas accounts payable generally fall due within a month, notes may be outstanding for 90, 180, or more days from the balance sheet date. This requires, for interim reporting purposes, the accrual of interest expense on a monthly basis.

To illustrate the accounting procedures involved, assume that a hospital issues its 90-day, 10 percent note for $36,000 to a local bank on August 1, 20X1. The interest on this note is $900 ($36,000 × 10 percent × [90 days ÷ 360 days]). The maturity date of the note is October 30, 20X1. All necessary entries for the 90-day term of the note are summarized in Figure 17.9.

Prepaid Loan Expenses

In some instances, local banking practices may dictate that interest on loans be deducted in advance from the loan proceeds. This, in effect, means that the hospital is prepaying the interest expense. If that were the case for this loan, the proceeds would be only $35,100 ($36,000 – $900), and the $900 would be accounted for as prepaid interest expense, as illustrated in Figure 17.10. It should be noted here that the hospital is paying $900 interest for the use of $35,100 for 90 days; so the effective (true) rate of interest is actually higher than the 10 percent rate quoted by the bank.

Accounts Payable

Trade accounts payable originate from the purchase of supplies and services on account. In many such purchases, a cash discount is allowed to the hospital if the related invoices are paid within a specified period of time. It is important, therefore, that the accounting system provide assurance that invoices are paid, whenever possible, within the discount period. It can be a costly omission to fail to take these discounts. (It should be noted that **trade discounts**, which may be obtained from a supplier because of large-volume buying or other reasons, are always considered a reduction in cost. Only the billed price, net of any trade discount, should be recorded in the hospital's accounts.)

Purchase Discounts

To illustrate, assume that the hospital purchases $5,000 of supplies on account, with terms of 2/10, net 30, on October 31. This means that, if the invoice is paid within ten days (by November 10), a 2 percent cash discount can be taken by the hospital. The discount would amount to $100 (2 percent of $5,000), and a payment of only $4,900 ($5,000 – $100) would be required. If the hospital does not pay the invoice within 10 days, however, the supplier must be paid the full $5,000 within 30 days. So, if the hospital waits until, say, November 30 to pay the invoice, it is in effect paying an additional $100 (or 2 percent) for delaying its payment for 20 days. Because there are roughly 18 periods of 20 days in a year, missing the discount would be the equivalent of paying 36 percent interest (18 periods × 2 percent) per year on purchases.

The procedure described in earlier chapters is indicated by the following journal entries:

FIGURE 17.9

Accounting for
Notes Payable
Interest Not
Prepaid

Cash Receipts Journal

8/1	Cash—general checking account	10110	$36,000	
	Notes payable	20200		$36,000
	Issuance of 90-day, 10% note			
	to a local bank for a short-term loan			
	of $36,000			

General Journal

8/31	Interest expense	60800	$ 300	
	Accrued interest payable	10300		$ 300
	Accrual of interest expense on note			
	for August: $36,000 × 10% ×			
	(30 days ÷ 360 days)			

General Journal

9/30	Interest expense	60800	$ 300	
	Accrued interest payable	20300		$ 300
	Accrual of interest expense on			
	note for September			

Voucher Register

10/30	Interest expense	60800	$ 300	
	Accrued interest payable	10300	600	
	Notes payable	20200	36,000	
	Accounts payable	20100		$36,900
	Issuance of voucher for payment			
	of note and interest to maturity date			

Cash Disbursements Journal

10/30	Accounts payable	20100	$36,900	
	Cash—general checking account	10110		$36,900
	Issuance of check in payment			
	of note and interest			

Voucher Register

10/31	Supplies expense	60200	$5,000	
	Accounts payable	20100		$5,000
	Voucher for purchase of			
	supplies on account			

Cash Disbursements Journal

11/10	Accounts payable	20100	$5,000	
	Purchase discounts earned			$ 100
	Cash—general checking			
	account	10110		4,900
	Check issued in payment of			
	voucher			

FIGURE 17.10

Accounting for
Notes Payable
Interest Prepaid

Cash Receipts Journal

8/1	Cash—general checking account	10110	$35,100	
	Prepaid interest		900	
	Notes payable	10900		$36,000
	Issuance of 90-day, 10% note to a			
	local bank for a short-term loan of			
	$36,000, with interest prepaid			

General Journal

8/31	Interest expense	60800	$ 300	
	Prepaid interest	10900		$ 300
	Recognition of interest expense			
	on note for August ($900 × 1/3)			

General Journal

9/30	Interest expense	60800	$ 300	
	Prepaid interest	10900		$ 300
	Recognition of interest expense			
	on note for September			

Voucher Register

10/30	Interest expense	60800	$ 300	
	Notes payable	20200	36,000	
	Prepaid interest expense			$ 300
	Accounts payable			36,000
	Issuance of voucher for payment of			
	note and to recognize interest			
	expense for October			

Cash Disbursements Journal

10/30	Accounts payable	20100	$36,000	
	Cash—general checking account	10110		$36,000
	Issuance of check in payment of note			

Notice here that purchase discounts are recorded only when taken, and they are treated as other operating income. If we can assume that all available discount opportunities will be taken, this procedure has a number of weaknesses. First, the voucher register entry overstates both the cost of the supplies and the amount of the liability. Second, income is not earned by purchasing. Third, if the discount is missed, no recognition is given to the discount lost in the accounting records. That is, the cash disbursements journal entry would be simply a debit to accounts payable and a credit to cash for $5,000.

Recording Supplies at the Amount the Hospital Should Pay

An alternative procedure designed to overcome the weaknesses of the system is indicated by the following entries:

Voucher Register

10/31	Supplies expense	60200	$4,900	
	Accounts payable	20100		$4,900
	Voucher (net of discount) for purchase of supplies on account			

Cash Disbursements Journal

11/10	Accounts payable	20100	$4,900	
	Cash—general checking account	10110		$4,900
	Check issued in payment of voucher			

In this way, the supplies and the related liability are recorded at the amount that the hospital should pay; no discount earned is recorded if the invoice is paid on time. If the discount is missed, however, the payment entry will be as follows:

Cash Disbursements Journal

11/10	Accounts payable	20100	$4,900	
	Purchase discounts lost	61000	100	
	Cash—general checking account	10110		$5,000
	Check issued in payment of voucher after discount period has elapsed			

Here, the use of the purchase discounts lost account (which is treated as a financial expense) points up an inefficiency in the hospital's processing of its accounts payable. Thus, management's attention is drawn to a situation that requires corrective action. Management should be more interested in the amount of purchase discounts lost than in the amount of discounts taken.

Current Maturities of Long-Term Liabilities

Mortgages, bonds, and other long-term obligations of the hospital should be reported as current liabilities to the extent that they are to be paid within one year from resources classified as current assets. In many instances, such as with mortgage notes and bonds that mature in annual installments, a portion of the total obligation is presented as a current liability, and the balance of the debt remains in the long-term liability classification. Assume, for example, that a hospital issues $5 million of bonds on January 1, 20X1, and that $500,000 of this bond issue matures each year for ten years, beginning January 1, 20X2. The December 31, 20X1, balance sheet therefore should report $500,000 among the current liabilities and $4.5 million as long-term debt.

Accrued Liabilities

Accrued liabilities are obligations that arise as a result of past transactions—usually ones involving contractual commitments and tax legislation. Included in this balance sheet classification are accrued salaries and wages payable, payroll withholdings and tax accruals, and various expense items such as interest and rent. Because of their materiality, accrued payroll and payroll-related liabilities typically are reported separately from other accrued liabilities. Accounting procedures for these liabilities were discussed in several earlier chapters, particularly Chapters 5 and 13.

Deferred Revenues

Hospitals sometimes receive cash advances from patients, third-party payers, and others for services that are to be provided in the future. Prepayments of this kind, which include patients' admission deposits, advances from third-party reimbursement agencies, and tuition, rent, and interest received in advance, are recorded as liabilities when they are received. If the provision of such future services will involve significant costs to be financed from the hospital's current resources, these advances are properly classified as current liabilities.

It sometimes has been the practice to report all deferred revenues in a balance sheet classification separately located between current liabilities and long-term liabilities. This practice, however, should be avoided. Deferred revenues should be identified as either current or long-term liabilities and be reported in the balance sheet accordingly.

Preferred Balance Sheet Listing of Deferred Revenues

Internal Control

The key to effective internal control over liabilities lies in (1) an appropriate authorization of purchase, borrowing, payroll, or other transactions giving rise to liabilities, and (2) an accurate determination of the amounts in which such liabilities are recorded. The voucher system employed should require that authorizations and approvals be fully evidenced in writing before any liabilities are recorded and before disbursements are made to discharge them. Appropriate subsidiary ledger records should be maintained by employees who are independent of the general ledger accounting function. These detailed records should be reconciled with the related general ledger control accounts on a regular basis.

Questions

Q17.1. Indicate some of the major requirements for a good system of internal control over hospital inventories.

Q17.2. Distinguish between the periodic inventory system and the perpetual inventory system. What are the advantages and disadvantages of each system? Which system should be used by hospitals?

Q17.3. Indicate the reasons that a considerable amount of importance should be assigned to inventory accounting and management in a hospital.

Q17.4. Distinguish between the FIFO and LIFO inventory costing methods. In a period of rising prices, which method would tend to result in the recording of the highest costs for supplies used? In a period of rising prices, which method would tend to result in the highest end-of-period inventory?

Q17.5. Quiet Hospital had a 20X1 excess of revenues over expenses of $164,000. The cost of supplies used during the year totaled $713,000. The hospital's inventory of supplies increased by $27,000, and accounts payable to suppliers increased by $39,400 during the 20X1 year. What was the amount of cash payments to suppliers during 20X1?

Q17.6. Because of an error, Quest Hospital's December 31, 20X1, inventory was understated by $19,000. What is the effect of this error on the hospital's reported excess of revenues over expenses for 20X1 and its balance sheet at December 31, 20X1? What effect, if any, will this error have on the hospital's 20X2 excess of revenues over expenses?

Q17.7. Define *current liabilities*. Give six examples of accounts that are reported in the current liability section of the hospital's balance sheet.

Q17.8. What are the financial consequences of a continued failure to take advantage of cash discount opportunities in the payment of accounts payable?

Q17.9. Quaint Hospital purchased supplies on account and paid the related invoice within the specified discount period. The following entries were made:

Supplies expense	$3,000	
Accounts payable		$3,000
Accounts payable	$3,000	
Purchase discounts		$60
Cash—general checking account		2,940

From a theoretical and practical point of view, what is wrong with these entries? Briefly explain the alternative "discounts lost" procedure.

Q17.10. What are some of the major features of a satisfactory system of internal control over hospital liabilities?

Exercises

E17.1. Quitt Hospital provides you with the following information relating to its activities for January:

Accounts payable to suppliers, 1/1	$ 10,000
Inventory, 1/1	14,000
Payments on accounts payable to suppliers	80,000
Revenues	335,000
Inventory, 1/31	17,000
Accounts payable to suppliers, 1/31	15,000
Operating expenses (excluding cost of supplies used)	233,000

Required: What amount should the hospital's January statement of operations report as excess of revenues over expenses?

E17.2. Quirk Hospital made inventory errors as follows:

- December 31, 20X1 inventory overstated by $400
- December 31, 20X1 inventory understated by $100

Required: (1) By what amount was the hospital's 20X2 excess of revenues over expenses overstated or understated due to these errors? (2) By what amount were the hospital's net assets (fund balance) overstated or understated at December 31, 20X2 due to these errors?

E17.3. Quark Hospital issues its 12 percent, 90-day, $100,000 promissory note to a local bank to obtain a short-term loan on April 1. Interest was not prepaid.
Required: Prepare, in general journal form, the necessary entry on June 30 to record payment of the note and interest.

E17.4. Answer the following multiple-choice questions:

1. The use of a discounts lost account indicates that the recorded cost of a purchased inventory item is its

a. Invoice price.

b. Invoice price plus the purchase discount lost.

c. Invoice price less the discount taken.

d. Invoice price less the discount allowable, whether or not it is taken.

2. A hospital has been using the FIFO method of inventory valuation for 15 years. Its inventory at the end of the 15th year was $26,000, but it would have been $15,000 if LIFO had been used. Thus, if LIFO had been used during the 15-year period, the hospital's excess of revenues over expenses would have been

a. $11,000 less over the 15-year period.

b. $11,000 greater over the 15-year period.

c. $11,000 less for the 15th year.

d. $11,000 greater for the 15th year.

3. A hospital's inventory valuation in its balance sheet was lower using FIFO than LIFO. Assuming no beginning inventory, in what direction did the unit cost of purchases move during the period?

a. Up.

b. Down.

c. No change.

d. Cannot be determined from the information given.

4. The September 30 physical inventory of a hospital properly included $13,000 of supplies that were not recorded as purchases until October. What effect will this error have on September 30 assets, liabilities, net assets (fund balance), and excess of revenues over expenses for the year then ended, respectively?

a. No effect; overstate; understate; understate.

b. No effect; understate; understate; overstate.

c. Understate; no effect; overstate; overstate.

d. No effect; understate; overstate; overstate.

Problems

P17.1. Quick Hospital provides you with the following information for a single supply item purchased and used in its radiology department:

			Units	Unit Cost
May	1	Inventory	400	$7
	8	Usage	300	
	15	Purchase	200	$8
	22	Purchase	200	$9
	27	Usage	200	

Required: Compute the cost of supplies used in May, assuming (1) periodic LIFO costing, (2) perpetual LIFO costing, (3) periodic FIFO costing, and (4) periodic weighted-average costing.

P17.2. Given the following data relating to a single billable supply item purchased and sold by Quack Hospital:

	Units	Cost Per Unit	Total
Inventory, 10/1	200	$1.00	$ 200
Purchases:			
10/5	200	2.00	400
10/15	400	3.00	1,200
10/25	200	4.50	900
Sales:			
10/10	300		
October 20	400		

Required: Compute the cost of supplies sold to patients during October and the inventory valuation at October 31, assuming the following:

1. Periodic inventory system
   a. Weighted-average costing
   b. FIFO costing
   c. LIFO costing
2. Perpetual inventory system
   a. Weighted-average costing
   b. FIFO costing
   c. LIFO costing

P17.3. Queen Hospital began operating a new department on April 1. This department purchased and issued a single supply item as follows:

			Units	Unit Cost
April	1	Purchased	500	$5
	5	Issued	300	
	10	Purchased	200	$6
	15	Purchased	300	$7
	25	Issued	400	

Required: Assuming that this supply item is billed to patients at $10 per unit, compute the gross profit made by this department during April if the department uses (1) a perpetual FIFO costing method or (2) a perpetual LIFO costing method.

P17.4. Quip Hospital issues its 90-day, 10 percent note to a local bank for a short-term loan of $48,000 on September 1, 20X1. Interest on the note was not deducted in advance. The hospital's fiscal year ends on September 30.

Required: Prepare, in general journal form, all necessary entries for 20X1 in connection with this note.

P17.5. Quinn Hospital issues its 120-day, 12 percent note to a local bank for a short-term loan of $75,000 on October 1, 20X1. Interest on the note was deducted in advance. The hospital's fiscal year ends on December 31.

Required: Prepare, in general journal form, all necessary entries for 20X1 and 20X2 in connection with this note.

P17.6. Quaker Hospital provides you with the following information about the purchase and usage of one of its billable supply items:

			Units	Cost Per Unit	Total
June	1	Inventory	300	$4.00	$1,200
	5	Purchase	500	4.60	2,300
	10	Usage	400		
	15	Purchase	450	5.20	2,340
	20	Usage	550		
	27	Purchase	200	5.50	1,100

This supply item is billed to patients at $8.00 per unit.

Required: Assume that Quaker Hospital employs the perpetual LIFO system of accounting for this supply item. (1) Prepare an inventory ledger card for the month of June. (2) Prepare, in general journal form, all necessary entries for the month of June. (3) Assume that the physical inventory at June 30 indicates that 480 units are on hand in the inventory. What adjusting entry, if any, would you suggest?

PLANT ASSETS AND DEPRECIATION

A hospital's plant assets consist of land, land improvements, buildings, and equipment. Other descriptive terms such as fixed assets, capital assets, and tangible assets also are often used as synonyms for this classification of resources. In any event, these assets are not intended for sale in the normal course of business but are held for use over a period of years in the provision of hospital services. Except for land, plant assets deteriorate with use and the passage of time; they eventually wear out. This "wearing out" process, as you already know, is recognized in accounting through depreciation, the rational and systematic allocation of the cost of plant assets to expense over their useful lives.

Previous chapters gave only minimum attention to the problems of accounting for plant assets and depreciation. We should now explore in some detail the accounting concepts and procedures employed by hospitals in recording the acquisition, depreciation, and disposal of plant properties. These are matters of considerable significance, because it is not at all unusual to find a very large portion of a hospital's assets invested in land, buildings, and equipment. Developing and maintaining adequate records of these long-lived and costly assets clearly must be one of the imperatives of hospital accounting.

Plant assets are usually defined by two criteria: the cost and useful life of the asset. Every hospital has its own policy regarding plant assets, but in general, the asset should have a cost of at least $500 (many hospitals use $1,000 or $2,500) and a useful life greater than one year. Since 1998, the Medicare program has allowed hospitals to set the capitalization minimum as high as $5,000. Anything acquired for less than the minimum stated in the hospital policy will be expensed.

Acquisition of Plant Assets

Hospitals generally acquire plant assets either by purchase or by donation. A purchase of plant assets should result only from a budgetary process and a carefully constructed program of capital expenditures. The amounts that can be spent for this purpose are limited, and the available funds must be allocated in the most effective manner consistent with the long-range objectives of the hospital. This program should also include an ongoing effort to secure plant assets by donation so that donors are encouraged to contribute in a form and manner best suited to the hospital's real needs. All plant asset acquisitions, whether by purchase or by donation, should also require the approval of the governing board of the hospital.

As plant assets are acquired, appropriate accounting records should be established. This requires a proper account classification of the assets and an accurate determination of their "cost." In addition to the general ledger record, a suitable subsidiary ledger record also must be maintained for accounting and internal control purposes.

Classification of Plant Assets

Hospital plant assets, with the related accumulated depreciation accounts, traditionally have been classified in the following manner:

Account
Numbers

12000	Land
12050	Land improvements
12100	Accumulated depreciation—land improvements
13000	Buildings and building improvements
13100	Accumulated depreciation—buildings and building improvements
14000	Fixed equipment
14100	Accumulated depreciation—fixed equipment
14200	Major movable equipment
14300	Accumulated depreciation—major movable equipment
14400	Minor equipment
14500	Accumulated depreciation—minor equipment

This classification, or some variation of it, probably is employed by a majority of hospitals. Let us briefly examine the nature and content of each of the six primary asset accounts.

Land
The land account includes the cost of earth surface owned by the hospital and used in the ordinary course of hospital operations. It includes all land used for building sites, yards and grounds, and parking areas. Land acquired for future expansion and not currently in use should not be included in the land account but should be reported among the long-term investments in the hospital's balance sheet. Because land does not deteriorate with use or the passage of time, it is not subject to depreciation.

Land Improvements
Land improvements consist of the cost of on-site water and sewer systems, fencing and walls, sidewalks, shrubbery and trees, and paving of roadways and parking lots. These costs are depreciable and therefore should be separately recorded in the accounts to distinguish them from land costs that are not depreciable.

This account should reflect the cost of all buildings owned by the hospital and used in its normal day-to-day activities. Included in this account are the hospital buildings themselves, personnel residences, garages and storage houses, and utility structures, such as an outlying heating and cooling plant. A building that has been donated to the hospital for endowment investment purposes and that is not used in regular hospital activities should be reported among the assets of the endowment fund. All hospital buildings, of course, are depreciable.

Buildings

The fixed equipment account includes the cost of equipment that is affixed to, and constitutes a structural component of, the hospital building. Another characteristic of fixed equipment is that it is not subject to transfer or removal from its fixed location. Equipment in this classification includes such items as mechanical and electrical systems, elevators, generators, pumps, boilers, and refrigeration machinery. All of this equipment is depreciable over a relatively long life.

Fixed Equipment

The following are general characteristics of equipment included in this category:

Major Movable Equipment

- A capability of being readily moved from one location to another in the hospital
- A unit cost sufficiently large to justify the expense incident to control by means of a subsidiary equipment ledger
- A minimum useful life usually exceeding one year

Some examples of major movable equipment are desks, chairs, beds, automobiles and trucks, accounting machines, sterilizers, operating tables, and radiology equipment. Major movable equipment items are depreciable over lives generally much shorter than for fixed equipment.

Minor equipment items include wastebaskets, bedpans, glassware, sheets, basins, buckets, silverware, and most surgical instruments. As a matter of expedience, many accounting systems provide that only the cost of the original supply of minor equipment should be charged to this asset account. This original cost generally is depreciated over a short period (perhaps three years), with all additional purchases charged to expense at acquisition. Other hospitals record all minor equipment (both the original supply and replacement purchases) to the asset account and depreciate it over a three-year period. Because it is not feasible to attempt to inventory this equipment annually and the costs involved are relatively immaterial, no other accounting procedures are generally workable.

Minor Equipment

Determination of Cost

The cost of a purchased plant asset includes all expenditures related to the acquisition of the asset, bringing it to the desired location, and making it ready for use in hospital activities. Such costs may include the following:

- The billed price of the asset, net of any trade or cash discounts allowed
- Freight charges
- Sales taxes
- Fees and commissions paid
- Installation costs

The cost of a purchased plant asset, however, generally should not include interest. A hospital, for example, may acquire expensive equipment under a conditional sales or other deferred payment plan requiring a series of installment payments that include interest. Such interest charges should be excluded from asset cost, being recorded instead as interest expense. When a hospital constructs a building, however, interest costs incurred during the construction period are capitalized as a part of the cost of the building.

Recording Donated Plant Assets

When plant assets are acquired by gift or donation, the assets should be recorded at their fair market values as of the date of donation. The offsetting credit is made directly to the unrestricted net assets balance account, not to a revenue account. All receipts of plant assets by donation are considered contributions to the permanent capital of the hospital. Depreciation should be recorded on donated plant assets as if the assets had been purchased.

Accounting Procedure

To illustrate the accounting procedure for plant asset acquisitions, let us assume that on January 1, 20X1, Hopewell Hospital purchased a new item of radiology equipment for $75,000. This equipment has an estimated useful life of five years and an estimated salvage value of 20 percent, or $15,000. The necessary entries to record the acquisition are the following:

Voucher Register

1/1/X1	Major movable equipment	14200	$75,000	
	Accounts payable	20100		$75,000
	Voucher for purchase of new item of radiology equipment			

Cash Disbursements Journal

1/1/X1	Accounts payable	20100	$75,000	
	Cash—general checking account	10110		$75,000
	Check issued for purchase of new radiology equipment			

The major movable equipment account, as you know, is a general ledger control account whose balance reflects the cost of all hospital equipment items in the major movable equipment classification. Detailed information concerning these individual items of equipment is contained in some form of plant asset subsidiary ledger record.

One form of subsidiary ledger record is illustrated in Figure 18.1. When an item of equipment is acquired, it is entered on one of these cards. This provides a detailed record that includes a full description of the equipment, cost, date of acquisition, salvage value, estimated life, depreciation method and amounts, and whatever additional information may be desired. Such records support the periodic depreciation charges, and the balance sheet asset valuations provide the basis for insurance coverage and claims, permit the accurate recording of asset retirements and disposals, and assist in securing effective internal controls over the plant asset investment. **Subsidiary Ledger Records**

Notice that the plant ledger card indicates that the x-ray equipment was assigned identification number 60260–60700–67. As you may recall, 60260 is the expense account number for the radiology department, and 60700 is the account number for depreciation expense. The 67 indicates that this equipment is the 67th item of equipment in the department. Numbering systems, of course, vary; this is simply an example. A metal tag showing this number is attached to the equipment to facilitate its identification with the accounting records whenever an inventory is taken of the hospital's equipment.

Even when automated electronic information systems are employed, it still may not be feasible to attempt to maintain this type of separate subsidiary record for each individual item of equipment. Instead, similar items of equipment may be grouped on a single card. All beds in a particular nursing unit, for example, might be entered on one card. In other systems, a separate plant asset subsidiary record is maintained for the equipment in each department. When one of these variations is found, depreciation often can be computed on a group or composite basis, such as is described later in this chapter.

Depreciation of Plant Assets

When Hopewell Hospital purchased the equipment, it acquired a "bundle of services" at a cost of $75,000. Each year, as this equipment is used in hospital activities, a portion of its total service capability is expended. After five years of use, it is estimated that this bundle of services will have been exhausted. Clearly, the cost of the services consumed each year should be recognized as an expense to be matched against the revenues produced by those services. As noted before, this consumption of cost, or expense, is depreciation. Depreciation is fully as valid an expense as is the hospital payroll. But how is it measured?

Three Factors in Determining Periodic Depreciation
The determination of periodic depreciation charges is dependent on three important factors: (1) depreciable cost, (2) service life, and (3) choice of depreciation method. In past years, hospitals have employed various techniques of

FIGURE 18.1

Plant Asset
Subsidiary
Ledger Card

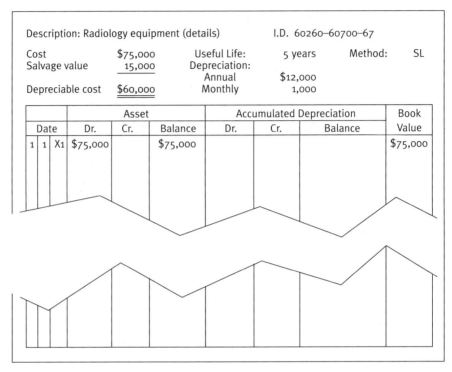

Description: Radiology equipment (details)   I.D. 60260–60700–67

Cost	$75,000	Useful Life:	5 years	Method:	SL
Salvage value	15,000	Depreciation:			
		Annual	$12,000		
Depreciable cost	$60,000	Monthly	1,000		

			Asset			Accumulated Depreciation			Book
	Date		Dr.	Cr.	Balance	Dr.	Cr.	Balance	Value
1	1	X1	$75,000		$75,000				$75,000

depreciation, including the straight-line method and accelerated methods, such as the declining balance method and the sum-of-years'-digits method. All of these methods are in conformity with GAAP and are widely used by industrial commercial firms for accounting and income tax purposes. The use of accelerated depreciation methods by hospitals for cost reimbursement purposes, however, will be disallowed by governmental and certain other third-party payers. For this reason, the discussion in this book is limited to the straight-line depreciation method.

Depreciable
Cost

The **depreciable cost**, sometimes called the *depreciation base* or *basis*, of a plant asset is its acquisition cost minus its estimated salvage value, as follows:

Acquisition cost – Salvage value = Depreciable cost

The residual salvage value of a depreciable plant asset is the estimated amount for which the asset can be sold when it is retired from use in hospital activity. There is no simple formula by which salvage value determinations can be made. It is largely a matter of judgment applied by the individual hospital in view of its plant asset retirement policy and experience, expected future market conditions for used or scrapped equipment, and other factors. Some assistance, however, may be obtained from the hospital's auditors and from equipment manufacturers.

The useful service life of a plant asset ordinarily is expressed in terms of years. In selecting a service life, consideration should be given to both the functional and the physical factors that limit the service life. The functional factors include obsolescence resulting from technological change, growth in the scale of a hospital's activities, and major changes in methods of delivering health-care services. The physical factors include wear and tear resulting from use and deterioration caused by the elements. As was true of salvage value determinations, however, the determination of service lives also is largely a matter of judgment and depends heavily on the individual hospital's plant asset retirement policy and experience. Although a plant asset remains in very sound condition, its economical service life may be at an end from the standpoint of a particular hospital. Various guides are published by hospital associations and governmental agencies that offer assistance in establishing useful service lives.

Service Life

The straight-line (SL) method of depreciation assigns an equal amount of depreciation to each year of useful life. The following formula is used to calculate annual depreciation:

Basic Straight-Line Depreciation Method

$$\frac{\text{Cost} - \text{Salvage value}}{\text{Estimated useful life}} = \text{Annual depreciation expense}$$

Application of the formula to the data assumed in this example for the new item of equipment produces annual depreciation expense of $12,000, as follows:

$$\frac{\$75,000 - \$15,000}{5} = \$12,000$$

Thus, each year of the 20X1–20X5 period would be charged with $12,000 of depreciation expense for this item of equipment.

Because monthly financial statements should reflect all expenses, including depreciation, the following adjusting entry is required at the end of each monthly reporting period:

General Journal

Depreciation expense	60700	$1,000	
Accumulated depreciation—			
major movable equipment	14300		$1,000
Monthly straight-line depreciation expense			
on radiology equipment ($12,000 × 1/12 months)			

Although the entry is posted to the general ledger accounts, monthly postings generally are not made to the plant asset subsidiary ledger cards. The plant asset subsidiary ledger cards ordinarily are posted only on an annual basis, as shown in Figure 18.2. The information in the subsidiary ledger is reconciled with the balances of the general ledger control accounts

FIGURE 18.2

Depreciation Posting to Plant Ledger Card

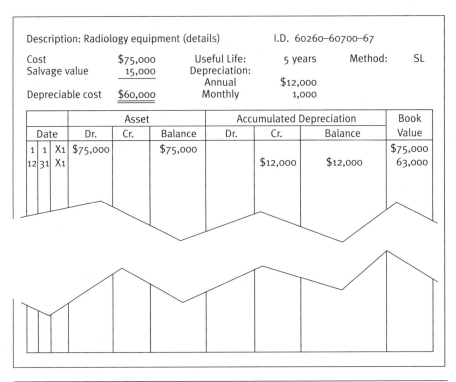

Description: Radiology equipment (details)		I.D. 60260–60700–67		
Cost	$75,000	Useful Life:	5 years	Method: SL
Salvage value	15,000	Depreciation:		
		Annual	$12,000	
Depreciable cost	$60,000	Monthly	1,000	

Date	Asset			Accumulated Depreciation			Book Value
	Dr.	Cr.	Balance	Dr.	Cr.	Balance	
1 1 X1	$75,000		$75,000				$75,000
12 31 X1					$12,000	$12,000	63,000

(for plant assets, depreciation expense, and accumulated depreciation) at the end of each fiscal year.

Recording a Half-Year's Depreciation on Plant Asset Additions

A special policy may be followed in recording depreciation on plant assets acquired during the course of a fiscal year. Because depreciation expense is, after all, merely an estimate, it is acceptable to adopt a policy of a half-year's depreciation on all plant asset additions in the year acquired, regardless of the month of acquisition. Once this policy is adopted, however, it should be consistently followed.

The procedure described so far has assumed **unit depreciation**—that is, the straight-line method was applied to a single unit or item of equipment. Because the computation of depreciation on an item-by-item basis involves considerable clerical effort, hospitals often find it more efficient to compute depreciation by groups of related plant assets. The procedure (known as **group depreciation**, or *composite depreciation*) involves the application of a single depreciation rate to the total cost of a combined group of assets.

Group Rates Under the group depreciation method, a number of similar plant assets are depreciated as a single unit. All the beds in a particular nursing unit, for example, might be grouped on a single subsidiary ledger record. Depreciation is then computed as if these beds were a single plant asset. If these beds have a total depreciable cost of $45,000 and an average service life of 15 years, the annual depreciation expense is $3,000 ($45,000 ÷ 15 years).

Under the composite depreciation method, a number of dissimilar assets may be depreciated as a single unit. To illustrate, assume that six different equipment items are acquired on January 1, 20X1, for a particular department of a hospital. Each equipment item has a different cost, salvage value, and useful life. When acquired, these items are entered on a single subsidiary ledger record, and a composite rate of depreciation is determined, as shown in Figure 18.3. The composite rate of depreciation for this departmental group of assets is 11.2 percent ($8,000 ÷ $71,400); the composite life is 8.925 years ($71,400 ÷ $8,000). Thus, $8,000 of depreciation expense is recorded each year so that, at the end of 8.925 years, accumulated depreciation will amount to $71,400.

Composite Rates

Funding of Depreciation

The funding of depreciation refers to the process by which cash resources are set aside periodically and accumulated for the purpose of financing the renewal or replacement of plant assets. The following illustrates the procedure, assuming that Hopewell Hospital's depreciation expense for a particular year is $185,000:

Depreciation expense	60700	$185,000	
Accumulated depreciation	13100		$185,000
Depreciation expense for the year			

Now assume that the funding of depreciation by the hospital is a voluntary action prescribed by the governing board. The following is the appropriate entry, assuming 100 percent funding:

Unrestricted net Assets (Board Designated)	30110	$185,000	
Cash—general checking account	10110		$185,000
Funding of depreciation expense for the year			

Thus, $185,000 is transferred from the hospital's general checking account and set aside in a special board-designated cash account within the unrestricted fund. Although these resources are earmarked for a specific purpose, the future use of this money remains entirely under the control of the board. It would be improper to transfer the $185,000 to the plant replacement and expansion fund as if it were donor-restricted.

The hospital, of course, may fund more or less than the amount recorded as depreciation expense. The amount actually funded, however, has no bearing whatever on the amount of depreciation expense to be recorded. Naturally, the cash set aside in this way should be invested until such time as new plant assets are required. Income earned on such investments is accounted for as

Amount Funded Is Distinct from Depreciation Expense

FIGURE 18.3
Computation
of Composite
Depreciation
Rate

Asset	Acquisition Cost	Salvage Value	Depreciable Cost	Useful Life (Years)	Annual Depreciation
A	$ 4,000	$ 400	$ 3,600	4	$ 900
B	22,000	2,000	20,000	20	1,000
C	9,000	-0-	9,000	5	1,800
D	20,000	4,000	16,000	8	2,000
E	6,000	1,200	4,800	6	800
F	19,000	1,000	18,000	12	1,500
	$80,000	$8,600	$71,400		$8,000

Composite depreciation rate = $8,000 ÷ $71,400 = 11.2%

unrestricted resources and must be reported as nonoperating revenues in the hospital's statement of operations. This income, however, may be designated by the board for the purchase of new plant assets and added to board-designated assets.

It should be pointed out that the funding of depreciation is the only means through which the value of plant assets is maintained and converted into cash during the assets' useful lives. The alternative is to do nothing, allowing the plant asset values to decline over time; this, in reality, gradually depletes and impairs the hospital's permanent capital.

Disposal of Plant Assets

It is important to make an accurate accounting of disposals of plant assets through normal retirement, sale, or exchange. Each of these possibilities is examined in this discussion. As a basis for the illustrations, we again assume that radiology equipment was acquired for $75,000 on January 1, 20X1. The equipment, which has an estimated useful life of five years and a $15,000 salvage value, is depreciated by the straight-line method.

Normal Retirement

If the equipment's useful service life ends on December 31, 20X5, as was estimated, and its expected salvage value is realized, the entry to record the retirement of the equipment is as follows:

Cash Receipts Journal

12/31/X5 Cash—general checking account	10110	$15,000	
Accumulated depreciation—major movable equipment	14300	60,000	
Major movable equipment			$75,000
Retirement of equipment			

FIGURE 18.4
Retirement
Recorded on
Plant Ledger
Card

Description: Radiology equipment (details)   I.D. 60260–60700–67

Cost	$75,000	Useful Life:	5 years	Method:	SL
Salvage value	15,000	Depreciation:			
		Annual	$12,000		
Depreciable cost	$60,000	Monthly	1,000		

| | Asset | | | Accumulated Depreciation | | | Book |
Date	Dr.	Cr.	Balance	Dr.	Cr.	Balance	Value
1 1 X1	$75,000		$75,000				$75,000
12 31 X1					$12,000	$12,000	63,000
12 31 X2					12,000	24,000	51,000
12 31 X3					12,000	36,000	39,000
12 31 X4					12,000	48,000	27,000
12 31 X5					12,000	60,000	15,000
12 31 X5		$75,000	-0-	$60,000			-0-

Retired 12/31/X5; salvage value was $15,000.

In addition to the general ledger postings arising from this entry, suitable notations are made on the plant ledger card, as indicated in Figure 18.4. At this time, the card is removed to an inactive file and retained for the period of time required by the hospital's record retention policies.

Should the actual salvage value prove to be more or less than $15,000, the entry just shown would include an account for the recognition of a gain or loss on retirement of the asset. If the salvage proceeds proved to be $16,500, for example, the entry would include a credit to a "gain on retirement of plant assets" account for $1,500. This gain would be reported among the nonoperating revenues in the hospital's 20X5 statement of operations.

In cases where fully depreciated assets remain in service, the usual practice is to take no further depreciation and to make no adjustment of previously recorded depreciation. The cost of such assets and the related accumulated depreciation remain on the books until the assets are eventually retired from service.

**Handling Fully
Depreciated
Assets
Remaining
in Use**

Sale of Plant Assets

A plant asset may be sold prior to the end of its scheduled useful service life for reasons not anticipated when it was acquired. Assume, for example, that the equipment is sold for $49,400 on May 1, 20X3:

Cash Receipts Journal

5/1/X3	Cash—general checking account	$49,400	
	Accumulated depreciation—		
	major movable equipment	28,000	
	Major movable equipment		$75,000
	Gain on sale of plant assets		2,400
	Sale of item of equipment:		
	Cost	$75,000	
	Accumulated depreciation:		
	20X1 (12 months)	12,000	
	20X2 (12 months)	12,000	
	20X3 (4 months)	4,000	
	Total	28,000	
	Book value	47,000	
	Sale proceeds	49,400	
	Gain	$ 2,400	

If this equipment had been sold on this date for an amount less than its $47,000 book value, the transaction would have produced a loss on sale of plant assets. Such losses usually are treated as reductions of nonoperating revenues in the statement of operations.

Exchanges (Trades) of Plant Assets

In certain instances, an old plant asset may be given up (along with cash) in exchange for a new plant asset. To illustrate, assume that the radiology equipment along with $33,800 cash is given in exchange for a new item of radiology equipment. The necessary accounting entry, assuming that the exchange occurs on May 1, 20X3, is as follows:

Cash Receipts Journal

5/1/X3	Major movable equipment	$80,800	
	Accumulated depreciation	28,000	
	Major movable equipment		$75,000
	Cash—general checking account		33,800
	Acquisition of new equipment in exchange		
	for old equipment and cash as follows:		

Book value of old equipment	$47,000	
Cash paid	33,800	
Cost of new equipment	$80,800	

The general accounting rule is that the cost of an asset received in an exchange is the fair market value of the assets given up or the fair market value of the asset received, whichever is more clearly evident. Any gain or loss is recognized. An exception to that general principle is made when, as in this case, the noncash assets exchanged are similar in nature and use. In such cases, the cost of the asset received is the book value of the noncash asset given up, plus cash paid, and no gain or loss is recognized. There are other exceptions, but a discussion of them is beyond the scope of this book.

Questions

Q18.1. Distinguish between land and land improvements.

Q18.2. Distinguish between fixed equipment and major movable equipment. Give examples of the types of equipment that are includable in each of these classifications.

Q18.3. Describe briefly the proper accounting procedure for minor equipment.

Q18.4. List five items that generally should be included in the cost of purchased equipment. Should interest be included in the cost of equipment purchased on an installment or deferred payment plan?

Q18.5. Rex Hospital obtained an item of equipment by donation. At the date received, the equipment had a fair market value of $25,000. This equipment has an estimated useful life of eight years and a 20 percent salvage value. Make the entry to record the acquisition of the equipment. Compute the annual depreciation to be recorded on this equipment.

Q18.6. What are the advantages of maintaining a detailed subsidiary ledger for plant assets?

Q18.7. How is each of the following determined?
  a. Depreciable cost
  b. Useful life
  c. Salvage value

Q18.8. "Depreciation expense is a measure of the decline in the value of plant assets during an accounting period." Do you agree or disagree? Explain your answer.

Q18.9. Distinguish briefly between the group depreciation method and the composite rate depreciation method.

Q18.10. What is meant by the "funding" of depreciation? What entry is made to record the funding of, say, $79,000 of depreciation?

Q18.11. Righton Hospital purchased an item of equipment for $40,000 on January 1, 20X1. This equipment has an estimated useful life of eight years and a 10 percent salvage value. On June 30, 20X4, the equipment is sold for $23,100. Assuming the straight-line depreciation method, prepare the necessary entry to record the sale of the equipment.

Q18.12. Ragtag Hospital purchased an item of equipment for $60,000 on January 1, 20X1. This equipment has an estimated useful life of ten years and a 20 percent salvage value. On October 1, 20X5, this equipment is traded, along with $26,000 cash, for similar equipment having a list price of $72,000. Assuming the straight-line depreciation method, prepare the necessary entry to record the trade.

Q18.13. Summarize briefly the accounting procedure to be followed when an existing item of equipment having a book value of $40,000 and a fair market value of $45,000 is traded, along with $13,000 cash, for a new item of equipment having a list price of $60,000.

Q18.14. Ritter Hospital purchased an item of equipment on April 1, 20X1. This equipment has an estimated useful life of 12 years and a 10 percent salvage value. The accumulated depreciation on this equipment on March 31, 20X4, was $18,000. Assuming straight-line depreciation has been recorded, what was the acquisition cost of the equipment?

Exercises

E18.1. Right Hospital purchased a new item of equipment for $800 on May 1, 20X1. The equipment has an estimated useful life of eight years and an estimated salvage value of $80. This equipment was sold for $535 on July 1, 20X2. The equipment is depreciated by the straight-line method.

Required: What was the loss on the sale of the equipment?

E18.2. Ready Hospital provides you with the following list of depreciable assets acquired at the beginning of the current year:

Asset	Cost	Estimated Salvage Value	Estimated Useful Life (Years)
A	$4,000	$400	3
B	1,500	300	4
C	7,000	750	5

Required: What is the composite depreciation rate on cost?

E18.3. Realgood Hospital purchased a new item of equipment for $800 on January 1, 20X1. The equipment has an estimated salvage value of $80 and an estimated useful life of eight years. The equipment, which was depreciated by the straight-line method, was traded on January 1, 20X4 for a similar item of equipment. Cash "boot" of $420 was paid to effect the trade. The old equipment had a fair

value of $530; the new equipment had a fair value of $950.
Required: What is the cost of the new equipment?

E18.4. Realfine Hospital provides you with the following information about one of its depreciable assets at December 31, 20X3:

Year of acquisition	20X1
Estimated useful life	5 years
Cost	$70,000
Estimated salvage value	14,000
Accumulated depreciation	33,600

The hospital takes a full year's depreciation in the year of a depreciable asset's acquisition, and no depreciation in the year of a depreciable asset's disposition. On June 30, 20X4, this depreciable asset was sold for $28,000.
Required: What is the gain (loss) on the sale?

Problems

P18.1. On January 1, 20X1, Rainy Hospital acquired five items of Problems equipment, as follows:

Asset	Acquisition Cost	Salvage Value	Useful Life (Years)
1	$10,000	$2,000	8
2	45,000	5,000	10
3	24,000	4,000	5
4	30,000	6,000	12
5	19,000	1,000	6

Required: Prepare a depreciation table, similar to the one illustrated in Figure 18.3, showing a computation of the composite rate of depreciation and the composite life of these five items of equipment.

P18.2. On January 1, 20X1, Restful Hospital acquired an item of equipment for $90,000. This equipment has an estimated useful life of five years and a 20 percent salvage value. On March 1, 20X4, this equipment is sold for $44,000.
Required: Assume that Restful Hospital's fiscal year ends on December 31 and that adjustments for depreciation are made only at the end of each year. (1) Prepare all necessary journal entries from January 1, 20X1, through March 1, 20X4. (2) Draw up and complete a plant ledger card for this item.

P18.3. Redhot Hospital purchased an item of laboratory equipment on October 1, 20X1, at a billed price of $20,000. In addition, the hospital paid $200 for freight and $800 for the construction of a wooden base and for making the proper electrical connections. The estimated useful life of the equipment is six years with no salvage value. The hospital's fiscal year ends September 30.

Required: Prepare journal entries to record (1) the purchase of the equipment, (2) depreciation expense for the first year, (3) the write-off of the fully depreciated equipment after six years, and (4) the funding of depreciation at the end of the first year.

P18.4. Roadway Hospital's preadjusted trial balance at December 31, 20X3 (the end of the hospital's fiscal year), includes the following accounts:

	Dr.	Cr.
Land	$ 13,000	
Land improvements	18,000	
Accumulated depreciation— land improvements		$ 2,000
Buildings and building improvements	900,000	
Accumulated depreciation— buildings and building improvements		28,800
Fixed equipment	300,000	
Accumulated depreciation— fixed equipment		20,000
Major movable equipment	440,000	
Accumulated depreciation— major movable equipment		60,000
Minor equipment	24,000	
Accumulated depreciation— minor equipment		16,000

The following additional information is available:

1. Roadway Hospital began operations on January 1, 20X1, when (with the exception noted below) all of its plant assets were acquired. The correct amounts of depreciation have been recorded for 20X1 and 20X2, but no depreciation entries have yet been made for 20X3.
2. The land improvements are being depreciated over an 18-year life with no expected salvage value.
3. The building has an estimated useful life of 50 years and an estimated salvage value of 20 percent.
4. The fixed equipment has an estimated useful life of 25 years and an estimated salvage value of $50,000.

5. An analysis of the major movable equipment account is as follows:

1/1/X1	Equipment purchased having an estimated useful life of 12 years and a 10% salvage value	$400,000
3/1/X3	Equipment purchased having an estimated useful life of eight years and a 20% salvage value	60,000
9/1/X3	Proceeds from sale of equipment purchased on 1/1/X1 for $20,000	(15,000)

6. Minor equipment is being depreciated over a three-year period with no salvage value expected.

Required: (1) Prepare the necessary journal entries at December 31, 20X3. (2) Prepare a presentation of the plant assets section of the hospital's December 31, 20X3, balance sheet.

LONG-TERM INVESTMENTS

Temporary, or short-term, investments in stocks and bonds are those that are readily marketable and that management intends to hold for only a short period (generally not in excess of one year). The proceeds from their disposition ordinarily are used to meet current obligations. Investments not meeting these criteria are separately classified in the balance sheet as long-term investments. Short-term investments were discussed in Chapter 16; this chapter is concerned with long-term investments.

Long-term investments may appear in any fund, but often they are found as assets of the endowment fund or of the plant replacement and expansion fund. The funding of depreciation by action of the hospital's governing board may result in long-term investments that are properly reported as board-designated assets in the unrestricted net assets. In any case, these investments typically consist of government bonds, corporate bonds, and corporate stocks.

When securities of a long-term investment nature are acquired by gift or by endowment, they are recorded in the appropriate fund at their fair market value when received. The cost of bonds and stocks purchased, on the other hand, will include the quoted purchase price, brokerage fees, and other expenditures that are necessary to the acquisition. Income from long-term investments, usually consisting of interest and dividends, should be recognized on the accrual basis and in the appropriate fund. All income on unrestricted net assets investments and all unrestricted income on investments of the restricted net assets must be reported as nonoperating revenues of the unrestricted net assets. Donor-restricted investment income generally is recorded in either the specific purpose fund or the plant replacement and expansion fund. Gains and losses on the disposition of long-term investments usually are recorded in the fund in which the investments were carried as assets.

Since the publication of FASB Statement No. 124 in the mid-1990s, long-term investments in debt securities, regardless of the fund in which they are recorded, are recorded in the accounts at market value. On a periodic basis, usually monthly, the unrealized gain or loss from the prior period is recorded as a change in net assets, which is typically not considered a change to the organization's bottom line.

Investments in Bonds

A major part of the hospital investment portfolio is likely to consist of investments in government and corporate bonds because of the emphasis usually put on safety of principal and stability of income. Both government and corporate bonds are available in varying types and denominations, although bonds of $1,000 face, or maturity, value are most common. Bond interest is quoted at annual percentage rates of face value but often is paid to bondholders semiannually on specified dates six months apart.

Acquisition of Bonds

To illustrate the accounting procedures for long-term investments in bonds, assume that Goodcare Hospital purchases 60 of the $1,000, 8 percent, ten-year bonds of National Company on September 1, 20X1. The bonds have a May 1, 20X8, maturity date and pay interest semiannually on May 1 and November 1. Although bonds may be purchased at face value at times, it is more likely that the acquisition price will be either more or less than face value; that is, the bonds will be purchased either at a premium or at a discount. This occurs largely because the current market rate of interest (which changes frequently) is higher or lower than the fixed nominal, or coupon rate, of interest paid on the bonds.

Discount Acquisition If the current market rate of interest is in excess of 8 percent, the National Company bonds may be quoted at a price that is less than face value. Assume, for example, that the bonds are quoted at 92 percent of face value, or $55,200 (92 percent of $60,000). Let us also assume that brokerage fees and other acquisition costs total $400. The entries for the acquisition of the bonds therefore are as follows:

Voucher Register

9/1/X1	Investments—bonds	$55,600	
	Accrued interest rceivable	1,600	
	Accounts payable		$57,200
	Voucher for purchase of		
	National Company		
	bonds at a discount:		
	Quoted price		
	(92% of $60,000)	$55,200	
	Acquisition costs	400	
	Cost of bonds	55,600	
	Accrued interest:		
	($60,000 × 8% ×		
	4/12 months)	1,600	
	Disbursement	$57,200	

Cash Disbursements Journal
9/1/X1 Accounts payable $57,200
            Cash—general checking account $57,200
        Check issued for purchase of
        National Company bonds

Notice that the brokerage fees and other acquisition expenditures are treated as a part of the cost of the bonds. Note also that because these bonds were purchased between interest payment dates, the hospital must pay the seller the amount of interest accrued since the last interest payment date (May 1, 20X1). This, however, will be recovered by the hospital on November 1, 20X1, as National Company will always pay a full six months' interest on each interest payment date, regardless of the number of months the bonds have been held by the investor. (This was explained earlier in Chapter 16.) If these bonds had been purchased on an interest payment date (May 1 or November 1 in this example), no accrued interest would have been involved in the acquisition.

Handling Brokerage Fees and Acquisition Expenditures

In instances where the nominal or coupon rate of interest is higher than the current market rate of interest, bonds tend to sell at a **premium**, a price greater than the face value. Assume, for example, that Goodcare Hospital purchased the above National Company bonds at 105 percent and that acquisition costs were $600. The following shows the necessary entries:

Premium Acquisition

Voucher Register
9/1/X1 Investments—bonds $63,600
            Accrued interest receivable   1,600
                Accounts payable $65,200
            Voucher for purchase of
            National Company bonds at a premium:
                Quoted price
                  (105% of $60,000) $63,000
                Acquisition costs   600
                Cost of bonds   63,600
                Accrued interest
                  ($60,000 × 8% ×
                  4/12 months)   1,600
                Disbursement $65,200

Cash Disbursements Journal
9/1/X1 Accounts payable $65,200
            Cash—general checking account $65,200
        Check issued for purchase of
        National Company bonds

Observe that Goodcare Hospital will receive annual interest of $4,800 (8 percent of $60,000). Because $63,600 was paid for the bonds, however, the effective (actual) rate of return on this investment to the hospital will be somewhat less than 8 percent. In the previous example, which assumed that the bonds were acquired at a cost of $55,600, the effective yield will be greater than 8 percent.

Bond Interest Income

The amount of bond interest to be recorded as investment income by Goodcare Hospital depends on whether the bonds were purchased at a discount or premium. This is because the amount of discount or premium must be amortized over the number of months between the date of acquisition and the maturity date of the bonds. Let us examine the amortization process through the following illustrations.

Amortization of Discount Again assume the purchase of the National Company bonds (details provided earlier) at a discount on September 1, 20X1. At the end of September (and at the end of each ensuing month), the hospital will make an adjusting entry to record bond interest income for the month. Assuming that the bond discount is amortized by the straight-line method, the following is the necessary entry:

General Journal

9/30/X1	Accrued interest receivable		$400	
	Investments—bonds		55	
	Bond interest income			$455

Accrual of interest and amortization of bond discount:

Nominal interest		
($60,000 × 8% × 1/12 months)	$	400
Discount amortization:		
Maturity value of bonds	60,000	
Cost of bonds	55,600	
Discount	4,400	
Divide by months to maturity	80	
Discount amortization	55	
Monthly interest income	$	455

Note that the discount ($4,400) will be taken into the accounts as bond interest income over the 80 months from the acquisition date to the maturity date of the bonds at the rate of $55 per month. The resulting $455 credit to income is a rough approximation of the effective amount of interest earned each month on the investment.

Notice also that the preceding entry debits the monthly amortization to the investment account, thereby increasing its carrying value by $55 each month. By the maturity date (May 1, 20X8), the investment account will have a balance of exactly $60,000, that is, $55,600 + ($55 × 80 months). So, when the face amount of the bonds is paid to the hospital on the maturity date by National Company, the following entry is made:

Debiting the Monthly Amortization

Cash Receipts Journal
5/1/X8 Cash—general checking account	$60,000	
Investments—bonds		$60,000
Receipt of face value of matured		
National Company bonds		

If the discount were not amortized over the 80-month period, the entire $4,400 discount would have to be recorded as 20X8 income in the above entry. It seems quite clear, however, that the discount is earned by the hospital ratably over the 80-month period rather than just in the year of maturity alone. Thus, long-term investments in bonds purchased at a discount are carried in the accounts at acquisition cost plus discount amortization to date.

On November 1, 20X1, the hospital will receive six months' interest on its investment in National Company bonds:

Cash Receipts Journal
11/1/X1 Cash—general checking account	$2,400	
Accrued interest receivable		$2,400
Receipt of semiannual interest on		
investment in National Company bonds		
($60,000 × 8% × 6/12 months)		

Remember that the accrued interest receivable account was debited for $1,600 on September 1, when the bonds were acquired, for $400 on September 30, in an adjusting entry, and for $400 again on October 31, in an adjusting entry. The resulting $2,400 debit balance is then cleared from the accounts by the credit in the cash receipts journal entry on November 1. The adjusting entry required at the end of each month to record the nominal monthly interest income also includes the monthly discount amortization.

To help you understand this process, Figure 19.1 shows the postings of all 20X1 entries relating to Goodcare Hospital's investment in the National Company bonds. The hospital's 20X1 statement of operations will report bond interest income of $1,820. Its December 31, 20X1, balance sheet will include $800 of accrued interest receivable and will report the long-term investment at $55,820 (acquisition cost plus discount amortization to date).

FIGURE 19.1

Accounting for Bonds Purchased at a Discount

Cash–General Checking Account		Accrued Interest Receivable		Investments–Bonds	
(5) 2,400	(2) 57,200	(1) 1,600	(5) 2,400	(1) 55,600	
		(3) 400		(3) 55	
		(4) 400		(4) 55	
		(6) 400		(6) 55	
		(7) 400		(7) 55	
		Bal. 800		Bal. 55,820	

Accounts Payable		Bond Interest Income	
(2) 57,200	(1) 57,200		(3) 455
			(4) 455
			(6) 455
			(7) 455
			Bal. 1,820

Posting references:
(1) 9/1/X1 acquisition of bonds—voucher register
(2) 9/1/X1 acquisition of bonds—cash disbursements journal
(3) 9/30/X1 adjusting entry—general journal
(4) 10/31/X1 adjusting entry—general journal
(5) 11/1/X1 receipt of interest—cash receipts journal
(6) 11/30/X1 adjusting entry—general journal
(7) 12/31/X1 adjusting entry—general journal

Amortization of Premium

Earlier, this section described the purchase of the National Company bonds on September 1, 20X1, at a cost of $63,600. At the end of each month, an adjusting entry will be required to record bond interest income and amortization of bond premium for the month. Assuming that the premium is amortized by the straight-line method, the entry at September 30, 20X1, is as follows:

General Journal

9/30/X1 Accrued interest receivable		$400	
Investments—bonds			$ 45
Bond interest income			355
Accrual of interest and amortization			
of bond premium:			
Nominal interest:			
($60,000 × 8% ×			
1/12 months)	$ 400		
Premium amortization:			
Cost of bonds	63,600		
Maturity value of bonds	60,000		
Premium	3,600		
Divide by months			
to maturity	80		
Premium amortization	45		
Monthly interest income	$ 355		

Exactly the same adjusting entry is made at the end of each month until the maturity date of the bonds. Notice that the amortization of bond premium has the effect of reducing bond interest income. The resulting $355 is roughly the effective amount of monthly bond interest income.

Notice that the adjusting entry credits the monthly amortization of premium to the investment account, thereby decreasing its carrying value by $45 monthly. By the maturity date of the bonds, the investment account will have a balance of precisely $60,000—that is, $63,600 – ($45 x 80 months). Thus, long-term investments in bonds purchased at a premium are carried in the accounts at acquisition cost minus premium amortization to date.

Monthly Premium Amortization Credited to the Investment Account

Figure 19.2 presents the postings of all 20X1 entries for Goodcare Hospital's investment (at a premium) in the National Company bonds. You should study this illustration in comparison with Figure 19.1.

The entry to be made when bond investments are held to maturity has been illustrated earlier. Suppose, however, that bonds held as long-term investments are sold prior to their maturity. Refer to the facts given earlier in this section relating to the purchase of the National Company bonds for $55,600 on September 1, 20X1, and now assume that the bonds are sold on April 1, 20X3, at 102 percent and accrued interest. The required entry is as follows:

Cash Receipts Journal

4/1/X3	Cash—general checking account	$62,725	
	Accrued interest receivable		$ 2,000
	Investments—bonds		56,645
	Gain on sale of investments		4,080
	Sale of investment in		
	National Company bonds:		
	Sales price (102% of		
	$60,000)	$61,200	
	Less brokerage fees	475	
	Net sales proceeds	60,725	
	Accrued interest:		
	($60,000 × 8% ×		
	5/12 months)	2,000	
	Cash received	$62,725	
	Net sales proceeds		
	(above)	$60,725	
	Book value of bonds:		
	Acquisition cost	55,600	
	Add amortized discount:		
	($55 × 19 months)	1,045	
	Book value of bonds	56,645	
	Gain on sale	$ 4,080	

FIGURE 19.2

Accounting for Bonds Purchased at a Premium

Cash–General Checking Account			Accrued Interest Receivable			Investments–Bonds		
(5) 2,400	(2) 65,200		(1) 1,600	(5) 2,400		(1) 63,600	(3)	45
			(3) 400				(4)	45
			(4) 400				(6)	45
			(6) 400				(7)	45
			(7) 400			Bal. 63,420		
			Bal. 800					

Accounts Payable		Bond Interest Income	
(2) 65,200	(1) 65,200		(3) 355
			(4) 355
			(6) 355
			(7) 355
			Bal. 1,420

Posting references:
(1) 9/1/X1 acquisition of bonds—voucher register
(2) 9/1/X1 acquisition of bonds—cash disbursements journal
(3) 9/30/X1 adjusting entry—general journal
(4) 10/31/X1 adjusting entry—general journal
(5) 11/1/X1 receipt of interest—cash receipts journal
(6) 11/30/X1 adjusting entry—general journal
(7) 12/31/X1 adjusting entry—general journal

As can be seen, the cash account is debited for the quoted price at which the bonds were sold (net of brokerage fees) plus the five months of bond interest accrued since the last interest payment date (November 1, 20X2). This accrued interest, of course, had previously been established in the accounts by the month-end adjusting entries. At the date of the sale, the bond investment account had a balance of $56,645, having been written up to that amount because of the amortization of discount at the rate of $55 per month for the 19 months since the date of acquisition. Then, the difference between this carrying amount and the net sales proceeds is recorded as the gain on the sale. Make special note of the fact that the accrued interest at the date of sale has no bearing on the amount of gain or loss on the sale.

Journal Entry for Sale of Some of the Bonds

Instead of selling all the bonds, let us now assume that only 40 percent (face value of $24,000) of the bonds are sold on April 1, 20X3, at 102 percent and accrued interest, with brokerage fees amounting to $200. The necessary entry is as follows:

Cash Receipts Journal
4/1/X3   Cash–general checking account $25,080

Accrued interest receivable	$800
Investments—bonds	22,658
Gain on sale of investments	1,622

Sale of 40% of the investment in
National Company bonds:

Sales price (102% of $24,000)	$24,480	
Less brokerage fees	200	
Net sales proceeds	24,280	
Accrued interest:		
($24,000 × 8% × 5/12 months)	800	
Cash received	$25,080	
Net sales proceeds (above)	$24,280	
Book value of bonds sold:		
(40% × $56,645)	22,658	
Gain on sale	$ 1,622	

Interest and discount amortization, of course, will continue on the remaining $36,000 face value of the National Company bond investment until these bonds are either sold or reach maturity. The monthly interest and discount amortization, however, will be only 60 percent of the amounts illustrated earlier. In other words, the monthly amortization will be $33 (60 percent of $55) and the monthly credit to bond interest income $273 (60 percent of $455), starting April 30, 20X3.

Bonds from Gifts or Endowments

The procedures described here are also applicable to bonds acquired by the hospital as a gift or an endowment. In these cases, the fair market value of the bonds at the date of donation is regarded to be their cost. If the fair market value is less than maturity value, accounting procedures are those described for bonds acquired at a discount. If the fair market value is greater than maturity value, the accounting procedure is that described for bonds acquired at a premium.

Investments in Stocks

The investment of hospital resources in corporate stocks involves some degree of risk with regard to price declines, but such investments may offer large rewards in the form of dividends and appreciation in value if they are managed intelligently. Investments may be made in either preferred or common stocks. Preferred stock has certain preferences over common stock, as the name implies. Dividends, for example, must be paid to a company's preferred stockholders before any dividends may be paid to its common stockholders. Accounting procedures for investments in capital stocks, however, are not much affected by the particular type of stock involved.

Acquisition of Stocks

Assume that Goodcare Hospital purchases 400 shares of Bluchip Company's common stock for $22,000 (including brokerage fees and other acquisition costs) on January 2, 20X1:

Voucher Register

1/2/X1	Investments—stocks	$22,000
	Accounts payable	$22,000
	Purchase of 400 shares of	
	Bluchip Company's common stock	

Cash Disbursements Journal

1/2/X1	Accounts payable	$22,000
	Cash—general checking account	$22,000
	Check issued for purchase of Bluchip	
	Company stock	

For investments in both bonds and stocks, a subsidiary ledger record should be maintained to provide the details of each investment and to support the general ledger investment control accounts. These subsidiary records sometimes are kept in the form illustrated in Figure 19.3.

Receipt of Dividends

Hospitals having capital stocks in their investment portfolios may receive cash dividends and perhaps stock dividends. We will illustrate the receipt of both types of dividends below with respect to Goodcare Hospital's investment in Bluchip Company stock.

Cash Dividends

A typical cash dividend announcement reads somewhat as follows:

On April 20, 20X1, the board of directors of Bluchip Company declared a cash dividend of $1.50 per share payable on May 19, 20X1, to common stockholders of record at May 5, 20X1.

You can find dividend announcements of this sort in the financial pages of newspapers, in business journals, and even in certain popular magazines. These announcements always provide three important dates:

1. The declaration date (here, April 20) is the date on which the board of directors voted dividend payment approval.
2. The payment date (May 19 in this case) is the date on which the company will mail out the dividend checks.
3. The record date (May 5 here) is the date on which a determination is made of the names of the stockholders entitled to the dividend on the basis of the company's records.

FIGURE 19.3

Subsidiary Ledger Record for Investments

SECURITY RECORD

Name of Security_____ Fund Account_____
Description and Other Data _____

Date of Issue _____ Interest Rate____ %   Interest or Dividend Dates_____
Principal Due on _____

DATE 20__	REFER-ENCE	BOND OR CERTIFICATE NUMBERS	ACQUISITIONS			SALES, MATURITIES, ETC.			BALANCE		
			PRICE	PAR VALUE OF BONDS OR NO. OF SHARES	AMOUNT	PRICE	PAR VALUE OF BONDS OR NO. OF SHARES	AMOUNT	PROFIT OR LOSS ON SECURITIES SOLD, ETC (ENTER LOSSES IN RED)	PAR VALUE OF BONDS OR NO. OF SHARES	AMOUNT

Once a dividend has been declared, it must be paid. It also should be noted that all stockholders listed as such in the company's records on the record date will receive the dividend, although they may sell their stock prior to the payment date. If the stock is purchased or sold between the declaration date and the record date, the quoted price per share includes the declared dividend. If the stock is purchased or sold after the record date, the per-share price does not include the dividend.

Entry for Cash Dividends at Declaration Date

An entry for cash dividends should be made at the declaration date by the investor, because the dividend has been earned at that time and because the payment of the declared dividend by the corporation is legally required. Goodcare Hospital's entry is as follows:

General Journal

4/20/X1 Dividends receivable	$600	
Dividend income		$600
Dividend income on Bluchip Company stock		
($1.50 × 400 shares)		

Assuming that the hospital continues to hold the 400 shares of Bluchip stock, no entry will be necessary at the record date. But when the dividend check is received on May 19, the following entry is made:

Cash Receipts Journal

5/19/X1 Cash—general checking account	$600	
Dividends receivable		$600
Receipt of cash dividends on Bluchip		
Company stock		

Carefully note that the stock's dividend income was recorded in April (the month in which the dividend was earned) whereas the cash receipt was recorded in May. This, you see, is accrual basis accounting; income is recorded in the time period in which it is earned rather than in the time period in which the income is received in cash.

Stock Dividends

In addition to paying cash dividends, corporations sometimes will distribute **stock dividends**—that is, their stockholders are given additional shares of stock without charge. As is true of cash dividends, there are three important dates in recording the distribution: the declaration date, the record date, and the stock distribution date. Announcements similar to those for cash dividends are made.

No Journal Entry Is Required for Stock Dividends

To illustrate, assume that on June 2, 20X1, Bluchip Company's board of directors declared a 10 percent common stock dividend to be distributed on July 10, 20X1, to common stockholders of record at June 26, 20X1. As a result, Goodcare Hospital receives 40 (10 percent of 400 shares) additional common shares without cost. No formal entry of any kind, however, is necessary because stock dividends do not give rise to income, regardless of the market value of the shares received. Stock dividends simply increase the number of shares outstanding without any change in the issuing corporation's net assets. Subsequent to a stock dividend, each shareholder has the same percentage ownership interest as before.

The effect of a stock dividend on the stockholder is simply to reduce the cost per share of stock. Goodcare Hospital, for example, had 400 shares of stock that had cost $22,000, or $55 per share. On receipt of the 40-share stock dividend, the hospital has 440 shares that cost $22,000, or $50 per share. Thus, the effect of the stock dividend in this example is simply an increase in the number of shares held and a decrease in the cost per share. Naturally, the subsidiary ledger investment records would be adjusted accordingly, but no journal entry is required.

Disposition of Stocks

When stock is sold, the difference between the proceeds of sale (net of any brokerage fees and other expenses of sale) and the cost of the stock (as it may be adjusted for stock dividends, if any) is recorded as a gain or loss of the fund in which the stock was carried as an investment.

  Assume, for example, that Goodcare Hospital sells 100 shares of the Bluchip Company common stock for $6,425 on September 4, 20X1. Assuming brokerage fees of $92, the entry to record the sale is as follows:

Cash Receipts Journal

9/4/X1	Cash—general checking account	$6,333	
	Investments—stocks		$5,000
	Gain on sale of investments		1,333
	Sale of 100 shares of Bluchip		
	Company stock:		
	Sales price	$6,425	
	Less brokerage fees	92	
	Net sales proceeds	6,333	
	Less cost of stock:		
	($50 × 100 shares)	5,000	
	Gain on sale	$1,333	

  The subsidiary ledger records should be properly adjusted for the shares sold. It should be clear that 340 shares (440 shares – 100 shares) of stock remain in the investment account at a cost of $17,000 ($50 × 340 shares).

Entries for Sale of Shares Purchased at Various Prices

Suppose, however, that the Bluchip stock had been acquired at different times and at different costs per share. In such cases, to determine the cost of shares subsequently sold, it may be necessary to assume FIFO or other costing methods (see Chapter 17) in much the same manner as is done for inventories of supplies. Of course, if the subsidiary record of investments provides a record of cost per share according to stock certificate numbers, a specific identification can be made to determine the cost of shares sold.

Valuation of Net Assets Investments

Since the publication of FASB Statement No. 124 in the mid-1990s, investments in net assets securities are recorded at market value. On a periodic basis, usually monthly, the unrealized gain or loss from the prior period is recorded as a change in net assets, which is typically not considered a change to the organization's bottom line.

Internal Controls

Suitable internal controls should be maintained to safeguard the hospital's investments in stocks and bonds, as well as the related interest and dividend income, against loss through fraud, error, or mismanagement. It is important that all purchases and sales of investment securities be authorized by the hospital's governing board or its investment committee. Once acquired, stock and bond certificates should be kept in a safe place, preferably in a bank safe deposit box with access requiring two hospital executives. Employees who can access the accounting records or cash should not, of course, have access to investment securities. Finally, regular reports of investments should be submitted to management and to the hospital's governing board.

Questions

Q19.1. Distinguish between temporary investments and long-term investments.

Q19.2. When securities of a long-term investment nature are acquired by donation, at what amount are such assets initially recorded in the hospital's accounts?

Q19.3. When securities are purchased for long-term investment purposes by the hospital, what is their cost?

Q19.4. In what fund should the hospital record income earned on long-term investments? In what fund should gains and losses on sales of long-term investments be recorded?

Q19.5. Explain what is meant by the declaration date, the record date, and the payment date with respect to corporate dividend distributions resulting from hospital investments in corporate stocks.

Q19.6. What are some of the major features of a satisfactory system of internal control over hospital investments in securities?

Q19.7. Sara Hospital holds an investment in the capital stock of an industrial corporation. The hospital receives 50 shares of the corporation's common stock as a dividend at a time when the stock is quoted on the market at $40 per share. Should Sara Hospital record $2,000 of dividend income? Explain your answer.

Q19.8. Saint Hospital owns investment securities that cost $100,000 but have a current market value of $140,000. At what amount should these securities be presented in the hospital's balance sheet? Explain your answer.

Q19.9. A hospital owns 300 shares of stock that were acquired as follows:

1/1/X1	100 shares purchased for $4,000
1/1/X2	100 shares purchased for $5,000

1/1/X3   100 shares purchased for $6,000

On February 1, 20X3, 150 of these shares are sold for $9,750. What is the amount of the gain on the sale?

Q19.10. When corporate bonds are purchased between interest payment dates, the hospital purchaser must pay accrued interest since the last interest payment date. Why?

Q19.11. When corporate bonds are purchased at a price higher or lower than face value, the premium or discount must be amortized by the purchaser. What is the purpose of amortizing bond premium or discount?

Q19.12. In what sections of the hospital balance sheet does one find the following accounts?
a. Temporary investments
b. Long-term investments—bonds
c. Accrued interest receivable
d. Long-term investments—stocks
e. Dividends receivable

Exercises

E19.1. Samson Hospital purchased $1,200 (face value) of the 5 percent bonds of XYZ Company at 92 percent on July 1, 20X1. Brokerage and other acquisition costs were $32. Interest is payable semiannually on May 1 and November 1. The maturity date of the bonds is November 1, 20X6. On September 1, 20X1, $480 (face value) of the bonds are sold at 95 percent and accrued interest; brokerage costs were $12.
Required: What was the gain (loss) on the sale?

E19.2. Sitdown Hospital purchased $900 (face value) of the 8 percent bonds of Robin Company at 109 percent on October 1, 20X1. Brokerage costs were $31. Interest is payable semiannually on June 1 and December 1. The maturity date of the bonds is June 1, 20X6. On January 1, 20X3, $450 (face value) of the bonds are sold at 114 percent and accrued interest; brokerage costs were $13.
Required: What was the gain (loss) on the sale?

E19.3. On November 1, 20X1, Sheraton Hospital purchased Maybell Company 10-year, 7 percent bonds with a face value of $50,000 for $49,167. Interest is payable semiannually on January 1 and July 1. The bonds mature on July 1, 20X8.
Required: What is the hospital's 20X1 interest income?

E19.4. On Janyary 1, 20X1, Sideway Hospital purchased 200 shares of Pickard Company stock for $5,760 plus brokerage costs of $240. An additional 200 shares were purchased on May 1, 20X1 for $6,912 plus brokerage costs of $288. On August 1, 20X1, Pickard declared and distributed a 20 percent stock dividend. On October 1, 20X1, Sideway sold 100 shares of the Pickard stock at $32⅜ less brokerage costs of $129.50.

Required: Assuming FIFO, what was the gain on the sale?

E19.5. On October 1, 20X1, Safeway Hospital purchased 100 shares of Paul Company stock at $45 per share; brokerage costs were $26. A $3 per share cash dividend had been declared on September 25, 20X1 to be paid on October 18, 20X1 to stockholders of record at October 8, 20X1.

Required: At what amount should the investment in Paul stock be reported in Safeway's October 31, 20X1 balance sheet?

Problems

P19.1. Sample Hospital purchased 90 of the $1,000, 8 percent, ten-year bonds of ABC Company on August 1, 20X1, at 91 percent and accrued interest. Brokerage and other acquisition costs were $560. These bonds mature in 116 months and pay interest semiannually on April 1 and October 1. The hospital's fiscal year ends on December 31. Although the hospital intended to hold these bonds as long-term investments, the bonds were sold on January 1, 20X2, at 98 percent and accrued interest. Brokerage and other expenses of sale amounted to $610.

Required: Prepare a chart, such as the one illustrated in Figure 19.1, showing all necessary entries from August 1, 20X1, through January 1, 20X2.

P19.2. Simple Hospital purchased 90 of the $1,000, 8 percent, ten-year bonds of ABC Company on August 1, 20X1, at 108 percent and accrued interest. Brokerage and other acquisition costs were $572. These bonds mature in 116 months and pay interest semiannually on April 1 and October 1. The hospital's fiscal year ends on December 31. Although the hospital intended to hold these bonds as long-term investments, the bonds were sold on January 1, 20X2, at 102 percent and accrued interest. Brokerage and other expenses of sale amounted to $520.

Required: Prepare a chart, such as the one illustrated in Figure 19.2, showing all necessary entries from August 1, 20X1, through January 1, 20X2.

P19.3. Supple Hospital purchased $100,000 face value of XYZ Company bonds at 96 percent on May 1, 20X1. These bonds pay 6 percent interest per year, payable semiannually on April 1 and October 1. These bonds mature in 107 months. Brokerage fees and various other acquisition costs totaling $255 were paid. It was management's intent to hold these securities as long-term investments, but on January 1, 20X2, 60 percent of the bonds were sold at 94 percent and accrued interest, less brokerage fees and other expenses of sale amounting to $210.

Required: Prepare all necessary entries relating to this investment from May 1, 20X1, through January 1, 20X2.

P19.4. Setsail Hospital purchased $100,000 face value of XYZ Company bonds at 104 percent on May 1, 20X1. Brokerage and other acquisition costs were $280. These bonds pay 7.5 percent interest per year, payable semiannually on April 1 and October 1. The maturity date of the bonds is April 1, 20X6. It was management's intent to hold these securities as long-term investments, but on January 1, 20X2, 40 percent of the bonds were sold at 106 percent and accrued interest, less brokerage fees of $310.

Required: Prepare all necessary entries relating to this investment from May 1, 20X1, through January 1, 20X2.

P19.5. Signoff Hospital purchased 200 shares of the $10 par value common stock of Mohawk Company on May 15, 20X1, for $12,700. Brokerage fees amounted to $60. On June 1, the board of directors of Mohawk declared a cash dividend of $2.50 per share payable on June 18 to stockholders of record at June 10. On August 4, the board of directors of Mohawk declared a 10 percent stock dividend payable on August 30 to stockholders of record at August 15. As of August 4, Mohawk stock was selling on the market at $80 per share. On September 19, the hospital sold 120 shares of the Mohawk stock for $10,000, with brokerage fees amounting to $140.

Required: Prepare entries to record all matters relating to the investment in Mohawk Company stock for 20X1.

P19.6. Situp Hospital purchased Eastcoast Company common stock, as shown here:

Date	Shares	Price per Share	Brokerage	Total Costs
1/1/X1	20	$11.00	$20.00	$240.00
1/1/X2	20	14.50	30.00	320.00

On April 1, 20X2, Eastcoast Company declared a cash dividend of $1.50 per share payable May 1, 20X2, to stockholders of record as of April 20, 20X2. On July 2, 20X2, Eastcoast Company declared a 25 percent stock dividend distributable August 15, 20X2, to stockholders of record on July 21, 20X2. On October 3, 20X2, Situp Hospital sold ten shares of the Eastcoast Company stock for $160, less brokerage costs of $25.

Required: Prepare entries to record all matters relating to the investment in Eastcoast Company stock for 20X1 and 20X2.

LONG-TERM LIABILITIES

In addition to the current liabilities described in Chapter 17, a hospital has economic obligations that will not be discharged with resources classified in the balance sheet as current assets. These obligations are variously referred to as **long-term liabilities**, or *noncurrent*, or *fixed, liabilities*. Whereas current liabilities generally arise from informal contractual arrangements, long-term liabilities are ordinarily based on a written contract, such as a mortgage document, bond indenture, or lease agreement. A proper distinction between current and noncurrent liabilities in the balance sheet is of considerable importance in evaluating the financial position of a hospital as well as in managing its financial affairs.

Long-term liabilities typically consist of mortgages and bonds payable, long-term contracts and capital lease obligations, employee pension and retirement plan liabilities, and the noncurrent portion of deferred revenues. The discussion in this chapter will be limited, however, to accounting procedures relating to hospital bond issues.

Because many hospitals can no longer expect to obtain significant amounts of new long-term funds from philanthropy, public subscription, government grants, and other traditional sources, the only recourse is for the hospital to borrow through bond issues and then to repay with internally generated cash. The rapid increase in debt financing by hospitals in recent years provides sufficient documentation on this matter. This practice, encouraged by various state laws that enable hospitals to issue tax-free revenue bonds, naturally places a premium on superior financial management and its accounting prerequisites. It is largely for these reasons that we devote this chapter entirely to the subject of accounting for bonds payable.

Nature of Bonds Payable

The power of a hospital corporation to issue bonds arises in the corporation laws of the state and is exercised by authorization of the governing board. For state and municipal hospitals, bonded indebtedness also may require the approval of a majority of citizens. Many states have created statutory authority for issuing tax-exempt bonds to finance not-for-profit hospitals' long-term capital needs.

The Bond Indenture

Bonds ordinarily are issued in $1,000 denominations referred to as **face value**, or *maturity value*. The terms of a bond issue are spelled out in a contract known as a bond indenture. It details the rights and obligations of the bondholders and the hospital, names the agency that is to act as trustee to protect the rights and enforce the covenants and obligations of both parties, and describes the bonds as to security, interest rate, maturity date, and other matters. Although bonds may be sold directly to the general public, investment bankers or a syndicate of brokerage firms who market the bonds on a commission basis more often underwrite them.

Types of Bonds

Several different types of bonds may be issued by hospitals. **Registered bonds** are those on which interest is paid only to "bondholders of record" (that is, those whose holdings are recorded by the issuing hospital or its registrar agent). No record is kept of the owners of **coupon bonds**; rather, interest on coupon bonds is paid to all bondholders who present the periodic interest coupons that accompany the bond certificates. **Serial bonds** mature in installments over a period of years, whereas a **term bond** issue matures on a single fixed maturity date. Some bonds, at the option of the hospital, may be callable at specified times on payment of a "call price" that usually is higher than the face value of the bonds.

In addition, bonds may be either secured or unsecured. **Secured bonds**, often known as *mortgage bonds*, involve pledging specific plant assets under liens as security to bondholders. Hospital bond issues may also be secured in the sense that payment of principal and/or interest may be guaranteed by a governmental authority or some parent organization. The security for a hospital bond issue may also arise from the accumulation of a bond **sinking fund** (a pool of resources earmarked for the payment of interest charges and for the retirement of the bonds). In many instances, hospitals have issued **revenue bonds** on which interest is paid from specified revenue sources. Finally, hospitals having extremely high credit ratings may sometimes issue **general obligation bonds** that are secured only by the hospital's reputation and general financial resources. Unsecured bonds of this type are called **debentures**.

The decision to issue bonds is a critical matter. All relevant factors must be carefully considered and evaluated. It should be evident that the bond issue is the most desirable means of obtaining the necessary long-term funds at reasonable cost and on acceptable terms. There must be assurances that the debt burden, periodic interest charges, and principal retirement will not lead to financial embarrassment and endanger the hospital's ability to meet its obligations to the community it serves. In all cases, the assistance of reputable professional firms specializing in hospital financing should be obtained.

Issuance of Bonds

When the hospital corporation issues bonds, it contracts to pay (1) the face value of the bonds at a specified maturity date and (2) interest (expressed as a percentage of face value) at periodic intervals, usually every six months. This nominal, or coupon, interest rate is predetermined on the basis of expectations concerning the rate of interest investors will demand at the time the bonds are actually issued. The market rate of interest varies according to the degree of credit risk, the term of the bonds, the supply-and-demand situation for long-term money, and the taxability of the bond interest to investors, among other factors.

Premium and Discount Prices

If the nominal interest rate should equal the market rate, the hospital's bonds will sell at face value. There often is a difference, however, between the nominal and market rates of interest. Bonds sell at a premium (a price greater than face value) if the nominal interest rate is higher than the market rate; they sell at a discount (a price lower than face value) if they pay interest at a rate less than the market rate. Thus, differences between the contractual and market rates of interest are reflected in the prices investors are willing to pay for the bonds, thereby eliminating the need to amend the bond contract. Because issuing bonds at a discount or a premium is most common, we will discuss only those two possibilities.

Issuance at a Discount

To illustrate the accounting procedures for bonds issued at a discount, let us assume that Supercare Hospital issues $400,000 (face value) of 6 percent, 20-year bonds at 92.625 percent of face value, or $370,500, on August 1, 20X1. (Hospital bond issues generally are much larger amounts, but $400,000 is a convenient amount for purposes of illustration.) These bonds pay interest semiannually on April 1 and October 1. Semiannual interest payments are $12,000 ($400,000 × 6 percent × 6/12 months). The bonds are dated April 1, 20X1, so the maturity date is 20 years later. Also assume that bond issue costs amount to $17,700, which include sales commissions paid to investment bankers, legal and accounting fees, registration and filing fees, appraisal costs, and printing expenses.

As noted earlier, the bond certificates are dated April 1, 20X1, but the hospital postponed the actual sale of the bonds until August 1, 20X1, to take advantage of an expected decline in the market rate of interest. Assuming that all of the bonds are sold on August 1, 20X1, the following entries are made in the unrestricted fund accounts of the hospital:

Cash Receipts Journal

8/1/X1	Cash—general checking account	$378,500	
	Unamortized bond discount	29,500	
	Accrued interest payable		$ 8,000
	Bonds payable		400,000

Issue of $400,000 of 6%, 20-year bonds:

Face value	$400,000	
Proceeds:		
(92.625 % of		
$400,000)	370,500	
Discount	$ 29,500	
Proceeds (above)	$370,500	
Accrued interest:		
($400,000 × 6% ×		
4/12 months)	8,000	
Total cash received	$378,500	

Voucher Register

8/1/X1	Unamortized bond issue costs	$ 17,700	
	Accounts payable		$17,700
	Voucher issued for payment of bond		
	issue costs		

Cash Disbursements Journal

8/1/X1	Accounts payable	$ 17,700	
	Cash—general checking account		$17,700
	Check issued in payment of bond		
	issue costs		

If a balance sheet were prepared immediately after the bond issue, it would present the bonds as a long-term liability of Supercare Hospital's unrestricted fund in the following manner:

6% bonds payable	$400,000	
Less unamortized bond discount	29,500	$370,500

Thus, the unamortized bond discount is deducted from the face amount of the outstanding bonds in the long-term liability section of the balance sheet. The unamortized bond issue costs of $17,700, on the other hand, should be included in the noncurrent assets of the unrestricted fund in a "deferred charges" or "other assets" category. Only the unamortized bond discount should be shown in the contra liability position. It is never correct to classify the bond discount as an asset. Finally, the balance sheet also would present the $8,000 of accrued interest payable among the current liabilities of the hospital.

When bonds are issued (sold) between interest payment dates, as these bonds were, the issuing hospital collects accrued interest from the purchasers as a part of the transaction. This procedure enables the hospital to pay a full six months' interest at each semiannual interest payment date, regardless of how long individual bondholders may have held their bonds. It would be impractical for the hospital to try to compute the amount of interest actually due to each bondholder at each interest payment date. Accrued interest settlements are made between sellers and buyers of bonds at the trading date as an adjustment of the price to be paid by the buyers.

Issuing Bonds Between Interest Payment Dates

When the nominal interest rate is higher than the market rate of interest, bonds will be issued at a premium. Assume, for example, that Supercare Hospital issues $400,000 (face value) of 9 percent, 20-year bonds at 108.85 percent of $400,000, or $435,400, on August 1, 20X1. These bonds pay interest semiannually on April 1 and October 1, and are dated April 1, 20X1. Also assume that bond issue costs amounted to $23,600. If all of the bonds are sold on August 1, 20X1, the following entries are made in the unrestricted fund accounts:

Issuance at a Premium

Cash Receipts Journal

8/1/X1	Cash—general checking account	$447,400	
	Unamortized bond premium		$ 35,400
	Accrued interest payable		12,000
	Bonds payable		400,000

Issuance of $400,000 of 9% bonds:

Proceeds:

(108.85% of $400,000)	$435,400
Face value	400,000
Premium	$ 35,400
Proceeds (above)	$435,400

Accrued interest:

($400,000 × 9% × 4/12 months)	12,000
Total cash received	$447,400

Voucher Register

8/1/X1	Unamortized bond issue costs	$ 23,600	
	Accounts payable		$ 23,600
	Voucher issued for payment of bond issue costs		

Cash Disbursements Journal

8/1/X1	Accounts payable	$ 23,600	
	Cash—general checking account		$ 23,600
	Check issued in payment of bond issue costs		

If a balance sheet were prepared immediately after the above bond issue, it would present the bonds as a long-term liability of the unrestricted fund in the following manner:

9% bonds payable	$400,000	
Add unamortized bond premium	35,400	$435,400

Note that unamortized bond premium is added to the face amount of bonds outstanding, whereas unamortized bond discount was deducted in the previous illustration. The balance sheet also will include the unamortized bond issue costs of $23,600 in a noncurrent "deferred charges" or "other assets" classification and will report the $12,000 of accrued interest payable among the current liabilities.

Bond Interest and Amortization

The amount of bond interest expense to be recorded each month is influenced by the premium or discount recorded at the time the bonds are issued. Amortization of bond discount is regarded as an addition to periodic interest expense, whereas the amortization of bond premium is treated as a reduction of interest expense. This system is followed to obtain at least a rough approximation of the effective (actual) interest cost of the bonds. In practice, bond discount and premium may be amortized (allocated) evenly throughout the life of the bond issue by application of the straight-line, or average, method. (A theoretically superior procedure, called *the compound-interest or effective-yield method*, is also used in actual practice.) Bond issue costs are usually amortized to expense by application of the straight-line method.

Interest and Discount

Refer to the Issuance at a Discount discussion earlier in this chapter, where the proceeds of the $400,000, 6 percent bond issue amount to only $370,500. The resulting $29,500 of bond discount should be amortized by charges to interest expense over the 236-month life of the bond issue: the 236 months between the issue date and the maturity date. The idea is that, because the hospital received only $370,500 but must repay $400,000 at maturity, the $29,500 represents a cost that is properly allocable to the period that presumably benefits from the resources the bond issue provided. It is a matter of cost allocation and of matching costs and revenues on a periodic basis. A similar procedure applies to the $17,700 of bond issue costs.

At the end of each of the 236 months during which the bonds will be outstanding, adjusting entries will be made to amortize $125 ($29,500 ÷ 236 months) of bond discount and $75 ($17,700 ÷ 236 months) of bond issue costs. The required entries for August 31, 20X1, will illustrate the procedure:

General Journal

8/31/X1	Bond interest expense	$ 2,125	
	Unamortized bond discount		$ 125
	Accrued interest payable		2,000

Accrual of monthly bond interest
expense, including amortization of
bond discount:

Nominal interest:		
($400,000 × 6% ×		
1/12 months)	$2,000	
Discount amortization:		
($29,500 ÷ 236 months)	125	
Monthly interest expense	$2,125	

8/31/X1	Amortization of bond issue costs	$ 75	
	Unamortized bond issue costs		$ 75

Monthly amortization of bond issue costs
($17,700 ÷ 236 months)

Notice that the amortization of bond discount is a part of the debit to bond interest expense, which roughly approximates the effective monthly interest cost. Amortization of bond issue costs, however, is charged to a separate expense account. Such costs, being in the nature of prepaid expenses, should not be confused or combined with bond discount.

The same entries, of course, will be made on September 30, 20X1. Then, on October 1, 20X1, when Supercare Hospital pays six months' interest on the bonds, the interest payment entries are as follows:

Voucher Register

10/1/X1	Accrued interest payable	$12,000	
	Accounts payable		$12,000

Voucher for payment of semiannual
bond interest

Cash Disbursements Journal

10/1/X1	Accounts payable	$12,000	
	Cash—general checking account		$12,000

Checks issued to pay semiannual bond
interest

Recall that the accrued interest payable account was credited for $8,000 in the bond issue entry on August 1, 20X1, and was credited for $2,000 on August 31 and again on September 30, 20X1, in the month-end adjusting entries. The resulting credit balance of $12,000 is eliminated by the debit in the preceding voucher register entry of October 1, 20X1.

You also should recognize that the entire $29,500 of bond discount and the $17,700 of bond issue costs will have been charged to expense by the maturity date of the bonds. So, when the maturity date arrives and the bonds are retired, the entries are as follows:

Voucher Register

4/1/XX	Bonds payable	$400,000	
	Accounts payable		$400,000
	Voucher issued for retirement of bonds		

Cash Disbursements Journal

4/1/XX	Accounts payable	$400,000	
	Cash—general checking account		$400,000
	Checks issued to retire bonds		

In certain circumstances, all or part of a bond issue may be retired prior to its normal maturity date. This matter will be pursued later in this chapter.

Summary of Entries During Year of Bond Issuance Let us return for a moment to 20X1 and summarize all the entries that are made during the year for the $400,000 bond issue. These 20X1 entries are summarized in the general ledger accounts presented in Figure 20.1. Take note of the year-end account balances. The 20X1 statement of operations of Supercare Hospital will report $10,625 of bond interest expense and $375 of bond issue cost amortization (an expense). The December 31, 20X1, balance sheet will present the bonds as a long-term liability as follows:

6% bonds payable	$400,000	
Less unamortized bond discount	28,875	$ 371,125

This balance sheet also will report $17,325 of unamortized bond issue costs as an asset and $6,000 of accrued interest payable as a current liability.

Interest and Premium

Refer to Issuance at a Premium earlier in this chapter, where the proceeds of the $400,000, 9 percent bond issue amount to $435,400. At the end of each of the 236 months during which the bonds will be outstanding, adjusting entries such as the following will be made to amortize $150 ($35,400 ÷ 236 months) of bond premium and $100 ($23,600 ÷ 236 months) of bond issue costs:

General Journal

8/31/X1	Bond interest expense	$ 2,850	
	Unamortized bond premium	150	
	Accrued interest payable		$ 3,000
	Accrual of monthly bond interest		
	expense and premium amortization:		

Cash–General Checking Account		
(1) 378,500	(3)	17,700
	(9)	12,000

Unamortized Bond Issue Costs		
(2) 17,700	(5)	75
	(7)	75
	(11)	75
	(13)	75
	(15)	75
Bal. 17,325		

Accounts Payable			
(3)	17,700	(2)	17,700
(9)	12,000	(8)	12,000

Accrued Interest Payable		
(8) 12,000	(1)	8,000
	(4)	2,000
	(6)	2,000
	(10)	2,000
	(12)	2,000
	(14)	2,000
	Bal.	6,000

Bonds Payable	
	(1) 400,000

Unamortized Bond Discount		
(1)	29,500	(4)	125
		(6)	125
		(10)	125
		(12)	125
		(14)	125
	Bal. 28,875	

Bond Interest Expense	
(4)	2,125
(6)	2,125
(10)	2,125
(12)	2,125
(14)	2,125
Bal.	10,625

Amortization of Bond Issue Costs	
(5)	75
(7)	75
(11)	75
(13)	75
(15)	75
Bal.	375

Posting references:
(1) 8/1/X1 bond issue—cash receipts journal
(2) 8/1/X1 payment of bond issue costs—voucher register
(3) 8/1/X1 payment of bond issue costs—cash disbursements journal
(4) 8/31/X1 interest accrual and discount amortization—general journal
(5) 8/31/X1 amortization of issue costs—general journal
(6) 9/30/X1 interest accrual and discount amortization—general journal
(7) 9/30/X1 amortization of issue costs—general journal
(8) 10/1/X1 payment of semiannual interest—voucher register
(9) 10/1/X1 payment of semiannual interest—cash disbursements journal
(10) 10/31/X1 interest accrual and discount amortization—general journal
(11) 10/31/X1 amortization of issue costs—general journal
(12) 11/30/X1 interest accrual and discount amortization—general journal
(13) 11/30/X1 amortization of issue costs—general journal
(14) 12/31/X1 interest accrual and discount amortization—general journal
(15) 12/31/X1 amortization of issue costs—general journal

FIGURE 20.1

Accounting for Bonds Issued at a Discount

Nominal interest:
($400,000 × 9% ×
1/12 months) $ 3,000
Premium amortization:
($35,400 ÷ 236 months)   150
Monthly interest expense $ 2,850

8/31/X1 Amortization of bond issue costs $ 100
              Unamortized bond issue costs $ 100
         Monthly amortization of bond issue costs
         ($23,600 ÷ 236 months)

Notice that the amortization of bond premium reduces the amount to be debited to bond interest expense to obtain an approximation of the true monthly interest cost.

Interest Payment Entries   The same entries, of course, will be made on September 30, 20X1. Then, on October 1, 20X1, when Supercare Hospital pays six months' interest on the bonds, the interest payment entries are as follows:

Voucher Register
10/1/X1 Accrued interest payable $ 18,000
              Accounts payable $18,000
         Voucher issued for payment of semiannual
         bond interest: ($400,000 × 9% ×
         6/12 months)

Cash Disbursements Journal
10/1/X1 Accounts payable $ 18,000
              Cash—general checking account $18,000
         Checks issued to pay semiannual bond
         interest

Following this, the previously described monthly adjusting entries will be made on October 31, November 30, and December 31, 20X1. All the 20X1 entries for the $400,000 of 9 percent bonds issued at a premium are summarized in Figure 20.2.

Bonds Issued at Premium Reported as Long-Term Liability   Notice the year-end balances in Figure 20.2. The December 31, 20X1, balance sheet will present the bonds as a long-term liability as follows:

9% bonds payable $400,000
Add unamortized bond premium   34,650 $434,650

This balance sheet also will report $23,100 of unamortized bond issue costs as an asset and $9,000 of accrued interest payable as a current

Cash–General Checking Account		Unamortized Bond Issue Costs		Accounts Payable	
(1) 447,400	(3) 23,600	(2) 23,600	(5) 100	(3) 23,600	(2) 23,600
	(9) 18,000		(7) 100	(9) 18,000	(8) 18,000
			(11) 100		
			(13) 100		
			(15) 100		
		Bal. 23,100			

Accrued Interest Payable		Bonds Payable		Unamortized Bond Premium	
(8) 18,000	(1) 12,000		(1) 400,000	(4) 150	(1) 35,400
	(4) 3,000			(6) 150	
	(6) 3,000			(10) 150	
	(10) 3,000			(12) 150	
	(12) 3,000			(14) 150	
	(14) 3,000				Bal. 34,650
	Bal. 9,000				

Bond Interest Expense		Amortization of Bond Issue Costs	
(4) 2,850		(5) 100	
(6) 2,850		(7) 100	
(10) 2,850		(11) 100	
(12) 2,850		(13) 100	
(14) 2,850		(15) 100	
Bal. 14,250		Bal. 500	

Posting references:
(1) 8/1/X1 bond issue—cash receipts journal
(2) 8/1/X1 payment of bond issue costs—voucher register
(3) 8/1/X1 payment of bond issue costs—cash disbursements journal
(4) 8/31/X1 interest accrual and premium amortization—general journal
(5) 8/31/X1 amortization of issue costs—general journal
(6) 9/30/X1 interest accrual and premium amortization—general journal
(7) 9/30/X1 amortization of issue costs—general journal
(8) 10/1/X1 payment of semiannual interest—voucher register
(9) 10/1/X1 payment of semiannual interest—cash disbursements journal
(10) 10/31/X1 interest accrual and premium amortization—general journal
(11) 10/31/X1 amortization of issue costs—general journal
(12) 11/30/X1 interest accrual and premium amortization—general journal
(13) 11/30/X1 amortization of issue costs—general journal
(14) 12/31/X1 interest accrual and premium amortization—general journal
(15) 12/31/X1 amortization of issue costs—general journal

FIGURE 20.2
Accounting for Bonds Issued at a Premium

liability. The 20X1 statement of operations of Supercare Hospital will report $14,250 of bond interest expense and $500 of bond issue cost amortization (an expense).

Early Extinguishment of Debt

The normal retirement of term bonds at the scheduled maturity date was illustrated earlier. Let us examine here the procedure to follow when term bonds are reacquired and retired prior to the scheduled retirement date. Accounting for the refunding of bond issues—that is, the replacement of an outstanding bond issue with a new bond issue—and for the operation of bond sinking funds, however, will not be covered in this book.

A hospital may sometimes reacquire its own bonds in the market prior to maturity when bond prices and other factors make such action desirable. To illustrate, refer to the facts of the earlier example in which a $400,000 bond issue is sold at a premium on August 1, 20X1. Assume also that Supercare Hospital reacquires $80,000 (face value) of these bonds at 98 percent and accrued interest on June 1, 20X7, with brokerage and other reacquisition costs of $115 being paid. At the reacquisition date, the relevant accounts on the hospital's books have the following balances:

Accrued interest payable ($3,000 × 2 months)	$ 6,000	Cr.
Bonds payable	400,000	Cr.
Unamortized bond premium	24,900	Cr.
($35,400) − ($150 × 70 months)		
Unamortized bond issue costs	16,600	Dr.
($23,600) − ($100 × 70 months)		

The 70 months used in these computations of account balances are the number of months between the bond issue date (August 1, 20X1) and the bond reacquisition date (June 1, 20X7).

Recording a Reacquisition of Bonds

The entry to record the reacquisition requires the recognition of a gain (or loss) measured by the difference between the amount paid for the reacquired bonds (exclusive of accrued interest) and their book value at the date of reacquisition. The book value of the bonds reacquired and retired is computed as follows:

Book value of all bonds outstanding:		
Face value	$400,000	
Unamortized premium	24,900	
Unamortized issue costs	(16,600)	
Total		$408,300

Percentage of bonds reacquired:

($80,000 ÷ $400,000)	.20
Book value of bonds reacquired	$ 81,660

Journal Entries for Bond Retirement

The amount paid (exclusive of interest) to reacquire these bonds is $78,515 (98 percent of $80,000, plus $115 of brokerage fees and other costs of reacquisition). So, the gain on the reacquisition is $3,145 ($81,660 – $78,515). The necessary entries to record the reacquisition and retirement of the bonds are the following:

Voucher Register

6/1/X7	Bonds payable		$80,000	
	Accrued interest payable		1,200	
	Unamortized bond premium		4,980	
	Unamortized bond issue costs			$ 3,320
	Gain on reacquisition of bonds			3,145
	Accounts payable			79,715
	Voucher issued for reacquisition			
	and retirement 20% of bond issue:			
	Face value			
	(20% of $400,000)	$80,000		
	Unamortized premium:			
	(20% of $24,900)	4,980		
	Unamortized issue costs:			
	(20% of $16,600)	(3,320)		
	Book value of bonds			
	reacquired	$ 81,660		
	Reacquisition cost:			
	(98% of $80,000)	$78,400		
	Brokerage fees	115		
	Total	78,515		
	Accrued interest:			
	(20% of $6,000)	1,200		
	Cash disbursement	$ 79,715		

Cash Disbursements Journal

6/1/X7	Accounts payable	$ 79,715	
	Cash—general checking account		$79,715
	Check issued for reacquisition and		
	retirement of 20% of bond issue		

After this reacquisition, accounting continues as before until maturity with respect to the remaining $320,000 of bonds. The monthly amount of amortization and interest, however, will be reduced by 20 percent. The

FIGURE 20.3

Summary of Discount Amortization and Interest Expense, Bonds Outstanding Method

Year	Bonds Outstanding	Fraction	Bond Discount	Discount Amortization	5% Nominal Interest	Interest Expense
20X1	$ 400,000	40/120	$24,000	$ 8,000	$20,000	$28,000
20X2	320,000	32/120	24,000	6,400	16,000	22,400
20X3	240,000	24/120	24,000	4,800	12,000	16,800
20X4	160,000	16/120	24,000	3,200	8,000	11,200
20X5	80,000	8/120	24,000	1,600	4,000	5,600
	$1,200,000			$24,000	$60,000	$84,000

Fraction × Bond discount = Discount amortization
Discount amortization + 5% nominal interest = Interest expense

monthly interest expense will be $2,280, monthly premium amortization will be $120, and monthly amortization of bond issue costs will be $80 (rather than $2,850, $150, and $100, respectively). Similarly, the monthly addition to accrued interest payable will be $2,400 ($320,000 × 9 percent × 1/12 months).

Reporting Gains and Losses on Early Retirement of Bonds

It should be noted that gains and losses on the early extinguishment of debt are reported in the statement of operations as extraordinary items. A simplified illustration of the presentation follows:

Revenues (assumed)	$800,000
Less expenses (assumed)	(750,000)
Income before extraordinary items	50,000
Add extraordinary gain (disclosed details)	3,145
Excess of revenues over expenses for the year	$ 53,145

Serial Bonds

The illustrations prior to this point have assumed that the bonds in question have been term bonds—that is, that all bonds in the issue have the same maturity date. Some hospital bond issues, however, are serial bonds that mature in periodic installments. To illustrate, assume a simplified case in which Supercare Hospital issues $400,000 of 5 percent serial bonds on January 1, 20X1, at 94 percent. These bonds pay interest annually on January 1, and mature at the rate of $80,000 annually, starting January 1, 20X2. Issue costs were $14,400.

The Bonds Outstanding Method of Amortization

Figure 20.3 summarizes annual discount amortization and bond interest expense as computed by the "bonds outstanding" method. This method, rather than the straight-line method described earlier in this chapter, is used because the face amount of bonds outstanding each year varies. It provides for an amortization pattern that corresponds to the amount of bonds outstanding. Bond issue costs are amortized in the same pattern.

To illustrate the entries to be made for serial bonds, let us assume that Supercare Hospital makes entries for amortization and interest accruals only once each year on December 31. All of the necessary entries for 20X1 are summarized in Figure 20.4 on page 392.

Questions

Q20.1. How are current and long-term liabilities different?

Q20.2. Briefly identify each of the following:
   a. Bond indenture
   b. Registered bond
   c. Coupon bond
   d. Serial bond
   e. Term bond
   f. Secured bond
   g. Revenue bond
   h. Debentures

Q20.3. How should unamortized bond discount, unamortized bond premium, and unamortized bond issue costs be presented in the hospital's balance sheet?

Q20.4. On January 1, 20X1, a hospital issued serial bonds with a total face value of $1 million. These bonds mature annually in $200,000 amounts, beginning January 1, 20X2. Indicate how these bonds should be presented in the hospital balance sheet as of December 31, 20X1.

Q20.5. A hospital bond issue, dated April 1, 20X1, is actually issued for cash on June 1, 20X1. The purchasers of these bonds will pay the hospital for two months of accrued interest. Why?

Q20.6. Distinguish between the nominal (or coupon) rate of interest and the effective rate of interest for a hospital bond issue.

Q20.7. For what reasons might a hospital bond issue sell at a price that is higher or lower than face value?

Q20.8. If a hospital bond issue is sold at a discount, will the monthly charge to bond interest expense be greater or less than the nominal amount of interest per month? Explain your answer.

Q20.9. A hospital bond issue is sold at a premium on January 1, 20X1. Interest on the bonds is payable annually on December 31. Will the annual interest expense recorded on the hospital's books be

FIGURE 20.4

Entries for
Serial Bonds

Cash Receipts Journal

1/1/X1	Cash—general checking account	$376,000	
	Unamortized bond discount	24,000	
	Bonds payable		$400,000
	Issuance of 5% serial bonds		

Voucher Register

1/1/X1	Unamortized bond issue costs	$ 14,400	
	Accounts payable		$ 14,400
	Voucher issued for payment of bond issue costs		

Cash Disbursements Journal

1/1/X1	Accounts payable	$ 14,400	
	Cash—general checking account		$ 14,400
	Check issued for payment of bond issue costs		

General Journal

12/31/X1	Bond interest expense	$ 28,000	
	Unamortized bond discount		$ 8,000
	Accrued interest payable		20,000
	Accrual of bond interest expense and amortization of bond discount:		

	Nominal interest:		
	(5% of $400,000)	$ 20,000
	Discount amortization:	
	($24,000 × [40 ÷ 120])	8,000
	20X1 interest expense	$ 28,000

12/31/X1	Amortization of bond issue costs	$ 4,800	
	Unamortized bond issue costs		$ 4,800
	Amortization of bond issue costs for 20X1 ($14,400 × [40 ÷ 120])		

Voucher Register

1/1/X2	Accrued interest payable	$ 20,000	
	Bonds payable	80,000	
	Accounts payable		$100,000
	Vouchers issued for payment of 20X1 accrued interest and for retirement of bonds due 1/1/X2		

Cash Disbursements Journal

1/1/X2	Accounts payable	$ 100,000	
	Cash—general checking account		$100,000
	Checks issued for payment of 20X1 accrued interest and for retirement bonds due 1/1/X2		

Continued

FIGURE 20.4
(CONTINUED)
Entries for
Serial Bonds

General Journal

12/31/X2 Bond interest expense	$22,400	
Unamortized bond discount		$ 6,400
Accrued interest payable		16,000

Accrual of bond interest and
amortization of bond discount:
Nominal interest:
(5% of $320,000) — $ 16,000
Discount amortization:
($24,000 × [32 ÷ 120]) — 6,400
20X2 interest expense — $22,400

| 12/31/X2 Amortization of bond issue costs | $ 3,840 | |
| Unamortized bond issue costs | | $ 3,840 |

Amortization of bond issue costs for 20X2
($14,400 × [32 ÷ 120])

greater or less than the amount of annual interest actually paid to the bondholders? Explain your answer.

Q20.10. If the market rate of interest is higher than the nominal (or coupon) rate of interest specified in a hospital bond issue, will the hospital's bonds sell at a price that is higher or lower than face value? Explain your answer.

Exercises

E20.1. On January 1, 20X1, Sandy Hospital issued 500 of its 9 percent, $1,000 bonds at a rate of 95 percent. Interest is payable semiannually on July 1 and January 1, and the bonds mature in ten years. The hospital paid bond issue costs of $20,000.
Required: What amount of long-term debt should be reported for the bonds in the hospital's December 31, 20X1 balance sheet?

E20.2. On January 1, 20X1, Skippy Hospital issued 2,000 of its 10 percent, $1,000 bonds for $2,080,000. These bonds mature in ten years, but were callable at 101 percent any time after December 31, 20X5. The interest is payable semiannually on July 1 and January 1. On July 1, 20X6, the hospital called all of the bonds and retired them.
Required: What was the gain (loss) on this early extinguishment of debt?

E20.3. On January 1, 20X1, Sally Hospital issued $500 of 8 percent, five-year serial bonds at 94 percent. The bonds mature at the rate of

$100 annually, beginning January 1, 20X2. Interest is payable annually on January 1.

Required: What is the amount of 20X2 bond interest expense?

E20.4. On October 1, 20X1, Scott Hospital issued $1,000 (face value) of 7.2 percent, five-year term bonds at 100 percent and accrued interest. Issue costs were $55. Interest is payable semiannually, on May 1 and November 1, and the bonds mature on May 1, 20X6. On January 1, 20X2, $250 (face value) of these bonds were reacquired at 104 percent and accrued interest.

Required: What was the gain (loss) on the reacquisition of the bonds?

E20.5. On September 1, 20X1, Stepout Hospital issued $4,000 (face value) of five-year, 9.6 percent bonds at 111 percent and accrued interest. Interest is payable semiannually, on April 1 and October 1, and the bonds mature on April 1, 20X6. On February 1, 20X2, $1,000 of these bonds are reacquired at 108 percent and accrued interest.

Required: What was the gain (loss) on the reacquisition of the bonds?

E20.6. On September 1, 20X1, Stepup Hospital issued $4,000 (face value) of five-year, 4.8 percent bonds at 94.5 percent and accrued interest. Interest is payable semiannually on April 1 and October 1, and the bonds mature on April 1, 20X6.

Required: What is the 20X1 bond interest expense?

Problems

P20.1. Saltville Hospital issued $1 million of five-year, 6 percent bonds at 100 percent and accrued interest on August 1, 20X1. Issue costs were $56,000. Interest is payable semiannually, on April 1 and October 1. The maturity date of the bonds is April 1, 20X6. On February 1, 20X2, $200,000 of these bonds are reacquired at 98 percent and accrued interest.

Required: Prepare entries to record all matters relating to the bond issue from August 1, 20X1, through February 1, 20X2.

P20.2. Saltick Hospital issued $500,000 (face value) of 6 percent, ten-year bonds at 97.7 percent and accrued interest on October 1, 20X1. Bond issue costs amounted to $20,700. The bonds, dated May 1, 20X1, pay interest semiannually on May 1 and November 1. The hospital's fiscal year ends on December 31. On January 1, 20X2, the hospital reacquires 20 percent of these bonds by purchase in the open market at 92 percent and accrued interest, with brokerage and other reacquisition costs of $280 being paid.

Required: (1) Prepare a chart, such as the one in Figure 20.1, showing entries for all matters relating to this bond issue through December 31, 20X1. (2) Indicate how all matters relating to this bond issue should be presented in the hospital's 20X1 financial statements. (3) Prepare the necessary entry to record the reacquisition of 20 percent of the bonds on January 1, 20X2. (4) Compute the amount of bond interest expense for January 20X2.

P20.3. Salty Hospital issued $500,000 (face value) of 6 percent, ten-year bonds at 102.3 percent and accrued interest on October 1, 20X1. Bond issue costs amounted to $16,100. The bonds, dated May 1, 20X1, pay interest semiannually on May 1 and November 1. The hospital's fiscal year ends on December 31. On January 1, 20X2, the hospital reacquires 20 percent of these bonds by purchase in the open market at 101 percent and accrued interest, with brokerage and other reacquisition costs of $260 being paid.

Required: (1) Prepare a chart, such as the one in Figure 20.2, showing entries for all matters relating to this bond issue through December 31, 20X1. (2) Indicate how all matters relating to this bond issue should be presented in the hospital's 20X1 financial statements. (3) Prepare the necessary entry to record the reacquisition of 20 percent of the bonds on January 1, 20X2. (4) Compute the amount of bond interest expense for January 20X2.

P20.4. Saltrock Hospital issued $500,000 (face value) of 6 percent serial bonds on January 1, 20X1, at 94 percent. These bonds pay interest annually on January 1 and mature at the rate of $100,000 annually, starting January 1, 20X2. Issue costs amounted to $15,000. The hospital's fiscal year ends on December 31, at which time annual entries are made for amortization and accruals.

Required: (1) Prepare a table, such as the one illustrated in Figure 20.3, to summarize discount amortization and interest expense for the 20X1–20X5 period. (2) Prepare the necessary entries for 20X1 and 20X2 only. (3) Indicate how all matters relating to these bonds should be presented in the hospital's 20X2 financial statements.

P20.5. Saltmine Hospital issued $600,000 (face value) of 8 percent serial bonds on January 1, 20X1, at 106 percent. These bonds pay interest annually on January 1 and mature at the rate of $120,000 annually, starting January 1, 20X2. Issue costs amounted to $18,000. The hospital's fiscal year ends on December 31, at which time annual entries are made for amortization and accruals.

Required: (1) Prepare a table, such as the one in Figure 20.3, to summarize premium amortization and interest expense for the 20X1–20X5 period. (2) Prepare the necessary journal entries for 20X1 and 20X2 only. (3) Indicate how all matters relating to these bonds should be presented in the hospital's 20X2 financial statements.

P20.6. Saltless Hospital issued $600,000 (face value) of 6 percent, ten-year bonds at 94 percent and accrued interest on June 1, 20X1. Bond issue costs were $18,000. The bonds, dated June 1, 20X1, pay interest annually on June 1. The hospital's fiscal year ends on December 31. On January 1, 20X3, Saltless Hospital reacquires $150,000 (face value) of these bonds by purchase in the open market at 90 percent and accrued interest, with brokerage and other reacquisition costs of $300 being paid.

Required: Prepare the necessary journal entries at (1) June 1, 20X1; (2) June 30, 20X1; (3) June 1, 20X2; and (4) January 1, 20X3.

STATEMENT OF CASH FLOWS

A statement of operations presents the results of a hospital's operations in terms of revenues earned and expenses incurred during a given time period. The balance sheet presents the hospital's financial position in terms of the assets, liabilities, and net assets existing at a given point in time. The statement of changes in net assets provides a summary analysis of the factors causing increases and decreases in the individual net assets balances over a given period of time. For many years, these three financial statements were considered sufficient for the purposes of external financial reporting.

In 1971, the American Institute of Certified Public Accountants required that a fourth statement (a **statement of changes in financial position**) be included in the external reporting of the financial affairs and activities of an economic enterprise (see FASB Opinion No. 19, "Reporting Changes in Financial Position" [New York: AICPA, 1971]). This position subsequently was affirmed and specifically made applicable to hospital financial reporting by the Institute's Committee on Health Care Institutions (see *Hospital Audit Guide* [New York: AICPA, 1978], p. 38). The statement of changes in financial position generally was designed to present the sources and uses of working capital during a given period of time within the unrestricted (general) fund. In some instances, the statement was presented in a cash (or cash equivalents) format rather than in a working capital format.

In the late 1980s, the FASB issued Statement No. 95, which supersedes FASB Opinion No. 19. Statement 95 requires all business enterprises to include a **statement of cash flows** (SCF), rather than a statement of changes in financial position, as an essential component of a complete set of financial statements. The AICPA Health Care Committee made Statement No. 95 applicable to not-for-profit healthcare entities as well in the *AICPA Audit and Accounting Guide for Health Care Organizations* (1996). In this chapter, we examine the nature of this required statement and illustrate the procedures for its preparation.

Nature of the Statement of Cash Flows

Comparative statements of operations and balance sheets for Hopeful Hospital are presented in Figures 21.1 and 21.2. (The changes in the unrestricted net assets are assumed to consist only of net income as shown within

FIGURE 21.1

Hopeful Hospital Comparative Statement of Operations, Years Ended December 31, 20X2, and 20X1 (Non-GAAP)

	20X2	20X1
Gross patient services revenues	$9,490	$8,870
Less deductions from revenues	890	780
Net patient services revenues	8,600	8,090
Other operating revenues	633	519
Total operating revenues	9,233	8,609
Less operating expenses:		
Nursing services	3,188	2,995
Other professional services	2,030	1,920
Administrative services	3,070	2,910
Depreciation	540	465
Bad debt	0	0
Other operating expenses	315	292
Total operating expenses	9,143	8,582
Operating income	90	27
Nonoperating income, net	195	154
Excess of revenues over expenses	$ 285	$ 181

the net assets section of the balance sheets. Consequently, a separate statement of changes in net assets is not presented here.)

What the Statements Reveal

Clearly, these statements provide a considerable amount of important information concerning the operating results and financial position of the hospital. Intelligent decision making, whether by the hospital's management or by interested external parties, requires such information. Is the information provided in these statements alone sufficient to the needs of management and external users? Is the information complete? Does it clearly reflect all significant operating, investing, and financing activities of the hospital during 20X1 and 20X2? Do statements of operations and balance sheets alone adequately disclose the flow of cash resources into and out of the hospital enterprise? In each instance, the answer is no.

Certain important aspects of the operating, financing, and investing activities of Hopeful Hospital are not disclosed by or made clearly apparent from an examination of its statement of operations and balance sheets alone. For example, consider the following information drawn from the balance sheets in Figure 21.2:

	20X2	20X1
Assets		
Cash	$ 124	$ 280
Accrued interest receivable	45	30
Accounts receivable, net of allowance for uncollectible accounts of $210 at 12/31/X2 and $160 at 12/31/X1	1,536	1,340
Inventory	175	140
Prepaid expenses	32	40
Total current assets	1,912	1,830
Long-term investments	1,010	600
Plant assets, net of accumulated depreciation of $1,850 at 12/31/X2 and $1,340 at 12/31/X1	5,250	4,920
Total assets	$8,172	$7,350
Liabilities and Net Assets		
Accounts payable	$ 302	$ 370
Accrued expenses payable	208	220
Deferred revenues	77	60
Total current liabilities	587	650
Bonds payable	3,000	2,400
Total liabilities	3,587	3,050
Net assets, 1/1	4,300	4,119
Add net income for the year	285	181
Net assets, 12/31	4,585	4,300
Total liabilities and net assets	$8,172	$7,350

FIGURE 21.2

Hopeful Hospital Comparative Balance Sheets— Unrestricted Net Assets, December 31, 20X2, and 20X1

	20X2	20X1
Long-term investments	$1,010	$600

One might conclude from this presentation that new long-term investments costing $410 were purchased during 20X2. As you will shortly see, however, Hopeful Hospital purchased new long-term investments costing $450 and sold long-term investments (which had cost $40) for $49. Thus, the apparent $410 increase in long-term investments actually is the net difference between the costs of investments purchased and sold during 20X2.

Similar offsetting transactions typically are found in many of the other balance sheet accounts. These offsetting transactions, however, ordinarily are not determinable from the information provided in the balance sheet and statement of operations alone. If these financial statements are not to be misleading, such "hidden" information must be fully disclosed in some manner.

Purpose of the Statement of Cash Flows

The necessary disclosure is accomplished through the preparation of a statement of cash flows. It provides a summary of all significant cash flows relating to the operating, financing, and investing activities of the hospital. As noted above, many of these cash flows simply are not readily determinable (if at all) through an examination of balance sheet and statement of operations information alone.

Cash flow information has important implications for the hospital's creditors, reimbursement and planning agencies, and other external groups, as well as for internal management decisions. It can be used in estimating the cash flows that will be generated in the future and the growth potential of the hospital in terms of its ability to pay its existing obligations, finance expansion, and meet added indebtedness. Cash flow information also may indicate the need for external financing and clarify the difference between net income and cash flow from operating activities. The statement of cash flows is most useful, of course, when presented in comparative form for two or more years.

It should be noted that the term "cash," in the context of the statement of cash flows, is defined as cash plus cash equivalents—that is, short-term investments that are highly liquid, readily marketable, and convertible into definitely known amounts of cash. Some examples of cash equivalents include demand deposits in bank savings accounts, commercial paper, treasury bills, and money market funds. Generally, only investments in securities having original maturities of three months or less should be classified as cash equivalents. It also should be understood that the statement of cash flows should present the gross amounts of both cash receipts and cash disbursements from the hospital's operating, investing, and financing activities.

Categories of Cash Flows

In the statement of cash flows, cash receipts and cash disbursements are classified into three categories: operating activities, investing activities, and financing activities. The types of cash flow transactions to be reported in each of these three categories are indicated at a later point in this chapter.

Illustration Data

Figure 21.3 presents a summary of the financial activity of Hopeful Hospital for the year ended December 31, 20X2. This summary worksheet begins with the December 31, 20X1, postclosing balances you saw earlier in the hospital's December 31, 20X1, balance sheet (Figure 21.2). The following two columns of the worksheet provide a summary of the 20X2 transactions; the next two columns show the adjustments required at the end of 20X2, and the last two columns contain the preclosing account balances at the end of 20X2. These preclosing balances appeared in the hospital's 20X2 financial statements illustrated in Figures 21.1 and 21.2.

To assist you in your study of this worksheet, the 20X2 transactions and adjustments are presented here in general journal form:

(1)	Accounts receivable	$ 9,490	
	Patient services revenues		$ 9,490
	Gross revenues from services to patients		
(2)	Cash	8,404	
	Deductions from revenues	840	
	Accounts receivable		9,244
	Revenue deductions and cash collections on patients' accounts		
(3)	Cash	49	
	Gain on sale of investments		9
	Long-term investments		40
	Sale of long-term investments (cost: $40) for $49		
(4)	Cash	54	
	Loss on sale of plant assets	16	
	Accumulated depreciation	30	
	Plant assets		100
	Sale of plant assets (cost: $100; accumulated depreciation: $30) for $54		
(5)	Cash	3,830	
	Other operating revenues		650
	Nonoperating revenues		180
	Bonds payable		3,000
	Other cash receipts, including proceeds from new 6% bond issue		
(6)	Nursing services expenses	3,000	
	Other professional services expenses	1,900	
	Administrative services expenses	2,500	

	Other operating expenses	300	
	Accounts payable		7,700
	Vouchers issued for operating expenses		
	(including employee salaries and wages		
	of $4,500) other than supplies		
(7)	Inventories	935	
	Long-term investments	450	
	Plant assets	940	
	Bonds payable	2,400	
	Accounts payable		4,725
	Other vouchers issued for purchase		
	of inventory, purchase of long-term		
	investments, purchase of plant assets,		
	and retirement of 7% bonds		
(8)	Accounts payable	12,493	
	Cash		12,493
	Checks issued in payment of		
	vouchers issued for employee		
	salaries and wages, and all vouchers		
	recorded in entry (7) above		
(9)	Nursing services expenses	200	
	Other professional services expenses	130	
	Administrative services expenses	570	
	Inventory		900
	Cost of supplies used		
(10)	Depreciation expense	540	
	Accumulated depreciation		540
	Depreciation expense for 20X2		
(11)	Accrued interest receivable	15	
	Nonoperating revenues		15
	Adjustment for increase in		
	accrued interest receivable		
(12)	Deductions from revenues	50	
	Allowance for uncollectible accounts		50
	Adjustment for required increase in allowance		
	for uncollectible accounts		

FIGURE 21.3 Hopeful Hospital Worksheet, Year Ended December 31, 20X2

	12/31/X1 Balances Dr.	12/31/X1 Balances Cr.	20X2 Transactions Dr.	20X2 Transactions Cr.	12/31/X2 Adjustments Dr.	12/31/X2 Adjustments Cr.	12/31/X2 Balances Dr.	12/31/X2 Balances Cr.
Cash	280		(2) 8,404 (3) 49 (4) 54 (5) 3,830	(8) 12,493			124	
Accrued interest receivable	30				(11) 15		45	
Accounts receivable	1,500		(1) 9,490	(2) 9,244			1,746	
Allowance for uncollectible accounts		160				(12) 50		210
Inventory	140		(7) 935	(9) 900			175	
Prepaid expenses	40					(13) 8	32	
Long-term investments	600		(7) 450	(3) 40			1,010	
Plant assets	6,260		(7) 940	(4) 100			7,100	
Accumulated depreciation		1,340	(4) 30			(10) 540		1,850
Accounts payable		370	(8) 12,493	(6) 7,700 (7) 4,725				302
Accrued expenses payable		220			(14) 12			208
Deferred revenues		60				(15) 17		77
Bonds payable		2,400	(7) 2,400	(5) 3,000				3,000
Fund balance		4,300						4,300
Patient services revenues				(1) 9,490				9,490
Deductions from revenues			(2) 840		(12) 50		890	
Other operating revenues				(5) 650	(15) 17			633
Nursing services expenses			(6) 3,000 (9) 200			(14) 12	3,188	
Other professional services expenses			(6) 3,000 (9) 130				2,030	
Administrative services expenses			(6) 1,400 (9) 570				1,610	
Depreciation expense					(10) 540		1,460	
Other operating expenses			(6) 300		(13) 8		540	
Gain on sale of investments				(3) 9				9
Loss on sale of plant assets			(4) 16				16	
Nonoperating revenues				(5) 180		(11) 15		195
Totals	8,850	8,850	48,531	48,531	642	642	20,274	20,274

(13)	Other operating expenses	8	
	Prepaid expenses		8
	Adjustment for decrease in prepaid expenses		

(14)	Accrued expenses payable	12	
	Nursing services expenses		12
	Adjustment for decrease in accrued expenses		
	(assuming that expense items are nonlabor and		
	relate solely to nursing services)		

(15)	Other operating revenues	17	
	Deferred revenues		17
	Adjustment for increase in balance of deferred revenues		

Recognize that certain liberties have been taken in these entries in an effort to simplify and reduce the size of the illustration. It is assumed, for example, that there were no accrued salaries and wages payable either at the beginning or end of 20X2. As you trace the journal entries through the worksheet (See Figure 21.3), however, you should concern yourself only with acquiring a general knowledge of Hopeful Hospital's 20X2 financial activities.

Equation for the Statement of Cash Flows

The basic accounting equation, discussed in Chapter 1, can be stated as follows: $A = L + NA$. In other words, assets equal liabilities plus hospital net assets. Now, let us expand this equation to read as follows:

$$CE + OA = L + NA$$

Here, CE means cash and cash equivalents, and OA represents all other assets (assets other than cash and cash equivalents). Remember, as noted earlier, that cash equivalents include some, but not all, short-term investments. So, OA (other assets) includes short-term investments that are not cash equivalents, receivables, inventories, prepaid expenses, long-term investments, plant assets, and so on. Purchases and sales of short-term investments that are not cash equivalents are reported as investing activities in the statement of cash flows.

Now, let us subtract OA (other assets) from each side of the equation:

$$CE = L + NA - OA$$

Given this equation, how can the value of the left side of the equation increase? The answer is easy: by increasing the value of the right side of the equation. Given this equation, how can the value of the left side of the equation decrease? By decreasing the value of the right side of the equation.

Cash Inflows

Cash inflows normally result from an increase in the value of the right side of the equation—that is, an increase in liabilities (L), an increase in net assets (NA), or a decrease in other assets (OA). So, increases in liabilities (L), increases in net assets (NA), and decreases in other assets (OA) generally produce cash inflows (or, at least, defer cash outflows into the future, thereby preserving current cash balances).

Why is an increase in liabilities (L) considered to be a source or inflow of cash? Obviously, if the hospital issues bonds or borrows money from a bank (either for the short or long term), cash inflows result. But what about an increase in, say, accounts payable to suppliers? How can this be viewed as a cash inflow? Well, the hospital has acquired assets (inventory) without an immediate expenditure of cash. This temporary "saving" (retention) of cash is treated as an equivalent of cash inflow. As indicated later, however, certain increases in liabilities may not result in cash inflows.

Temporary Retention of Cash from Increasing Liabilities

An increase in hospital net assets (NA) generally arises from an excess of revenues over expenses (net income), and net income eventually results in a net cash inflow. In a very few instances, as noted later, certain increases in hospital net assets (NA) may not result in cash inflows.

Decreases in noncash assets ordinarily generate cash inflows. If long-term investments or plant assets are sold, for example, the sales proceeds increase the hospital's cash balances.

Cash Outflows

Cash outflows normally result from a decrease in the value of the right-hand side of the equation—that is, a decrease in liabilities (L), a decrease in net assets (NA), or an increase in other assets (OA).

Why is a decrease in liabilities (L) considered to be a use or outflow of cash? Obviously, if the hospital makes payments on accounts payable, repays the principal amount of bank loans, or retires long-term debt, cash outflows result. As indicated later, however, there may be certain transactions that decrease liabilities but do not require disbursements of cash.

A decrease in hospital net assets (NA) generally arises from an excess of expenses over revenues (net loss), and the net loss eventually results in a net cash outflow. In a very few instances, as noted later, certain decreases in hospital net assets (NA) may not result in cash outflows.

Net Assets Decreased by Net Losses

Increases in noncash assets ordinarily require cash outflows. If new long-term investments or plant assets are purchased, for example, such purchases generally result in cash disbursements.

Classification of Cash Flows

As noted earlier, cash receipts and cash disbursements are classified within the statement of cash flows into three types of economic activity: operating activities, investing activities, and financing activities.

Operating Activities

Hospital operating activities are those directly or indirectly related to the provision of healthcare services to patients. Cash flows from operating activities generally result from revenue and expense transactions that enter into the determination of the hospital's net income (or net loss).

Cash Flows from Operating Activities Cash inflows from operating activities include collections of accounts receivable arising from healthcare services provided to inpatients and outpatients, cash receipts related to other operating revenues, and certain cash receipts (interest and dividend income, for example) that are related to nonoperating revenues. Cash outflows from operating activities include cash disbursements for employee salaries and wages, inventory items and purchased services, interest on borrowings, taxes to governmental agencies, and other types of operating and nonoperating expenses. These cash inflows and outflows may arise from revenues and expenses that were recognized in a prior period, ones recognized in the current period, or some that will be recognized in one or more future periods.

Investing Activities

The investing activities of a hospital generally consist of transactions in which the hospital purchases and sells investments in securities (that are not cash equivalents) and plant assets. Investing activities may also include lending money and collecting the principal amount. (Receipts of interest income on such loans are classified as cash inflows from operating activities.)

Financing Activities

Financing activities generally are transactions that involve the acquisition and repayment of resources obtained through short-term and long-term borrowings in the form of bonds payable, mortgages payable, and notes payable (interest payments on these debts are treated as cash outflows relating to operating activities). Investor-owned hospitals include the proceeds from issuance of net assets securities and the payment of dividends to stockholders as financing activities.

Form and Content of the Statement of Cash Flows

Figure 21.4 presents a statement of cash flows for Hopeful Hospital. Observe that the cash flows during the year ended December 31, 20X2, are classified into the three types of economic activity: operating, investing, and financing. The net cash outflow for the year is $156, which accounts for the decrease in cash indicated in Figure 21.2. Also note that this schedule provides a reconciliation of net income and the net cash inflows from operating activities.

Net Cash Flow from Operating Activities

During 20X2, Hopeful Hospital had a net cash inflow from operating activities of $531:

1. Cash received from patients and third-party payers (see transaction 2 under Illustration Data), $8,404
2. Cash received from other operating revenue sources (see transaction 5), $650
3. Cash received from nonoperating revenue sources (see transaction 5), $180
4. Cash payments to employees (see transactions 6 and 8), $4,500
5. Cash payments to suppliers of goods and services (see the computation that follows), $4,203

   In this illustration, the dollar amounts for the first four items are given. (Recall that we have assumed that there were no accrued salaries and wages payable at either the beginning or the end of 20X2.) The dollar amount of Item 5, however, requires the following computation:

Cash payments on accounts payable (see transaction 8 under Illustration Data)	$12,493
Less:	
Payments of vouchers issued for purchase of long-term investments, purchase of plant assets, and retirement of bonds payable (see transaction 7)	(3,790)
Payments of vouchers issued for employee salaries and wages (see transactions 6 and 8)	4,500
Cash payments to suppliers of goods and services	$ 4,203

There may be situations where other dollar amounts of cash flows from operating activities must be computed. Consider, for example, the following facts:

Computing Cash Flows from Operating Activities

FIGURE 21.4

Hopeful Hospital Statement of Cash Flows Unrestricted Fund (Direct Method), Year Ended December 31, 20X2

Cash Flows from Operating Activities:

Cash received from patients and third-party payers	$8,404
Cash received from other operating revenue sources	650
Cash received from nonoperating revenue sources	180
Cash payments to employees	(4,500)
Cash payments to suppliers of goods and services	(4,203)

Net cash inflow from operating activities (see Schedule A)	$ 531

Cash Flows from Investing Activities:

Cash payments for purchase of plant assets	(940)
Cash payments for purchase of long-term investments	(450)
Proceeds from sale of plant assets	54
Proceeds from sale of long-term investments	49

Net cash outflow from investing activities	(1,287)

Cash Flows from Financing Activities:

Proceeds from issuance of 6% bonds payable	3,000
Cash payment for retirement of 7% bonds payable	(2,400)

Net cash inflow from financing activities	600

Net decrease in cash	$ (156)

Schedule A:

Net income	$ 285
Depreciation expense	540
Increase in accrued interest receivable	(15)
Increase in accounts receivable	(196)
Increase in inventories	(35)
Decrease in prepaid expenses	8
Decrease in accounts payable	(68)
Decrease in accrued expenses payable	(12)
Increase in deferred revenues	17
Gain on sale of long-term investments	(9)
Loss on sale of plant assets	16

Net cash inflow from operating activities	$ 531

Accounts receivable, net, 12/31/X1	$1,340
Accounts receivable, net, 12/31/X2	1,536
Net patient services revenues for 20X2	8,600

The computation of cash received from patients and third-party payers is as follows:

Accounts receivable, net, 12/31/X1	$1,340
Net patient services revenues for 20X2	8,600
Total	9,940
Accounts receivable, net, 12/31/X2	1,536
Cash received from patients and third-party payers during 20X2	$8,404

Figure 21.4 illustrates the use of the **direct method** of reporting cash flow from operating activities. Under this method, cash receipts and disbursements are presented by major classes of revenues and expenses. In Schedule A, the resulting net cash flow from operating activities is proven by a reconciliation of net income to the net cash flow. This reconciliation is required by FASB Statement No. 95 when the direct method of presentation is employed.

An alternative to the direct method is the **indirect method** of reporting cash flow from operating activities. Under the indirect method, the reconciliation is moved up into the body of the statement and is substituted for the presentation of cash inflows and outflows from operating activities.

Placement of Reconciliation Using the Indirect Method

Cash Flow from Investing Activities

In its 20X2 statement of cash flows, Hopeful Hospital reports a net cash outflow ($1,287) from investing activities composed of the following:

1. Cash payments for purchase of plant assets (see transaction 7 under Illustration Data), $940
2. Cash payments for purchase of new long-term investments (see transaction 7), $450
3. Cash proceeds from sale of plant assets (see transaction 4), $54
4. Cash proceeds from sale of long-term investments (see transaction 3), $49

All of the dollar amounts for cash flows from investing activities are given in this illustration. In some instances, however, one or more of the dollar amounts must be computed.

Assume, for example, the following facts:

Long-term investments, 12/31/X1	$600
Long-term investments, 12/31/X2	1,010
Purchase of long-term investments during 20X2	450
Gain on sale of long-term investments during 20X2	9

Proceeds from sale of long-term investments during
20X2   40

The necessary computation is as follows:

Long-term investments, 12/31/X1	$ 600
Purchase of long-term investments during 20X2	450
Total	1,050
Less long-term investments, 12/31/X2	1,010
Cost of long-term investments sold during 20X2	40
Gain on sale of long-term investments	9
Proceeds from sale of long-term investments	$ 49

Cash Flow from Financing Activities

Hopeful Hospital had a net cash inflow from its financing activities during 20X2, as follows:

1. Proceeds from issue of 6 percent bonds (see transaction 5 under Illustration Data), $3,000
2. Cash payment to retire 7 percent bonds (see transaction 7), $2,400

Although not included in this illustration, cash flows from the financing activities of a hospital also may include borrowings by the unrestricted (general) fund from donor-restricted funds and repayments of such borrowings.

Reconciliation Schedule

Schedule A, presented at the bottom of Figure 21.4, consists of a reconciliation of net income and the net cash flow from Hopeful Hospital's operating activities. Increases in current assets other than cash or cash equivalents are treated as deductions from net income; decreases in these accounts are added to net income. Increases in current liabilities (other than short-term borrowings) are treated as additions to net income; decreases are deducted from net income. The logic for this procedure was discussed earlier in this chapter. Why, however, were depreciation expense and the loss on sale of plant assets added to net income? Why was the gain on sale of long-term investments deducted from net income?

Depreciation expense ($540) and the loss on sale of plant assets ($16) were deducted in determining net income. Neither, however, required the use of cash (or cash equivalents). Net income, therefore, is an understatement of the amount of cash inflow generated from operations. Thus, these two items must be added back to net income. The gain on the sale of long-term investments ($9) was included in net income. The gain, however, did not provide (increase) cash; the proceeds of sale did. Net income, therefore, is an overstatement (by $9) of the amount of cash inflow from operations. Thus, the gain must be deducted from net income.

FIGURE 21.5
Hopeful
Hospital
Statement of
Cash Flows
Unrestricted
Net Assets
(Indirect
Method)

Cash Flows from Operating Activities:

Net income	$ 285	
Depreciation expense	540	
Increase in accrued interest receivable	(15)	
Increase in accounts receivable	(196)	
Increase in inventories	(35)	
Decrease in prepaid expenses	8	
Decrease in accounts payable	(68)	
Decrease in accrued expenses payable	(12)	
Increase in deferred revenues	17	
Gain on sale of long-term investments	(9)	
Loss on sale of plant assets	16	
Net cash inflow from operating activities		$ 531

Cash Flows from Investing Activities:

Cash payments for purchase of plant assets	(940)	
Cash payments for purchase of long-term investments	(450)	
Proceeds from sale of plant assets	54	
Proceeds from sale of long-term investments	49	
Net cash outflow from investing activities		(1,287)

Cash Flows from Financing Activities:

Proceeds from issuance of 6% bonds payable	3,000	
Cash payment for retirement of 7% bonds payable	(2,400)	
Net cash inflow from financing activities		600
Net decrease in cash		$ 156

Figure 21.5 presents a statement of cash flows under the indirect method for Hopeful Hospital's unrestricted net assets. In effect, Schedule A is substituted for the operating cash flows reported in Figure 21.4.

Exchange (Noncash) Transactions

Hospitals sometimes enter into significant financing and investing transactions that do not directly or immediately affect cash. A plant asset, for example, may be acquired in exchange for a long-term note payable. Here, we have a transaction that results in an increase in a noncash asset (but no decrease in cash) and an increase in a liability (but no increase in cash).

Another example is the receipt of a plant asset donated in kind. The entry for this transaction is a debit to plant assets and a direct credit to the unrestricted (general) net assets account. As a result, we have an increase in a noncash asset (but no decrease in cash) and an increase in hospital net assets (but no increase in cash). Transactions of these types, if significant, are disclosed in a schedule or note accompanying the statement of cash flows.

Questions

Q21.1. If a hospital's annual financial report includes a balance sheet, statement of operations, and statement of changes in net assets, why should a statement of cash flows also be included?

Q21.2. State the equation for the statement of cash flows.

Q21.3. In the context of the statement of cash flows, list the three major possible sources of cash inflows. Give an example of each.

Q21.4. In the context of the statement of cash flows, list the three major possible sources of cash outflows. Give an example of each.

Q21.5. Under the indirect method, depreciation expense is added back to net income to obtain the net cash flow from operating activities. Is depreciation expense a source of cash inflows? Explain your answer.

Q21.6. What is the purpose of a statement of cash flows?

Q21.7. Explain what is meant by the following:
   a. Operating activities
   b. Investing activities
   c. Financing activities

Q21.8. Distinguish between the direct and indirect methods of reporting cash flows from operating activities. Which do you prefer? Explain your answer.

Q21.9. A hospital acquired an item of equipment in exchange for a long-term note payable. How should this transaction be reported in the statement of cash flows?

Q21.10. Do all expenses in the statement of operations represent cash outflows in the current period? Do all revenues in the statement of operations represent cash inflows in the current period? Explain your answer.

Exercises

E21.1. Gras Hospital reported a net income of $87,400 for 20X1. The statement of operations included the following items, among others:

Loss on sale of long-term investments	$ 13,900
Depreciation expense	141,600
Gain on sale of plant assets	8,300

Required: In the hospital's 20X1 statement of cash flows, what amount should be reported as "net cash inflow from operating activities"?

E21.2. Refer to Exercise 1, but assume that Gras Hospital reported a net loss of $87,400 for 20X1.

Required: In the hospital's 20X1 statement of cash flows, what amount should be reported as "net cash inflow from operating activities"?

E21.3. Carole Hospital's balance sheets provide the following information:

	12/31/X2	12/31/X1
Long-term investments	$288,300	$262,700

During 20X2, the hospital sold certain long-term investments at a gain of $14,600 and purchased new long-term investments at a cost of $87,500.

Required: In the hospital's 20X1 statement of cash flows, what amount should be reported as a cash inflow from its investing activities?

E21.4. The following information was drawn from the general ledger of Frumer Hospital:

	12/31/X2	12/31/X1
Accounts receivable	$400,000	$340,000
Inventory	30,000	45,000
Prepaid expenses	5,000	4,000
Accounts payable to suppliers	50,000	46,000
Accrued wages payable	10,000	12,000
Revenues	850,000	
Employee compensation	560,000	
Cost of supplies used	25,000	
Depreciation expense	15,000	
Other expenses	200,000	

Required: Prepare the cash flow from the operating activities section of the 20X2 statement of cash flows, assuming the direct method of reporting operating cash flows.

E21.5. Refer to the data of E21.4.

Required: Prepare the cash flow from the operating activities section of the 20X2 statement of cash flows, assuming the indirect method of reporting operating cash flows.

Problems

P21.1. Barbara Hospital provides you with the following comparative balance sheets at December 31, 20X2 and 20X1:

	12/31/X2	12/31/X1
Cash	$ 180	$ 100
Other current assets	420	400
Long-term investments	440	450
Plant and equipment	7,900	7,600
Accumulated depreciation	(1,740)	(1,550)
Total	$7,200	$7,000
Current liabilities	$ 534	$ 250
7% bonds payable	2,800	3,000
Net assets	3,866	3,750
Total	$7,200	$7,000

The following additional information is available:

1. The 20X2 statement of operations reports a net income of $116.
2. Long-term investments that had cost $60 were sold for $75 in 20X2.
3. In 20X2, plant and equipment was purchased for $500.
4. Depreciation expense for 20X2 was $280.
5. During 20X2, plant and equipment items were sold for $100.

Required: Prepare, in good form, a statement of cash flows for Barbara Hospital for the year ended December 31, 20X2.

P21.2. Linda Hospital provides you with the following comparative balance sheets at December 31, 20X2 and 20X1:

	12/31/X2	12/31/X1
Cash	$ 160	$ 30
Other current assets	160	70
Long-term investments	400	350
Plant and equipment	2,000	1,860
Accumulated depreciation	(900)	(780)
Total	$1,820	$1,530
Current liabilities	$ 90	$ 40
8% long-term notes payable	-0-	500
7% long-term notes payable	600	-0-
Net assets	1,130	990
Total	$1,820	$1,530

The 20X2 statement of operations shows a net income of $80. Long-term investments were purchased at a cost of $90; other investments were sold for $54. Plant and equipment that had cost $100 (and was 60 percent depreciated) was sold for $32. In 20X2, $60 was transferred from the hospital's plant replacement and expansion fund to the unrestricted fund for the purchase of plant assets.

Required: Prepare, in good form, a statement of cash flows for Linda Hospital for the year ended December 31, 20X2.

P21.3. Tracy Hospital's preclosing trial balance at December 31, 20X1, is as follows:

	Dr.	Cr.
Cash	$ 310	
Accrued interest receivable	40	
Accounts receivable	1,460	
Allowance for uncollectible accounts		$ 170
Inventory	180	
Prepaid expenses	35	
Long-term investments	990	
Plant assets	6,100	
Accumulated depreciation		1,300
Accounts payable		390
Accrued expenses payable		210
Deferred revenue		50
Bonds payable		2,500
Net assets		4,825
Patient services revenues		8,900
Deductions from revenues	800	
Other operating revenues		670
Nursing services expense	3,200	
Other professional services expense	2,100	
General services expense	1,600	
Fiscal and administrative services expense	1,500	
Depreciation expense	570	
Other expenses	320	
Nonoperating revenues		190
	$19,205	$19,205

The following information relates to 20X2 activities:

1. Patient services revenues totaled $9,600.
2. Collections were as follows on accounts receivable:

Cash	$8,600
Deductions from revenues	750
Credited to accounts receivable	$9,350

3. The hospital sold long-term investments (cost $50) for $58.
4. The hospital sold plant assets (cost $250; accumulated depreciation $170) for $65.
5. Other cash receipts were as follows:

Other operating revenues	$ 680
Nonoperating revenues	170
Proceeds of new bond issue	3,500

6. Operating expenses vouchered were as follows:

Nursing services	$ 3,100
Other professional services	2,000
General services	900
Fiscal and administrative services	1,500
Other operating expenses	260

7. Depreciation expense for the year was $550.
8. Vouchers issued for other items were as follows:

Purchase of inventory	$ 900
Purchase of long-term investments	500
Purchase of plant assets	1,500
Retirement of long-term debt (bonds payable)	2,500

9. Checks issued in payment of vouchers totaled $12,300.
10. Cost of supplies used during the year was as follows:

Nursing services	$ 210
Other professional services	140
General services	490
Fiscal and administrative services	70

11. Accrued interest receivable at December 31, 20X2, is $55.
12. The allowance for uncollectible accounts at December 31, 20X2, should be adjusted to a balance of $195.
13. Prepaid expenses at December 31, 20X2, total $49.
14. Accrued expenses payable at December 31, 20X2, total $234 (make the necessary adjustment through nursing services expense).
15. Deferred revenues at December 31, 20X2, total $75 (make the necessary adjustment through other operating revenues).

Required: (1) Prepare a summary worksheet, such as the one in Figure 21.3, for the year ended December 31, 20X2. (2) Prepare a statement of cash flows, such as the one in Figure 21.4, for the year ended December 31, 20X2.

P21.4. Bennett Hospital provides you with the following comparative balance sheets:

	12/31/X2	12/31/X1
Cash	$ 140	$ 290
Accrued interest receivable	50	40
Accounts receivable	1,800	1,600
Allowance for uncollectible accounts	(200)	(180)
Inventories	170	130
Prepaid expenses	60	70
Long-term investments	1,000	750
Plant assets	7,000	6,800
Accumulated depreciation	(1,900)	(1,300)
Total	$ 8,120	$ 8,200
Accounts payable	$ 300	$ 290
Accrued expenses payable	210	240
Deferred revenues	80	90
Bonds payable	3,000	3,000
Net assets	4,530	4,580
Total	$ 8,120	$ 8,200

The following additional information is available:

1. During 20X2, certain long-term investments were sold at a loss of $40, and new long-term investments were purchased for $400.
2. During 20X2, certain plant assets (cost $250; accumulated depreciation $240) were sold for $22.
3. During 20X2, an old $3,000, 7 percent bond issue was retired at face value, and a new $3,000, 6 percent bond issue was sold at face value.
4. The 20X2 income reported a net loss of $50.

Required: Prepare a statement of cash flows for 20X2.

ANALYSIS AND INTERPRETATION OF FINANCIAL STATEMENTS

The foregoing chapters of this book were concerned primarily with the fundamental mechanics of the accounting process and with the basic accounting concepts underlying the financial statements of the hospital enterprise. The discussion has been directed mainly toward performing accounting operations and developing internal financial reports from the information generated by those operations. In this final chapter, the discussion is directed toward the analysis and interpretation of financial statements for the purpose of evaluating the hospital's financial position and operating results.

To introduce the subject of financial analysis and interpretation, let us briefly examine the Handy Hospital financial statements presented in Figures 22.1 and 22.2. Take a moment to study these statements, noticing the amounts (in thousands of dollars) reported as revenues, expenses, assets, liabilities, and net assets. On the basis of the information provided in these statements, what (if anything) can you conclude about Handy Hospital's 20X5 operating results and its financial position at December 31, 20X5? Are the operating results satisfactory? Is the hospital's financial position strong?

If you were a member of Handy Hospital's executive management team or governing board, what would be your reaction to the reported 20X5 operating results? Are revenues too low? Are expenses too high? Note that the excess of revenues over expenses for 20X5 is $894,000. Is this good or bad? Is it exciting or disappointing? How can a hospital executive make judgments about the financial impact of operating results for 20X5?

Similarly, how would you evaluate the hospital's financial position? The balance sheet, for example, reports $2.45 million of receivables. Is this amount too large or about right? What does it tell you, if anything, about the quality of the hospital's credit and collection efforts? Also reported in the balance sheet are inventories totaling $220,000. What, if anything, does the balance sheet indicate about the quality of inventory management at Handy Hospital? Is the hospital over-invested in this asset, or are the inventories at a dangerously low level? As a final observation, note that the hospital has $3.006 million of liabilities. Do you regard this as an excessive amount of debt?

As these questions reveal, the accounting function does not end with the accumulation of economic data and the communication of that information in financial statements. Once the financial statements are developed, the

FIGURE 22.1

Handy
Hospital
Statement of
Operations,
Year Ended
December 31,
20X5

Gross patient services revenues	$14,517
Less deductions from revenues	1,742
Net patient services revenues	12,775
Other operating revenues	1,225
Total operating revenues	14,000
Less operating expenses:	
Nursing services	4,460
Other professional services	3,361
Administrative services	2,263
Other operating services	3,150
Total operating expenses	13,234
Operating income	766
Nonoperating income, net	128
Excess of revenues over expenses for the year	$ 894

FIGURE 22.2

Handy
Hospital
Balance Sheet,
December 31,
20X5

Assets

Cash	$ 296
Temporary investments	110
Receivables, net	2,450
Inventories	220
Prepaid expenses	24
Total current assets	3,100
Long-term investments	430
Plant and equipment, net	6,370
Total assets	$ 9,900

Liabilities and Net Assets

Notes payable	$ 50
Accounts payable	366
Accrued expenses payable	651
Other	139
Total current liabilities	1,206
Long-term debt	1,800
Total liabilities	3,006
Net Assets	6,894
Total liabilities and net assets	$ 9,900

information they contain should be analyzed and interpreted to answer the kinds of questions posed in the above paragraphs. The answers can be extremely useful to hospital management and external groups in evaluating a hospital's operations and financial status for decision-making purposes. Hospital accountants, either directly or indirectly, are closely involved in the decision-making process by providing relevant information and by assisting in its proper interpretation.

Basic Analytical Techniques

In the analysis and interpretation of an item of financial information, one must have a basis of comparison. Consider, for example, the following item from Handy Hospital's December 31, 20X5, balance sheet:

Receivables, net $2,450

What does this mean? Is the amount too high, too low, or about what it should be? Standing alone, this bit of information is almost meaningless. There is no way to evaluate a single figure in isolation. It must be compared with or measured against something, usually another figure that provides a relevant and useful standard.

It would be helpful, for example, to compare the amount of December 31, 20X5, receivables with that of December 31, 20X4. Or, we could compare the actual amount of receivables at December 31, 20X5, with the amount budgeted for that date. Another possibility would be to compare the amount of December 31, 20X5, receivables with the amount of total assets at December 31, 20X5. In addition, the December 31, 20X5, receivables might be compared with net patient services revenues for 20X5. Each of these comparisons would be relevant and useful in evaluating the level of receivables at the end of 20X5.

Such comparisons involve the use of three basic analytical techniques:

1. Horizontal analysis
2. Vertical analysis
3. Ratio analysis

This section illustrates each of these techniques.

Horizontal Analysis

Horizontal analysis consists of the comparison of two or more figures across a single line of a financial statement. The following is an example:

	20X5	20X4	Increase (Decrease) Amount	Increase (Decrease) Percent
Net patient services revenues	$12,775	$12,045	$730	6.1%

In this analysis, we see that net patient services revenues in 20X5 were higher than in 20X4. The columns on the right indicate the dollar amount of the increase as well as the percentage increase. The percentage increase (or decrease) is determined by dividing the dollar amount of change by the base-year figure (the earliest year in the comparison, 20X4 in this example)—that is, $730 ÷ $12,045 = 6.1 percent. Where the base-year figure is zero or a negative value, the dollar change cannot be expressed as a percentage.

What Horizontal Analysis Reveals

Figures 22.3 and 22.4 illustrate the horizontal analysis technique applied to Handy Hospital's statement of operations and balance sheet. In each case, both dollar changes and percentage changes are provided to show the absolute as well as the relative changes. Although not illustrated here, a similar analysis could be made of the hospital's statements of changes in net assets and statements of cash flows. Whatever the statement may be, the purpose of horizontal analysis is to direct the statement reader's attention to those items exhibiting the greatest absolute and relative changes compared to the prior year. Significant changes should be fully investigated and explained.

Uncovering Trends in the Data

When more than two years are included in horizontal analysis, trend percentages can be developed. Examine, for example, the illustration in Figure 22.5 of a trend analysis of Handy Hospital's condensed statement of operations for a five-year period. In this method of analysis, the figures in the base-year statement are considered to represent 100 percent. The base year in this example is 20X1. The corresponding figures of each succeeding year are expressed as percentages of the base-year figures.

The net patient services revenues of 20X5 are 165.9 percent of 20X1 net patient services revenues ($12,775 ÷ $7,702 = 165.9 percent). Such percentages can be extremely useful in bringing out unusual relationships and trends that might go unnoticed in an examination of dollar amounts alone. The technique, of course, can also be applied to balance sheets and other financial statements.

Vertical Analysis

Vertical analysis involves the development of component percentages that express the relationships among related data within a particular statement. This procedure also is referred to as *common-size analysis*. Figures 22.6 and 22.7 illustrate the application of vertical analysis to Handy Hospital's statement of operations and balance sheet.

Total Operating Revenue as Base Figure

In the vertical analysis of a statement of operations, total operating revenue usually is selected as the base figure for the computation of component percentages. All other figures (with the possible exception noted below) in the statement are expressed as percentages of this base figure. In Figure 22.6, for

	20X5	20X4	Increase (Decrease) Amount	Percent
Gross patient services revenues	$14,517	$13,534	$983	7.3%
Less deductions from revenues	1,742	1,489	253	17.0
Net patient services revenues	12,775	12,045	730	6.1
Other operating revenues	1,225	955	270	28.3
Total operating revenues	14,000	13,000	1,000	7.7
Less operating expenses:				
Nursing services	4,460	4,269	191	4.5
Other professional services	3,361	3,167	194	6.1
Administrative services	2,263	1,953	310	15.9
Other operating services	3,150	3,129	21	.7
Total operating expenses	13,234	12,518	716	5.7
Operating income	766	482	284	58.9
Add nonoperating revenues	128	120	8	6.7
Excess of revenues over expenses for the year	$ 894	$ 602	$292	48.5

FIGURE 22.3

Handy Hospital Comparative Statement of Operations Horizontal Analysis, Years Ended December 31, 20X5, and 20X4

instance, the 20X5 base figure is $14,000 of total operating revenues, and each other figure in the 20X5 statement of operations is reported as a percentage of the $14,000 base figure. Similarly, in the 20X4 statement of operations, the $13,000 of total operating revenue serves as the base figure. All figures in the 20X4 statement of operations (with the possible exception noted shortly) are expressed as a percentage of this $13,000 base figure.

As can be seen at the top of the statement of operations in Figure 22.6, deductions from gross patient services revenues may be presented as a percentage of gross patient services revenues (rather than of total operating revenues). Otherwise, the component percentage would be distorted to the extent of other operating revenues to which the deductions are not related. In other words, although 20X5 deductions are 12.4 percent of total operating revenues ($1,742 ÷ $14,000), it is perhaps more meaningful to say that revenue deductions are 12 percent of gross patient services revenues ($1,742 ÷ $14,517), or 12 cents of each dollar of services rendered to patients.

Notice also in Figure 22.6 that operating expenses are reported both in a functional and in a natural (or "object of expenditure") classification. In their external reports particularly, hospitals often present operating expenses in a natural classification because the general public better understands that form of classification. The percentages indicated for the natural classification in Figure 22.6 are based on total operating expenses simply to illustrate the use of an acceptable alternative base figure.

Natural Classifications for Operating Expenses

FIGURE 22.4

Handy Hospital
Comparative
Balance Sheets
Horizontal
Analysis,
December 31,
20X5, and 20X4

	December 31 20X5	December 31 20X4	Increase (Decrease) Amount	Increase (Decrease) Percent
Current assets:				
Cash	$ 296	$ 230	$ 66	28.7%
Temporary investments	110	80	30	37.5
Receivables, net	2,450	2,145	305	14.2
Inventory	220	234	(14)	(6.0)
Prepaid expenses	24	11	13	118.2
Total current assets	3,100	2,700	400	14.8
Long-term investments	430	390	40	10.3
Plant and equipment, net	6,370	6,010	360	6.0
Total assets	$9,900	$9,100	$800	8.8
Current liabilities:				
Notes payable	$ 50	$ 200	$(150)	(75.0)
Accounts payable	366	431	(65)	(15.1)
Accrued expenses payable	651	545	106	19.5
Other	139	124	15	12.1
Total current liabilities	1,206	1,300	(94)	(7.2)
Long-term debt	1,800	1,800	-0-	—
Total liabilities	3,006	3,100	(94)	(3.0)
Net assets	6,894	6,000	894	14.9
Total liabilities and net assets	$9,900	$9,100	$800	8.8

**What
Vertical
Analysis
Reveals**

Vertical analysis can be quite useful in appraising the various components of the statement of operations. In Figure 22.6, for example, we see that nursing services expenses increased from $4,269 in 20X4 to $4,460 in 20X5. But we also see that nursing services expenses, as a percentage of total operating revenues, decreased from 32.8 percent in 20X4 to 31.8 percent in 20X5. On the other hand, administrative services expenses increased both absolutely and in relation to total operating revenues. Observations such as these give perspective to the evaluation of financial statement figures and tend to pinpoint areas for further investigation.

The results of vertical analysis can be viewed in another way. In Figure 22.6, the 20X5 operating expenses may be appraised in terms of "cents per dollar of operating revenue." In other words, of each $1 of operating revenue, 31.8 cents went for nursing services, 24.0 cents was expended for other professional services, 16.2 cents was employed for administrative services, and 22.5 cents was taken by other operating services. Thus, out of each dollar of 20X5 operating revenues, Handy Hospital was able to "bring down" only 5.5 cents into operating income.

	20X5	20X4	20X3	20X2	20X1
Amounts					
Gross patient services revenues	$14,517	$13,534	$11,630	$10,250	$8,440
Less deductions from revenues	1,742	1,489	1,245	996	738
Net patient services revenues	12,775	12,045	10,385	9,254	7,702
Other operating revenues	1,225	955	846	782	646
Total operating revenues	14,000	13,000	11,231	10,036	8,348
Less operating expenses:					
Nursing services	4,460	4,269	3,916	3,528	3,084
Other professional services	3,361	3,167	3,074	2,997	2,905
Administrative services	2,263	1,953	1,788	1,433	937
Other operating expenses	3,150	3,129	2,144	1,993	1,265
Total operating expenses	13,234	12,518	10,922	9,951	8,191
Operating income	766	482	309	85	157
Add nonoperating revenues	128	120	211	70	43
Excess of revenues over					
expenses for the year	$ 894	$ 602	$ 520	$ 155	$ 200
Trend Percentages					
Gross patient services revenues	172.0	160.4	137.8	121.4	100.0
Less deductions from revenues	236.0	201.8	168.7	135.0	100.0
Net patient services revenues	165.9	156.4	134.8	120.2	100.0
Other operating revenues	189.6	147.8	131.0	121.1	100.0
Total operating revenues	167.7	155.7	134.5	120.2	100.0
Less operating expenses:					
Nursing services	144.6	138.4	127.0	114.4	100.0
Other professional services	115.7	109.0	105.8	103.2	100.0
Administrative services	241.5	208.4	190.8	152.9	100.0
Other operating services	249.0	247.4	169.5	157.5	100.0
Total operating expenses	161.6	152.8	133.3	121.5	100.0
Operating income	487.9	307.0	196.8	54.1	100.0
Add nonoperating revenues	297.7	279.1	490.7	162.8	100.0
Excess of revenues over					
expenses for the year	447.0	301.0	260.0	77.5	100.0

FIGURE 22.5
Handy Hospital Trend Analysis of Statement of Operations, 20X1–20X5

FIGURE 22.6

Handy Hospital Comparative Statement of Operations Vertical Analysis, Years Ended December 31, 20X5, and 20X4

	20X5 Amount	20X5 Percent	20X4 Amount	20X4 Percent
Gross patient services revenues	$14,517	100.0	$13,534	100.0
Less deductions from revenues	1,742	12.0	1,489	11.0
Net patient services revenues	12,775	88.0	12,045	89.0
Other operating revenues	1,225	8.7	955	7.3
Total operating revenues	14,000	100.0	13,000	100.0
Less operating expenses*:				
Nursing services	4,460	31.8	4,269	32.8
Other professional services	3,361	24.0	3,167	24.4
Administrative services	2,263	16.2	1,953	15.0
Other operating services	3,150	22.5	3,129	24.1
Total operating expenses	13,234	94.5	12,518	96.3
Operating income	766	5.5	482	3.7
Add nonoperating revenues	128	0.9	120	0.9
Excess of revenues over expenses for the year	$ 894	6.4	$ 602	4.6
*Natural classification of expenses:				
Salaries and wages	$ 8,364	63.2	$8,024	64.1
Supplies	1,606	12.1	1,423	11.4
Utilities	1,945	14.7	1,702	13.6
Depreciation	583	4.4	563	4.5
Interest	138	1.0	120	1.0
Other expenses (including bad debts)	598	4.6	686	5.4
Total operating expenses	$13,234	100.0	$ 12,518	100.0

Total Assets as Base Figure

In the Handy Hospital balance sheets illustrated in Figure 22.7, the base figure for asset analysis is total assets, and all other asset figures in the statements are expressed as percentages of total assets. The December 31, 20X5, cash balance of $296, for example, is 3.0 percent of total assets ($296 ÷ $9,900).

The base figure for the analysis of liabilities and net assets is their total (the same as total assets), and each component item is converted to a percentage of that base. It can be said, for example, that December 31, 20X5, accounts payable comprises 3.7 percent of total assets (or of total liabilities and net assets). This type of analysis is helpful in evaluating the balance sheet in terms of management's allocation of resources and in terms of the sources from which the assets have been financed. It can also determine whether the

	December 31, 20X5		December 31, 20X4	
	Amount	Percent	Amount	Percent
Current assets:				
Cash	$ 296	3.0	$ 230	2.5
Temporary investments	110	1.1	80	0.9
Receivables, net	2,450	24.8	2,145	23.6
Inventory	220	2.2	234	2.6
Prepaid expenses	24	0.2	11	0.1
Total current assets	3,100	31.3	2,700	29.7
Long-term investments	430	4.3	390	4.3
Plant and equipment, net	6,370	64.4	6,010	66.0
Total assets	$9,900	100.0	$9,100	100.0
Current liabilities:				
Notes payable	$ 50	0.5	$ 200	2.2
Accounts payable	366	3.7	431	4.7
Accrued expenses payable	651	6.6	545	6.0
Other	139	1.4	124	1.4
Total current liabilities	1,206	12.2	1,300	14.3
Long-term debt	1,800	18.2	1,800	19.8
Total liabilities	3,006	30.4	3,100	34.1
Unrestricted net assets	6,894	69.6	6,000	65.9
Total liabilities and net assets	$9,900	100.0	$9,100	100.0

FIGURE 22.7

Handy Hospital Comparative Balance Sheets Vertical Analysis, December 31, 20X5, and 20X4

hospital's ratios are better or worse than those of comparable (peer) hospitals through the use of benchmarks.

For certain analytical purposes, however, it may be more useful to develop component percentages for current assets, using total current assets as the 100 percent figure. This is illustrated in Figure 22.8, where it can be seen, for example, that the cash balance is 9.5 percent of total current assets at December 31, 20X5. Similar analyses could be made, of course, of current liabilities or total liabilities.

Preparing Component Percentages for Current Assets

Regardless of whether the horizontal or vertical analytical method is used for comparing items on the financial statement, these methods merely serve as tools to assist in determining where problems may exist and where a more thorough examination of underlying financial data may be desirable.

FIGURE 22.8
Handy Hospital
Component
Percentage
Analysis of Cur-
rent Assets,
December 31,
20X5, and 20X4

	December 31, 20X5		December 31, 20X4	
	Amount	Percent	Amount	Percent
Cash	$ 296	9.5	$ 230	8.5
Temporary investments	110	3.5	80	3.0
Receivables, net	2,450	79.0	2,145	79.4
Inventory	220	7.1	234	8.7
Prepaid expenses	24	0.9	11	0.4
Total current assets	$3,100	100.0	$2,700	100.0

The key question is why unusual relationships appear between various amounts in the financial statements. Later on in this chapter, techniques for finding the answers to such questions will be described.

Ratio Analysis

A ratio is the quotient that results when one number is divided by another. It is one number expressed in terms of another; the ratio expresses the quantitative relationship between two numbers. A ratio may be stated as a common fraction, decimal, or percentage form. If, for example, we divided Handy Hospital's December 31, 20X5, current assets of $3,100 by its December 31, 20X5, current liabilities of $1,206, we obtain a ratio known as the **current ratio**. This ratio may be expressed as 3,100 ÷ 1,206, as 2.57, or as 257 percent. It may be said, then, that the current ratio is 257 percent, or 2.57 to 1, or that the hospital has $2.57 of current assets for each dollar of current liabilities.

Uses of Ratios Ratios are used in financial analysis to expedite comparisons and make relationships more understandable. Many different ratios can be computed from the data in financial statements. One does not, however, compute all possible ratios. Many, such as the ratio of prepaid expenses to nonoperating revenues, would be totally meaningless for analytical purposes. We must select those ratios that have significance and relevance for the purpose of the analysis. Our discussion here is directed toward the selection, computation, and interpretation of a number of ratios commonly employed in hospital financial analysis.

Analysis of Operating Results

The management of a hospital is charged with the task of maintaining a satisfactory relationship between revenues and expenses. Opinions differ as to precisely what this relationship should be. Some have argued that a not-for-profit hospital's financial operating objective should be to break even—that is, to maintain an equality between revenues and expenses. Given the pressures of demand for more and better services, advancing technology, inflation, inadequate reimbursement systems, and other socioeconomic forces, however, others (including this writer) are convinced that a reasonable profit (or margin) objective is both necessary and justifiable. In view of current and emerging conditions in the hospital industry, a no-profit fiscal objective seems totally unrealistic if the individual hospital is to avoid the erosion of its real capital and its ability to continue to provide the volume and quality of services desired by the community it serves.

Evaluation of Profitability

Because a profit should be regarded as necessary and desirable for a particular hospital, a judgment must be made about what that profit should be. A hospital management is likely to have in mind an absolute dollar amount of profit as a financial operating objective. This amount is determined to be the figure required to produce the cash flow needed to meet specific financial requirements, such as the payment of bond interest charges, the retirement of long-term debt, the acquisition of new plant assets, the development of new healthcare programs, and the generation of additional necessary working capital. In addition, a percentage relationship between operating income and operating revenues or between operating income and total assets, for example, could be established as a goal or standard against which actual operating results might be measured. For this purpose, the ratios described here are managerially useful.

One frequently used measure of profitability is the **operating profit margin**, which is derived by dividing operating income by total operating revenues. A computation of this ratio for Handy Hospital follows:

Operating Margin

	20X5	20X4
1. Operating income	$ 766	$ 482
2. Total operating revenues	14,000	13,000
3. Operating income ratio (1 divided by 2)	5.47%	3.71%

Thus, in terms of the ratio of operating income to operating revenues, Handy Hospital was more profitable in 20X5 than in 20X4. In 20X5, the hospital was able to earn an operating income that was 5.47 percent of operating revenues; in 20X4, the operating income ratio was only 3.71 percent. To put it another way, Handy Hospital's 20X5 operating income was about 5.5 cents per dollar of operating revenues; the 20X4 operating income was only 3.7 cents per dollar of operating revenues. This improved operating performance may be attributable to such factors as an increase in service rates, better management of operating expenses, an increased volume of service, and a more favorable service mix (in other words, relatively greater use of those patient services that generate revenues in excess of costs). Whatever the reasons for the improved ratio, they should be identified and evaluated by the hospital's management.

Looking at the Operating Expense Ratio

Emphasis sometimes is given to the **operating expense ratio**, the mathematical complement of the operating margin ratio. If the operating margin ratio is 5.5 percent, for example, the operating expense ratio must be 94.5 percent—that is, operating expenses consume 94.5 cents of each dollar of operating revenue. Naturally, the lower the operating expense ratio, the greater the operating margin ratio.

Return on Investment

A weakness of the operating margin as a measure of profitability is that it does not take into account the amount of resources invested in the hospital enterprise. Consider, for example, an investor-owned hospital having a 20X5 operating income of $100,000 and an operating margin of 10 percent that, by most standards, would indicate a high degree of profitability. Suppose, however, that the investor-owned hospital's average owners' net assets and average total assets were $5 million and $10 million, respectively, during 20X5. The rate of return (profit) on the owners' investment, then, is only 2 percent ($100,000 ÷ $5 million), and the rate of return on average total assets is only 1 percent ($100,000 ÷ $10 million).

In most types of business enterprises, such rates of return would be regarded as grossly inadequate to satisfy creditors, pay reasonable dividends to stockholders, attract new investment capital, obtain new long-term debt, or even justify a continuation of the business. Thus, the best and most useful indicator of profitability is the rate of return on the amount of assets invested and employed in an enterprise.

Computing the Rates of Return

The rates of return on Handy Hospital's average net assets and average total assets for 20X5 are computed as follows:

1. Excess of revenues over expenses for the year $ 894
2. Average net assets ([$6,000 + $6,894] ÷ 2)   6,447
3. Average total assets ([$9,100 + $9,900] ÷ 2)   9,500
4. Rate of return on net assets (1 divided by 2)   13.9%
5. Rate of return on total assets (1 divided by 3)   9.4%

In other words, Handy Hospital earned a 20X5 excess of revenues over expenses that was about 14 cents per dollar of net assets and 9.4 cents per dollar of assets. These rates of return probably would be regarded as quite satisfactory by a majority of profit-seeking businesses.

Significance of the Rate of Return

Although Handy Hospital is a not-for-profit corporation, these ratios are not at all without significance or managerial usefulness. Although there are no stockholder-owners interested in cash dividends and appreciation in the value of their stock holdings, Handy Hospital does have constituents: the people of the community it serves. These people presumably are interested in the continuation of the hospital as a financially sound and efficient provider of healthcare services. The hospital's employees are interested in adequate compensation. Banks, hospital bondholders, and other creditors are concerned with the hospital's ability to meet its financial obligations. Management must find the means to finance the acquisition of expensive equipment demanded by advancing medical technology. If philanthropy and government subsidies can be ruled out as important sources of new capital funds, the future of the voluntary not-for-profit hospital is likely to be dependent on the earning and reinvestment of adequate amounts of profit. It is for this reason that the rate-of-return concept cannot be ignored by the management of any hospital enterprise.

A profitability ratio of particular concern to current and potential investors in hospital bond issues is the times interest earned ratio. The computation of the ratio for Handy Hospital is as follows:

Times Interest Earned

	20X5	20X4
1. Excess of revenues over expenses for the year (operating income may be used)	$ 894	$602
2. Bond interest expense (assumed)	108	108
3. Total (1 + 2)	1,002	710
4. Times interest earned (3 divided by 2)	9.3	6.6

Thus, the hospital earned its bond interest charges 9.3 times in 20X5 and 6.6 times in 20X4. This is an indicator of the ability of the hospital to pay the annual interest charges on its outstanding bonds. The higher the ratio, the more favorably will investors regard the hospital's bonds as investment opportunities.

Internal Analysis of Revenues and Expenses

In addition to the ratios just explained that may be used by groups external to the hospital as well as by management, certain other analytical techniques can be applied by management to evaluate various revenue and expense items. The discussion here will be limited to actual versus budget comparisons and variance analysis.

Assume that Handy Hospital's 20X5 patient services revenues of $14,517 million include $487,275 of daily patient services (routine services) revenues earned in a 20-bed nursing unit referred to as "Three South." The 20X5 revenue budget for this unit was $439,600. A management report may present these facts as follows:

Analysis of Revenues

			Variance	
	Actual	Budget	Amount	Percent
Daily patient services revenues:				
Three South	$487,275	$439,600	$47,675	10.8

As can be seen, the revenues of this nursing unit were $47,675, or 10.8 percent, in excess of budgeted revenues. The management question is, why? What were the factors that caused this favorable revenue variance? How much of the variance is attributable to each factor?

To answer these questions, let us assume that 6,280 patient days of service were budgeted and that actual patient days in this unit were 6,497. Knowledge of the statistical units of service permits the following computation of actual and budgeted average revenue per patient day:

	Actual	Budget
1. Revenues	$487,275	$439,600
2. Patient days	6,497	6,280
3. Average revenue per day (1 divided by 2)	75	70

Factors Causing the Budget Variance Assuming this nursing unit offers private accommodations only, it is clear that service rates were increased during the year. So, we become aware that the budget variance is caused by two factors: (1) an increase in service rates and (2) a higher volume of service than budgeted. The dollar amount of revenues attributable to each of these factors is computed in Figure 24.9. A similar analysis could be made, of course, in a comparison of 20X5 actual with 20X4 actual.

Analysis of Expenses Assume that Handy Hospital's 20X5 general services expenses of $2,263,000 include $484,106 of dietary department expense. The 20X5 expense budget for the dietary department was $492,750. A management report may present these facts as follows:

			Variance	
	Actual	Budget	Amount	Percent
Operating expenses:				
Dietary department	$484,106	$492,750	$8,644	1.75%

Thus, dietary department expenses for 20X5 are seen to be $8,644, or 1.75 percent, less than was budgeted. Why? What were the factors that caused this favorable budget variance? How much of the variance is attributable to each factor?

The statistical unit of service for this department is a served meal. So, let us assume that 328,500 served meals were budgeted and that the actual number of meals served during the year was 336,185. This information permits the following computation of the actual and budgeted average cost per meal served:

Budget volume variance:		
Patient days of service		
20X5 actual	6,497	
20X5 budget	6,280	
Excess of actual days over budgeted days	217	
Budgeted revenue per patient day	× $70	
Budget volume variance (favorable)		$ 15,190
Budget rate variance:		
Average revenue per patient day		
20X5 actual	$75	
20X5 budget	70	
Excess of actual average revenue		
over budgeted average revenue	$5	
Actual patient days for 20X5	× 6,497	
Budget rate variance (favorable)		32,485
Total budget variance (favorable)		$47,675

FIGURE 22.9

Handy Hospital Analysis of Budget Variance Daily Patient Service Revenues- Three South, Year Ended December 31, 20X5

	Actual	Budgeted
1. Total expense	$484,106	$492,750
2. Number of meals served	336,185	328,500
3. Average cost per meal served (1 divided by 2)	$1.44	$1.50

Now we can see that, although the volume of service was 7,685 meals higher than was budgeted (336,185 − 328,500), the average cost per meal was six cents less than budgeted ($1.50 − $1.44). The effects of these factors on 20X5 dietary department expenses are shown in Figure 22.10.

Offsetting Volume with Lower Cost per Meal

Note that the unfavorable effect of a higher-than-budgeted volume was more than offset by the favorable effect of the lower-than-budgeted cost per meal.

Analysis of Financial Position

While operating results and financial position are treated separately here, both are important considerations, regardless of one's point of view. The information in the balance sheet cannot be ignored when appraising operating results; neither should the statement of operations be bypassed entirely in evaluating the financial strength of a hospital. Careful attention also should be given the data provided in statements of changes in net assets and in statements of cash flows.

Budget cost variance:		
Average cost per meal		
20X5 budget	$1.50	
20X5 actual	1.44	
Excess of budgeted cost over actual cost	$0.06	
Actual number of meals served	× 336,185	
Budget cost variance (favorable)		$20,171
Budget volume variance:		
Number of meals served		
20X5 actual		336,185
20X5 budget		328,500
Excess of actual over budget	7,685	
Budgeted cost per meal served	× $1.50	
Budget volume variance (unfavorable)		(11,527)
Net budget variance (favorable)		$ 8,644

Evaluation of Current Financial Position

The current financial strength of a hospital is a matter of great importance not only to its management but also to various external groups. If the hospital is to be able to repay bank loans and meet its short-term obligations to other creditors, it must maintain a sound current financial position. The hospital must have an adequate amount of working capital, it must maintain a satisfactory degree of liquidity, and it must not overinvest in receivables or inventories. Some of the ratios usually applied to obtain insights into the presence or absence of these desired conditions are presented here, using the financial statements of Handy Hospital as a basis for illustration.

Current Ratio One of the most widely used measures of current financial strength is the current ratio, which indicates the number of dollars of current assets per dollar of current liabilities. It shows the number of times the current assets will pay off the current debts of the hospital. A computation of Handy Hospital's current ratio is as follows:

	December 31	
	20X5	20X4
1. Current assets	$3,100	$2,700
2. Current liabilities	1,206	1,300
3. Current ratio (1 divided by 2)	2.57	2.08

Thus, in terms of the current ratio, Handy Hospital's current debt paying ability appears somewhat stronger at the end of 20X5 than at the end of 20X4. There is, however, no one value for the current ratio that is applicable to, or desirable for, all hospitals. What may be an adequate current ratio for one hospital may be dangerously low for another. It also is worth noting that although a particular current ratio may be satisfactory at the end of one year, it may not be satisfactory for the same hospital at the end of the next year.

Quick Ratio

A weakness of the current ratio is that it does not take into account the composition of either current assets or current liabilities. The quick ratio is a more valid test of current debt-paying ability than the current ratio in that it gives some consideration to the composition of the hospital's current assets. The computation is as follows:

	December 31	
	20X5	20X4
1. Cash	$ 296	$ 230
2. Temporary investments	110	80
3. Receivables, net	2,450	2,145
4. Quick assets (1 + 2 + 3)	2,856	2,455
5. Current liabilities	1,206	1,300
6. Quick ratio (4 divided by 5)	2.37	1.89

Difference Between Quick Ratio and Current Ratio

The basic difference between the quick ratio and the current ratio is simply that the computation of the quick ratio excludes inventories and prepaid expense items. An extreme modification of the quick ratio is the division of cash, or the total of cash and temporary investments, by current liabilities.

Current Asset Turnover

The current asset turnover is said to be an indicator of how hard the management of the hospital works the current assets—that is, the intensity of current assets usage. Handy Hospital's turnovers for 20X5 and 20X4 are computed as follows:

	20X5	20X4
1. Total operating revenues	$14,000	$13,000
2. Current assets, 12/31	3,100	2,700
3. Current asset turnover (1 divided by 2)	4.52	4.81

What the Turnover Indicates

Some analysts make the computation using total operating expenses rather than revenues as the numerator; others prefer to use working capital (current assets minus current liabilities) as the denominator (that is, a working capital turnover). In any event, a high turnover generally is indicative of efficient and productive employment of current resources.

Analysis of Receivables

The amount of receivables from patient services in a hospital's balance sheet should not exceed a reasonable proportion of the charges made to patients' accounts during the same period of time. This relationship may be illuminated by computation of the accounts receivable turnover as follows:

	20X5	20X4
1. Net patient services revenues	$12,775	$12,045
2. Average receivables, net	2,298	1,983
3. Receivables turnover (1 divided by 2)	5.56	6.07

What Ratio Reveals About Collections

This ratio indicates roughly the number of times during the year the receivables from patients were turned over, or collected. An increase in the turnover generally may be regarded as favorable with respect to the effectiveness of the credit and collection functions.

A more widely used ratio employed by hospitals in the analysis of accounts receivable involves the number of days' charges uncollected and in receivables. This ratio is computed for Handy Hospital as follows:

	20X5	20X4
1. Net patient services revenues	$12,775	$12,045
2. Average daily charges (1 divided by 365 days)	35	33
3. Receivables, net, 12/31	2,450	2,145
4. Number of days' charges uncollected (3 divided by 2)	70	65

One may tentatively conclude that on the average, the quality of receivables management may have declined somewhat between 20X4 and 20X5. Yet it must be recognized that this ratio is an average; some patients' accounts may be 200 days old and others may be only a few days old. It also is extremely informative to compute by major categories of patients and third-party payers (where the necessary information is available) both the receivables turnover and the number of days' charges uncollected.

Analysis of Inventories

As is true of receivables, a hospital can have an excessive investment in inventories. A reasonable relationship should be maintained between inventories and total current assets. In addition, the relationship between inventories and total cost of supplies used may be computed as the inventory turnover as follows:

	20X5	20X4
1. Total cost of supplies used	$ 1,606	$ 1,423
2. Average inventories (1/1 inventories plus 12/31 inventories, divided by 2)	227	209
3. Inventory turnover (1 divided by 2)	7.07	6.81

The fact that Handy Hospital turned over its inventories a greater number of times in 20X5 than in 20X4 generally is a favorable indication about the quality of inventory management.

What Inventory Turnover Reveals

In addition to inventory turnover, the average number of days' supply in inventories may be calculated as follows:

	20X5	20X4
1. Total cost of supplies used	$1,606	$1,423
2. Average daily usage (1 divided by 365 days)	4.4	3.9
3. Inventories, 12/31	220	234
4. Number of days' supply in inventories (3 divided by 2)	50	60

In evaluating inventories, it must be understood that a hospital can be understocked as well as overstocked. Either extreme is undesirable. Note also that, where the information is available, both the inventory turnover and the number of days' supply should be computed by major categories of inventory to take into account the differing characteristics of various types of supplies.

Evaluation of Long-Term Financial Position

Many external users of hospital financial statements are interested in the hospital's long-run financial strength as well as in its current financial position. Hospital bondholders and mortgagees, for example, are concerned not only with the ability of the hospital to pay current interest charges but also with the long-run safety of their investments. An intelligent appraisal of a hospital's long-term financial position is also essential to sound long-term financing decisions and long-range planning on either an individual-hospital or an area-wide basis. Such an analysis is helpful as well in evaluating the consequences of long-term commitment decisions (bond issues and plant asset acquisitions, for example) that have previously been made and implemented.

In studying a hospital's long-run financial position, an analysis is usually made of (1) changes in the absolute and relative amounts invested by the hospital in the various categories of assets, and (2) changes in the absolute and relative amounts of the sources (debt and net assets) of its assets. This analysis may take the form of a five- or ten-year study of the hospital's common-size balance sheets and statements of changes in financial position. Particular attention is given to detecting substantial shifts in the allocation of resources between the current and noncurrent classifications.

A study of the hospital's asset structure should also include an examination of assets held in the temporarily and permanently restricted net assets accounts. This is particularly true with respect to the plant replacement and expansion fund, where material amounts might be available for the financing

Temporarily and Permanently Net Assets

of future construction and equipment needs. Should the hospital have term endowments, their amounts and termination dates should also be considered in evaluating the hospital's long-run financial strength.

An appraisal of a hospital's long-run financial position must necessarily include the detection and investigation of substantial shifts noted in the capital structure, that is, the relative amounts of debt and net assets. For this purpose, debt ratios and net assets ratios may be computed as follows:

	December 31	
	20X5	20X4
1. Total liabilities	$3,006	$3,100
2. Hospital net assets	6,894	6,000
3. Total liabilities and net assets (assets)	9,900	9,100
4. Debt ratio (1 divided by 3)	30.4%	34.1%
5. Net asset ratio (2 divided by 3)	69.6%	65.9%

At the end of 20X5, we see that 30.4 percent of Handy Hospital's assets were financed by debt and 69.6 percent through net assets. This position is more conservative (less risky) than that which existed at the end of 20X4, when a somewhat greater percentage of the assets was being supplied by creditors.

Debt/Net Assets Ratio In some cases, the above ratios are combined into a single debt/net asset ratio (total liabilities divided by total net assets). The debt/net asset ratio at the end of 20X5, for example, is 43.6 percent ($3,006 ÷ $6,894), meaning that the hospital has about 44 cents of debt for each dollar of net assets.

The hospital's asset and capital structure as reflected in its balance sheet should always be viewed in conjunction with its statement of cash flows. This statement should preferably be presented in comparative form covering several prior periods so that trends in the sources and uses of cash resources may be clearly discerned. This permits an appraisal of the effectiveness of management's past operating, investing, and financing policies in bringing the hospital to its present financial position.

Above all, it must be recognized by all external groups that a successful hospital seldom remains the same. It either changes and grows, or it stagnates and declines. It moves in new directions, developing new programs and services in response to changes in demand and improved technology. This requires adequate financing, satisfactory operating results, and a sound financial position.

Questions

Q22.1. What are common-size financial statements?

Q22.2. Niceplace Hospital's nursing services expenses were $957,400 in

20X2 and $898,300 in 20X1. Prepare a horizontal analysis of the Niceplace Hospital data.

Q22.3. What is meant by a vertical analysis of the balance sheet? The statement of operations?

Q22.4. "A hospital with a current ratio of 4 to 1 has greater current financial strength than does a hospital with a current ratio of only 2 to 1." Do you agree or disagree? Explain your answer.

Q22.5. State how each of the following is computed and explain what might be indicated by the results of the computation:
a. Operating income ratio
b. Operating expense ratio
c. Return on investment
d. Times interest earned

Q22.6. State how each of the following is computed and explain what might be indicated by the results of the computation:
a. Current ratio
b. Quick ratio
c. Current asset turnover

Q22.7. State how each of the following is computed and explain what might be indicated by the results of the computation:
a. Accounts receivable turnover
b. Number of days' charges uncollected
c. Ratio of accounts receivable to total current assets

Q22.8. State how each of the following is computed and explain what might be indicated by the results of the computation:
a. Inventory turnover
b. Average number of days' supply in inventories
c. Ratio of inventory to total current assets

Q22.9. How is the debt/net asset ratio computed? Explain what might be indicated by the results of the computation.

Exercises

E22.1. Fineplace Hospital provides you with the following information:

	Actual	Budget
Daily patient services revenues	$367,500	$360,000
Patient days of service	4,375	4,500

Required: Prepare an analysis of the budget variance in the manner illustrated in Figure 22.9.

E22.2. Highplace Hospital provides you with the following information:

	Actual	Budget
Laboratory expense	$628,100	$500,000
Number of examinations	114,200	100,000

Required: Prepare an analysis of the budget variance in the manner illustrated in Figure 22.10.

E22.3. Goodplace Hospital has a current ratio of 2 to 1 on June 30, 20X1. On July 1, 20X1, the hospital obtains a $150,000 short-term loan from a local bank.

Required: What is the effect of the loan on the (1) current ratio, (2) quick ratio, and (3) working capital?

E22.4. The December 31, 20X1 balance sheet of Goodwork Hospital is as follows.

Cash	$ 25,000
Receivables, net	?
Inventory	?
Plant assets, net	294,000
	$432,000
Accounts payable	?
Other current payables	25,000
Long-term debt	?
Hospital net assets	?
	$432,000

The following additional information is available:

Current ratio	1.5 to 1
Total liabilities divided by hospital net assets	0.8
Inventory turnover based on cost of supplies used and ending inventory	15 times

These are the only accounts in Goodwork's balance sheet. Amounts indicated by a question mark (?) can be calculated from the information given.

Required: What was Goodwork Hospital's long-term debt as of December 31, 20X1?

E22.5. Verygood Hospital collected a $3,000 account receivable that had previously been written off as a bad debt against the allowance for uncollectible accounts.

Required: Which of the following describes the comparison of the current ratio before this collection (X) with the current ratio after the following collection (Y)?

a. X greater than Y
b. X equals Y
c. X less than Y
d. The answer cannot be determined from the information given

E22.6. Getwell Hospital has a current ratio of 3 to 1. An account payable recorded last month is paid this month.

Required: Which of the following is the effect of this payment on the current ratio and working capital, respectively?

a. Rise and decline
b. Rise and no effect
c. Decline and no effect
d. No effect on either

E22.7. Gotwell Hospital has a current ratio of 4 to 1. A transaction reduces the current ratio.

Required: Which of the following describes the comparison of the working capital before this transaction (X) and the working capital after this transaction (Y)?

a. X greater than Y
b. X equals Y
c. X less than Y
d. The answer cannot be determined from the information given

Problems

P22.1. Greatplace Hospital provides you with the following financial statements for 20X2 and 20X1:

	December 31	
	20X2	20X1
Cash	$ 240	$ 120
Temporary investments	210	180
Receivables, net	1,400	1,150
Inventory	300	370
Prepaid expenses	50	80
Total current assets	2,200	1,900
Plant assets, net	5,800	5,100
Total	$8,000	$7,000
Current liabilities	740	475

Long-term debt	3,530	3,205
Net assets	3,730	3,320
Total	$8,000	$7,000

	Year Ended 12/31	
	20X2	20X1
Gross patient services revenues	$6,600	$6,000
Deductions from revenues	790	500
Net patient services revenues	5,810	5,500
Other operating revenues	700	500
Total operating revenues	6,510	6,000
Less operating expenses:		
Nursing services	2,100	1,900
Other professional services	1,600	1,500
Administrative services	1,300	1,100
Other operating services	1,100	1,400
Total operating expenses	6,100	5,900
Excess of revenues over		
expenses for the year	$ 410	$ 100

Operating expenses include the $900 cost of supplies used, $400 of depreciation, and $240 of bond interest expense.

Required: (1) Develop a horizontal analysis of these statements. (2) Convert the above financial statements to common size. (3) Prepare a ratio analysis of 20X2 operating results. (4) Prepare a ratio analysis of the December 31, 20X2, financial position.

P22.2. Careplace Hospital supplies you with the following information relating to the 20X1 operations of its radiology department:

	Actual	Budget
Revenues	$966,400	$930,000
Expenses	393,600	372,000
Number of examinations	60,400	62,000

Required: Prepare an analysis of the budget variances for the radiology department's revenues and expenses for 20X1

P22.3. Wellplace Hospital provides you with the following financial statements for 20X2 and 20X1:

| | December 31 | |
	20X2	20X1
Cash	$ 168	$ 211
Temporary investments	126	34
Receivables—patients, net	1,011	893
Inventory	296	315
Prepaid expenses	25	29
Total current assets	1,626	1,482
Long-term investments	466	442
Plant assets, net	8,126	8,185
Other assets	167	88
Total	$10,385	$10,197
Current portion of long-term debt	$ 180	$ 180
Notes payable	125	75
Accounts payable	196	202
Accrued expenses payable	238	217
Payroll taxes withheld	81	63
Advances from third-party payers	75	55
Other	42	29
Total current liabilities	937	821
Long-term debt	1,718	1,865
Total liabilities	2,655	2,686
Net assets	7,730	7,511
Total	$10,385	$10,197

| | Year Ended 12/31 | |
	20X2	20X1
Gross patient services revenues	$ 8,830	$ 7,326
Deductions from patient		
services revenues	1,430	1,465
Net patient services revenues	7,400	5,861
Other operating revenues	505	407
Total operating revenues	7,905	6,268
Less operating expenses:		
Nursing services	2,560	2,197
Other professional services	2,050	1,615
Administrative services	1,350	1,033
Other operating services	1,925	1,614
Total operating expenses	7,885	6,459
Operating income (loss)	20	(191)
Nonoperating revenues, net	224	176
Excess of revenues over expenses		
(loss) for the year	$ 244	$ (15)

The other operating services include expenses of $520 of depreciation, $110 of interest expense, and $790 of insurance expense.
Required: (1) Develop a horizontal analysis of these statements. (2) Convert the above financial statements to common size. (3) Prepare a ratio analysis of 20X2 operating results. (4) Prepare a ratio analysis of the December 31, 20X2 financial position.

P22.4. Starplace Hospital provides you with the following information:

	December 31 20X2	December 31 20X1
Cash	$ 50,000	$ 35,000
Temporary investments	80,000	50,000
Receivables, net	140,000	110,000
Inventory	35,000	28,000
Prepaid expenses	12,000	16,000
Long-term investments	230,000	190,000
Plant assets, net	420,000	421,000
	$967,000	$850,000
Notes payable	$ 75,000	$ 25,000
Accounts payable	21,000	19,000
Accrued expenses payable	33,000	28,000
Other current liabilities	7,000	22,000
Long-term debt	500,000	450,000
Net assets	331,000	306,000
	$967,000	$850,000

	Year Ended 12/31 20X2	Year Ended 12/31 20X1
Total operating revenues	$840,000	$780,000
Cost of supplies used	210,000	186,000
Depreciation expense	90,000	90,000
Bond interest expense	30,000	27,000
Net patient services revenues	960,000	890,000
Excess of revenues over expenses	25,000	16,000

Required: (1) Prepare a ratio analysis of operating results for 20X2. (2) Prepare a ratio analysis of the hospital's financial position at December 31, 20X2.

P22.5. Rightplace Hospital supplies you with the following information relating to the 20X1 operations of one of its nursing units:

	Actual	Budget
Revenues	$753,300	$750,000
Expenses	502,200	500,000
Patient days of service	9,300	10,000

Required: Prepare an analysis of the budget variances for revenues and expenses for 20X1.

APPENDIX A: HFMA PRINCIPLES AND PRACTICES BOARD STATEMENTS

As of May 1, 2006

All HFMA P & P Board statements have been published in *Healthcare Financial Management (HFM)*, the journal of the Healthcare Financial Management Association, and are currently online at HFMA's website at www.hfma.org/library/accounting/reporting/PPB_pubs.htm. The following table identifies the title of each statement.

Statement Number	Title	HFM Publication Date
Statement 20	Healthcare Mergers, Acquisitions, and Collaborations	10/97
Statement 19	Transactions Among Affiliated Entities Comprising an Integrated Delivery System	6/96
Statement 18	Public Disclosure of Financial and Operating Information by Healthcare Providers	8/94
Statement 17	Assessments and Arrangements Similar to Taxes on Tax-Exempt Institutional Healthcare Providers	5/94
Statement 16	Classifying, Valuing, and Analyzing Accounts Receivable Related to Patient Services	5/93
Statement 15	Valuation and Financial Statement Presentation of Charity Service and Bad Debts by Institutional Providers	2/93
Statement 11	Accounting and Reporting by Institutional Providers for Risk Contracts	8/89
Statement 5	Accounting and Reporting for Agency Relationships	12/83

Withdrawn Statements

Statement 1:   Uniform Accounting and Uniform Reporting in Hospitals (*HFM*-6/77)

Statement 2:   Defining Charity Service as Contrasted to Bad Debts (*HFM*-7/78)
Note: Statement 2 was replaced by Statement 15

Statement 3:   Supplementary Reporting of Hospital Financial Requirements (*HFM*-12/80)

Statement 4:   Reporting of Certain Transactions Arising in Connection with the Issuance of Debt (*HMF*-6/82)

Statement 6:   How to Measure Working Capital: Classification and Definition Issues (*HFM*-9/84)

Statement 7:   The Presentation of Patient Service Revenue and Related Issues (*HFM*-4/86)

Statement 8:   The Use of Fund Accounting and the Need for Single Fund Reporting by Institutional Healthcare Providers (*HFM*-6/86)

Statement 9:   Accounting and Reporting Issues Related to Continuing Care Retirement Communities (*HFM*-11/86)

Statement 10:   Accounting and Reporting Issues Related to Corporate Reorganizations Involving Tax-Exempt Institutional Healthcare Providers (*HFM*-2/89)

Statement 12:   Accounting for Resource Transfers Among Affiliated Entities (*HFM*-10/90)
Note: Statement 10 was replaced by Statement 19

Statement 13:   Timing Differences Pertaining to Third-Party Payment (*HFM*-1/92)

Statement 14:   The Presentation of Patient Service Revenue and Related Issue (*HFM*-10/92)

APPENDIX B: HFMA PRINCIPLES AND PRACTICES BOARD ISSUE ANALYSES

As of May 1, 2006

In addition to the preceding statements of position, the HFMA P & P Board also releases issue analyses, which provide short-term assistance to the healthcare industry on emerging issues. Issue analyses are not sent out for public comment prior to their release, which is the practice with statements of position.

The HFMA Board of Directors assigns issues for analysis to the P & P Board. Current issues being analyzed by the P & P Board include disclosure; mergers, acquisitions, and collaborations; and managed care risk-contracting.

When completed, all P & P Board issue analyses are available for purchase as monographs from the HFMA website at www.hfma.org /library/accounting/reporting/PPB_pubs.htm. The following issue analyses are available from the website at this time.

Issue Analysis Number	Title	Monograph Publication Date
IA 05-01	The Relationship of Community Benefit to Hospital Tax-Exempt Status	4/05
IA 02-01	Recognition of Other-than-Temporary Decline in Investments for Tax-Exempt Organizations	11/02
IA98-01	Compliance with Laws and Regulations for Healthcare Organizations	6/98
IA97-01	Assessing Managed Care Contracting Risk	4/97
IA95-01	Acquisition of Physician Practices	9/95

GLOSSARY

Accounts payable. Amounts owed by the hospital to suppliers and other trade creditors for merchandise and services purchased from them but for which the hospital has not yet paid. (Chapter 1)

Accounts receivable. The amount of money due the hospital from patients and their third-party sponsors for services provided to them but for which the hospital has not yet been paid. (Chapter 1)

Accrual basis. Under this system of accounting, revenues are recognized and recorded in the time period in which they are earned by the hospital in rendering services and selling products to patients and others, regardless of when (if ever) the related inflow of cash occurs. Expenses are recognized and recorded in the time period in which they are incurred, or consumed in revenue-producing activities of the hospital, regardless of when (if ever) the related outflow of cash occurs. It is a GAAP that should be employed by all hospitals. (Chapter 4)

Accrued expenses. Expenses that have been incurred but for which the hospital has not yet paid. (Chapter 5)

Accrued expenses payable. Liabilities for expenses that have been incurred by the hospital but for which the hospital has not yet paid. Also called *accrued liability*. (Chapter 1)

Accrued revenues. Revenue items that the hospital has earned but for which the hospital has not recorded a receivable or collected cash. (Chapter 6)

Accumulated depreciation. The amount of plant asset costs consumed by the use of the assets and treated as an operating expense of the hospital during the time that has elapsed since the assets were acquired. (Chapter 1)

Accumulation. The process of recording and classifying the business transactions and financial events that occur in the economic life of the hospital. (Chapter 1)

Adjusting entry. An entry made at the end of an accounting period to assign income and expenses to a different period. These entries are made under the accrual accounting system to correctly reflect the timings of income and expenditure. (Chapter 5)

Allowance for uncollectible accounts. Amounts extimated to be uncollectible in the future due to bad debt expense, contractual adjustments, and charity services adjustments. This is a contra asset acount to the accounts receivable account on the balance sheet. (Chapter 7)

Assets. The economic resources of the hospital that are recognized and measured in conformity with GAAP. (Chapter 1)

Bad debt. Arises from services rendered to patients who are able but unwilling to pay. For GAAP reporting purposes, bad debt is presented as an operating expense, not as a revenue deduction. (Chapter 7)

Balance sheet. A presentation of the financial position of a hospital at a particular point in time. Also referred to as a statement of financial condition (*or position*). (Chapter 1)

Board-designated assets. Certain assets that are earmarked by the board for a specific purpose. Assets that are so designated, however, are unrestricted assets and must be reported as a part of the hospital's unrestricted fund. (Chapter 15)

Board of directors. The term used in for-profit hospitals to describe the governing board at the top of the hospital's organizational structure. (Chapter 1)

Board of trustees. The term used in not-for-profit hospitals to describe the governing board at the top of the hospital's organizational structure. (Chapter 1)

Cash. The amount of actual money and other immediately available resources or credit instruments generally accepted as a medium of exchange and used as money equivalents. (Chapter 16)

Cash basis. In this system of accounting, revenues are recorded in the time period in which they are received in cash; expenses are recognized and recorded in the time period in which they are paid in cash. It is not appropriate for hospitals. (Chapter 4)

Charity care adjustment. The difference between the hospital's established rates for services provided to the financially indigent and the amount collected (if any). In compliance with GAAP, charity care is reported as a note to the financial statements. (Chapter 7)

Closing entries. Entries made in the journal and posted to the ledger to eliminate the revenue and expense account balances and accomplish the closing of the books. (Chapter 4)

Closing the books. This procedure consists of the closing of revenue and expense accounts in the hospital's ledger and the adjustment of the hospital net assets to the balance at which it is stated in the year-end balance sheet. (Chapter 4)

Communication. The process of reporting recorded information to those who use it. (Chapter 1)

Community hospitals. Defined by the American Hospital Association as all nonfederal short-term general and other special hospitals whose facilities and services are available to the public. (Chapter 1)

Compound entries. Entries having more than one debit or credit. (Chapter 2)

Contra asset accounts. A negative asset account. It has a credit balance and offsets the debit balance of the corresponding asset. (Chapter 7)

Contractual adjustments. The amount of the differences between full rates and contractual agreements with third-party payers. (Chapter 16)

Coupon bond. A long-term liability in which no record is kept of the owners of the bond; rather, interest on coupon bonds is paid to all bondholders who present the periodic interest coupons that accompany the bond certificates. (Chapter 20)

Credit. An entry or a balance on the right side of an accounting record. (Chapter 2)

Current assets. Consist of cash plus other assets that will be converted into cash or consumed by operations within one year from the balance sheet date. (Chapter 1)

Current liabilities. Obligations that mature and will be paid by the use of current assets within one year from the balance sheet date. (Chapter 1)
Current ratio. Obtained by dividing current assets by current liabilities. (Chapter 22)

Debentures. Unsecured bonds, such as those that are secured only by the hospital's reputation and general financial resources. (Chapter 20)

Debit. An entry or balance on the left side of an accounting record. (Chapter 2)

Deferred income. Income that has been received in cash by the hospital but that the hospital has not yet earned and for which it is obligated to provide some specific service in the future. (Chapter 1)

Deferred revenues. Revenue items for which cash has been received but that the hospital has not yet earned. Sometimes called *deferred income, prepaid income,* or *revenues received in advance.* (Chapter 6)

Depreciable cost. The acquisition cost of a plant asset minus its estimated salvage value. Also known as *depreciation base* or *depreciation basis.* (Chapter 18)

Depreciation. An accounting procedure by which the cost (less salvage value, if any) of certain plant assets is allocated to expense over the estimated useful lives of such assets in a systematic and rational manner. (Chapter 7)

Depreciation expense. The amount of plant asset cost allocated to a particular accounting period. (Chapter 7)

Direct method. Method of reporting cash flow where cash receipts and disbursements are presented by major classes of revenues and expenses. (Chapter 21)

Endowment. Consists of contributed resources that, by donor restriction, are not to be expended but are to be held intact for the production of income. (Chapter 15)

Excess of revenues over expenses. The difference between the revenues and expenses of the period. It also may be referred to as *net income* or *net margin.* (Chapter 1)

Expenses. The costs of services, supplies, and other items purchased and consumed by the hospital in the provision of patient care services during a given period of time. (Chapter 1)

Face value. The nominal dollar amount assigned to a security by the issuer. Also known as *maturity value.* (Chapter 20)

Financing activities. Generally are transactions that involve the acquisition and repayment of resources obtained through short-term and long-term borrowings in the form of bonds payable, mortgages payable, and notes payable. (Chapter 21)

Fund accounting. A system of accounting in which the resources (and related obligations) of a hospital are segregated in the accounting records into self-balancing sets of accounts ("funds") for the purpose of carrying on specific activities or attaining particular objectives in accordance with legal and other restrictions. (Chapter 15)

General obligation bonds. Bonds issued by hospitals having extremely high credit ratings that are secured only by the hospital's reputation and general financial resources. (Chapter 20)

Generally Accepted Accounting Principles (GAAP). A body of rules, conventions, concepts, and standards that accountants must observe in reporting financial information. (Chapter 1)

Group depreciation. Application of a single depreciation rate to the total cost of a combined group of assets. Also known as *composite depreciation*. (Chapter 18)

Hospital accounting. The accumulation, communication, and interpretation of historical and projected economic data relating to the financial position and operating results of a hospital enterprise, for purposes of decision making by its management and other interested parties. (Chapter 1)

Indirect method. Method of reporting cash flow where the reconciliation is moved up into the body of the statement and is substituted for the presentation of cash inflows and outflows from operating activities. (Chapter 21)

Interim and/or internal statements. The financial statements that are issued during the course of a year. (Chapter 1)

Internal control. Comprises the plan of organization and all of the coordinated methods and measures adopted within a business to safeguard its assets, check the accuracy and reliability of its accounting data, promote operational efficiency, and encourage adherence to prescribed managerial policies. (Chapter 1)

Interpretation. The effort made by accountants to analyze and evaluate reported information so that it may be better understood and more easily used by decision makers. (Chapter 1)

Inventory. The cost of food, fuel, drugs, and other supplies purchased by the hospital but not yet used or consumed. (Chapter 1)

Investing activities. Generally consist of transactions in which the hospital purchases and sells investments in securities (that are not cash equivalents) and plant assets. (Chapter 21)

Journal. A chronological record of financial events in the economic life of the hospital. (Chapter 3)

Journalizing. The process of recording transactions in the journal. (Chapter 3)

Land, buildings, and equipment. The original acquisition costs of tangible plant assets used in hospital operations. (Chapter 1)

Liabilities. The economic obligations of the hospital that are recognized and measured in conformity with GAAP. (Chapter 1)

Long-term investments. The cost of governmental and corporate securities that the hospital owns and intends to hold for a period of time in excess of one year. (Chapter 1)

Long-term liabilities. Economic obligations that will not be discharged with resources classified in the balance sheet as current assets. Long-term liabilities are ordinarily based on a written contract, such as a mortgage document, bond indenture, or lease agreement. Also known as *noncurrent liabilities* or *fixed liabilities*. (Chapter 20)

Matching principle. The revenues of the hospital are matched with the accounting period during which they are earned. The expenses of the hospital are matched to the extent practicable with the revenues to which they are related. There is a matching of expenses with revenues in each accounting period to permit a meaningful and useful measurement of periodic net income. (Chapter 5)

Natural business year. A fiscal year or accounting period that ends June 30 or September 30. (Chapter 5)

Net assets. The excess of hospital assets over hospital liabilities. Is sometimes called *equity, capital,* or *net worth*. (Chapter 1)

Net assets accounting. The FASB Statement No. 117's provision that each of the individual internal funds in an organization must be classified into one or more of the three broad classes of net assets (unrestricted net assets, temporarily restricted net assets, and permanently restricted net assets). (Chapter 15)

Nominal (temporary) accounts. The statement of operation accounts, all revenue and expense accounts, which are closed when closing the books. (Chapter 4)

Noncurrent assets. Assets that will not be consumed within the next year. (Chapter 1)

Noncurrent liabilities. A debt not due to be paid within the next year. Also known as *long-term liabilities* or *fixed liabilities*. (Chapter 1)

Not sufficient funds (NSF). Memo produced when there is an insufficient amount of funds in a checking account to cover the checks written. (Chapter 16)

Notes payable. Short-term borrowings by the hospital from banks and other financial institutions. (Chapter 1)

Operating activities. Activities directly or indirectly related to the provision of healthcare services to patients. (Chapter 21)

Operating expense ratio. The mathematical complement of the operating income ratio. (Chapter 22)

Operating profit margin. Obtained by dividing the operating income by the total operating revenues. Also known as the *operating income ratio*. (Chapter 22)

Postclosing trial balance. A trial balance of the ledger to determine whether the accounts are in balance after the books are closed. (Chapter 4)

Posting. The process of transferring journalized information into the accounts in the hospital's ledger. (Chapter 3)

Preadjusted trial balance. The trial balance taken after all transaction entries have been journalized and posted. (Chapter 5)

Preclosing trial balance. A trial balance of the ledger to determine whether the accounts are in balance before the books are closed. (Chapter 4)

Premium. A price greater than the face value. (Chapter 19)

Prepaid expenses. Expenditures made by the hospital for goods and services not yet consumed or used in hospital operations. Sometimes called *deferred expenses* or *deferred charges*. (Chapter 5)

Quick assets. Consist of cash and those other assets (temporary investments and receivables) that can be quickly and directly converted into cash. (Chapter 16)

Real (permanent) accounts. Balance sheet accounts that are not closed. The balances of these accounts—assets, liabilities, and net assets—are carried over into the next year as the opening balances for that year. (Chapter 4)

Receivables. The realizable cash value of the hospital's legal claim against its patients, third-party payers, and others. (Chapter 16)

Registered bonds. Bonds on which interest is paid only to bondholders of record (i.e., those whose holdings are recorded by the issuing hospital or its registrar agent). (Chapter 20)

Responsibility accounting. Relies on the basic principle that each organizational unit (e.g., division, department, section) of the hospital is a responsibility center that performs an activity or function and is headed by an individual responsible for attaining its mission. (Chapter 10)

Responsibility reporting. The procedure of classifying hospital expenses on a primarily functional basis to associate the expenses with the organizational units and individuals who are responsible for them. (Chapter 1)

Restricted resources. Donated resources received by hospitals that are restricted by donors to specific uses and purposes. Such resources are not available for any purpose other than that specified by the donor. The term should be used only to refer to resources that are externally restricted. (Chapter 15)

Revenue. Economic values earned by the hospital through the provision of services and sales of products to patients. (Chapter 1)

Revenue bonds. A long-term liability on which interest is paid from specified revenue sources. (Chapter 20)

Revenue centers. Centers that generate revenues through the provision of patient services for which a specific charge is made. (Chapter 10)

Reversing entries. In some accounting systems, these entries are prepared on the first day of each new accounting period to reverse certain previously recorded adjusting entries. The reversing entries are made to avoid certain complications in the accounting routine. (Chapter 5)

Routine services. The provision of room, board, and normal nursing services to inpatients. Also known as *daily patient services*. (Chapter 12)

Salvage value. The amount, if any, for which an asset can be sold at the end of its useful life. Also called *residual value*, or *scrap value*. (Chapter 7)

Secured bonds. Bonds that involve pledging specific plant assets under liens as security to bondholders. Also known as *mortgage bonds*. (Chapter 20)

Serial bonds. Bonds that mature in installments over a period of years. (Chapter 20)

Sinking fund. A pool of resources earmarked for the payment of interest charges and for the retirement of bonds. (Chapter 20)

Statement of cash flows. Used to report the basic reasons for the changes in the organization's short-term balance sheet cash. Required by FASB Statement No. 95 as an essential component of a complete set of financial statements. (Chapter 21)

Statement of changes in financial position. Required in 1971 by the American Institute of Certified Public Accountants to be included in the external reporting of the financial affairs and activities of an economic enterprise. The statement was designed to present the sources and uses of working capital during a given period of time within the unrestricted fund. (Chapter 21)

Statement of changes in net assets. Used to report the summary reason for the changes in the three most common net assets. (Chapter 1)

Statement of operations. A presentation of the operating results of a hospital for a specified period of time. Also may be referred to as the *income statement*, the *statement of revenues and expenses*, the *profit-and-loss statement*, or simply the *operating statement*. (Chapter 1)

Stock dividends. Stockholders are given additional shares of stock without charge. (Chapter 19)

Straight-line depreciation. A method of calculating the depreciation of an asset by subtracting the salvage value of the asset from the purchase price, and then dividing this number by the estimated useful life of the asset. (Chapter 7)

Temporary investment. An investment that can be quickly and directly converted into cash. (Chapter 16)

Term bonds. Bonds that mature on a single fixed maturity date. (Chapter 20)

Term note receivable. Indicates that the face amount of the note and all interest is payable in a single sum on the maturity date of the note. (Chapter 16)

Trade discounts. Discounts obtained from a supplier because of large-volume buying or other reasons. (Chapter 17)

Unit depreciation. Applying the straight-line method of depreciation to a single unit or item of equipment. (Chapter 18)

Unrestricted fund. This fund includes all hospital resources, with related obligations, that are not restricted by any external authority or donor. All of the resources of this fund are available for general operating activities at the discretion of the hospital's governing board. In addition, the accounts of the unrestricted fund include all the revenues and expenses to be reported in the hospital's statement of operations. (Chapter 15)

Unrestricted net assets. Resources with no stipulation or restriction by the donor about the specific purpose for which the money is to be used. (Chapter 15)

Voucher. A document prepared for approving disbursements that includes the auditing of invoices and the securing of authorizations. (Chapter 11)

Voucher system. Before a check is written, an investigation is made of the proposed disbursement, and (if approved) a credit is made to a liability account (accounts payable). When the check is written, an entry is made in the cash disbursements journal. (Chapter 11)

Worksheets. Device used by accountants to facilitate the preparation of financial statements. Sometimes called *working papers*. (Chapter 4)

INDEX

ABOUT THE AUTHOR

Michael Nowicki, Ed.D., FACHE, FHFMA, is a professor of health administration and director of graduate studies in the department of health administration at Texas State University, where he has received numerous university awards for his teaching, research, and service. He has taught for universities in California, Indiana, Kentucky, Missouri, and New Jersey, as well as for associations such as the American College of Healthcare Executives, the Healthcare Financial Management Association, the American Hospital Association, VHA, and the Association of University Programs in Health Administration.

Prior to joining academia full time in 1986, Dr. Nowicki was director of process management in the hospital division of Humana. Dr. Nowicki has also held a variety of administrative positions at Valley Medical Center in Fresno, Hutzel Hospital in Detroit, Georgetown University Medical Center, and Lubbock Medical Center.

Dr. Nowicki received his doctorate in educational policy studies and evaluation from the University of Kentucky, his master's in healthcare administration from The George Washington University, and his bachelor's in political science from Texas Tech University. Dr. Nowicki is board certified in healthcare management and a Fellow of the American College of Healthcare Executives, and has served as founder and advisor of student chapters, founder and president of the Central Texas Chapter, and chair of the national Book-of-the-Year Committee. Dr. Nowicki is also board certified in healthcare financial management and a Fellow in the Healthcare Financial Management Association (HFMA), and has served as president of the South Texas Chapter, chapter liaison representative for five-state Region 9, and as a director on the national board of directors serving as chair of both the Chapter Services Council and the Council on Forums. Dr. Nowicki also served on the HFMA Board of Examiners, serving as chair in 2001.

Dr. Nowicki has presented financial management seminars to audiences worldwide, including the Russian Ministry of Health in Moscow, Russian hospital executives in Golitsyno, Estonian hospital executives in Tallin, and Indonesian hospital executives visiting the University of Massachusetts, as well as numerous audiences in the United States.

In addition to *HFMA's Introduction to Hospital Accounting*, Dr. Nowicki published the third edition of *The Financial Management of Hospitals and Healthcare Organizations* in 2004. Dr. Nowicki is a frequent contributor to numerous journals, including *HFM* (the journal of the Healthcare Financial Management Association) and *HealthLeaders*.

Dr. Nowicki and his wife, Tracey, and children, Hannah and David, live in New Braunfels, Texas.